Love and Modernity

Scandinavian Literature, Drama and Letters

Essays in Honour of Professor Janet Garton

Some other books from Norvik Press

Love and Modernity

Scandinavian Literature, Drama and Letters

Essays in Honour of Professor Janet Garton

Edited by C. Claire Thomson and Elettra Carbone

Norvik Press
2014

Norvik Press Series A: Scandinavian Literary History and Criticism, No. 33.

A catalogue record for this book is available from the British Library.

ISBN: 978-1-870041-99-7

Norvik Press
Department of Scandinavian Studies
University College London
Gower Street
London WC1E 6BT
United Kingdom
Website: www.norvikpress.com
E-mail address: norvik.press@ucl.ac.uk

Managing editors: Sarah Death, Helena Forsås-Scott, Janet Garton, C. Claire Thomson.

Cover image: *Academic Procession*, Kathleen McFarlane
150 x 334 cm, Wool Tapestry.
Reproduced by kind permission of Sainsbury Centre for Visual Arts, University of East Anglia, Norwich.
Cover design: Elettra Carbone.
Layout: Elettra Carbone, Marita Fraser, C. Claire Thomson.

Contents

II. Travels

III. Communities

IV. Textualities

V. Bodies

Introduction

C. Claire Thomson and Elettra Carbone

This Festschrift is presented to Professor Janet Garton on the occasion of the fiftieth anniversary of the founding of the University of East Anglia, the institution at which she has been based during her long and successful career. We congratulate you, Janet, on your outstanding and inspiring contribution to research, teaching and leadership in Scandinavian Studies and European literature at UEA and worldwide.

Now Professor Emerita of European Literature, Janet Garton's major publications include *Jens Bjørneboe: Prophet without Honor* (1985); *Norwegian Women's Writing 1850-1990* (1993); the acclaimed three-volume edition of Amalie and Erik Skram's letters, *Elskede Amalie* (2002); two further volumes of Amalie Skram's correspondence with other authors and with her publishers (2005, 2010); and most recently, a biography of Amalie Skram, *Amalie. Et forfatterliv* (2011). She has also translated works by, amongst others, Knut Faldbakken, Bjørg Vik, Johan Borgen, August Strindberg and Kirsten Thorup into English, and edited and translated a selection of Amalie Skram's letters (2003). Janet has served as Editor of the journal *Scandinavica*, as Managing Editor of Norvik Press, as Secretary and President of the International Association of Scandinavian Studies, and as Dean of the School of Language, Linguistics and Translation Studies at UEA. Her services to Scandinavian literature and culture have been recognised with an MBE. In 2007 she received a Fritt Ords award from the Freedom of Expression Foundation, Oslo, for her work in Norwegian literature and language and in 2009 was awarded a Knight First Class from the Kongelige Norske Fortjenstorden.

The contributors to this volume were asked to write an essay which touched on the themes of modernity, decadence and love, themes which were central to a popular course in fin-de-siècle literature which

Janet taught at UEA for many years. This brief resulted in a wide-ranging selection of essays on literature, drama, letters, travels, and visual and bodily culture. The voices of women writers, such as Amalie Skram, and the great figures of Norwegian literature, whose work Janet's research has done so much to illuminate, echo through the collection of essays.

This Festschrift was originally mooted as a project in 2008, in the context of Janet's retirement from UEA. We are very grateful to the contributors for their patience and flexibility while publication of the volume was delayed, in large part due to the relocation of Norvik Press from UEA to UCL during this period, and the consequent changes in staffing and production schedules. We acknowledge with gratitude the support of UCL Enterprise for the production post held by Marita Fraser, who has been instrumental in designing and producing the book. It is very appropriate that Elettra Carbone, a member of the emerging generation of Norwegian literary scholars and also Office Manager for Norvik Press, has come on board as co-Editor. Launching the Festschrift at this time enables us to raise a glass to the future of Scandinavian Studies and to Norvik Press – and to Janet's continuing leadership in both enterprises!

Janet Garton
and
the University of East Anglia

Jean Boase-Beier
University of East Anglia, Norwich

It was the late summer of 1991 and I had been at UEA only a few weeks, in the School of Modern Languages and European Studies (EUR). The late W.G. (Max) Sebald, Professor of German Literature, had arranged a meeting of everyone interested in helping me set up an MA in Literary Translation. Among the many people I met for the first time that morning was an energetic young woman with a brisk smile, a Northern accent, and a very forthright manner. This was Janet Garton, and I took to her straight away. I learned that she taught Scandinavian Studies, liked the poetry of German poet Christian Morgenstern, and came from somewhere near Scunthorpe. Of all the new colleagues I got to know in those first weeks, Janet was the one who struck me as the most even-tempered and level-headed; here was someone who felt certain of how she fitted in to the scheme of things, who enjoyed her work enormously but never let it consume her to the detriment of her personal life, someone who took triumphs and setbacks in her stride with good humour and poise. Of course, that cannot have been the whole picture, and I expect Janet will smile when she reads this and say 'If you only knew.' But it is an impression that has persisted. This is the face she has chosen to present to the world and there is no doubt that in many respects it is her true one.

Janet's equanimity came in no small measure from the fact that, when I first met her in 1991, she had already been at UEA for over twenty years. Asked in 1968 by the late James McFarlane, always known as Mac, the first Professor of European Literature at UEA, to help develop the Scandinavian Studies programme in EUR, she threw herself whole-heartedly into the design and development of courses in Norwegian, Danish and Swedish language and literature. From the start she played an important role in the running of the Scandinavian Sector. She taught various aspects of the Scandinavian languages, especially Advanced Translation, but focussed mainly on Scandinavian Literature, with a particular emphasis on modern writing. The Scandinavian Sector was always well-run, its courses coherent, well-managed, and popular, and the sense was of an area in which teaching, research and administration managed to achieve a fusion that other Sectors would have liked to emulate. Though the reality is never really this unproblematic, nevertheless, looking back, there was a confidence and cohesion in Scandinavian Studies which was quite remarkable. It is clear that Janet, right from the start, was a major factor in that clarity of purpose and strength of organisation.

Soon after taking up her post at UEA, Janet became involved with the journal *Scandinavica*, first as Assistant Editor, later as Editor. In 1986, together with Mac, she set up Norvik Press, which was always – or at least as far back as I can remember – run from a small, overflowing office in the Arts Building, next to the offices of the Scandinavian Studies teachers. Like *Scandinavica*, Norvik Press always attracted a great deal of external funding, and indeed one of the successes of Janet's career at UEA was the large amount of funding she was awarded for the various Scandinavian projects, whether in research or publishing, with which she was involved.

One of Janet's great strengths is networking. She has organised and attended many conferences and events in England, in Scandinavia, and in other parts of the world, and this activity made UEA known for the excellence of its research and teaching in Scandinavian Studies. This has been borne in upon me through the reaction of colleagues at various national and international events in literature, languages or translation studies. Whenever I meet anyone who has anything to do with Scandinavian Studies, the first thing they say, on learning I am from UEA, is always 'You must know Janet Garton.' I have heard her several times described as the most famous English person in Norway. I once could not resist passing this description on to Janet; she replied, in her inimitable no-nonsense way: 'Well, it's a small country.' I wondered whether she meant Norway or England. I suspect she was just uncomfortable with the implied praise.

Small country or not, Janet has always been passionate about Norway, and things Norwegian. She has translated its plays, letters and novels and she has taught and researched on many different aspects of its literature and its language. She has talked about its churches, worn its clothes, and served its food. And this is an interest that extends to the whole of Scandinavia, as can be seen both from her publications and from the contributions to this volume.

Scandinavian Studies, because of the excellence of its teaching, and its 5* rating in the Research Assessment Exercise, was often praised as 'the jewel in the crown' of EUR, a phrase originally used, I believe, in an external Quality Assurance report. Sadly, Scandinavian went the way of German and Linguistics at UEA and elsewhere: discontinued because, despite high ratings, it was not a subject that attracted large numbers of students. But like those other subjects, it never ceased to play a significant part in later UEA courses, living on as an important element in both the MA in Literary Translation and the undergraduate literature options in the School of Literature and Creative Writing, to which Janet moved some years before her retirement.

But however great Janet's contribution to international Scandinavian Studies has been, and to UEA's long association with the world of Scandinavian letters, it is not possible to talk of her time at UEA without mentioning the other areas of her work. Some of these will be familiar to Scandinavian scholars, combining as they do that central focus with her interests in, for example, women writers, literary translation, and life-writing. Her vast project on the correspondence of Norwegian writer Amalie Skram with Danish writer Erik Skram is a good example of the way she has combined these various interests. Her teaching was not only in Scandinavian language and literature but also took in European literature in a wider sense; as a student at Cambridge, she had taken French and German, as well as Norwegian. One of her early books was on European Modernism. And in the years leading up to her retirement, she taught a popular undergraduate module on modern dystopia, utopia and fantasy, dealing with works as diverse as Orwell's *Nineteen Eighty-Four* and Tolkien's *Lord of the Rings*.

She also continued to play an important role in the MA in Literary Translation, ever since that first meeting in 1991. From the start she taught one of its core seminars, on case studies of translated texts, and developed various different strands within that seminar, including gender and translation, the translation of children's writing, and translating drama. Much of this work formed the basis for the MA module taught by my current colleague, BJ Epstein, also a Scandinavianist. Janet has held numerous workshops as part of the MA programme, and continues to do so in retirement, on the translation of Paal-Helge Haugen's poetry, the translation of Ibsen, and of course the translation of the letters of Erik and Amalie Skram. She has supervised and examined many MA and PhD students in widely varying areas of Translation Studies, including those working on Japanese women's writing, on Greek children's literature, on

Turkish translations of modern English novels, and on French drama. She several times took over the running of the programme with typical efficiency and complete lack of fuss when I was on study leave. To me, it is this latter quality which epitomises what must surely be one of her most important contributions to life at UEA: her outstanding ability as an impartial leader and an imperturbable organiser.

Janet filled a number of very different organisational roles during her time here: she was not only Head of the Scandinavian Sector, but also Dean of EUR, and Humanities Associate Dean for Postgraduate Research. She carried out all the associated tasks with great energy and complete even-handedness. Although Janet was always keen to promote Scandinavian Studies, and very successful in doing so, this was never at the expense of other subject areas. Back in the early 1990s, when Scandinavian Studies was under threat at UEA as elsewhere in England, I was very struck by the way she always argued for the good of the School, and never merely for that of her own subject. As Deputy Dean during the Deanship of Roger Fowler, who was also Professor of Linguistics in the School, there was no sense of conflict between their subject areas, even when money was tight, and structure precarious. Indeed, Roger Fowler used to say often how easy he found her to work with, and how fair and reasonable she was. When she took over the Deanship of the newly-formed School of Language, Linguistics and Translation Studies on Roger Fowler's sudden death, she was an extremely just and careful leader, adapting with ease (or at least with good grace) to the new subject constellation. And in more recent years, after her move to what is now the School of Literature, Drama and Creative Writing, where until her retirement she was Professor of European Literature, she both continued to support her former colleagues in her old School, and also quickly became fully involved in the life of the new School. To adapt constantly to changing structures, while still preserving the identity of one's own subject, is something academics have become used to. But I have rarely seen anyone manage this mix of change and continuity quite so well. And it was all done with humour, energy and the exercise of considerable organisational skills. In fact, I often suspected that she would like to organise several other areas of UEA; perhaps they would have been better run if she had. She never made a secret of her impatience when colleagues were disorganised, or things that were planned didn't happen. But she has also, throughout her career, always been ready to stand up for the interests of others, and would protest firmly on behalf of her colleagues if she felt they were being given an inequitable workload.

Overall, her involvement in four decades of UEA life was an extremely active one, going beyond her subject area, her School and the Humanities Faculty, to include important work at University level on Assembly Standing Committee, and a number of other University committees.

And during all this time, as well as since her retirement, Janet Garton has continued to be one of the leading figures in international Scandinavian Studies. For me personally, as for many of my former and present colleagues, she has been the friend who has offered unflagging support, brisk and sensible advice, and a great deal of practical help. She is showing little sign of slowing down since her retirement, and is involved in a number of projects, including several translations for Norvik Press. And I am sure her next projects are already clearly mapped out.

I

Loves

A Footnote to
The Lady from the Sea,
and the Heroic

Marie Wells
University College London

Dear Janet,

When I came to New Hall in Cambridge in 1970 to do my PhD, everyone asked me, 'do you know Janet Mawby, because she too did Norwegian? I did not know you then because you had been head-hunted by 'Mac' (Professor James MacFarlane) and had gone off to the recently-founded University of East Anglia. Gradually we met at the Biennial Conferences of Teachers of Scandinavian in the UK (there were enough of us then for there to be such conferences) and later we acted as External Examiners at each other's universities and met at inter-university seminars. For a long time our lives ran on parallel tracks, but in recent years those tracks have crossed more and more often for all sorts of reasons.

You have an impressive career behind you, teaching, taking over and running Norvik Press after Mac's death, and more recently fighting to save Scandinavian Studies at UEA. All that is apart from your academic output, and it is to that I turn now. The culmination of your career has been your work on Amalie Skram, first of all editing her letters to Erik Skram and to friends and publishers (five volumes in all) and then writing her biography from the time she married Erik Skram in 1884 and moved to Copenhagen. Further back in time there was your very useful book *Norwegian Women's Writing 1850-1990* which I used when I taught a course on the works of Norwegian women writers and it was, of course, on the students' reading list. Likewise your chapter on 'The Middle Plays' in *The Cambridge Companion to Ibsen* where you write something I want to take as the starting point of this short essay. In the section on *Lady from the Sea* you write of the 'the reckless passion which laughs at society's laws and conventions, the white heat of sexual desire which melts [...] will power and has nothing to do with the settled domesticity of the village' (Garton 1994: 116). This, you write, is what Dr Wangel cannot offer Ellida, but is what the Stranger had offered, and your memorable comment is that, 'there must be some part of most women that would like her to have gone with the Stranger' (118). Instead of that, as you write, Ellida will now have a home in Wangel's house, 'ties to his children and a more equal partnership.' However, because Wangel was attracted to Ellida's feyness, you argue that both Wangel and Ellida lose something in this seemingly happy resolution of Ellida's neurosis.

Ibsen certainly championed the right of women to be equal partners in marriage and not to be treated as property, but where passion is concerned I would argue that he was in fact rather conservative, and believed that passion could only lead to tragedy. He shows this time and again in his plays. In both *The Lady from the Sea* and *Rosmersholm* (the play that precedes *The Lady from the Sea*), passion is associated with the sea and death. In *The Lady from the Sea* not only does the Stranger admit to having murdered the captain of the ship he was on at the time when he first met Ellida, but it is the sea and a ship-wreck that gave Lyngstrand the 'weakness in the chest' that will soon kill him. In *Rosmersholm*, Rebecca, who comes from northern Norway, compares the passion for Rosmer that overwhelmed her and drove her to lure Beate into suicide to a storm up in the north. In *Little Eyolf* too, the sea is associated with death, and while in *Hedda Gabler* there are no links to the sea, there is certainly passion of a very destructive nature. I would also (tendentiously, perhaps) include Nora's absolute passion for finding out who she is as an individual and her concomitant removal of feeling from Torvald at the end of *A Doll's House* as an example of tragic passion.

But why are we so fascinated by these tragic protagonists? John Northam would say that we are fascinated by the protagonist (whom he calls an idealist) who is 'prepared to sacrifice all the normal expectations of life and happiness in pursuit of some end which *for him* represents a higher value' (Northam 1966: 11). (One should point out that unlike Atle Kittang, Northam does not limit his idealists or tragic protagonists to men, as it might appear from the above quotation, and indeed one of his main examples in arguing his case is Hedda Gabler). Closer to our own day, Michael Robinson writing specifically about Ibsen, could still find it useful to quote Northrop Frye: 'what makes tragedy tragic and not simply ironic, is the presence of a counter movement of being that we call heroic, a capacity for action and passion, for doing and suffering which is above ordinary experience' (Robinson 1981: 171). Feminist critics tend to be less interested in tragedy *per se* than in analysing the social circumstances that lead to certain of Ibsen's female protagonists facing a tragic end.

But several of Ibsen's plays have female characters who demonstrate a heroism in the everyday round that does not lead to death. Prime among these is Ellida at the end of *The Lady from the Sea,* who courageously commits herself to the challenges of life. Other such everyday heroes are Mrs Linde in *A Doll's House* and Thea Elvsted in *Hedda Gabler*. Because of our taste for tragedy, it is perhaps no accident that *The Lady from the Sea* with its 'happy ending' was for many years regarded as a less interesting play than those that preceded and followed it, and scant attention has been paid to Mrs Linde and Thea Elvsted. Therefore in the short space available I intend to consider *A Doll's House, The Lady from the Sea* and *Hedda Gabler* and to highlight the courage of certain characters in them, and a heroism that does not end in death.

In a recent article Margaret D. Stetz admits that in the Third Wave feminism of the 1990s 'we have seen a sharp turn away from the notion that any one woman – or any one woman's consciousness – can stand in for all others' (Stetz 2007: 151). With this I would agree; indeed it is a fundamental part of the argument of this essay that Ibsen in many of his plays gives us two contrasted female characters, and one cannot necessarily assume that one is only a foil for the other. This is all the more true today when we can read Ibsen's plays as text and can separate them from his own notes, which in the case of *A Doll's House* can lead the reader to see Nora through his eyes. But in relation to *A Doll's House* Stetz argues that Mrs Linde's joyous return to Krogstad in Act III is 'clear evidence of the survival of an ideology that had long proved disabling to women's ambitions and damaging to their autonomy [...] an ideology that defined women as the moral guardians of men and as the good angels necessary to their uplift' (159). Not only that, but Stetz argues that Ibsen's portrayal of Mrs Linde shows the limits of Ibsen's feminism because he lets her feel unhappy and unfulfilled in her life as a single working woman. She points to inconsistencies in what Mrs Linde says about her working life, and maintains that 'the representation of the middle-class woman as uninspired by her career, including her career as a teacher, runs directly counter to the historical evidence reported by feminist historians such as Martha Vicinus' (162). It seems that here Stetz has forgotten what she herself argued in the earlier part of her article, namely that one woman's consciousness cannot stand for all. Mrs Linde loved Krogstad, but married Linde because she had to consider her bed-ridden mother and younger brothers. It seems she never had any children by Linde, so it is surely not hard to believe she might feel unfulfilled after Linde's death and after three years of work, and be delighted by the prospect of finally being re-united with the man she loved and of acquiring some children, who, even though they are not her own, are those of the man she loved? Indeed, several of the late plays of Ibsen contain women forming strong bonds with children who are not theirs, but who are the children of the men they love: Ellida in *The Lady from the Sea*, Aasta Allmers in *Little Eyolf* and Ella in *John Gabriel Borkman* spring to mind in this connection. Finally, one must not underestimate the significance of the fact that Mrs Linde, who knows all about the rules of society, shows considerable independence, courage and heroism, in throwing in her lot with a man who has been a social outcast.

Nora by contrast rejects all inherited ideas about society, the law, religion, and her duties as mother and wife, and walks out into a hostile, wintry world, to try to work out 'who is right, society or me.' There are many examples in the plays of Ibsen of characters who try to withdraw from the world in order to reflect upon it: Mrs Alving, Gregers, Rosmer, Dr Stockmann. Some of these are tragic figures, others comic, but all are vulnerable, and rarely effective. Mrs Linde's choices and decisions in no way invalidate Nora's, but Stetz should remember what Gina says to Mrs Sørby in Act IV of *The Wild Duck*: 'Oh we women are so different, – some one way, and some another' (Ibsen, vol. VI: 210).

The case for regarding Ellida's decisions in *The Lady from the Sea* as heroic has recently been made by Toril Moi in her book, *Henrik Ibsen and the Birth of Modernism*. Instead of seeing the Stranger in terms of an Other who can arouse in Ellida a 'sexual desire which melts her willpower,' Moi sees him as 'a barely concealed metaphor for Ellida's yearning for the infinite and the absolute' (Moi 2006: 296), which is why she does not recognize him when he appears. These yearnings are, she argues, in dangerous opposition to finitude and necessity, which Ellida has up till now not accepted. Not only that, but Moi argues that in this play Ibsen is challenging the romantic absolutism of the promise that was made when the Stranger took one of Ellida's rings, and one of his own, tied them together and threw them into the sea, saying that now they were wedded to the sea. (The fact that he says they are wedded to the sea and not to each other is noteworthy and it seems like another example of the strange and suspect 'proposals' that Ibsen's male characters sometimes make, and which you, Janet, have commented on in relation to *Rosmersholm*.)

When the Stranger announces that he has come to fetch Ellida, and she responds with horror, the Stranger asks whether she does not want to go with him, to which she replies 'I will not! Never, never! I will not! I can't! I won't! [*In a lower voice*]. Besides, I daren't!' (Ibsen, vol. VII: 77). As Moi puts it, 'Against the Stranger's insistence that she owes him her faith, Ellida insists on her *will*' (2006: 305). When Wangel appears and asks the Stranger whether he is intending to take her by force, the Stranger replies 'if Ellida wants to come with me, then it must be of her own free will' (Ibsen, vol. VII: 80). This reply strikes Ellida with such force that she reiterates the phrase 'of my own free will' twice in a sort of amazed fashion as if it opened up a totally new perspective.

Moi's interpretation of these exchanges is that Ellida comes to realize that she has the power to defy the Stranger's 'compelling will,' 'not by mobilizing some superhuman effort of resistance, but by choosing finitude' (Moi 2006: 305). If Ellida had followed the Stranger before being given the freedom to choose in the final pages of the play, she would have been following him 'as she did once before, in the marriage ceremony with the rings – that is to say as in a trance, compelled by his unbending will' (307). But when Wangel offers Ellida the freedom to choose, her choice is between 'the Stranger's absolute, infinite, unbounded mad freedom' and Wangel's offer of 'finite, ordinary human freedom' (306). But, given the choice, had she *chosen* to go with the Stranger, he 'would be stripped of his mysterious allure, he would no longer be the infinite for Ellida, but just another man and considered as an ordinary man, as husband and lifelong partner, he is no match for Wangel' (307). Gail Finney, too, endorses the ending of *The Lady from the Sea*, stating that the play 'may stand as the last word on the question of Ibsen and feminism. For insofar as it reverses the pattern of *A Doll's House*, it does not present women with the choice between motherhood and solitary New Womanhood but rather powerfully advocates women's right to choose their identity and combine roles as they desire' (Finney 1994: 103).

In choosing Wangel, Ellida re-enters 'the human community, in all its fragility' according to Moi (2006: 307), and one can certainly ask if there is not as much risk and heroism in doing this as in succumbing to an absolute intransigent will. Ibsen has a series of characters who exercise this kind of will on others and they do not make an attractive gallery of figures. They range from Brand, to Gregers Werle in *The Wild Duck,* and to Hedda Gabler, though others could certainly be included.

Moving to *Hedda Gabler,* it is not difficult to see that Hedda lacks the creative will and courage to make something of her situation, and that her intransigence can only lead to death. But this article is not concerned with those whose choices lead to death, but those whose equally creative and heroic decisions lead to life.

The similarities between Mrs Linde and Thea Elvsted are striking. Both marry someone they do not love (though Mrs Linde loved Krogstad before she felt compelled to marry Linde, while Thea Elvsted met Løvborg after she had married Elvsted), and neither have children by their husband. In both plays the women show courage in attaching themselves to men whom polite society would consider unsuitable, though Thea Elvsted's courage is of a distinctly rasher order than Mrs Linde's, for she follows Løvborg to town while still married to Elvsted. Joan Templeton, however, tries to play down the significance of this, stating that, 'Thea's unconventionality is of the approved sort for women; she risked her reputation for a man' (Templeton 1997: 219).

One could easily extend what Margaret Stetz writes about Mrs Linde to Thea Elvsted, and see her as another of those women to whom Ibsen with his limited feminist perspective gives the role of being 'guardians of men and as the good angels necessary to their uplift.' Løvborg certainly became such a reformed character through his association with Thea that he could write his new book, but Ibsen lets Thea make it clear that she did not actively try to change Løvborg: 'I never dared do that. But he knew all right that I didn't like that sort of thing. And then he gave it up' (Ibsen, vol. VII: 194). Not only that, but the influence was not all one way, for he, according to her testimony, has 'made me into a sort of real person. Taught me to think ... and to understand a lot of things' (ibid). One could query what 'sort of' implies when attached to 'real person,' though it is possible that it only expresses Thea's unassumingness. Whatever it means, Thea speaks of the time she was able to help Løvborg with his book as a 'beautiful, happy time.' Again Joan Templeton is disparaging, saying 'Thea Elvsted is a sterling example of the nineteenth-century womanly ideal [...] the devoted companion who serves a man in his work (Templeton 1997: 220). Now, however, Thea has followed Løvborg to town because she is worried what he might do.

When Løvborg enters in Act III the morning after Brack's party, the first thing he does when he sees Hedda and Thea is roughly tell Thea that everything is over between them, and that he has no use for her any more because he no longer intends to work. At this point Thea, 'yielding to despair' as the stage instruction indicates, asks 'What am I to do with my life then?' While this could look as if Thea is in despair at the loss of her role as the good and supportive angel, this would be a less than adequate reading. Her relationship to Løvborg never was that of the supportive angel, for not only does she describe it as one of their being 'good companions,' but the very fact of helping him was an act of rebellion *against* her role of being the good angel for Elvsted. When Løvborg tells her that she must now try to live her life as if she had never known him and go back home to Elvsted, she does not plead, but 'in rebellion' – as the stage instructions state – she tells him that she will not be 'packed off like this! I want to be right here! To be together with you when the book comes out!' and two exchanges further on, 'I want to see you praised and honoured again. And the joy … I want to share the joy of it with you.' (Ibsen, vol. VII: 246). This is not the cry of a woman who has no vocation of her own, but the assertiveness of a woman who sees herself as a co-creator. When Løvborg then tells Hedda and Thea that he has torn up the manuscript and cast the pieces on the fjord, Thea faces him squarely and says, 'I want you to know, Løvborg, what you've done to the book … For the rest of my life it'll be for me as though you'd killed a little child' (247). When he agrees, she again turns to him accusingly and asks, 'But how could you then …! The child was mine, it was also mine!' There is a vehemence here which, if it does not quite match Hedda's when she burns the manuscript, at least tells us that Thea is not just a blonde, subservient, 'good angel.' At this point Thea, who just has received a devastating blow, not surprisingly leaves because for the present she can see 'nothing but darkness ahead' of her.

When she returns in Act IV because she is concerned about Løvborg, Brack first tells her that he has been taken to hospital, and her distress then is that they were not reconciled. When she learns that he shot himself she accepts that everything is over. But when, a short while after, Tesman bemoans the fact that he did 'not even leave behind him the work that would have made his name immortal' (Ibsen, vol. VII: 260). Thea's thoughts immediately turn to the manuscript and not only does she say that she wishes it could be put together again, but suggests it can. To some critics, this looks like too easy and fast a turnaround, as if Thea can transfer her loyalties from Løvborg to Tesman. But is it not more as if she has to find a foster- or step-father for a child? Thea is not a woman without a project of her own, who has to have a man whom she can serve as 'the good angel,' but a woman who wants to give something to the future, and can only do so in co-operation with someone else, and one has to ask if this is less valid than having a solo project of one's own? Again one should remember Stetz's observation (which she does not follow herself) that we no longer believe that 'any one woman's consciousness – can stand in for all others.'

In this short essay I have tried to present a few arguments against those critics who would limit Ibsen's feminism to his portrayal of the rebellious women who cannot find a place for themselves in the society of their day, and who denigrate those women who do not have a solo project, but find fulfilment in co-operation with, and relationship to, another human being. I would argue that Ibsen lets us see that these women show a creative courage and heroism in accepting and transforming everyday reality that is as valid as the intransigent heroism of those female characters who cannot do so.

Best wishes,

Marie

References

Finney, G. (1994): 'Ibsen and feminism.' In J. McFarlane (ed.), *The Cambridge Companion to Ibsen*, Cambridge: Cambridge University Press, pp. 89-105.

Garton, J. (1994): 'The Middle Plays.' In J. McFarlane (ed.), *The Cambridge Companion to Ibsen*, Cambridge: Cambridge University Press, pp. 106-125.

Ibsen, H. (1960-1977): *The Oxford Ibsen*. Edited by James McFarlane. London: Oxford University Press.

Moi, T. (2006): *Henrik Ibsen and the Birth of Modernism: Art, Theatre, Philosophy*. Oxford: Oxford University Press.

Northam, J. (1966): 'The substance of Ibsen's idealism.' In *Contemporary Approaches to Ibsen,* Vol 1, pp. 9-20.

Robinson, M. (1981): 'Ibsen and Possibility of Tragedy.' In *Scandinavica* 20 (2), pp. 171-182.

Stetz M. (2007): 'Mrs Linde, Feminism, and Women's Work, Then and Now.' *Ibsen Studies* VII(2), pp.150-168.

Templeton, J. (1997): *Ibsen's Women*. Cambridge: Cambridge University Press.

Maja's Freedom
in Ibsen's *Når vi døde vågner*

Tanya Thresher

If we accept the claim of many feminist critics such as Hélène Cixous[1] that death is the cultural position of Woman in patriarchy, then the mere title *Når vi døde vågner* (When We Dead Awaken) seems to promise much for the feminist scholar.[2] As women are also often considered to have been silenced in patriarchal tradition, then the opening dialogue in which Maja paradoxically claims to be able to hear the silence around her also seems to suggest that this dramatic epilogue might encourage a new form of listening that would allow women their own voice. The ambitious scholar might expect this play to provide a positive codicil to the woman question in the Ibsen corpus, particularly if we take into account previous Ibsen representations of women who challenge patriarchal norms such as Hedda Gabler or Nora Helmer. We might also take into account Ibsen's statement in an interview in *Verdens Gang* on December 12, 1899:

> Hvad jeg i denne Forbindelse har ment med Betegnelsen Epilog er blot dette, at Stykket danner Epilogen til den Række af mine dramatiske Arbejder, som tager sine Begyndelse med 'Et Dukkehjem,' og som nu afsluttes med 'Naar vi døde vaagner.' Dette siste Arbejde hører med til de Oplevelser, jeg har villet skildre i den hele Række. Denne udgjør en Helhed, en Enhed, og hermed er jeg nu færdig. Om jeg herefter kommer til at skrive noget, vil alt blive i en helt anden Forbindelse, maaske i en anden Form ogsaa.[3] (quoted in Seip 1928-57: 206)

> (What I mean in this connection by the term Epilogue is merely that the piece forms an epilogue to the series of my dramatic works that begins with 'A Doll House' and now ends with 'When We Dead

Awaken.' This last work belongs to the experiences I have wanted to depict in the entire series. This [series] comprises an entirety, a unity with which I am now finished. If I come to write something afterwards it will be in an entirely different connection, perhaps also in another form.)[4]

While this play certainly echoes themes raised in earlier Ibsen works and does problematize the hierarchical binary oppositions that support patriarchal ideology, the final outcome for the two female characters seems to offer troubling instances of an apparent reinstatement of that same ideology. Maja replaces one male oppressor with another seemingly more overt one all in the name of freedom, and Irene returns to a subservient role in relation to Rubek when she states in her penultimate line: '(*som forklaret*) Jeg følger villig og gerne min hersker og herre' (Ibsen, HU XIII: 283) ([*as if transfigured*] I follow my lord and master willingly and gladly). While these instances may raise questions for a scholar searching for an alternative to a tradition based upon oppositions which after all have proved disastrous for women in particular, a nuanced reading of them reveals, in my opinion, Ibsen's deep understanding both of the position of women in modern Western society and art, and of a relationship between the sexes that is commensurate with his humanism. This essay will detail Maja as a positive representation of a woman able to negotiate the patriarchal framework precisely because of her capability for change and her capacity for creative language use.

A reading of *Når vi døde vågner* in the context of binary oppositions is commonplace within Ibsen scholarship and is encouraged by the content of the play itself, since it is replete with doubles and pairings. Moreover, the play examines the relationships of art to reality, death to life, symbolism to realism, and ultimately, and most importantly for this investigation, of female to male. Nevertheless, as Lisbeth Wærp (1999: 101) points out, the characters in fact

> [v]iser seg å være splittet og typifiserer *begge* poler i motsetningsparene, avhengig av hvem man ser dem i forhold til, og i hvilken fase man ser dem i. [...] Ved nærmere ettersyn viser det seg likevel å være en dynamisk struktur av motsetninger som glir over i hverandre

> (reveal themselves to be divided and typify both poles in the oppositional pairs dependent upon who they are seen in relation

to and in which phase one sees them. [...] On closer inspection [the play] shows itself nevertheless to be a dynamic structure of oppositions which flow over into each other).

It is this view of the characters as part of a dynamic network of relations that blur the lines between opposites which Maja typifies.

Act III of *Når vi døde vågner* sets itself up as a battle between the sexes in that it is introduced by the very physical struggle of Maja and Ulfhejm on the mountain top. The relation of this space to the two male figures represents the very possibilities of female representation in a traditional patriarchal society. For Rubek it is a space to which he entices women, most importantly the young Irene, with the promise of showing them 'al verdens herlighed' (Ibsen, HU XIII: 252) (all the splendor of the world), a space in which his utopian vision of Woman is to be realized. For Ulfhejm on the other hand, the space has a practical usage that supports his very survival in that it is a hunting ground to which he takes his clients. Ulfhejm takes women to this space not to view an intangible concept, but rather to seduce them in the somewhat brutal manner romanticized in fairy tales, as Maja recognizes when she parallels the hunter's behaviour to that of the man who 'kom ind til kongedatteren i en skogbjørns lignelse' (Ibsen, HU XIII: 274) (came to the princess in the form of a forest bear). The hunting castle to which Ulfhejm takes women is, in fact, a tumbledown cabin which Maja refers to as 'svinestien' (ibid) (the pig sty). The physical reality of Ulfhejm's cabin exemplifies the disconnection between his verbal description of the building, a description that Maja initially finds so enticing, and its actual manifestation. Moreover, the cabin highlights the very ephemeral nature of relationships between the sexes. Outlining its function as a short-term shelter for a human couple, Ulfhejm refers to the cabin as a place in which 'et menneskepar kan dorme bort en sommernat nokså lunt derinde' (Ibsen, HU XIII: 274) (a human couple can doze away a summer night quite cozily in there). The recognition of the cabin as a space which is used temporarily contrasts starkly with Rubek's stagnant interpretation of the mountain as a space of the past, which in turn suggests Rubek's inability to conceive of change within his relationships, in particular to Irene.

The ability to change evidenced by Ulfhejm's relationship to the cabin may be read positively if we take into account Ibsen's earlier portrayals of change and how that relates to successful relationships between the sexes. Nora in *Et dukkehjem* expresses her desire for 'det vidunderligste' (Ibsen, HU VIII: 364) (the most wonderful thing), which she defines in the final moments of the play as the possibility that she and Torvald might 'forvandle oss således at vårt samliv kunne bli et ekteskap' (ibid) (change ourselves so that our life together could become a marriage). Ellida in *Fruen fra havet* mentions that 'det er forvandling i dette her' (Ibsen, HU: XI) (there is change in this) when talking of Wangel's release of her from the marriage contract, and suggests that change has permitted her the freedom to choose. Similarly, Rita in *Lille Eyolf* refers to positive aspects of the laws of change that allow her to move beyond mourning the death of her son and to accept a socially responsible role. While Ibsen never actually shows us the long-term outcome of such a change in relationships between the sexes, the implication with these examples is that it may occur and that it would be a positive alternative to the oppression these women have experienced. The ability to accept change is precisely what Maja and Ulfhejm embrace in their final appearance in the play, and what Irene and Rubek ultimately reject in their continued ascent up the mountain.

In accompanying Ulfhejm up the mountain, Maja has already altered her existence and has renounced her marriage to Rubek by embarking on what she calls an adventure that 'vil sætte livet i stedet for alt det andet' (Ibsen, HU XIII: 269) (would put life before everything else). She has changed her appearance, and thereby her suitability for movement within the mountain landscape, by wearing 'en flad turisthue, kort ophæftet skørt, som kun rækker til midt på læggen, og høje solide snorestøvler. I hånden har hun en lang springstav' (Ibsen, HU XIII: 243) (a flat tourist hat, short skirt that is hitched up and only reaches to midway up her thighs, and high, heavy laced boots. In her hand she has a long staff) in Act II. This contrasts with the 'elegant rejsedragt' (Ibsen, HU XIII: 215) (elegant travelling clothes) she wore in Act I. Moreover, her new vitality is also shown in the rosy cheeks that have replaced her tired appearance. Additionally, as Frode Helland notes, Maja has adopted some of Ulfhejm's verbal expressions, in particular the analogy of the sanatorium to 'flueskabet' (Helland 2000: 442) (the fly-trap). Maja's changed appearance and manner complement her growing awareness of otherness, and it is this very awareness that halts Ulfhejm's brutal sexual advances. The interaction between Maja and Ulfhejm concerning his identity reveals Maja's understanding of the human individual:

> FRU MAJA (undviger og måler ham med øjnene) Véd De, hvad de ligner for noget, godsejer Ulfhejm?
> GODSEJER ULFHEJM. Jeg tænker vel at jeg ligner nærmest mig

selv.
FRU MAJA. Ja det har De akkurat ret i. For De ligner livagtig en faun.
GODSEJER ULFHEJM. En faun – ?
FRU MAJA. Ja netop en faun.
GODSEJER ULFHEJM. En faun, – er ikke det et slags udyr? Eller sådan noget som en skogdævel at kalde for?
FRU MAJA. Jo just slig en som De er. En som har både bukkeskæg og bén som en gedebuk. Ja, og så har faunen horn også.
(Ibsen, HU XIII 273-4)

(MAJA [evasively, eyeing him up and down] Do you know what you resemble Squire Ulfhejm?
SQUIRE ULFHEJM I rather think I resemble mostly myself.
MAJA Yes, you're right in that. Because you look just like a faun.
SQUIRE ULFHEJM A faun – ?
MAJA Yes, precisely. A faun.
SQUIRE ULFHEJM A faun, – isn't that a sort of monster? Or something like a forest devil?
MAJA Yes, just like you are. Something that has both a goat's beard and legs like a goat. Yes, and there the faun has horns as well.)

Maja's description of Ulfhejm as a faun, forest devil and monster not only underlines a mythological connection to Pan, god of fertility, but also in a wider context shows an awareness of the dualistic nature of the hunter.[5] She acknowledges here Ulfhejm's animalistic side, a side also exposed in the way in which Ulfhejm fails to differentiate between animals and humans when he calls his hunting dogs 'mine nærmeste' (Ibsen, HU XIII: 230) (my closest friends), and in his very name, which means 'wolf-home,' bringing to mind Rubek's busts that contain an animal head beneath the human likeness. In contrast to Ulfhejm, however, Rubek fails to acknowledge a positive aspect to this duality, using it merely as an example of commercial art, the 'true' meaning of which the masses cannot possibly comprehend.

The way in which Maja verbalizes her perception of Ulfhejm's identity is an important example of her ability to create stories and verse: it represents a movement away from the silence that characterizes her relationship to Rubek, as well as an improvement in her ability to negotiate the conditions of her existence. Her desire to go on an adventure in which she 'vil sætte livet i stedet for alt det andet' (Ibsen, HU XIII: 269) (wants to put life before everything else), finds its expression in a simple rhyming verse which she creates:

> FRU MAJA: (synger og jubler) Jeg er fri! Jeg er fri! Jeg er fri! / Mit fangenskabs liv er forbi! / Jeg er fri som en fugl! Jeg er fri! / Ja for jeg tror, jeg er vågnet nu – endelig (ibid)

> (MAJA: [sings jubilantly] I am free! I am free! / My life of captivity is over! / I am free as a bird! I am free / Yes, because I think I have woken up now – finally).

This verse comprises in fact the final lines of the play: it is heard as the curtain closes, and consequently carries much weight for the audience. As an example of poetry or creative language it falls into the narrative framework that Irene elucidates when she refers negatively to Rubek as a 'digter' (poet) instead of a 'kunstner' (artist), after discovering the changes he made to the original sculpture (Ibsen, HU XIII: 264). While Irene's accusation is intended as a derogatory designation of Rubek, it can be re-evaluated in light of Maja's verse and the parallel motivations of the two characters to put life before everything else. The changes made to the sculpture, in fact, exemplify art as a complex representation of life in its multiplicity conditioned by observation, and if the changes are thereby classified as 'digtning' (poetry), then that too carries with it positive implications for interpretation.

Rubek changed the sculpture after Irene left, a departure instigated according to Irene by the insistence their collaboration was but an 'episode,' something that indicates its very ephemeral nature, which Irene could not accept. Motivated by his desire to put life before everything else, Rubek marries Maja and alters the original sculpture which then is deemed a masterpiece by the general public. According to Rubek, the original version of 'Oppstandelsens dag' (Resurrection day) represents a pure woman who awakens to a state of ecstatic sameness and lack of change:

> den rene kvinde således, som jeg syntes hun måtte vågne på opstandelsens dag. Ikke undrende over noget nyt og ukendt og uanet. Man fuldt af en helligdoms glæde over at genfinde sig selv uforvandlet, – hun, jordkvinden, – i de højere, finere, gladere egne – efter den lange, drømmeløse dødssovn (Ibsen, HU XIII: 230)

> (the pure woman as I thought she would awaken on resurrection day. Not wondering about anything new and unknown and

unimagined. But full of sacred joy in finding herself unchanged, – her, earth woman, – in the higher, finer happier realms – after the long, dreamless sleep of death).

With Irene's absence and an increased awareness of the world, Rubek has changed the piece to reflect that 'som jeg rundt omkring mig i verden så med mine øjne' (HU: 262) (which I saw with my own eyes in the world around me). From a portrayal of one woman, Rubek has expanded the base of the sculpture:

> – så den blev stor og rummelig. Og på den lagde jeg et stykke af den buede, bristende jord. Og op af jordrennerne vrimler der nu mennesker med dulgte dyreansigter. Kvinder og mænd, – slig som jeg kændte dem ude fra livet (ibid)

> (– so it became large and spacious. And on it I made a piece of the curved, cracking earth. And people with hidden animal faces are now teeming up out of the cracks of the earth. Women and men, – just as I knew them from life).

Additionally, Rubek has pushed the woman into a 'mellemgrundsskikkelse' (Ibsen, HU XIII: 263) (a figure in the middle ground), and included a depiction of himself as a 'skyldbetinget mand, som ikke kan komme helt løs fra jordskorpen' (ibid) (guilt-ridden man who cannot quite break free from the earth's crust). It is this sculpture that depicts the very multiplicity of life in that it, in parallel to Rubek's portrait busts, recognizes the complexity of human existence. Furthermore, as Michael Goldman (2006: 392-3) states, 'Rubek's statue in its final form, with its imagery of guilt, animal sexuality and violence, is truer to Irene's life than either the version of innocent beauty she insists on or the fantasy image Rubek now projects on her.' Additionally, the final sculpture highlights the necessary communal existence of individuals and relegates the idealized woman figure from a central position to a transitional one. Irene's accusation of 'poet' seems, in light of the changes, a positive designation, even if it is not intended, or taken, as such.

The importance of poetry and of telling stories is further reiterated in Maja and Ulfhejm's final conversation together. In order to fend off Ulfhejm's rough, almost violent sexual advances, Maja convinces the hunter, the loner who has preferred the company of dogs to people, to tell his story. Maja's interest in Ulfhejm's stories contrasts with Rubek the artist who tells Maja very little, and as Maja notes is 'ingen selskabsmand'

(Ibsen, HU XIII: 248) (not one for good company). As Maja observes of Rubek: 'du [g]åer helst sån for dig selv og tumler med dit eget. Og jeg kan jo ikke tale ordentlig med dig om dine sager' (ibid) (you keep mostly to yourself and are occupied with your own things. And I can't really talk to you properly about your things). While Maja's relationship to Rubek is characterized by a lack of communication and silence, her attraction to Ulfhejm, on the other hand, stems precisely from

> alt det vidunderlige, han fortæller om fjeldet. Og om livet deroppe! Stygt, fælt, skrækkelig afskyeligt er det meste af det, han lyver sammen -. Ja, for jeg tror næsten at han lyver. Men så vidunderlig dragende er det alligevel. (Ibsen, HU XIII: 240)

> (all the wonderful things he tells about the mountain. And about life up there! Most of what he fabricates is ugly, disgusting, horribly loathsome. Yes, because I almost think that he is lying. But it is so wonderfully fascinating, nevertheless.)

Ulfhejm's narrative becomes all the more meaningful to Maja when he personalizes it and explains that he

> tog engang et ungt tøsebarn, - løfted hende op av gadesølen og bar hende på mine arme. På hænderne bar jeg hende. Vilde bære hende slig gennem hele livet; - på det at hun ikke skulde støde sin fod på nogen sten. For hun havde svært tyndslidte sko den tid jeg fandt hende -. [...] Tog hende op af skidtet og bar hende som jeg højest og varligst kunde. Og vét De, hvad jeg fik til tak for det? [...] Hornene fik jeg. Hornene, som De grangivelig kan se. (Ibsen, HU XIII: 275-6)

> (once took a young wench – lifted her up from the mire of the streets and carried her on my arms. I carried her with my hands. I wanted to carry her thus throughout life; - so that she shouldn't stub her foot on any stones. Because she had very worn out shoes when I found her- . [...] Took her up out of the dirt and carried her as highly and carefully as I could. And do you know what thanks I got for that? [...] I got the horns. The horns that you can see so precisely.)

Maja recognizes in his story a certain parallel to her own situation, one the audience may already suspect because of the clear similarity drawn between Ulfhejm and her husband. Both men, Ulfhejm claims:

arbejder med et hårdt materiale [...] Han maser vel med marmorstenen, kan jeg tænke mig. Og jeg maser med spændte, dirrende bjørnsene. Og begge så lægger vi materialet under os til slutt. Gør os til herre og mester over det. Gi'er os ikke før vi har vundet bugt med det, som strider så hårdt imod (Ibsen, HU XIII: 229)

(work with hard materials [...] He really slaves away with the marble, I imagine. And I slave away with taut, quivering bear sinews. And both of us eventually get the material under us. Make ourselves lord and master of it. Don't give up before we have the upper hand on that which struggles so much against us).

For Rubek this material is naturally the clay and marble he works with and for Ulfhejm it is the wild animals he hunts – and women are intricately connected to that material in both instances. Having listened to Ulfhejm's tale, Maja relates how she, in similar fashion to his street girl, was originally bought by Rubek with promises of accompanying him 'på det højeste berg, hvor der var lys og solskin over al måde' (Ibsen, HU XIII: 276) (to the highest mountain, where there was excessive light and sunshine). Calling herself a silly girl, she acknowledges the life Rubek led her to was 'et koldt, klamt bur, hvor der hverken var sol eller fri luft [...] men bare forgyldning og store, forstenede menneskespøgelser rundt væggene' (ibid) (a cold, oppressive cage, where there was neither sun nor fresh air. [...] But just gilding and huge ghostly humans that had been turned to stone around the walls). While Maja's storytelling depicts the presence of art as confining and lacking in life, it does so in a language and imagery reminiscent of a folktale. In this way it differs sharply from Ulfhejm's story, since it '[b]åde i form og innhold låner altså [...] grep fra eventyret, nok en gang er det kunstens domæne hun søker recurs til når hun skal finne uttrykk for sine tanker' (Helland 2000: 452) (both in form and content borrows [...] aspects from the folktale, once again it is the domain of art in which she seeks recourse when she wants to find expression for her thoughts). In contrast to Ulfhejm's first person confessional, Maja's begins in folktale tradition with '[d]er var engang' (Ibsen, HU XIII: 276) (once upon a time), and is told in a more impersonal third-person narrative in which characters are classified in general terms as 'et dumt pigebarn' and 'en stormægtig herremand' (ibid) (a silly little girl and a mighty nobleman).[6]

Maja's narrative brings about a change as Ulfhejm now calls her 'min gode jagtkammerat' (Ibsen, HU XIII: 277) (my good hunting companion) and halts his aggressive advances. The hunter, who now refers to himself as a 'lappeskrædder' (ibid) (tailor of patches) asks Maja, 'kunde vi to ikke prøve på at flikke fillerne sammen hist og her, – så vi fik ligesom et slags menneskeliv ud af det?' (ibid) (couldn't we two try and patch the rags together here and there – so we made a kind of human life out of it?) and suggests that when the relationship is worn out that 'så står vi der, frit og frejdigt, – som de, vi selv er!' (ibid) (then we will stand there freely and boldly, as we really are!). In addition to an acknowledgement of each individual identity that may come together in some sort of human life, there are positive connotations to Ulfhejm's patchwork metaphor. These have been enumerated by Sofie Gram Ottesen in her article 'Om at finde sin stemme. Melodrama som skepticisme i Ibsens *Når vi døde vågner*' (On Finding one's Voice. Melodrama as Scepticism in Ibsen's *When we Dead Awaken*) and I quote Ottesen's astute discussion of the connotations here at length:

> Ulfheims tilbud og Majas accept tyder på at de to ikke ønsker den ødelæggende enhed, men en sammenføjning 'hist og her' af deres to hidtil adskilte liv. Dermed ligger der en anerkendelse af den andens andethet indbygget i den ordning, de indgår i sammen. Endvidere tyder Ulfheims fremhævelse af, at det er et *menneskeliv*, han ønsker at skabe sammen med Maja, på, at han er klar til at indgå i en mellommenneskelig, sproglig relation med hende, og at han er klar over at hans hidtidige liv, har været først et slags 'engleliv' og siden et slags 'dyreliv'. (Ottesen 1999: 172)

> (Ulfhejm's offer and Maja's acceptance indicate that the two do not want a destructive unity, but a joining together 'here and there' of their two formerly separate lives. In the arrangement they are about to enter together there thus lies an acknowledgement of the difference of the other. Furthermore, Ulfhejm's emphasis that it is a *human life* he wants to create with Maja indicates that he is ready to enter into an inter-personal, linguistic relationship with her, and that he is aware that his life until now was initially a kind of 'angel life' and then a type of 'animal life'.)

With this in mind, we may interpret Maja's final poetic 'Jeg er fri! Jeg er fri! Jeg er fri! / Mitt fangenskaps liv er forbi! / Jeg er fri som en fugl! Jeg er fri!' (I am free! I am free! / My life in captivity is over! / I am free as a bird! I am free!) as an acknowledgement of life in all its multiplicity and temporality. Not only has Maja found a voice, which expresses itself differently in song, but her movement down the mountain signals her distancing from any idealized notion of Woman, away from art and into poetry. In contrast to the prostitute Ulfhejm carried up from the gutter – the ascent implying idealization just as was the case with Rubek and Irene when creating the statue – he will carry Maja down the mountain, from idealization to reality. This reality is not clouded by any preconceived notion of certainty or stability, something to which Maja has already suggested her own resistance in Act I with her reply to Rubek's statement that 'Hele verden véd ingenting! Forstår ingenting!' (Ibsen, HU XIII: 219) (The entire world knows nothing! Understands nothing!). Maja's response of 'Nå, så aner de da vel i alle fald noget –,' (ibid) (well, at least they have some idea –) indicates an ability on her part not to look for absolutes, and a flexibility that will enable her to embrace multiplicity. Moreover, in Act II, it is Maja who evasively and innocently proposes a solution to Rubek's dilemma of needing Irene to unlock his creative impulses. She questions Rubek's anxiety:

> FRU MAJA (sér uskyldig på ham) Men snille Rubek, – er det da værdt at gøre al den opstyr og alle disse her ophævelser for noget, som er en så ganske ligefrem sag?
> PROFESSOR RUBEK. Synes du at dette der er så ganske ligefrem?
> FRU MAJA. Ja det synes jeg da rigtignok. Slut du dig bare til den, du mest behøver.
> (nikker til ham)
> Jeg skal nok altid vide at finde mig en plads.
> PROFESSOR RUBEK. Hvad mener du?
> FRU MAJA (sorgløst, undvigende). Nå, – jeg kan jo bare flytte ud på villaen, hvis det blir nødvendigt. Med det blir det ikke. For inde i byen, – i hele vort store hus, må der da vel – med lidt god vilje – kunne bli' rum til tre.
> PROFESSOR RUBEK (usikker). Og tror du at det vil kunne gå i længden?
> FRU MAJA (i en let tone). Herregud, – går det ikke, så går det ikke. Der er ikke noget at snakke om den ting.
> PROFESSOR RUBEK. Og hvad gjør vi så, Maja, – hvis det nu ikke går?
> FRU MAJA (ubekymret). Så går vi to simpelt hen af vejen for hinanden. Helt væk. Jeg finder mig altid noget nyt et steds i verden. Noget frit! Frit! Frit! – Det har ingen nød med det, professor Rubek!
> (Ibsen, HU XIII: 254-55)

(MAJA [looking innocently at him] But dear Rubek, – it is really worth making all this fuss and bother over something that is so straightforward?

PROFESSOR RUBEK Do you think this is straightforward?

MAJA Yes, I really do think that. Just you attach yourself to the one you need most.

[nods to him]

I will always manage to find a place for myself.

PROFESSOR RUBEK What do you mean?

MAJA [unworried, evasively] Well – I can just move out to the villa, if it becomes necessary. But it won't. For in the town,– in our large house, there has to be – with a little good will – room for three.

PROFESSOR RUBEK [uncertain] And do you think that would work in the long run?

MAJA [in a light tone] Good Lord, – if it doesn't work, then it doesn't work. There is little point in talking about it.

PROFESSOR RUBEK And what will we do then, Maja, – if it doesn't work?

MAJA [unconcerned] Then we two will simply go our separate ways. Completely away from each other. I will always find myself a new place somewhere in the world. Something free! Free! Free! – There is no danger in that, Professor Rubek!)

Maja's easy tone – suggested in the stage directions 'sorgløs, undvigende, i en let tone, ubekymret' (unworried, evasively in a light tone, unconcerned) – along with the very suggestion that there should be room for three people in Rubek's house, for both the idealized woman and the woman who represents real life, are clear indications of Maja's propensity for change and her understanding of the necessary multiplicity of human existence. And it is precisely such an understanding that might allow society to awaken to new representations of gender beyond a binary oppositional framework, one Ibsen announces in this final piece in a jubilant female singing voice.

References

Cixous, H. (1975): *La jeune née*. Paris: UGE

Detering, H. (1989): 'Allegorisierun und Modernität in Ibsens Når vi døde vågner.' In *Skandinavistik* 19, pp. 1-19.

Goldman, M. (2006): 'When we Dead Awaken. A Scene that gets Out of Control.' In *Modern Drama* 49:3, pp. 387-395.

Helland, F. (2000): *Melankoliens spill. En studie i Henrik Ibsens siste dramaer*. Oslo: Universitetsforlaget

Ibsen, H. (1928-57): 'Når vi døde vågner.' In F. Bull, H. Koht & D. Arup Seip (eds.): *Henrik Ibsen Samlede verker. Hundreårsutgave XIII*. Oslo: Gyldendal, pp. 210-284.

Ibsen, H. (1928-57): 'Et dukkehjem.' In F. Bull, H. Koht & D. Arup Seip (eds.): *Henrik Ibsen Samlede verker. Hundreårsutgave XIII*. Oslo: Gyldendal.

Ottesen, S.G. (1999): 'Om at finde sin stemme. Melodrama som skepticisme i Ibsens *Når vi døde vågner*.' In L Wærp (ed.): *Livet på likstrå*. Oslo: LNU & Cappelen, pp. 149-178.

Seip, D.A. (1928-57): 'Inledning.' In F. Bull, H. Koht & D. Arup Seip (eds.): *Henrik Ibsen Samlede verker. Hundreårsutgave XIII*. Oslo: Gyldendal, pp. 187-210.

Wærp, L. (1999): 'Oppsandelsen som forføreriskmorder. Personifikasjon, allegori, parodi og ironi i Når vi døde vågner.' In L. Wærp (ed.): *Livet på likstrå*. Oslo: LNU & Cappelen, pp. 94-121.

Notes

1. See for example 'Sorties' in *La jeune née*.

2. Even Ibsen's original title of 'Oppstandelsensdag' [Resurrection day] and its relationship to the verbs 'å stå opp' and 'å oppstå,' meaning respectively to arise, stand up and to rise from the dead or come into existence, might similarly entice a scholar seeking a revival of a lost female existence.

3. In a letter dated March 5 1900 to Moritz Prozor, his French translator, Ibsen explained that Prozor was 'i grunden ret når De siger at den serie, som afsluttes med epilogen, egentlig begyndte med "Bygmester Solness."' Men mere indgående vil jeg ikke gerne udtale mig om dette' (HU XVIII, 447). (essentially

correct when you say that the series which concludes with the epilogue actually began with *The Master Builder*. But I do not wish to comment more extensively on this.' While there are close ties between Ibsen's last four plays, *Bygmester Solness, Lille Eyolf, John Gabriel Borkman* and *Når vi døde vågner*, there are also clear traces of Ibsen's earlier pieces. This leads me to not disavow Ibsen's initial statement.

4. All translations from Norwegian are my own.

5. Heinrich Detering (1989: 6) has also pointed out the mythological overtones in Ulfhejm's name.

6. Helland (2000: 452) also notes the allusion in Maja's tale to 'bergtaking' or being enchanted and taken into the mountain, which is a common motif in folktales and is even evident in Ibsen's *Peer Gynt*.

Amalie Skram's *Agnete* (1893): A Drama of Reconciliation

Jorunn Hareide
Universitetet i Oslo

Amalie Skram's most successful play, *Agnete* (1893), has been read as the story of broken illusions of love. Men and women in Amalie Skram's universe have such different ideas of love that they can never find happiness with each other; their dreams of long-lasting love relationships are doomed from the outset (Engelstad 1981: 32ff.; Tjäder 2004: 71). I subscribe to this interpretation, but will extend the argument to include a Christian aspect of love that seems to be crucial in *Agnete*. This is also a play about reconciliation, or rather, the utopia of reconciliation through the redeeming love of a beloved man.

A Tainted Heroine

Agnete is the name of the heroine of the drama. She is a divorced, attractive and seemingly well-to-do woman who lives with a married couple and a widow in an artist's apartment in Copenhagen. One day Mr. Berg, her former divorce lawyer, asks her to marry him, despite the fact that he greatly disapproves of what he calls Agnete's bohemian ways. He had decided to leave town when he had to admit to himself that he had fallen in love, for Agnete was upsetting his peace of mind: '[...] jeg måtte tænke paa Dem meget mere, end jeg vilde og havde tid til' (Skram 1893: 89) (I found myself thinking of you much more than I wanted to or had time for). But Berg returned when he found that he could not live without Agnete.

She happily accepts his offer of marriage. True to her ideals, and trusting his love for her, Agnete soon reveals to him that after her divorce she has been lying, swindling and stealing to keep up her previous standard of living. She wants to make a clean breast of it before they get married. Berg is shocked but at first stands by his offer. After considering the matter for a few days, however, he comes to the conclusion that her confessions are more than he can accept, and breaks off the engagement. Agnete decides to leave her present life and take up a post as housekeeper for her cousin, a widower with several small children living in Nordfjord in the outskirts of Western Norway. It is the worst fate she can imagine, but at least she will have to steal and lie no more.

The drama is structured not unlike one of Henrik Ibsen's modern plays, and has often been considered as a response to his *Et Dukkehjem* (A Doll's House), suggesting a more disillusioned and perhaps more truthful assessment of Nora Helmer's decision to leave her husband than is implied in Ibsen's drama (Engelstad 1981: 36f. ; Garton 2011: 212). *Agnete* is made up of realistic scenes in a realistic setting, with contemporary dialogue and few symbols.

For what it is worth, one may ponder the meaning of the name of the heroine. Agnete is a Danish and Norwegian version of the more common Agnes, originally a Latin form of the Greek name *Hagne*, derived from the adjective *hagnos*, meaning chaste. It is uncertain whether the author was aware of this, but she was of course familiar with the heroine Agnes in Ibsen's *Brand*, who is struggling to meet the demands of a strict pietistic code imposed upon her by her husband. 'Chaste' is perhaps not the first adjective that comes to mind concerning Amalie Skram's heroine. It may perhaps be interpreted as a refutation of all the vicious gossip surrounding her?

The name and its meaning may also throw some light on an interesting symbol appearing in something Berg tells Agnete in Act II, in the scene where he first declares his love for her. He tells her that he finds her changed after his return, more beautiful than ever, but with a new, strange look in her eyes. She reminds him of a painting he has once seen, maybe in Dresden, of a female martyr – unfortunately I have not been able to identify it, if it exists. The woman is depicted on her knees at the end of an open plain with some ragged blocks of sandstone in front of her, turning her head in horror towards the approaching persecutors. 'Blikket tindrer af angst og resignation,' Berg says (Skram 1893: 94) (Her gaze trembles with angst and resignation). Agnete reacts with an almost imperceptible shiver. Does she recognize her own situation in this image?

What may have been on Berg's mind? Does he simply think that being a divorced woman, chaste or not, makes her an easy prey to gossipers, while what he really has observed without being aware of it, is that Agnete is unhappy and anxious about her present, untruthful situation? Or is she a 'martyr' to her conviction that she must tell the truth at all costs – with its fatal consequences? However one interprets this, the essential point is that Amalie Skram has chosen a religious, mainly Christian concept to express Agnete's predicament. As we shall see, the martyr is not the only religious reference in Agnete.

The Utopia of Love: Love's Power to Forgive and Purify

Let us stop for a moment at a short dialogue between Agnete and her friend Doris, who knows that Agnete has stolen the money that her friends discover to be missing. Agnete knows that Doris knows, and in her agitation wants to confess that she is the thief. But Doris refuses to hear her confession. One should never confide in anyone, for the day always comes when one regrets it, she says. Then she goes on to remind Agnete of her noble behaviour as a child. 'Lad mig bare få lov til at tro på Dig. Du véd jo, hvorledes jeg holder af dig, Agnete,' she says, adding that whatever happened, she would 'holde meg til det gode, jeg kjender hos Dig' (Skram 1893: 61) (Let me just be allowed to believe in you. You know how much I care for you, Agnete ... [whatever may happen] I shall cling to the good I know there is in you).

Agnete does not listen to Doris. She will not keep anything from the man she loves, she tells Berg:

> For det eneste, jeg har higet og tragtet efter, det er at klæ mig selv åndelig nøgen for den mand, jeg elsker på jorden, for at han skal se mig ganske som jeg er, og om muligt holde af mig tiltrods for, at han kjender mig helt' (Skram 1893: 110)

> (For the only thing I have sighed and longed for is to strip myself spiritually naked before the one man I love on Earth, so that he can see me just as I am, and if possible love me despite knowing me totally).

But while Doris acknowledges the good sides of Agnete and dismisses her moral weaknesses out of love for her, Berg judges Agnete in the light of her worst sides. His love is not strong enough to forgive. He can find nothing to excuse or explain her acts, which are in fact criminal and could send her to jail:

At Du kunde *få* dig til det. – Det er den mørkeste gåde, noget menneske nogensinde har stirret på. Hvis du havde havt børn, som sulted, eller en mor, som led nød. – Men jeg ser ingen grund, som tvang Dig. Jeg spejder forgjæves efter en formildende omstændighed. (Skram 1893: 160f.)

(That you could do such a thing. – It is the darkest mystery anyone has ever beheld. Had you had children who were hungry, or a mother in need. – But I see no reason that compelled you. I search in vain for any mitigating circumstance.)

Here speaks the barrister, not the lover. But it is crucial for Agnete that the man she loves must love her *despite* her faults. This is underlined in her conversation with her other suitor, the slightly comical Mr. Egholm, who wants to know whether there is any truth in the scandalous rumours he has heard about her. If so he will not marry her. His love is strong, but not so strong. Agnete replies: 'Ja men ser De, den mand jeg skulde ha, hans kjærlighed måtte netop være så stærk. Forstår De? Netop så stærk, at han vilde ha mig, om jeg så havde bedrevet det værste i verden' (Skram 1893: 117) (Yes, but you see, the man I should have, his love must be so strong. Do you understand? So strong, that he would want me even though I have committed the worst things in the world). Here Agnete is probably thinking of Berg, whose love she at this point does not doubt.

Considering that Agnete lost her mother at the age of two, this quest for a man's unconditional love may also be interpreted as an echo of the child's longing for the unconditional love of its mother. A glimpse of Agnete's unspeakable loneliness and desire for love and understanding is revealed as she tells Doris, awaiting Berg's final decision in desperation: 'Men min mor var så god. Hun var fuld av kjærlighed. Den, som har kjærlighed, forstår alt' (Skram 1893: 141) (But my mother was so good. She was full of love. The one who has love understands everything). It seems almost like a regression to childhood, as the love of a parent for her or his child seems to be the only possible unconditional love existing in this universe. But even this love is uncertain. Doris tries to warn Agnete that not all mothers are like that, hinting perhaps that not all men are like that either. But again Agnete will not listen to her.

As it turns out, Berg's love is not of this kind. He soon has to admit that he cannot bear so much truth, and wishes that she had not told him: 'Jeg er ikke mand for det, Agnete. Den, som skulde være min hustru, måtte ingen flekker ha.' (Skram 1893: 154) (I cannot do it, Agnete. The one who is to be my wife must have no blemishes). Agnete acknowledges that he is right: 'Nei, Du er ikke mand for at elske. [...] Du har aldrig kjendt noget til den hemmelighed, at to mennesker kan elske hinanden rene.' (Skram 1893: 154) (You have no ability to love [...] You have never known the secret that two people can love each other pure). This is an interesting autobiographical reference, as this last phrase seems to have been taken from a letter that Amalie Skram's second husband Erik wrote to her before they were married.[1]

After the final break, Berg complains that his future life seems to lie before him like a desert. But Agnete does not pity him. She believes that this situation will suit him well: 'Du vil leve rolig og uanfægtet og utilfredsstillet gjennem din ørken. For Du er skabt for ørkenen.' (Skram 1893: 155) (You will live quietly and unconcerned and unsatisfied on your way through your desert. For you are made for the desert). This is a harsh judgement on the part of Agnete, and a sign that she has seen through his pedantry and moralism. Has Agnete simply stopped loving Berg for this very reason? This was at least Amalie Skram's opinion. In a letter to Bjørnstjerne Bjørnson she wrote:

> Naturligvis er kjærligheden mellem Berg og Agnete ikke af den slags som holder ud eller står sig i kamp. Ikke hos hende heller. Derfor opgir hun ham jo straks. Hun blir jo så inderlig ydmyg at hun står der og citerer budene og snakker om at hun fortjener straf, hun som dagen i forvejen så prægtigt har forsvaret sig selv, dengang kjærligheden til Berg gjorde hende stærk og ryggesløs. Ved afskeden er kjærligheden alt vække, uden at hun véd det selv, og derfor er hun opi ingenting. (Letter of April 25, 1893. Quoted in Anker and Beyer 1981: 84)

> (Naturally, the love between Berg and Agnete is not of that kind which prevails or puts up a defence. Nor in her case, either. Therefore she gives him up immediately. She humbles herself so much that she stands there citing the commandments and saying that she deserves to be punished, whereas the day before she had defended herself so well, when her love for Berg made her strong and reckless. When they part, love is already gone, without her knowing it, and therefore it is hopeless for her.)

Before walking out of his life, Agnete puts Berg to a last test, proposing that she move with him to Christiania without being married to him; he can perhaps find her some suitable work there. This he rejects, at first seemingly out of concern for her reputation, but finally admitting that he must think of himself: 'Men også for min skyld, Agnete. En mand i min stilling – det vilde skade min anseelse' (But also for my sake Agnete. A man in my position – it would harm my reputation). He thereby confirms that he is more concerned with convention than with love, and Agnete replies: 'Ja, det er sant, hvert øjeblik står jeg her og glemmer, hvordan Du er, og hvorfor Du støder mig bort' (Skram 1893: 156) (Yes, it is true, how could I forget how you are, and why you are rejecting me).

An Enigmatic – and Repentant – Woman

How should we understand the character Agnete? Do we react as Bjørnstjerne Bjørnson did? In a series of letters exchanged between Skram and Bjørnson in April 1893 (Anker and Beyer 1982: 74-80), Bjørnson tells Skram he did not like the play, and considered it a flop. First of all, he did not believe in Agnete's love for Berg: 'At hun ælsker det korrekte, det rene viljeliv i ham, skjønner jeg; men det tørre, snobbete, fantasitomme...' (That she loves the correct, the pure life of the will, in him, I see; but the dry, snobbish, unimaginative ...).

As mentioned above, Amalie Skram more or less agreed with Bjørnson that Agnete could no longer love Berg when she finally fathomed his character. But in their correspondence, she defends her drama:

> Er Du blit så gammel i kundskab og verdenserfaring som Du er? og véd ikke endnu at elskovs og kjærligheds begyndelse og ende kan ingen udforske. Du og jeg véd at Berg ikke var noget for Agnete. Men hun selv, den stakker!

> (Have you really become as old and knowledgable and experienced as you are, and still do not know that no-one can fathom the beginning and end of passion and love? *You and I* know that Berg was no good for Agnete. But what about her, the poor thing!)

Amalie Skram posits that Berg at first seemed to Agnete a haven compared to the life she was leading, 'i en sump af laster' (in a swamp of vice), but after a while he would have made her unhappy. Therefore he shall not have her. The development of this conflict and the final exchanges between Agnete and Berg were much admired by the public at the staging of the play in Copenhagen, she adds in conclusion to this argument, to support her point of view.

Bjørnson's other main objection to the play was that a lady like Agnete would never resort to petty thefts. It is improbable: 'Du experimenterer for stærkt; for nejgu, om du vet det der av nogenslags erfaring, at en kvinne av det slag stjæler.' (You are experimenting too much; for surely you do not know from experience that ladies of that kind steal).

Amalie Skram's reply is interesting as it reveals a naturalistic set of ideas. She had known a woman who behaved like this and she was only depicting a scene from real life, just as it was. '[...] fordi hun holdt så meget af mig at hun klaget sin nød for mig, derfor har jeg kunnet skrive Agnete' ([...] because she cared for me so much that she poured out her troubles to me, and that is why I was able to write *Agnete*). Furthermore, she strongly disapproves of Bjørnson's notion that women can be categorized according to specific qualities: 'Dette her, at man tar den og den slags kvinder og tildeler dem den og den slags egenskaber – føj! for satan! –' (This idea that one can take this and that kind of woman and attribute to them this and that quality – like hell!).

But Bjørnson persisted. After Amalie Skram's death in 1905 he told Antonie Tiberg that if she intended to mention his name in connection with the biography she was planning, she must include the following paragraph:

'Jeg tror ikke det mindste paa det psychologiske grundlag i 'Agnete'; jeg maa naturligvis medgi at et menneske som stjæler ved siden derav i mange henseender kan være et udmerket menneske, og da navnlig et høit begavet menneske med mange idealer. Men det er tyveriets art som det kommer an paa. Det smaatyveri i andres lommer ute paa gangene og i stadig gjentagelse til visse bestemte tider, – aldrig kunde et menneske av den aandshøihet og redelige hjertevarme som Agnete har, indlate sig paa det. Det hele er en umulig konstruktion.'

(I do not believe at all in the psychological basis of *Agnete*; I must of course concede that people who steal can in many respects be fine people, not least a highly gifted person with many ideals. But it is the kind of theft that matters. This petty thieving from other's pockets in the corridors, recurring at given times – never could a person of such spiritual and genuine warmth as Agnete carry this out. All in all this is an impossible construction.)

Antonie Tiberg (1910: 215) comments laconically that medical and literary authorities have had no such objections, and that Bjørnson often showed a lack of understanding faced with Amalie Skram's psychological insight.

The portrayal of Agnete is not clinical, not neutral in a strictly naturalistic sense. She is portrayed with a certain compassion, and above all with understanding: her behaviour is not acceptable, but the reader or spectator will eventually forgive her and feel sorry for her, perhaps even grow fond of her. Why?

A tentative answer may be found in the expressions of reconciliation and redemption with which the play and Agnete's personal drama conclude. The solution to Agnete's predicament may have seemed more obvious, and appealed more directly to a contemporary public mainly brought up in accordance with Christian ethics, than it would to the more secular audiences of today. Agnete finally comes to understand that she does not deserve happiness; she has behaved immorally, and must atone for it. 'Jeg forstår det nu. Du skal ikke lyve, ikke stjæle, ikke bedrage – de bud står fast. Og den, som går udenom, fortjener sin straf' (Skram 1893: 159) (I understand now. You shall not lie, nor steal, nor swindle – those commandments stand. And anyone who disobeys them deserves her punishment). She accordingly decides to put an end to her former life and to compensate for her misdeeds by taking upon herself the fate that she feared most of all. This way of thinking is not grounded in law, but in a Christian moral order.

It may seem that Amalie Skram in her letter to Bjørnson quoted above dismisses this development in Agnete as the rather unhealthy effect of Berg's influence upon her. But Agnete's use of Christian metaphors and a biblical vocabulary in the dialogues with Berg will support my point of view. She 'citerer budene' (quotes the commandments), as Amalie Skram pointed out to Bjørnson, but this is not all.

Amalie Skram's language – in fiction as well as in non-fiction – is full of quotations and semi-quotations from the Bible. One does not always notice this, because many biblical expressions have become part of our everyday language – or at least were so in Amalie Skram's day. All the same these expressions give her texts a religious dimension, as they are only seemingly mere figures of speech, void of original meaning. This is also the case with *Agnete*.

When Berg first tells her that he will marry her in spite of what she has disclosed of her past, at the end of Act II, Agnete reacts by bursting into biblical language:

> Jeg er så fuld af taknemmelighed, ja af andagt. Et ord står for mig, som jeg ofte har tænkt på: 'Om eders synder var røde som blod, de skulde blive som den hvide uld.' Nu fatter jeg den salighed, de frelste tænkes at føle ved at bli tilgit og regnet for fuldgod af den

gud, for hvem intet er skjult. Ja, dette er lykke, og intet andet kan nævnes ved det navn. (Skram 1893: 111f.)

(I am so full of gratitude, yes, of devotion. I am reminded of one phrase, which I have often pondered:'Be your sins as red as blood, they shall be like white wool.' Now I grasp that grace felt by those who are saved and whose sins are forgiven and atoned for in the eyes of God, for whom nothing is hidden. Yes, this is bliss, and nothing else.)

The quotation is taken from Isaiah in the Old Testament, 1: 18, in a slightly altered version: 'Kommer dog og lader os gaa irette (med Hinanden)! siger Herren; dersom Eders Synder (end) vare som Purpuret, de skulle blive hvide som Sneen; om de (end) vare røde som Skarlagenets (Farve, da) skulle de (dog) blive som den (hvide) Uld' (Come now, and let us reason together, saith the Lord; though your sins be as scarlet, they shall be white as snow; though they be red like crimson, they shall be as wool.)[2]

Amalie Skram has strengthened the symbolic aspect of the text by substituting *blood* for the red colours *crimson* and *scarlet*. Isaiah's point is that if people would 'cease to do evil,' if they 'Learn to do well; seek judgment, relieve the oppressed, judge the fatherless, plead for the widow,' then God will cleanse them of their sins (Is. 1, 16-17). Agnete's present happiness now that Berg has forgiven her takes on religious dimensions. She is as blissful as if pardoned by God himself.

Agnete also uses biblical references when the break with Berg is a fact. Another sentence had been ringing in her ears since the day he promised to marry her despite her confessions: 'Det var som et kor af englerøster: Gak ind til din herres glæde, gak ind til din herres glæde' (Skram 1893: 159) (It was like a choir of angelic voices: enter thou into the joy of thy Lord, enter thou into the joy of thy Lord). This is a quotation from the story of the faithful and unfaithful servants in the gospel of St. Matthew in the New Testament. Their lord says to his faithful servant:'Vel, du gode og tro Tjener! Du har været tro over Lidet; jeg vil sætte dig over Meget; gak ind til til din Herres Glæde!' (St. Matthew, 25.21-30) (His lord said unto him, Well done, good and faithful servant; thou hast been faithful over a few things, I will make thee ruler over many things: enter thou into the joy of thy lord.)

But the words 'enter thou into the joy of thy lord' change their value when Agnete finally understands that Berg will let her down: 'Og siden, da jeg ante hvad der skulde ske med mig, er det blet ved at lyde som en bitterlig grådfuld klage' (Skram 1893: 159) (And ever since I understood what would happen to me, it has sounded like a bitter mournful complaint). Only the good and faithful servant can enter into 'din Herres Glæde,' the joy of the lord. The unfaithful servant is thrown 'into outer darkness,' where there shall be 'weeping and gnashing of teeth.' As Agnete has not been good and faithful, this will also be her fate. She accepts this, if not with joy.

A Defence of Nora Helmer

To substantiate my analysis I will take a brief look at Amalie Skram's critique of Henrik Ibsen's *Et Dukkehjem* (A Doll's House), which appeared in the Norwegian newspaper *Dagbladet* in January 1880. Amalie Skram was then 33 years old and had recently set out on a career as writer and reviewer, after a mental breakdown in the wake of the separation from her first husband August Müller. This very competent review, written some fourteen years prior to the publication of *Agnete*, expresses strong support for Nora's decision to leave her husband. Knowing Amalie Skram's situation it is not difficult to detect an autobiographical aspect here.

But there are other interesting observations to be made. The biblical references that we found in *Agnete* have parallels in this review of *A Doll's House* and demonstrate that biblical language was part of Amalie Skram's way of expressing herself throughout her career as a writer. In defence of Nora she points out that Nora has seen through her husband's vanity and egotism and with horror detects that she has loved 'den klingende Malm og den lydende Bjelle' (the clanging brass and ringing cymbal). She can love him no more, and no longer be his wife.

'Den klingende Malm og den lydende Bjelle' is a verbatim echo of Paul's first letter to the Corinthians in the New Testament, the well known dictum about the nature of love. Paul's version goes like this: 'Though I speak with the tongues of men and of angels, and have not charity, I am become as sounding brass, or a tinkling cymbal.' At first one may think that 'clanging brass and ringing cymbal' refers to Helmer's social and personal vanity, but it is a much harsher judgement. The point is that Helmer cannot love. A person lacking the ability to love, is poor beyond all understanding, Paul goes on to state in verse two in his letter to the Corinthians: 'And though I have the gift of prophecy, and understand all mysteries, and all knowledge; and though I have all faith, so that I could remove mountains, and have not charity, I am nothing.' Furthermore: 'And though I bestow all my goods to feed the poor, and though I give my body to be burned, and have not charity, it profiteth me nothing.' Paul closes this chapter by hailing love as the most important of a number of excellent qualities: 'And now abideth faith, hope, charity, these three; but the greatest of these is charity.'

Amalie Skram seems to have been more than commonly preoccupied with religious questions in her youth, strongly influenced by her mother and younger brother Ludvig, and by her teacher, rector O. E. Holck (Tiberg 1910: 28). Her judgement of Helmer might just as well have been directed at Agnete's suitor, the prudent, moralistic and pedantic lawyer Rikard Berg. By directly referring to the Bible in her own drama Amalie Skram extends the boundaries of an earthly, erotic love and introduces the belief in an all-comprehensive Christian, altruistic love that 'beareth all things, believeth all things, hopeth all things, endureth all things' (Corinthians 13.6) – a belief that is thwarted when put to the test.

In *Agnete* love does not replace religion as the road to salvation, but carnal, erotic love takes on a religious dimension and subtly changes into the compassionate *caritas*, charity. In Agnete's imagination the figure of Berg the man blends with the figure of Jesus Christ the Redeemer. Agnete is the repentant sinner who hopes to be saved through Berg's love for her, just as Christ would save all of mankind through his love for them.

Agnete is a more serious, more profound drama than it first appears to be. It obviously deals with social questions, comparing a bohemian lifestyle to that of the bourgoisie, exposing the double moral standards for men and women, and questioning conventional limits for decent behaviour. But more significantly it deals with no less than the existential quest for an all-comprehensive, all-forgiving love, which in this literary universe no human being can offer. Only Jesus Christ or God Almighty can do that. Therefore *Agnete* is deeply pessimistic on behalf of humanity.

A Biographical Endnote

Skram's first biographer, Antonie Tiberg, underscores the fact that Amalie Skram seems to have been more than commonly preoccupied with religious questions in her youth, strongly influenced by her mother and younger brother Ludvig, and by her teacher, rector O. E. Holck (d. 1909) (Tiberg 1910: 28). In his religious teaching he especially emphasized 'forsoningen i Kristus,' reconciliation in Christ. It was from Holck that Amalie Skram (then Müller) sought advice prior to her second long voyage aboard her husband's ship, this time to Australia, Peru and Constantinople. She had misgivings as her marriage was becoming increasingly loathsome to her, but encouraged by her old teacher, who emphasized that it was her duty to go with her husband, she finally gave in. 'Hun skulde holde sig til sin Gud og vente hans hjelp i tunge stunder. Hendes gamle lærer vilde følge hende i tanker og forbøn' (She should cling to God and expect his help in difficult times. Her old teacher would keep her in his thoughts and prayers). It was to Holck that she poured out her thoughts and heart in a number of sorrowful, pained letters during this two-year-long voyage. For the most part these letters were preoccupied with questions of her duties as a Christian, of her anguish at not being able to fulfill those duties, and of vacillating feelings of hope and resignation about her marriage (Tiberg 1910: 49ff., 86ff.).

Her brother Ludvig Alver, who had been close to her since childhood, and with whom she had discussed religious questions since that time, became her spiritual anchor in the difficult years around her separation and later divorce from August Müller. During her stay with her brother in Fredrikshald (Halden) at the end of the 1870s and as a result of a severe crisis, she broke with Christian orthodoxy and for a number of years seems to have been spiritually adrift. The language of her letters, reviews and articles from this time was nevertheless prolific with exuberant quotations and sentences from the Bible. Antonie Tiberg (1910, ch VI) suggests that she seemed to intoxicate herself in these expressions, while at the same time beginning to question the rationality and truth of Christian doctrines.

Through her marriage with Erik Skram in 1884 she became part of the radical elite in Copenhagen, and religion seems to have played a lesser role in her life and thoughts, although she never quite stopped pondering religious matters, according to Tiberg (1910: 23). After her beloved brother Ludvig Alver's death in 1897 she again drifted toward 'en slags religiøsitet, som vel i grunden aldrig havde sluppet taket i hendes sind nogen gang' (a kind of religiosity, which she had after all never really abandoned). Letters to her mother from this period seem to confirm a return to religion, but Skram scholars suggest that she was probably hoping to please her deeply religious mother. Or maybe she was really trying to find her way back to her old belief, in her search for a strong foothold? At the same time she seems to have been looking for something to replace religion, for during these years she also became interested in spiritualism. She was hoping that she might get in touch with Ludvig after his death as he had promised, but she was bitterly disappointed. There was no 'prestelig bistand' (religious ministry) at her cremation and funeral service in March 1905; apparently she had not wanted a Christian ceremony (Tiberg 1910: 23, 163, 253; Garton 2011: 302). But refusing the ministrations of the church does not necessarily mean a refutation of religion as such.

Even if one may safely assume that Amalie Skram had left the church and its rules by the time she wrote *Agnete*, it seems safe to also assume that her thinking was so imbued with Christian doctrines and biblical references that she could not escape them. This is notable for example in *Fru Inés* (1891), in which the notions of compassion and reconciliation are evoked at the end. Fru makes it clear already at the start of the novel that she is an ardent Christian: 'Jeg er romersk katholsk og vel at mærke en oprigtig troende' (Skram 1907: 15) (I am Roman Catholic and a sincere believer). But it is only at the end of the story, when about to die after a miscarriage, that she can feel some compassion for her husband, whom she has always despised and detested. Her prolonged suffering in the wake of her lover's suicide, and her anxiety when finding herself pregnant by him, have mollified and purified her to the extent that she can finally embrace the Holckian admonition of 'forsoningen i Christus' (reconciliation in Christ).

In some of her early literary critique of Bjørnson, Amalie Skram maintained that his works were the kind of 'Bodsprædiken,' sermons of penance, that she longed for but no longer heard from the pulpit when celebrating Mass. The church and the clergy had failed to make people understand that they had a personal responsibility for their own miserable, compromised situation and for society as a whole. In her opinion modern literature must take over the function of moral enlightenment that the church no longer seemed to provide (Tiberg 1910: 143, 148).

Maybe *Agnete* can be read in the light of such ideas. In this drama Amalie Skram portrays a man who is unable to forgive the person he loves despite himself; he has a moral flaw. In reality she herself was unable to forgive the man she loved. She could never fully trust Erik Skram after he admitted that he had had a mistress for many years, and even insisted on keeping her until Amalie consented to marry him. Amalie could neither understand nor forgive, was constantly jealous during their years of marriage, and totally failed to 'elske ham ren' (love him pure). In the end he grew tired of her jealousy and continuous reproaches, Amalie herself was torn between love and bitterness, and finally they were divorced. A similar conflict was the subject matter of many of her novels and short stories, for example 'Post Festum' from 1896, in which the female character blames herself for not having loved her husband as she should have, and as he deserved. Now he has left her, and she must sadly accept her punishment.

Maybe the gender distance made it easier for the author to ironically expose the frailties of Berg. His punishment is subtle: his life will go on as before. But it no longer seems attractive; it lies before him like a barren, lifeless desert. Agnete's life will change drastically for the worse, at least outwardly, for even she must atone. But in a higher moral (and Christian) perspective Agnete's faults are trifles compared to his. The charged accusations, clad in biblical language, that she directs against herself, may be interpreted as an expression of a deeper and more existential feeling of guilt on the part of the author than petty thefts would call for.

References

Anker, Ø. and E. Beyer (eds.) (1982): *Brevvekslingen mellom Bjørnstjerne Bjørnson og Amalie Skram*. Oslo: Gyldendal.

Bibelen (1879). Det norske Bibelselskab, Christiania: Grøndahl & Søn.

Engelstad, I. (1981): 'Sannhetskrav og kjærlighetsdrøm. Amalie Skrams *Agnete.*' In I. Engelstad og J. Øverland (eds.): *Frihet til å skrive. Artikler om kvinnelitteratur fra Amalie Skram til Cecilie Løveid*, Oslo: Pax, pp. 24-38.

Garton, J. (ed.) (2002): *Elskede Amalie. Brevvekslingen mellom Amalie og Erik Skram*, vol. I 1882-september 1883. Oslo: Gyldendal.

Garton, J. (2011): *Amalie. Et forfatterliv*. Oslo: Gyldendal.

Holy Bible, The (1945): The Authorized King James Version, The World Publishing Company, Cleveland and New York.

Losnedahl, K.G. (1996): 'Teatret hadde jeg aldri lyst til'. In E. Aasen, (ed.): *Amalie Skram. 'Silkestrilen sin datter.'* Oslo: Pax, pp. 85-110

Macé, N. (1977): 'Det ufullendte opprør.' Afterword in *Agnete. Skuespill i tre akter*. Oslo: Pax, pp. 85-92.

Skram, A. (1893): *Agnete*. Kjøbenhavn: Schubothes Boghandel.

Skram, A. (1907 [1891]): 'Fru Inés'. In *Kjærlighed i Nord og Syd*, 2nd Edition. Kjøbenhavn: Schubothes Boghandel.

Skram, A. (1987 [1880]): 'En Betragtning over 'Et Dukkehjem'.' *Dagbladet*

19.1.1880, re-printed in I. Engelstad (ed.): *Optimistisk Læsemaade. Amalie Skrams litteraturkritikk,* Oslo: Gyldendal, pp. 32-44.

Tiberg, A. (1910): *Amalie Skram som kunstner og menneske.* Kristiania: Aschehoug.

Tjäder, P.A. (2004): 'Att söka sin glädje – Amalie Skrams *Agnete.*' In Y. Leffler (ed.): *Det moderna genombrottets dramer. Fem analyser.* Lund: Studentlitteratur, pp. 63–76.

Notes

1. Letter of Sept. 10th [1882]. Erik Skram writes that two honest persons can love each other pure. (Garton 2002: 70). Janet Garton draws attention to the fact that this phrase has been used by Amalie Skram in her play.

2. All Bible quotations in Norwegian are from Bibelen (1879). English translation of passages in this chapter is by CCT, except where taken from The Holy Bible (1945) as indicated.

The Imprint of Lutheran Pietism on the Writing of Amalie Skram

Katherine Hanson
University of Washington

Amalie Skram's early encounter with pietistic religion left an indelible impression on her life and work.[1] During her lifetime she moved from ardent belief to overt skepticism, an evolution that can be seen in letters to her former schoolmaster Ole E. Holck, among others, and in the review articles she wrote on contemporary literature from 1880-1887. Skram's religious conflicts are also reflected in her novels, particularly *Constance Ring* (1885), *Lucie* (1888), *Forraadt* (1892, Betrayed), and *Hellemyrsfolket* (1887-1898, The People of Hellemyr). In these fictional works Skram revisits her early faith and explores the ways religious upbringing can shape adult personality and form attitudes about sexuality and marriage. Skram's break with the State Church was never repaired, and yet, though she may have called herself a free thinker, she never lost her religious sensibilities. Life experiences and religious teachings combined to produce a profound awareness of suffering and grief; her body of work is infused with emotional struggle and pessimism about the possibility of earthly happiness.

Skram's infatuation with Lutheran pietism began in her teens. In letters to her colleagues Peter Nansen and Georg Brandes, Skram confessed that she had been 'alvorlig religiøst grepet' (Kielland 1955: 14) (seriously in the grip of religion) and 'en troende pietist' (68) (a believing pietist) in her youth. Her brother Ludvig Alver wrote to Gerhard Gran that he remembered his sister being 'sterkt religiøst paavirket, [hun] tog kristendommen efter dens absolute ideale fordring' (greatly affected by religion, [she] embraced Christianity's absolute ideals).[2]

Lutheran Pietism

The dominant religion of Western Norway in the nineteenth century was a strict and authoritarian version of Protestantism. Pietism had characterized the Lutheran Church in Norway ever since the reign of Christian VI (1731-1746), the monarch who commissioned Erich Pontoppidan to write an Explanation to Luther's cathechism. In 1736 King Christian had declared that confirmation was mandatory for everyone, and Pontoppidan's questions and answers were to ensure that the instruction was uniform and in accordance with the King's pietistic beliefs. Pontoppidan's *Forklaring*, published in 1737, was required reading for young people throughout Denmark and Norway. For many, Pontoppidan was the first book they learned to read, or, if they never learned to read, to know by heart.

Toward the end of the eighteenth century Danish theologians and clergymen were increasingly receptive to rationalism and the ideas of the Enlightenment, and in the 1790s Pontoppidan's *Forklaring* was replaced in Denmark by an Explanation that was less strict, less authoritarian. In Norway, however, the predominantly rural and largely conservative population was resistant to change. To be sure there were important exponents of rationalism in Norway during the eighteenth century.[3] Until a Norwegian university opened in Christiania (1813), the clergy received their education at the University in Copenhagen and their theological training was thereby influenced by rationalistic, enlightened thought.[4] Clergymen brought these ideas to Norway where they found fertile ground among educated parishioners, but in the late eighteenth and early nineteenth centuries the educated represented but a small segment of the country's population. A much more powerful influence on the Norwegian laity came from revivalist Hans Nielsen Hauge (1771-1824). A critic of the State Church, Hauge provoked the Church hierarchy with his prayer meetings and his call for a deeper religious fervour among believers, but he insisted that the lay movement he initiated in 1796 remain within the framework of the State Church. Pontoppidan's *Forklaring* was a central pillar in Hauge's faith as it was for the lay preachers he inspired throughout the country and well into the nineteenth century.

The importance of Pontoppidan's instruction is evidenced by the many references in Amalie Skram's work to his *Forklaring*. The title of Pontoppidan's Explanation is *Sandhed til Gudfryktighed*. These words were taken from Paul's letter to Titus: Paul introduces himself as 'Guds tjener og Jesu Kristi apostel for at vække tro hos Guds udvalgte og erkendelse af den sandhed, der sigter til gudfryktighed' (Brøndsted 1965: 48) (God's servant and Jesus Christ's apostle, [who shall] awaken faith among God's elect and acknowledge the truth that points the way to godliness). The essence of pietism is revealed here: the true doctrine leads to a pious and God-fearing life, knowledge about God leads the believer to God's presence. Strict adherence to Lutheran pietism demanded the renunciation of wordly pleasures. True Christians, that is pietists, should see themselves as 'Guds barn' (children of God), as opposed to 'verdens barn' (children of the world). They were the elect and as such should strive to lead righteous, sober, chaste lives, shun the obvious vices, and also forsake secular culture, e.g., art, theatre, novels, modern scientific ideas that questioned or were at variance with Christian doctrine. Also setting the pietists apart from other Christians was their concept of salvation. According to Pontoppidan's *Forklaring*, salvation is contingent upon 'omvendelse' (conversion). Only when a sinner sincerely and fervently repents can he/she experience God's grace and be born again. 'Botskamp' (an anguished admission and repentence of one's sins and sinful nature) is a prerequisite for true faith. 'Å omvende seg,' Pontoppidan explains, 'er hjertelig å kjenne, føle, angre og hate sine begåtte synder, ja all sin syndige naturs vanart, inderlig lenges etter Guds nåde i Kristus og alvorlig få i sinne å forbedre sitt levnet' (Oftestad et al. 1993: 159) (To convert is to feel, repent and hate in one's heart the sins one has committed, indeed, all the depravity spawned by one's sinful nature, to fervently long for God's mercy in Christ and be seriously mindful of improving one's life). Central to this recipe for 'omvendelse' and, therefore, salvation, is the exhortation to experience sorrow and suffering intensely.

Amalie Müller took this to heart, as evidenced in the confessional letters she wrote to her former teacher. As an author, Amalie Skram had an affinity for characters who suffered and were overcome with sorrow. She felt compelled not only to tell their stories, but also to show her readers the anatomy of their sorrow and anguish.

Pontoppidan's *Forklaring* was not the only source of spiritual guidance for Norwegian pietists in the middle of the nineteenth century. They read the Bible, of course, and during worship services at church and prayer meetings at home they sang 'salmesanger' (hymns). The hymns were important teaching devices in that they convey Church doctrine, but beyond that the music and poetry of the hymns had an emotional appeal. If pietism had the negative effect of sequestering believers, turning them away from and against the world and focusing attention on human sinfulness and wretchedness, it also encouraged believers to open themselves to their inner lives, to look inward and feel their emotions keenly and fervently. 'Salmesanger' were key to putting people in touch with their inner lives and for Amalie were an early affirmation that a person's emotional life could be a subject for literature.

'Andaktsbøker' (devotional literature) also encouraged reflection and soul-searching. The writings of German author Johann Arndt (1555-1624) were, according to Tarald Rasmussen in *Norsk kirkehistorie*, very popular in Norway from the mid seventeenth century to the end of the nineteenth. Like the pietists who came after him, Arndt preached that true Christianity must be heartfelt and emotional. He taught that the true believer is to model his life on Jesus' life on earch, including the Passion and Crucifixion of Christ. Rasmussen quotes from a prayer book Arndt wrote, *Paradiss Gårtlein*, in which he teaches believers how they should pray, not superficially, but from the depths of their souls. He describes five stages that must be followed, step by step. At step five, the pinnacle, the believer will pray with a burning love and experience oneness with God. The first step is heartfelt acknowledgment of sin in a spirit of true repentence and sorrow. At step three, the mid-point, one should pray with heavy sighs, like Hannah in 1st Samuel, and with bitter tears, like the Mary Magdalen, whose tears were prayers without words (Oftestad et al. 1993: 136-138). The influence of Arndt is strongly suggested in the letters Amalie wrote to her former school teacher Ole Holck.

Letters to Ole E. Holck, September 1869 – March 1871

When she was barely eighteen, Amalie Alver married the Bergen seacaptain August Müller, a man with excellent prospects, but whom she scarcely knew. Her family's financial crisis seems to have been the primary motive for the marriage, but for the inexperienced, religious girl, the reality of sex and marriage proved traumatic. Two children followed in quick succession and in the fall of 1869 the young wife and mother set out on a trip around the world with her husband and two sons. During the long voyage she wrote four letters to her former schoolmaster Holck. Her letters are a cry for help during a difficult period in her life. Her ecstatic embrace of religious submission had not prepared her for the reality of marriage to a sexually experienced older man. The letters are filled with thanks for Holck's prayers and guidance in bringing her closer to God. They are also punctuated with emotional outbursts of despair.

She entreats Holck to pray for her that she might receive the strength and grace to deny her own will and win over her stubborn heart for Christ. She longs to be one with Christ, to have him always in her heart.

The image of Jesus conveyed in these letters is of Jesus suffering in Gethsemane and bearing the cross. In her first letter Amalie describes for Holck the picture in their cabin: a large copperplate engraving of Jesus in Gethsemane, kneeling and hands folded, 'dødstræt og sjeleangst' (tired unto death, his soul filled with angst), and yet at peace. She confides to her teacher that she looks at this picture for affirmation of her salvation from Hell: 'Naar jeg kun med Troens Øie, ser hen til den lidende Jesus, saa er jeg jo frelst' (Kielland 1955: 23) (I have only to look at the suffering Jesus with believing eyes, and I am saved). The image of the suffering Christ appears again in her last letter. She admits to feeling utterly despondent, filled with fear and sorrow. Holck's letter has dispelled the darkness and renewed her resolve to take up the cross and follow Christ: 'jeg blev saa fuld af Haab og Glæde at det tyktes mig en let Sag at tage Korset op og følge Jesum efter. Gud give Naade til at følge i hans trange Fotspor, til ufravendt at fæste Blikket paa ham, det store Guddomsideal …' (28) (I was so filled with hope and joy that it seemed to me an easy matter to take up the cross and follow Jesus. By God's grace I will follow his narrow path and keep my gaze steadfast on Him, the divine ideal …).

Feelings of being inadequate and unworthy vis-à-vis her faith are other emotions Amalie admits to in letters to Holck. In one she writes about a girlfriend, also a pupil of Holck's, who had struggled in vain to 'naa frem til Fulkommenhed' (achieve perfection), but who now had a clearer understanding of what is meant by 'barnetroen' (25) (childlike faith). One gets the sense the struggle has been Amalie's as well. In another letter she deplores her failure to always love Jesus as passionately as she should. How does a woman who yearns to love Jesus, her 'store Guddomsideal,' reconcile herself to a pledge to love, honor and obey an earthly and imperfect husband?

Marital and Mental Crisis

Marriage to August Müller opened Amalie's eyes to the wider world, and it opened the fault lines in her pietistic beliefs. At sea and in the ports they visited, the beautiful and intelligent young wife of Captain Müller was much admired. She enjoyed dressing up in beautiful clothes and elaborate coiffures and she was a voracious reader always ready to discuss ideas and opinions. The wider experience in the years of sea travel partly papered over the troubles in the Müller marriage, but after the family had established a home in Bergen, in the mid '70s, the couple became increasingly estranged.

In Bergen she socialized with a group of radical intellectuals associated with the theatre and the newspaper, *Bergens Tidende*, and was thereby introduced to a new way of thinking. She read and discussed contemporary literature and was, by her own admission, deeply moved by *Magnhild*, Bjørnstjerne Bjørnson's novel defending a woman's moral right to divorce an unworthy husband. Self subjugation was no longer possible for Amalie, given her belief in Müller's infidelity. Her request for a divorce rebuffed by Müller and his family, she suffered a nervous breakdown, and was hospitalized at Gaustad Asylum in Christiania. After her release, she left Bergen with her two sons and never returned to Müller. Her new life would be as a single woman, separated from her husband, in the more liberal environment of Eastern Norway.

In pursuing a divorce Amalie had set herself up against the authority of the State Church, a topic she would later dramatize in *Constance Ring*. But even though she had been influenced by modern ideas, her faith in God remained intact. We know this from the many letters she wrote to Elisa Knudtzon in the period following her release from Gaustad. She felt exhausted and depressed, she wrote Elisa on January 14, 1879, but her faith gave her inspiration and strength:' […] du tror ikke på ånd og evigt liv, -- men det gjør jeg, og denne tro begeistrer mig, og giver mig kraft til at leve: uden den måtte jeg dø, -- ja, uden den var det simpelthen intet andet for mig at gjøre end at gå hen og begå selvmord' (52) ([…] you don't believe in spirit and eternal life – but I do, and this belief inspires me and gives me strength to live: without it I would die, without it there would be nothing else for me to do but go off and kill myself).

Correspondence with Bjørnson

Amalie was released from Gaustad in mid-February, 1878. A week later, February 22, she wrote a letter to Bjørnson and enclosed an essay she had written about his play *Kongen* (The King). She had thought to publish the essay in the newspaper, but only if Bjørnson approved. Given her situation and the condition of her health, this was an amazing act of courage and initiative. Did she write to Bjørnson on an impulse, or was she reaching out for a helping hand, much like she had done nine years earlier when she wrote to Holck?

As the author of *Magnhild*, Bjørnson had played a critical role in Amalie's decision to leave her husband, but he had also written other things that I believe were equally important to her. In the spring of 1876 Bjørnson had published three articles in *Oplandenes avis* that unleashed a lengthy newspaper debate in Norway and Denmark. Bjørnson signed the articles 'En kristen' (A Christian) to underscore that he was a Christian in spite of his differences with the Church. He attacked pietism as a dark, conservative, dogma-ridden religion that turned believers away from the world and stood in the way of democracy and progress. At the center of Bjørnson's religion was a God of love who manifested himself in humanitarian work and in the pursuit of freedom and opportunity for all.

Amalie would certainly have followed this debate in the press. Likewise she would have read about the public speech Bjørnson made in Christiania in October 1877: 'Om at være i Sandhed' (Being in Truth). Bjørnson admonished his countrymen not to confuse the pursuit of truth with reverence for the status quo. Christianity's demand for truth must be extended to include the cultural and political sphere, he argued. Bjørnson's vision for Norway was of a nation and a people who would build their future on the combined principles of democracy and Christian morality.

It seems a reasonable assumption that Amalie Müller would have been open and receptive to this vision in the winter of 1877-78. The truths on which she had built her former life had failed her. In recent years she had become disposed to many of the ideas she had encountered in her reading and yet she clung to her belief in God. Bjørnson imagined a harmonious marriage of modern ideas and Christianity, and in him Amalie saw the hope of a new teacher.

Bjørnson proved to be a willing teacher. He basked in the warm enthusiasm of his new admirer and she carefully followed her new mentor as he moved through his own religious crisis. Bjørnson experienced his religious crisis publicly, in lectures, letters to the press, books – he was looking to win converts to 'a new system.' Amalie's private letters and review articles published in various newspapers provide a record of how her views were evolving. Bjørnson had recommended the 'nuværende videnskab' (contemporary science) in his second letter to Amalie and on May 30, 1878 she replied that she was not interested in that kind of study: 'resultaterne af tidens forskning kaster en stakkels menneskesjæl ifra det ene bundløse tvivlens hav til det andet, uden på noget hold at kunne give et standpunkt til gjengjæld for det der berøves os ...' (the results of current studies only cast a poor soul from one bottomless sea of doubt to another without providing anything to hold onto in return for what it takes from us …). She longed only for clarity and truth and sought to find that in 'kristendommens evige sandhed' (the eternal truth of Christianity), which she believed 'passer til alle tider, når vi blot forstår den riktig' (Anker and Beyer 1982: 9) (is relevant for all times when only we understand it correctly). Over the next couple of years Amalie Müller's views on the 'nuværende videnskab' and 'tidens forskning' shifted dramatically, her thoughts about 'kristendommens evige sandhed' less so.

Finding Spiritual Guidance in Contemporary Literature

In April 1880 she submitted a long article to *Dagbladet*: a review of Bjørnson's drama *Det ny System* (The New System). The reviewer's zeal for the play and the playwright borders on the fanatical. She bristles with indignation over the hypocrisy of the conservative Christians portrayed in the play and rails against their pietistic Church. As she warms to her subject, her language becomes religious. In *Det ny System*, she proclaims, Bjørnson has raised 'et Tempel for den ideale Sandhedskultus' (Anker and Beyer 1982: 163) (a temple for the ideal worship of truth). Playwright becomes prophet who preaches 'Omvendelse fra Løgnen' (conversion from hypocrisy). Bjørnson is, declares the reviewer, 'Norges største nulevende Botsprædikant' (170) (Norway's greatest living preacher of repentance).

Her language betrays the raw emotion of someone aggrieved. Amalie had accepted Christianity's absolute claim of the ideal, to paraphrase her brother Ludvig, and then learned that the institution and its pillars claiming to represent Christianity were false. As her focus turned from salvation in the hereafter to ethics and moral behaviour, she came to view the sceptics, more than the believers, as the true Christians. Throughout 1880 Amalie Müller moved further and further away from the religious beliefs and community she had once embraced, a process she alludes to in articles on J.P. Jacobsen's novel *Niels Lyhne* in January and February 1881. Her struggle to find her place among the sceptics is reflected in the language of the articles; she presents her arguments clearly, and, for the most part, dispassionately, and yet the subject of religion triggers emotions and language from her old life. Whether it's because she didn't choose to or wasn't able to, Amalie had not yet rid herself of language and expressions rooted in her pietistic upbringing.

In an article on *Gengangere* (Ghosts) from April 1882, the focus is again on morality. Amalie Müller accuses 'Den herskende religion' (the prevailing religion) in Norway of having failed to instill 'nogen levende Følelse af et Menneskes personlige Ansvar' (Skram 1987: 73) (any real feeling of an individual's personal responsibility). Instead, the Church instructs believers on the importance of duty and obedience to authority. The consequences of this are made clear through the fate of Mrs. Alving: 'bedraget og beløjet og mishandlet' (betrayed and lied to and abused) because she has acted in 'Lovlydighed mod de vedtægter, der lever af at hvile paa en "kristelig Grund"' (74) (obedience to those principles which are based on a "Christian foundation"). By enclosing 'kristelig Grund' in quotation marks, Amalie ironically implies a disconnect between the prevailing religion and Christian ideals, thus opening the way for her to make a connection between contemporary writers (e.g. Ibsen) and morality. Ibsen's drama is 'en opskræmmende Bodsprædiken' (74) (an alarming sermon of repentance) and the dramatist is likened to Christ who was also received with 'Stenkast og Smædeord og ... det gamle Raab: Korsfæst! Korsfæst!' (76) (stones and insults ... and the old cry: Crucify! Crucify!).

Amalie was surely conscious of the dramatic and provocative effect these religious references would have on the vast majority of her readers. But if she was willfully irreverent on the one hand, she was equally sincere in her belief in Christian values as guiding principles for humanity on the other. In 1887 she again defended a writer who had come under attack for a publication and hailed him as one of the 'moderne tænknings mænd' (modern thinkers) who, from a purely humane point of view promote 'Nazaræerens lære' (110) (the teachings of the Nazarene). The author was Christian Krohg, the book *Albertine*.

Skram was deeply moved by Krohg's depiction of a lower class girl whose fall into prostitution is facilitated and monitored by city officials. Her indignation over social injustice and the hypocrisy of 'den bestånde religions vogtere' (111) (guards of the established religion) is still warm, but in Krohg's novel she has found another, more positive message: the power of compassion and Christian charity. While Bjørnson preaches virtue, and Ibsen calls for greater personal responsibility, Skram concludes, 'Krohg søger i sin "Albertine" at puste liv i barmhjertighedsfølelsen og den kristelige næstekjærlighed' (110) (Krohg seeks in Albertine to breathe life into compassion and Christian charity).

These articles about contemporary literature are the best record we have of Amalie Skram's spiritual development from an ardent believer to a sceptic. Early reviews, from November and December 1878, reveal a woman who was seeking spiritual guidance from books with religious content. For example, in a book about the eighteenth century German pietist August Hermann Francke, founder of a school and orphanage for homeless children, she finds inspiration in 'hvad ét menneske i tro til Gud har kunnet udrette' (17) (what one person with belief in God has accomplished). Contemporary fiction opened other perspectives and just a few months later, in March 1879, she wrote an enthusiastic review of stories by Bret Harte, an author who 'søger midlet til individets og samfundets forædling udelukkende i menneskets eget bryst' (27) (seeks the means to improve the individual and society in the human heart alone). It was the dramas of Bjørnson and Ibsen that probably had the greatest influence on her thinking as she struggled to start a new life, severed from her Church and former faith, yet based on ideals and a striving for truth. Skram found common cause with the 'moderne tænknings mænd' because they were outspoken critics of an authoritarian and hypocritical church, and because they were advocates of an ethics and morality that she identified as essentially Christian.

'Om Albertine' (About *Albertine*), published in December 1887, represents a postscript in Skram's relatively short career as a book reviewer. Nearly four years had gone by since her last article appeared, and in the interim she had married Erik Skram, moved from Christiania to Copenhagen, and earned a reputation as an author of controversial books. She had succeeded in starting a new life in a more sophisticated and secular society, but had at the same time held onto her Norwegian identity. And an integral part of that identity was her history as 'en troende pietist.' Skram's views about the Church and Christian ethics in the article on *Albertine* are consistent with those formulated years earlier. Church leaders and members who profess to be Christians are criticized for failing to live and act according to the teachings of Christ, which for Skram continue to have relevance for contemporary society. Krohg's novel has impressed upon her how 'barmhjertighedsfølelsen og den kristelige næstekjærlighed' (compassion and Christian charity) can open eyes and hearts to a clearer understanding of how an honest girl from the lower class can end up on the streets.

Pietism Revisited in Skram's Fiction

Amalie Skram's preoccupation with the religious belief she struggled with and rejected in the early 1880s is present in works throughout her career. Her treatment of religious topics and themes seems to follow a development similar to the one traced in her review articles – from passionate condemnation of the Church and its clergymen to a willingness to acknowledge a Christianity based on charity and compassion.

In *Constance Ring*, Skram's first novel, published in 1885, the author openly attacked the Church through the person of Reverend Huhn. Constance had sought the counsel of her pastor, certain that he would share her outrage over Ring's adulterous behavior and intervene to save her from an immoral marriage. But the clergyman, though he did express his dismay, instructed Constance to stay in her marriage and strive to be a good influence on her husband. Constance was persuaded to do as the pastor said, much against her will. As a result she felt humiliated and demoralized, but this did not cause her to question her faith, or even to think about religion at all.

In subsequent stories and novels about unhappy marriages Skram explored the ways religious upbringing and belief affect attitudes and behavior. Ory, the young bride in *Forraadt* (Betrayed), entered marriage with no knowledge of sexual relations between husband and wife. Sexual aversion and trauma only intensified when Captain Riber tried to educate his child-wife by exposing her to the bawdy atmosphere of London's dance halls, places that to her 'stanket av fordervelse' (Skram 1976: vol 5, 69) (stank of depravity). Ory's way of coping with the horror and disgust that filled her was to interpret the situation and her emotions within a religious framework – she had been taken to 'satans eneveldige rike' (70) (Satan's absolute monarchy). Riber's willingness to confess his past relationships with women only encouraged Ory to assume the role of religious authority, and to assign him the role of wretched sinner. Her religion was a stern and sin-focused pietism where Pontoppidan's words counted for more than the Holy Scripture. Though the Bible taught that the love that forgives and endures is the greatest of all, Pontoppidan warned fornicators that they would be punished with eternal damnation: '... i *Forklaring* stod det at utukt var den verste av alle synder' (137) (in the Explanation it said that fornication was the worst sin of all).

Riber also turned to religion, but a milder, more compassionate form of Christianity. He read the Bible and found comfort in Jesus' words to the prostitute whom He did not condemn, and in the promise that Christ's death was for the salvation of all. 'Skriftens trøst er jo for alle' (The comfort of the Scriptures is for all), he tells Ory. 'For alle de angrende' (140) (For all who repent), she retorts. Ory had expected a confession according to Pontoppidan's formula, full of anguish and remorse, a genuine 'botskamp.' Her position had clearly been informed by this question in Pontoppidan's Explanation: 'Kan en ikke ha tro til Kristus og trøste seg ved Ham uten at en føler fortrytelse over synden? – Nei, den tro som skal fatte Kristus, må vekkes opp i følelsen av vår syndige jammer; for ellers er vi av de innbilte friske og sunne, som ikke trenger til lege. Matt. 9,12.' (Oftestad et al. 1993: 159) (Can one not believe in Christ and find comfort in Him without first feeling contrition for one's sins? – No, the belief that shall comprehend Christ must be awakened by feeling and acknowledging our sinful wretchedness; for otherwise we are like those who imagine they are whole and need not a physician). Until Riber felt 'så skamfull og ydmyk, at han gjerne hadde latt sig tråkke på' (Skram 1976: vol 5, 159) (so full of shame and humility that he would let himself be trampled upon), his confession was not complete and he could receive no forgiveness.

Who gets the last word in this struggle? Though Riber's voice was silenced when he leapt through the porthole, his words about Jesus on the night he was betrayed, and about forgiveness, his own and Ory's, are the ones that conclude the narration. Many scholars have commented on the ambiguity of the book's title, *Betrayed*: it refers both to Ory who was betrayed by those entrusted with preparing her for adulthood, and to Riber who was betrayed by the child-woman to whom he opened his heart and soul. To that I would add that both characters were betrayed by a harsh, pietistic interpretation of Christianity. At the end of the novel Skram's sympathy is with Riber and the compassionate and forgiving God he believes in.

Lucie is another example of a novel with religious overtones, as well as undertones. Mrs. Reinertsen's brother, Pastor Brandt, defends the double standard with Old Testament stories of patriarchs and others upon whom the Lord had bestowed virgins, and complains bitterly about pietistic parishioners who are leaving his congregation to find a personal relationship with Christ; Lucie experiences a conversion and joins the Free Church after she has been impregnated by a rapist and then humiliated by Knut; and Theodore Gerner, Lucie's tyrannical husband, has the disposition and demeanor of a strict, authoritarian clergyman. His name, Theodore, means 'gift of God,' and his project of educating and moulding Lucie into a fine lady is essentially a wish to convert her. His desire is that her past, the 'old' Lucie, be obliterated so that she might be 'born again,' and become a woman without a past. As a teacher he is a punishing disciplinarian who refuses to relent until his pupil has prostrated herself before him like a penitential Magdalene.

Skram's treatment of religion in *Hellemyrsfolket* (The People of Hellemyr) is quite different. The novel is epic in scope, a sociological snapshot over several generations, and religious rituals and beliefs are depicted as part of the background. In the character of Sivert Myre, Skram portrays a spiritual development that follows a trajectory similar to her own. Raised in a pietistic home, Myre is seemingly incapable of following the strict tenets of his parents' faith and as a consequence is beset with feelings of guilt, remorse and unworthiness. At the end of his life he finally experiences a God who grants him absolution from his sins and with his last words praises 'Guds uransagelige barmhjertighet' (Skram 1976: vol 3, 342) (God's inscrutable compassion).

Amalie Skram's fiction was clearly informed by her life experiences: her childhood and adolescent years growing up in Bergen, sea voyages as a young wife and mother, marriage and divorce, mental breakdown and hospitalization. To this list we must add the years of intense religious experience as 'en troende pietist,' years that extended from adolescence well into adulthood. Her letters offer a window into how deeply she embraced her faith and how that faith was a source of both solace and suffering. In her reviews on contemporary literature we can follow her spiritual development from ardent belief to scepticism. I have merely hinted here at the opportunities for interpretation and analysis of religious themes and motifs in Skram's fiction. The author's preoccupation with religion in her work, not only as it relates to Lutheran pietism but also more broadly, is as yet mostly uncharted territory.

References

Amdam, P. (1977): *Bjørnson og kristenarven. 1875-1910. Selvhevdelse og Selverkjennelse.* Trondheim: Universitetsforlaget.

Amdam, P. (1993): *Bjørnstjerne Bjørnson. 1832-1880.* Oslo: Gyldendal.

Anker, Ø. and E. Beyer (1982): *"Og nu vil jeg tale ut" – "Men nu vil jeg også tale ud." Brevvekslingen mellom Bjørnstjerne Bjørnson og Amalie Skram.* Oslo: Gyldendal.

Brøndsted, M. (1965):'Historien om Pontoppidans Forklaring i Danmark og Norge.' In *Fund og Forskning*, XII, pp. 47-66.

Flint, J.T. (1990): *Historical Role Analysis in the Study of Religious Change: Mass Educational Development in Norway, 1740-1891*, Cambridge: Cambridge University Press.

Kielland, E. (1955): *Mellom slagene. Brev i utvalg*. Oslo: Aschehoug.

Oftestad, B., T. Rasmussen and J. Schumacher (1993): *Norsk kirkehistorie*. Oslo: Universitetsforlaget.

Rasmussen, J.E. (1981):'Amalie Skram as Literary Critic.' In *Edda* 81, pp. 1-11.

Skram, A. (1976): *Samlede verker*, vols. 1-6. Oslo: Gyldendal.

Skram, A. (1987): *Optimistisk Læsemaade. Amalie Skrams litteraturkritikk*, ed. Irene Engelstad. Oslo: Gyldendal.

Notes

1. I would like to thank Judith Messick for insightful comments and suggestions on an earlier draft, a paper given at SASS 2007.

2. This letter from Ludvig Alver to Gerhard Gran, dated 14.9.1896, is housed in the University Library in Oslo, Brevs.117.

3. Johan Ernst Gunnerus was perhaps the foremost advocate of rationalism and enlightenment in the eighteenth century. He was Bishop in Trondheim from 1758 to 1773 and was instrumental in establishing the Academy of Science (det Throndhjemske Selskab later called Det klg. Norske videnskabers selskab) in 1760. See Oftestad et al. 1993: 170.

4. The Theology Faculty at the new university in Christiania came to be dominated by two Professors, Svend Borchmann Hersleb (1784-1834) and Stener Johannes Stenersen (1789-1835). Hersleb and Stenersen favoured a Bible oriented Christianity as opposed to Rationalist Christianity with its focus on morals, ethics and enlightenment. In 1849 Gisle Johnson was appointed to the faculty and 'his neo-orthodox/Pietist Lutheran Confessionalism' had a tremendous impact on Norwegian theological students. This period in Norwegian history corresponds to the years Amalie Alver was growing up in Bergen and is also the time period in which Amalie Skram sets her fiction (Flint 1990: 35).

Sacramental Imagination in Sigrid Undset's Literary Work[1]

Liv Bliksrud
Universitetet i Oslo

Sigrid Undset's literary work – especially her historical novels, for which she was awarded the Nobel Prize – were greatly admired by Norwegian literary scholars until the late 1960s. In the 1970s, feminism sparked innovative studies of her contemporary fiction, particularly to shed light on her reactionary tendencies. This might be seen as a necessary reaction to the former glorification of Undset's art, but regrettably it left it languishing under the category of 'women's literature,' a pigeon hole far too constricted for her work. Today, Norwegian scholars do not know quite how to categorize Undset's writings. Her Catholic perspective and realistic style straddle national, liberal, feminist and modernist literary categories, to which most Norwegian literature is ascribed. Undset is therefore no longer a self-evident writer to be discussed in university courses devoted to the literature of the twentieth century. One obvious reason is that she is regarded as an anti-feminist writer, and another may be the lack of provocative modernism in her work. Undset does not attract interest from a formal perspective, writes the Undset scholar, Christine Hamm.[2] In Norwegian literary criticism, modernism has become a virtue, a sort of dogmatism. The ideology of modernism seems to denigrate realism, considering realism as politically conservative, unsophisticated, and naïve in its belief in the power of language to reflect reality. In her book *Henrik Ibsen and the Birth of Modernism* (2006) Toril Moi writes 'that the modernist attack on realism is motivated by the need to defend the philosophical skepticism that underpins the ideology of modernism.' Moi underlines that realist writing does not have 'a built-in commitment to any particular philosophical position, and that realism can coexist with the deepest skepticism in relation to the power of words to make sense' (Moi 2006: 23-24). Undset's writing exemplifies that realism can coexist with a religious viewpoint and a transcendent position as well.

To understand Undset's realism we have to leave modernist dogmatism aside and ask the question why she is and has always been one of Norway's most loved authors, in spite of the critics' skepticism towards her work. Her books appear regularly in new editions both in Norway and abroad. She is one of the few Norwegian authors who has an enduring world reputation, and has proved to fascinate her readers for more than one hundred years. One aspect of the fascinating power of her art is obviously her Catholic faith. Religion gives her a particular vantage point (Bliksrud 2006: 180). On the other hand she does not allow religious scruples to obscure the real psychological insights of her penetrating grasp of life's instinctive aspects. As an artist Undset must be understood in her own right, that is: as a Catholic writer.

However, Undset's readers do not have to accept her Catholic ideas in order to realize the value of these ideas in her work (Bliksrud 2005: 77, Monroe 1941: 140). All of her books have a dramatic situation at their core, but the effect of Christianity on her writing tends to add spiritual obligations that intensify and deepen the human drama.[3] Undset remains a great author because of, not in spite of, her faith, which gave her an exceptionally deep insight into the universal aspects of human mentality and into man's basic experiences: love, parenthood, childhood, family conscience; the phases of life in its ripening, in mysticism and religion, and in life and death. Her insights go deeper than those of the popular gurus among other authors of her time. Her models were not contemporary superstars like Freud or William James. Undset found her inspiration in pre-modern personalities like Chaucer and Shakespeare and the Swedish botanist Carl Linnaeus. Other models were Catholic saints – St. Augustine, St. Thomas Aquinas and St. Teresa of Avila, the latter being 'the sharpest brain God had ever put into a woman's head,' according to Undset (cited in Bliksrud 2005: 77, 81).

In other words: Undset is unique as an incorruptible realist writer, as well as an incorruptible Catholic writer. This may appear to be a paradox. However, this paradox might, in my opinion, provide an important key to understanding the power of fascination of her art. This power is based on what I shall call a *sacramental imagination* in her literary work.

Undset turned to the Catholic Church as the only reliable authority, because the inherent logic of its teachings appealed to her intellect. But Catholic perspectives on the world and man's role in it also appealed to her creative powers as an *artist*, and to her *imagination*, which might be characterized as sacramental. A 'sacrament' consists of two elements:

the *sacramentum*, or 'sign', and the *res*, or 'reality', hence sacraments are the liturgical and supernatural, but still outward and visible signs, of an inward and spiritual grace. Thus, sacramental imagination is a challenge to a naturalist's world. For the naturalist, reality is what we perceive, i.e. matter; for the sacramentalist what we perceive – matter – is not reality, but rather a sign – *sacramentum* – that points to, and carries, a deeper, invisible reality. Since Christ has done his sanctifying work upon the physical world, it is restored and made worthy to function sacramentally, i.e. to be 'the stuff' of sacraments.

I came across the expression 'sacramental imagination' in an online article (Butorac, n.d.) about the American Catholic author Flannery O'Connor, in which Andrew Greeley's 1990 book, *The Catholic Myth*, was referred to. In the third chapter of his book, Greeley poses this question: 'Do Catholics imagine differently?' He proceeds to explain that, yes, indeed they do: Religion, he writes, is imagination before it is anything else. The Catholic imagination is different from the Protestant imagination. Greeley defines the confessional difference between the two kinds of imagination in this way: The Catholic imagination is 'analogical' and the Protestant imagination is 'dialectical'. As to how the Catholic imagination is different, Greeley writes:

> The central symbol (of religion) is God. One's 'picture' of God is in fact a metaphorical narrative of God's relationship with the world and the self as part of the world. [...] The Catholic 'classics' assume a God who is present in the world, disclosing Himself in and through creation. The world and all its events, objects, and people tend to be somewhat like God. The Protestant classics, on the other hand, assume a God who is radically absent from the world, and who discloses (Himself) only on rare occasions (especially in Jesus Christ and in Him crucified). The world and all its events, objects, and people tend to be radically different from God. (Greeley 1990: 45)

By an analogical imagination Greeley means that a Catholic mind-set, more or less consciously, tends toward analogy, where the physical reality speaks of another, spiritual, reality. Greeley's position is that of the long tradition of Christian exegesis, developed and practiced above all in the Middle Ages. Applied to contemporary culture, Greeley's observations may seem too simplified and stereotyped, but nevertheless they convey a basic understanding of Undset's writing. In her work artistic creativity and religious faith are closely linked. Catholic dogmas are instruments of her penetrating reality. This Catholic perspective seems to be profoundly embodied in her realistic fiction, even in the works written several years before her conversion to the Catholic Church in 1924 – one can perhaps say that Catholicism enhanced her instinctive realism (Bliksrud 2005: 72). Undset's fiction presents a skillful and deliberate merging of the spiritual with the physical. She penetrates the concrete world in order to find in its depths the image of its source, the image of the ultimate divine reality. She is interested in all the events of life from the greatest to the smallest, because they serve as a bridge between the two orders of life: the temporal and the eternal. Events in every human's life are understood as channels of grace through which man is prepared for eternity. This philosophy manifested in her fiction is based on the conviction that a metaphysical principle works through the physical world. In her novel *The Wild Orchid*, a Catholic priest, Harald Tangen, explains Catholicism to the main character: Divine grace, says Tangen, does not change nature. It makes it perfect again. Tangen does not refer directly to Thomas Aquinas in his statement, but he is obviously repeating Thomas' well known statement from *Summa Theologica*: 'Gratia non tollit, sed supponit et perficit naturam' (Grace does not destroy nature, but perfects and elevates it) (Bliksrud 1986: 26, Whitehouse 1999: 106).

Like Saint Thomas, Undset was always convinced that there is an essential link between the world of the senses and the world of the spirit. This conviction is a function of her sacramental imagination, and an important theme in her writing from its very beginning. Undset's stories proceed on two levels. In her interesting study *The Novel and Society* from 1941, N. Elizabeth Monroe writes that Undset's reader can enjoy these narratives without regard to their respective level, or without believing in the supernatural destinies that her characters are working out in their lives:

> but the literary effectiveness of having natural motives reinforced by supernatural motives cannot be denied. Although intensely interested in ideas, Undset never lets ideas take the place of the story. She knows how to set characters into action and to involve them in tense situations. The characters' ideas are enthralling because they lead to action, or deflect the course of action, or call for deep resources of spiritual energy to motivate the rest of life. They never turn ideas over in their mind as a mere form of intellectual exercise […], their ideas are given only when they help to determine their lives.' (Monroe 1941: 48)[4]

The nature of sacramental imagination in fiction is determined by the nature of the writer's perceptive apparatus and abilities. In her book on Catholic fiction, *Mystery and Manners* (1957), Flannery O'Connor says: 'The beginning of human knowledge is through the senses, and the fiction writer begins where human perception begins' (O'Connor 1957: 67). This is a fundamentally Aristotelian and Thomistic point of view. We remember Saint Thomas' basic epistemological formula: 'Nihil est in intellectu quod non prius fuerat in sensu' – i.e. approximately 'There is nothing in the mind which has not first been in the senses.'

In my doctoral thesis I pointed out that Undset belongs to an Aristotelian tradition in European intellectual history, also known as the 'orphic' tradition, which includes her favorite mentors, among them Linnaeus and Shakespeare. Like Orpheus they 'sing' the creation into a dynamic, divine order (Bliksrud 1988: 44-45, 51). These authors' logical and imaginative ways of thinking work together. They do not use their mind only to gather knowledge and establish interpretations of man and the world. The body, physical and sensual experiences are essential to this method, which is called 'post-logic'. The method bears a close relationship to sex and fertility; one might say that 'love' is a necessary part of its working. Its aim is the discovery of the world, and it is this which gives it all the beauty it has.[5] Undset's art is characterized by a similar approach to man and the world, giving her writings a multi-sensory, almost tactile quality. Undset's depiction of nature is always religious in this 'orphic' way. From her earliest years she saw the manifestation of God in the beauty of nature. Her concept of nature corresponds to that of the Swedish botanist Carl Linnaeus. Her almost passionate love of plants led her to study – and unconditionally savor – Linnaeus' work. His classifications in the field of botany, his taxonomic method and his 'universal science of order' struck a deep chord with Undset. Her fiction reinforces our sense of the supernatural by grounding it in concrete, observable reality, and a typical feature in her almost endless descriptions of nature are small epiphanies of its innate divinity.

Sacramental imagination depends first of all on a special ability or achievement of the eye. In an essay on the Swedish naturalistic writer Elin Wägner, Undset herself defines art as a result of a visual transformation of the world and human beings. Art is a work of perception of the inner eye. An artist, she writes, must retell what he sees with his heart and mind, and not only what he sees with his eyes; that is the essence of art (Undset 2004: 307). Flannery O'Connor confirms this view in *Mystery and Manners*

(1957) where she writes about Catholic fiction as if she were Undset's literary soulmate. In an essay entitled 'The Church and the Fiction Writer' O'Connor says: 'For the writer of fiction, everything has its testing point in the eye, an organ which eventually involves the whole personality and as much of the world as can be got into it. [...] The roots of the eye are in the heart' (O'Connor 1957: 144).

Undset believed that an attitude of 'pretending not to see' was underlying the hypocrisy and moral anarchy she observed in her own time. She, however, had the courage to see, and she followed her vision of Truth in an uncompromising way. She did not choose to shut her eyes to what she saw around her about the reality of human life, how narrow-minded and egotistical people become when they have nothing but themselves to believe in. Indeed, her novels of modern life present a psychological analysis of this phenomenon. In a letter to an American literary scholar during her Second World War exile in America Undset writes: 'If I had not always been insatiably curious about the quaint ways human beings go about the business of living, the mess they make of it, if I had been satisfied with a superficial knowledge, and a desire to skip unpleasant conclusions, I should probably have been as much of an atheist today as I was at thirty' (cited in Daniloff 1974: 127). Undset's clear-sightedness and honesty saved her from the cult of the self and the wishful thinking of her time, not at least in sexual matters. She was opposed to any puritanical morality which preferred to ignore the sexual instinct in human experience, and also to the modern, secular and feminist morality with its over-emphasis on innocence. In her novel *Jenny* Undset depicts the ghost-ridden character of sex and shows that sex can become a demonic force. She knew, with the American feminist philosopher Camille Paglia, a critic who is relevant to understanding Undset, that sex is a far darker power than feminists have dared to realize. Sex, Paglia writes, is the point of contact between man and nature, where morality and good intentions fall victim to primitive urges. As sexual beings we are infected with dark forces. The element of free will in sex and emotion is slight, and falling in love is irrational (Paglia 1990: 4). These insights are communicated in Undset's novels, most of all in *Kristin Lavransdatter*. Kristin's passion for Erlend is a wild power, which forces her and her lover to betrayal, defeat and murder. Undset knew that passionate love does not create any laws, it breaks them all, as she states in her essay on the Brontë sisters: 'Elskoven skaper ingen lover, den bryter alle' (Undset 2004: 261).

In Catholicism Undset found an open attitude toward the realities of life. The Church does not ignore the dark forces of sexuality, and knows that man cannot cope with the forces of human nature without supernatural, sacramental help. Long before her conversion Undset thought of the erotic relationship between man and woman as a mystery, which includes the possibility of bringing the lovers to heaven or hell. Already in a burlesque poem written in her early youth, 'Evig kjærlighet' (*Eternal Love*), she displays inter-textual insights from Dante's *Inferno*. In the Catholic theology of human and divine love and its teaching of marriage as a sacrament, Undset found a confirmation of what she had thought and believed in the atheistic period of her life. There is no other ideal strong enough to keep man and woman together than the sacrament which has the power to raise fallen nature and make it perfect again.

This point of view is closely linked to Christianity's dogma of incarnation and the sacrament of the Eucharist. The nature of Undset's fictional writing is intrinsically rooted in the Incarnation of Christ. To her this was a historical fact, not a metaphorical statement. She acknowledges that God, Himself spirit, became human at a certain point in history. The abstract and supernatural Word became natural, physical flesh. This doctrine has a very far-reaching effect: it redeems the physical world, and Undset felt it to be the essential basis of Catholic fiction. In an address, 'Truth and Fiction,' delivered in New York in May 1942, she writes that the Catholic writer will feel life from the standpoint of the central Christian mystery: that despite all its horror, God found human life worth dying for. But if a Catholic writer hopes to reveal this mystery, he will have to do it by describing truthfully what he sees from where he is. He cannot do it by statements about his belief in a given Catholic dogma. That Undset calls placing 'the cart before the horse' (cited in Daniloff 1974: 137). She gave these words of literary advice to other Catholic writers:

> Tell the truths you have, even if they are grim, preposterous, shocking. After all, we Catholics ought to acknowledge what a shocking business human life is. Our race has been revolting against its Creator since the beginning of time. Revolt, betrayal, denial, or indifference, sloth, laziness – which one of us has not been guilty in one or more of all these sins one time or other? But remember you have to tell other and more cheerful truths, too: of the grace of God and the endeavor of strong and loyal, or weak but trusting souls, and also of the natural virtues of man created in the image of God, and this image is very hard to efface entirely. (Quoted from Bayerschmidt 1970: 156, translation into Norwegian in Undset 2008)

To do Undset's authorship justice, it must be seen in the light of the twentieth century's Catholic renaissance in European literature. This was a literary movement based on the New Thomism of Jacques Maritain, comprising great European authors like Georges Bernanos, François Mauriac, G. K. Chesterton, Graham Greene, Evelyn Waugh, and I will also include the American writer Flannery O' Connor. In his book *Literary Converts* (1999) Joseph Pearce writes: 'Taken as a whole this network of minds represented a potent Christian response to the age of unbelief. It produced some of the century's great literary masterpieces and stands as a lasting testament to the creative power of faith' (Pearce 1999: xii).

All these writers turned to the Catholic Church as their sole authority, because its teachings of the sacramental dimension of life appealed and corresponded both to their intellect and to their creative powers as artists, to their imagination.

References

Bayerschmidt, C.F. (1970): *Sigrid Undset*. Colombia University. New York. Twayne Publishers.

Bliksrud, L. (1986): 'Opposisjon ex auditorio.' In *Edda* 1. Oslo: Universitetsforlaget.

Bliksrud, L. (1995 [1988]): *Natur og normer hos Sigrid Undset*. Oslo: Aschehoug.

Bliksrud, L. (2005): 'Norsk utakt. Sigrid Undset i litteraturvitenskapen.' In *Norsk Litteraturvitenskapelig Tidsskrift* 1. Oslo: Universitetsforlaget.

Bliksrud, L. (2006): 'Sigrid Undset (Literature 1928).' In O. Njølstad (ed.), *Norwegian Nobel Prize Laureates*. Oslo: Universitetsforlaget.

Butorac, N. (n.d.): 'The Sacramental Imagination and Catholic Literature.' http://www.alyosha.com/si/. Accessed July 21, 2013.

Daniloff, J.F. (1974): *Sigrid Undsets litteratursyn, hovedoppgave i nordisk litteratur*. Universitetet i Oslo.

Greeley, A. (1990): *The Catholic Myth. The Behavior and Beliefs of American Catholics*. New York. Scribner.

Hamm, C. (2006): 'The Maiden and the Knight: Gender, Body and Melodrama in Sigrid Undset's Kristin Lavransdatter.' In *Scandinavica* 45(1), pp. 5-27.

Monroe, N.E. (1941): *The Novel and Society. A Critical Study of the Modern Novel*. Chapel Hill: The University of North Carolina Press.

O'Connor, F. (1957): *Mystery and Manners. Occasional prose selected by Sally and Robert Fitzgerald*. New York: Farrar Straus Giroux.

Paglia, C. (1990): *Sexual Personae. Art and Decadence from Nefertiti to Emily Dickinson*. Yale University Press, Penguin Books.

Pearce, J. (1999): *Literary Converts. Spiritual Inspiration in an Age of Disbelief.* London: Harper Collins Publishers.

Sewell, E. (1960): *The Orphic Voice. Poetry and Natural History. New Haven*: Yale University Press.

Undset, S. (2004): *Sigrid Undsets essays og artikler 1910-1919*, ed. Liv Bliksrud. Oslo: Aschehoug.

Undset, S. (2007): *Sigrid Undsets essays og artikler 1930-1939*, ed. Liv Bliksrud. Oslo: Aschehoug.

Undset, S. (2008): *Sigrid Undsets essays og artikler 1940-1949*, ed. Liv Bliksrud. Oslo: Aschehoug.

Whitehouse, J.C. (1999): *Vertical Man. The Human Being in the Catholic Novels of Graham Greene, Sigrid Undset, and Georges Bernanos*. London: The Saint Austin Press.

Notes

1. This essay is based on my paper 'The Sacramental Imagination of Sigrid Undset's Writings' at the 95th Annual Meeting of the Society for the Advancement of Scandinavian Study, May 5-7, 2005, Portland State University, Portland, Oregon. A more elaborate version is published in Norwegian: 'Sigrid Undsets diktekunst og poetikk,' in *Gymnadenia. Årsskrift for Sigrid Undset Selskapet.* 2005. Lillehammer.

2. See Hamm 2006: 6. Hamm puts it this way: 'In combination, these two aspects become critical, a fact that becomes especially clear when comparing Undset's status to that of Virgina Woolf. Born in the same year as Undset, Woolf is seen as an accomplished modernist [...]' (ibid) Undset writes in her essay 'Den hellige Angela av Merici – en kvinnesakskvinne' (1931) that she dislikes Woolf's *A Room of ones own*. But in 1937 she states in a note to her own essay: 'Siden dette ble skrevet, har jeg lest adskillig av Virginia Woolf. At hun ikke bare er en ytterst interessant og talentfull forfatterinne, men en artist av høy rang – det er en av de største overraskelser jeg har opplevd i retning av bøker.' (Since this was

written, I have read various works by Virginia Woolf. That she is not only an extremely interesting and talented author, but an artist of high rank - this is one of the greatest surprises I have experienced with books) Cf Undset 2007: 135.

3. Monroe (1941: 41) compares Undset with Edith Wharton: 'Edith Wharton has this same sense of drama, but her characters are bound only by a morality that has been cut loose from its supernatural foundations and by the conventions of a well-to-do, compact society.'

4. Carl Bayerschmidt comments on Monroe's statement as follows: 'Because of the author's profound religious experience she wishes to write of the "unbending realism" of Christianity and the rediscovery of the eternal. At the same time she realizes that most men and women never lose their contact with the commonplace and react to the problems confronting them in a practical manner and usually without any spiritual motivation. As a realistic writer Undset is able to generate a flow of narrative at this lower level and to introduce characters whose thinking and actions conform to such commonplace circumstances.' (Bayerschmidt 1969: 136).

5. The term 'orphic' is a core concept in Elizabeth Sewell's study *The Orphic Voice. Poetry and Natural History* (1960). About the 'post-logic method' Sewell writes: 'The post-logic method is a way of using mind and body to build up dynamic structures (never fixed or abstract patterns) by which the human organism sets itself in relation to the universe and allows each side to interpret the other. The mind's relation to its structure or myth is inclusive and reflective. It is not detached; the working mind is part of the dynamic of the system, and it is united, by its forms, to whatever it is inquiring into in the universe. The process of making the interpretative myths is carried on in language, and the structure of language in its dynamic with the mind both conditions and is conditioned by this mutual interpretation' (Sewell 1960: 404-405).

Love and Passion in some pre-1870 Danish Literature

Tom Lundskær-Nielsen
University College London

Introduction

Many of the writers in the pre-Romantic and Romantic age in Denmark grappled with representations of love and relationships between the sexes, and these presentations span the whole spectrum between portrayals of passionate physical love on the one hand, and more idealistic 'other world' attitudes – sometimes complete repudiation of carnality – on the other. This chapter aims to present a very brief survey of the development that took place in this area from the 1770s to the Modern Breakthrough of the 1870s, as seen in the works of some of the most prominent writers.

Obviously, it is only possible to deal with a small sample of texts within this limited scope, but there are a number of critical treatments of erotic love and passion covering this period of Danish literature.[1]

Background

Dualism can be traced back to the earliest records of human culture. Throughout history it has involved some of the most fundamental contrastive sets of concepts or forces in human life, such as those between body and soul/spirit, physicality/sexuality and spirituality, heaven and earth, realism and idealism, etc., where the emphasis has tended to be on one or the other of these opposites. An early example of emphasis on the unearthly aspects in Western culture is found in Plato's system of 'ideas,' according to which the worldly phenomena are merely shadows and reflections of the eternal ideas, as seen most clearly in his famous parable of the cave; hence the term 'idealism.' The emphasis on such 'platonic' aspects of life has cast a long shadow down the Western tradition; the notion of life on earth being only a pale shadow (cf. Macbeth's utterance 'Life's but a walking shadow')[2] of the higher world of ideas took on many forms of which the declamation by Faust, 'Am farbigen Abglanz haben wir das Leben' (we experience life in the colourful reflection)[3] is one of the more famous literary expressions, though by no means the only one even in Goethe's own works.

In a religious context, the downgrading of physical and material life in Western civilisation goes back to the account of the Fall in Genesis, when Adam and Eve suddenly realised the shame of their nakedness, and it was adopted by Christianity during most of its existence. Although it could take different forms, there was never any doubt that life on earth was essentially a vale of tears, at best a preparation for 'true' life after death, and that the fate of each individual was determined by his or her moral conduct in life, to be assessed on Judgement Day.

One of the key aspects of life that for centuries was viewed in such moralistic-religious terms was the concept of love. This, in itself, could mean different things. The highest sphere was that of all-embracing spiritual love, such as that of God for the creation and mankind, whose ultimate incarnation was the death of Jesus on the cross in order to expiate human sins. But such emotions could also be reversed, as in people's love of God and their longing for Heaven, and leading an unblemished life in accordance with the scriptures and the teaching of the Church (which was not always the same thing) was regarded as the ultimate meaning of life.

Because of the complexity of feelings and relationships between the two sexes, representation of them in writing was not easy, but all the more interesting for that. The strict moral code preached by the Church ensured that the physical, sexual side of relationships was tolerated only within marriage. It was of course necessary for procreation – indeed in times of high infant mortality, producing a large number of children was the norm rather than the exception – but sexual gratification in its own right, for the sole purpose of pleasure, was condemned, and was not normally to be talked (or written) about, certainly not in any detail. Moreover, when it took place outside marriage, whether it was adultery or 'just' fornication, it was a sin and the perpetrators, women in particular, were often treated harshly. This, of course, did not stop such activities from taking place and girls in socially inferior positions were especially prone to being the victims of such liaisons, whether entered into voluntarily or by coercion. Yet, on the European scene, particularly as we approach the Renaissance, positive literary descriptions of the pleasures of the flesh, such as those found in Boccaccio's *Decameron* (1358), set during the flight from the Black Death in Florence in 1348, and in Chaucer's *Canterbury Tales* from the end of the fourteenth century, begin to appear. Two hundred years later such relationships are depicted in Shakespeare and the English baroque drama and, after the English Civil War, in the Restoration drama, though here in a more 'sophisticated' social environment. It is clearly a topic that has interested all ages, but how far the portrayals could go in this direction varied considerably from country to country, as too much focus on the subject was considered offensive to good taste.

Love between the sexes was further complicated by the widespread practice of 'arranged marriages', which took place within all social classes. Thus 'marrying for love', certainly when viewed as the norm, is a relatively modern concept which in plays (e.g. Shakespeare and Holberg) is nearly always the result of a rebellion against the authority of the parents and thus a challenge to the established order. In tragedies such attempts usually have disastrous consequences, cf. *Romeo and Juliet*, while in comedies we witness the triumph of the young lovers over the grumpy elders and their traditional values.

In (pre-)Romantic Danish literature, the fundamental dualism between erotic love and a more 'idealistic' attitude takes different forms, from attempts to bridge the gap between the two to seeing them as incompatible. They are usually referred to as *eros* and *agape*, respectively. In the rest of this chapter I shall trace some of the stages of this development.

Pre-Romanticism

In the last few decades before the breakthrough of the Romantic movement, two writers were instrumental in changing the style of Danish poetry and prose, and in not too dissimilar ways: Johannes Ewald (1743-81) and Jens Baggesen (1764-1826). Ewald's all-too-brief life was dominated by the painful conflict between the pietism of his upbringing and his increasingly strong attraction to a hedonistic lifestyle. The pivotal experience of his youth, the meeting with Arendse Huulegaard and his hopeless infatuation with her, became the catalyst both for his conduct in adult life and for some of the most sublime poems and prose passages in Danish literature. Thus his famous description in *Levnet og Meeninger* (Life and Opinions)[4] of the stages of love shows an intriguing blend of self-mocking realism and soaring idealism. What stands out, in particular, is his rapturous account of Arendse's graceful shape and how he suddenly composes himself in the middle of his eulogy of her breasts and starts praising her virtue and blameless soul as the most important things about her. All this is conveyed by means of a lively, almost incoherent and idiosyncratic syntax, the first of its kind in Danish literature, full of enumerations, interruptions and apostrophes:

> En Arendse, med store mørkebruune, straalende Øyne, med en lille kroged Næse, en Mund hvorpaa Gratierne syntes at skjærtse, tykke kastaniebruune Lokker, som beskyggede en sneehviid Hals, to runde, elastiske, svulmende --- o Himmel! – jeg glemmer mig! – men det vigtigste! – En Arendse, med en dydig, en vittig, en satt og en høy Sjæl – en Arendse, med det ømmeste Hjerte, som nogentid har slaaet bag ved et Snørliv! Jeg havde hende – O Himmel! – o mine Læsere! [...] (Ewald 1964:142)

> (An Arendse with big dark-brown, radiant eyes, with a small, hooked nose, a mouth on which the graces seemed to jest, thick chestnut-coloured ringlets that shaded a snow-white neck, two round, elastic, swelling --- oh, Heaven! – I forget myself! – but the most important thing! – an Arendse with a virtuous, sensible, demure and elevated soul – an Arendse with the tenderest heart that has ever beaten behind a corset! I had her – oh, Heaven! – oh, my readers! [...])[5]

This is a masterful, seemingly involuntary erotic portrayal of a teenage girl (she was 15) by a young man of the same age who is simultaneously bowled over by her attractions and trying, rather unsuccessfully, to convince himself – as well as the readers of whom he is clearly well aware – that her spiritual sides are more important than her bodily charms; in other words, an adolescent man thrown into a turmoil of feelings that he cannot properly understand and cope with, and yet they are recollected, not in Wordsworthian tranquillity but with all the passionate experience of the moment. This, in essence, shows Ewald's unreconciled strife between body and soul (cf. his late poem 'Til Sielen – en Ode' (1780; To the Soul – an Ode)) and between the erotic and the spiritual aspects of life. This dualism also manifests itself in his plays, notably in *Balders Død* (1775; Death of Balder) where the demi-god Balder's pursuit of the human Nanna, who in turn is in love with Hother the king, is as hopeless as it is unsuitable and can only end in tragedy.

There are many parallels between Ewald and Baggesen, though the latter lived long enough to witness the end of High Romanticism in Denmark. Baggesen, too, had frequent mood swings that alternated between exultation and extreme exhaustion or defeatism. His numerous infatuations were generally of a spiritual nature and at times triangular, involving married women to whom he would write passionate, suggestive love poems, laying bare all his feelings, real or imagined. And yet, like Ewald's 'spontaneous' passages in *Levnet og Meeninger*, most of Baggesen's seemingly impromptu outpourings are carefully crafted for maximum effect, whether they are addressed to individual women or form part of the highly egocentric, lyrical descriptions in his most famous work, the travelogue *Labyrinten*.

Romanticism ('romantik')

An even starker and completely irreconcilable dualism is found in arguably the first Danish Romantic poet, Schack von Staffeldt, whose love poetry is almost exclusively platonic and idealistic in its nature while the rare descriptions of a consummated union are invariably followed by bitterness and disillusion. Only the eternal expectation and the union of the souls, rather than the bodies, can be worthy of praise, and perfection is restricted to an ideal world where the sexual instinct is absent or sublimated. This was an extreme stance which deprived Staffeldt of critical attention until relatively recently, but it hints at the kind of split personality characteristic of the later 'romantisme.'

However, the central figure of Danish Romanticism is unquestionably Adam Oehlenschläger (1779-1850), who virtually burst on to the literary scene with his collection *Digte* (1803; Poems), inspired by the lectures given by Henrik Steffens in Copenhagen in 1802 on the new Romantic School in Germany, published as *Indledning til philosophiske Forelæsninger* (1803; Introduction to Philosophical Lectures), and by his own subsequent conversations with Steffens (who also happened to be Grundtvig's cousin). From the start, Oehlenschläger was therefore imbued with the predominant spirit among the early German Romantics (the so-called Jena School) in his search for a synthesis between body and soul, which had already been attempted, for example, in Friedrich Schlegel's *Lucinde* and in Novalis's novel fragment *Heinrich von Ofterdingen* with its central Romantic symbol of 'die blaue Blume' (the blue flower); cf. the term *Universalromantik*.

These aspirations are clear in Oehlenschläger's 'Sanct Hansaften-Spil' (in *Digte* 1803; A Midsummer Night's Play), where the ending is a pantheistic woodland apotheosis, a quasi-religious fusion of love and nature, body and spirit, not couched in the idealistic idiom of most of his predecessors. In his seminal work, the play *Aladdin* (1805), the physical attraction between Aladdin and Gulnare is clear from the moment they first set eyes on each other (echoes of *Romeo and Juliet*), but it is only when Aladdin has suffered the loss of wife and palace and has overcome his suicidal thoughts that he is mature enough to regain it all in his struggles with the forces of darkness, Noureddin and his brother Hindbad, and thus to combine the dualistic aspects of life.

It is also possible to see the multi-genre trilogy *Helge* (1814), *Hroars Saga* (1817; The Saga of Hroar) and *Hrolf Krake* (1828) as an early imbalance between raw, ruthless power (Helge) and spiritual idealism (Hroar), which are combined into a synthesis by Hrolf.

Poetic Realism

In the 1820s High Romanticism started giving way to a more realistic strain in Danish literature, known as 'poetic realism.' The two writers who have above all been saddled with this label are Poul Martin Møller and Steen Steensen Blicher. Poul Martin Møller (1794-1838) ended his career as Professor of Philosophy at Copenhagen University, where he became one of Søren Kierkegaard's important early influences. His literary production consists mainly in poetry and aphorisms, but he is best known for his incomplete novel *En dansk Students Eventyr* (1824; The Adventures of a Danish Student), inspired by Goethe's *Wilhelm Meister* and the episodic, picaresque novels of the eighteenth century, though on a reduced scale. On his rather aimless wanderings its protagonist, the carefree Aladdin-like student Fritz visits a number of different places and comes across various character types that are treated with a good deal of irony, as are the erotic situations. Being an impulsive and easily affected person, Fritz himself is prone to falling in love at any moment, his chief infatuation being Marie, who is far more balanced and natural in her behaviour than any other character in the novel. Nevertheless she and Fritz form strong contrasts both to Jens Hansen with his insufferable self-sufficient, petit-bourgeois, egocentric view of life (and women) and to the learned 'licentiatus medicinæ,' a completely inept young man, described as 'denne aandelige og legemlige Krøbling' (this spiritual and physical cripple, Møller 1958: 64), whose thoughts are as paralysed as his actions. The incompleteness of the text makes it impossible to know the intended ending, but in the extant fragment the only real love interest is centred on the skirmishes between the likeable but very immature Fritz (only the other young girl, Sophie, surpasses him in childishness) and the more sensible Marie. However, this relationship has none of the depth and passion that are found in contemporary and later Danish fiction.

One of these contemporary writers is Steen Steensen Blicher (1782-1848), whose short stories take place in the bleak moorland scenery of central Jutland, a hill-less Danish Brontë-like countryside where passions rage and fates unfold with no less tragic consequences. A case in point is 'Hosekræmmeren' (1829; The Hosier), in which a wealthy hosier not only rejects the neighbouring poor, young Esben's proposal to his beautiful if mentally fragile daughter, Cecilia, but also the former's earnest request not to let Cecilia marry someone else before his return from Holstein (where he hopes to make his fortune). Nevertheless the father accepts another and richer suitor, but the daughter does not and the agitation has driven her insane by the time the third banns are read in church. The shamefulness to the family of the cancelled wedding takes a new turn when Esben returns with a minor fortune, only to be confronted with Cecilia's state of madness. Even worse, her subconscious mind reveals her repressed sexuality and her rambling talk circles around their wedding night and life together in Paradise. Esben's hope of bringing her to her senses is dashed when his overnight stay results in Cecilia cutting his throat in the night, though she is quite unconscious of her deed. The shock of this action sends her father to his grave soon afterwards, which psychologically must have set her free, for on the day of his funeral she falls into a long, deep sleep and wakes up sane but without any recollection of the previous events, until her jilted lover reveals them to her and thus sends her back into insanity. Although all this happens in an isolated house on the heath, the passions aroused and the thwarted sexual instincts could hardly be stronger. This is further emphasised by the textual references to both Macbeth and exotic romances and by the contrast with the quiet but complex way in which the narration unfolds.

Blicher's first, and arguably finest, short story, 'Brudstykker af en Landsbydegns Dagbog' (1824; Fragments of the Diary of a Parish Clerk), is also essentially a story centred on an all-consuming passion. As a servant at a manor house, the narrator (diarist) Morten Vinge, a studious, mild-mannered, but inherently passive character, falls hopelessly (and comically, as he needs Ovid's *Ars amoris* to explain his 'illness') in love with the passionate and flirtatious daughter of the house, Sophie (modelled on the real-life noblewoman Marie Grubbe). The tragicomical climax of his life happens one night when Sophie unexpectedly enters his room and starts making ardent love to him, only to flee in panic when he utters the ironic words 'Evindelig min!' (mine for ever!, Blicher 1959:23). What was a heavenly, if very brief, experience turns into its opposite when Morten discovers that Sophie simply mistook his room for that of his mate, Jens, with whom she is in love and they elope immediately afterwards. However, Morten, who hopes to become a priest, is in emotional turmoil and longs to repeat the act which morally he has to condemn, so his denunciation of Sophie in biblical terms as 'Du falske Qvinde! Du Potiphars Hustru!' (you false woman! you wife of Potiphar!, ibid) is rather an indictment of his own lust. Towards the end of the story, Morten meets Jens and Sophie again, now living in wretched conditions following their social degradation during which Sophie had to resort to prostitution to survive financially, and yet showing no regrets. Thus love and lust become inextricably entangled, but if that can be construed as punishment for sinful behaviour, Morten's life is by contrast portrayed as sterile and futile after his departure from the manor house. Not even his modest ambition of priesthood is fulfilled and he ends up disillusioned as a mere clerk in his home parish.

'Romantisme'

The Danish term 'romantisme' differs from 'romantik' (Romanticism) as it denotes the trend in the 1830s and 1840s towards a more disharmonious outlook and the impossibility of embracing or accepting the Romantics' attempted monistic synthesis of body and soul. An increasingly irreconcilable schism arises between the two, often resulting in an inherent discord within some of these writers themselves, such as Byron par excellence but also Hoffmann, Heine, Musset, Hugo and others. This rift between the realism of the body and the idealism of the spirit can no longer be bridged and the result is either polarisation in the form of a more or less fanatic endorsement of one or the other extreme, the flesh or the soul, or inner destruction in a vain attempt to bring the two together. Terms like *spleen*, *Weltschmerz* and *tristesse* have all been used to describe this inner pain. The gulf that thus opens up also lends itself to ironic treatment, as seen among others in Byron and Heine, which is of a far more serious and destructive kind than was the case with the so-called 'Romantic irony.'

In Denmark, such a world-view is bound up with a peculiarly 'local' notion, namely that of 'det interessante' (what is interesting).[6] First coined and defined by Johan Ludvig Heiberg (1791-1860) – for decades the arbiter of taste and 'dannelse' (i.e. the values and the kind of educational background required and expected by the dominant literary circles in Copenhagen) – it highlights the increasing focus on aspects of life that are not obvious or in the limelight, and thus on what is left unsaid (e.g. in a drama) or is only intimated. It is obvious that in an age when there are limits to what you can say and write about erotic matters, 'det interessante' becomes an important notion in this context.

Few people would perhaps put Hans Christian Andersen (1805-75) high on their list of erotic writers, but there is no doubt from his autobiographies and especially his diaries that he had a lifelong fascination with this topic. For example, one need only point to his visits to the secret erotic collection in the National Archaeological Museum in Naples, his penchant in old age for talking (yes, just talking) to prostitutes in Paris brothels and, much earlier, the turmoil (his boiling blood) he was thrown into when he was offered young girls (and boys) on the streets of Naples during his first visit in 1834. On the other hand, Andersen's well-documented *Sexualangst* (perhaps sublimated in his strong urge to kiss all and sundry among his friends and acquaintances, often passionately on the mouth) may account for the general lack of sexual satisfaction among the protagonists in his works. His experiences from his first journey to Italy (1833-34) are transformed into the characters of his first novel *Improvisatoren* (1835; The Improvisatore), where the idealistic and innocent artist Antonio is complemented by the sensual and dynamic Bernardo, but it is the virtuous Antonio and the equally pure women, particularly his eventual wife Lara/Maria, who are held up as models, although their union is more one of souls and minds than of bodies. This contrast between body and soul is shown clearly, if symbolically, in the scene (in Naples, of course) between Antonio and the voluptuous and mature married woman Santa, who is in the process of seducing him when a painting of the Virgin Mary (no less!) falls down and hits him on the head, thus miraculously preventing an act of depravity (1987:185-86).[7]

In his third novel, *Kun en Spillemand* (1837; Only a Fiddler), Andersen juxtaposes the somewhat talented but feeble and passive Christian (a 'tame bird') and the socially superior, brave, strong-minded and free-spirited Naomi (a 'free bird') of dubious and demonic origin, in their roles of joint protagonists. Here too the dualistic framework is clear, so although they have known each other from childhood and at one level become soulmates, their characters are as radically different as are their fates. Christian is too weak to overcome the problems he encounters, including in his relationships with women, while Naomi at every stage displays her independence and takes the initiative both in her career and in sexual matters, at one point teaming up with the dashing but ruthless and sadistic riding master Ladislaus, whom she leaves the moment he touches her with his whip (no Marie Grubbe-like masochism in her!), but her actions catch up with her in the end and force her into the power of, and a loveless marriage to, a cynical nobleman. They can thus both be seen as losers in life, but Naomi's passion, assertiveness and fearless behaviour contrast strongly with Christian's indecision and fear of life. In the end, the dualistic divergence is all too obvious.

In his stories and fairy tales, there are further examples of Andersen's reluctance to create a synthesis of body and soul, a happy union of physical and spiritual life. Where the two are in conflict, it is as a rule the spiritual, sometimes in the form of the religious, side that is triumphant. Examples of this can be seen in the endings of tales as diverse as 'Den lille Havfrue' (1837; The Little Mermaid), 'Dyndkongens Datter' (1858; The March King's Daughter) and 'Iisjomfruen' (1861; The Ice Maiden), as well as in the rejections and failed unions in 'Den standhaftige Tinsoldat' (1838; The Steadfast Tin Soldier), 'Svinedrengen' (1842; The Swineherd), 'Kjærestefolkene' (1844; The Lovers) and 'Sneemanden' (1861; The Snowman), to name but the most obvious ones. 'The Snowman,' in particular, demonstrates the impossibility of passionate, sexual feelings coming to fruition in the doomed, and admittedly one-sided, 'relationship' between the snowman and the hot stove, while the chilling tale 'Skyggen' (1847; The Shadow) more clearly than any other displays graphically the dualistic split between man and shadow.[8]

Frederik Paludan-Müller (1809-76) started his literary career as a true child of the licentious side of 'romantismen,' to which – like Andersen – he was at first tempted and drawn although, in accordance with the spirit of the time, anxiety and longing for earthly love and sexual satisfaction are countered by reflections of superficiality and constant disappointment, even by disillusion with it all, thus creating the fashionable dissonant note. His early 'romantistiske' phase is most clearly expressed in the Byron-inspired verse epic *Danserinden* (1833; The Danseuse). It is the story of a fearless and natural love relationship between a fêted female ballet dancer, Dione, and a dashing but ultimately feckless count, Charles, who deserts her for a socially more advantageous match, only to die in a duel fought for Dione before the planned wedding, while for Dione this outcome leads to madness and death. It thus contains plenty of the ingredients of 'romantismen' and was immensely popular, but five years later a spiritual crisis, followed by marriage, propelled Paludan-Müller into a repudiation of his former life and work and the adoption of a strict idealistic outlook which dominates his subsequent works and finally leads him into an ascetic world-view. Of these works, I shall confine myself to mentioning his undisputed masterpiece, the verse epic *Adam Homo* (Part I: 1842, Parts II-III: 1849), where these values are clearly displayed. In it, the weak and increasingly hollow eponymous hero – a Mr Average, having the Greek and Latin words for 'man' as his name – is easily led astray by worldly ambition and flirtatious women and keeps choosing the 'wrong' (i.e. non-idealistic) path in life. Some of his actions are quite despicable, such as his violent seduction of the poor servant girl Lotte, which leads her into prostitution. Adam's infatuation with some physically attractive and emancipated women, in particular the two noblewomen Clara and Mille, is shown as shallow and ill-founded, and his interest in the hedonistic values of the depraved old 'grey Galt' is no more edifying. He even sacrifices the one chance he has of a much better life with the good, composed and self-effacing Alma, whose undemanding, profound and 'higher' love goes well beyond anything Adam will ever encounter. Of the three kinds of love mentioned, only Alma's possesses the inner, evolutionary and spiritual strength that marks it out from the two others which are based, respectively, on imagination and raw sensuality. It therefore seems almost too much when this wretched weakling, whose pursuit of superficiality in life brings him social success but moral bankruptcy, having rejected (or redefined) 'the ideal,' is saved at the after-death judgement by the ever-forgiving Alma, in a way strongly reminiscent of both Beatrice and Dante, and Gretchen and Faust, but with much less justification. Or is this perhaps a remnant of the 'romantistiske' sarcasm?

His contemporary Søren Kierkegaard (1813-55) underwent a development not unlike that of Paludan-Müller. He too moved inexorably towards a strict version of idealism and a renunciation of the world, based on his firm religious beliefs. He became more and more extreme in his arguments about the right course in life. He was also strongly influenced by his background (the black and pessimistic outlook) and his feeling of guilt at his one visit to a brothel and not least his treatment of Regine Olsen (the broken engagement). Nevertheless, Kierkegaard published some of the most intense and fascinating studies of eroticism in Book I of *Enten – Eller* (1843; Either – Or).[9] In 'De umiddelbare erotiske Stadier eller det Musicalsk-Erotiske,' using Mozart's operas as his frame of reference, the fictitious writer 'A' distinguishes three stages of desire (Kierkegaard

1994: 77-78), which he characterises with the words (i) 'drømmende' (dreaming), associated with the page Cherubino in *The Marriage of Figaro*; (ii) 'søgende' (searching), linked to Papageno in *The Magic Flute*; and (iii) 'attraaende' (desiring), with reference to the title character in *Don Giovanni* who really subsumes the two others. Only in the third stage does desire have a clear object. The writer 'A' even sees Don Juan (Giovanni) and Faust as 'Middelalderens Titaner og Giganter' (the titans and giants of the Middle Ages) and claims that Don Juan is 'Udtrykket for det Dæmoniske bestemmet som det Sanselige' (the expression of the demonic determined as the sensual), while Faust is 'Udtrykket for det Dæmoniske bestemmet som det Aandelige' (the expression of the demonic determined as the spiritual) (Kierkegaard 1994: 86). However, the point about Don Juan is that he is a naïve and spontaneous, i.e. unreflecting, seducer. For him sensuality equals seduction, and sensual love is by its very nature faithless since it loves (and seduces) not one person but all. It only lives in and for the moment.

This makes Don Juan completely different from the reflecting seducer, whom we meet in the shape of Johannes in the later part of *Enten – Eller* called 'Forførerens Dagbog' (The Diary of a Seducer).[10] Suffice it to say that where Don Juan has not even reached the first of Kierkegaard's three general 'stages' in life, i.e. the aesthetic one, this is the stage where Johannes finds himself in his all-consuming preoccupation with pleasure. For him pleasure does not just consist in seducing a girl (and then another, etc.) – that merely becomes a matter of repetition, a notion which plays an important part in Kierkegaard's later thinking – it must be done in such a devious and sophisticated way that the girl at the end is willing to sacrifice herself unconditionally, but once she has surrendered, body and soul, she is completely vanquished – and thus no longer of any interest to the reflecting seducer. That, laid out in painstaking detail, is the cynical game that Johannes plays with the innocent Cordelia.

Finally, the two most important lyrical poets between Oehlenschläger and the Modern Breakthrough must be mentioned briefly. Christian Winther (1796-1876), stepbrother of Poul Martin Møller, lived his life as a bohemian poet, but was no revolutionary in a time of political turmoil. He is particularly known for his erotic love poetry, such as the cycle of poems *Til Een* (begun in 1841; To One), but his principal work remains the long historical verse epic *Hjortens Flugt* (1855; The Flight of the Hart), set in the early fifteenth century during the reign of Erik of Pomerania. Here the otherwise (reasonably) peaceful Danish nation and nature are being threatened by a poisonous foreign influence in the shape of the demonic but extremely seductive, gypsy-like Rhitra, who has the King in her power and previously had others in her net, but cannot conquer the pure and upright Squire Strange. In revenge, she engineers the imprisonment of Strange's beloved and chaste Ellen. The symbol of Rhitra's (erotic) power is the phallic golden serpent, which she wears as a ring in her ear. The plot has many complications before the happy ending that includes the expulsion of Rhitra, but it is worth taking a look at Rhitra's demonic origin, which is quite extraordinary. She was fathered by no less a figure than the four-headed Wendish god Svantevit, who every year mates with a virgin brought out to an isolated grotto by the sea. Such a virgin was Gulitza, the mother of Rhitra, when she was violated by Svantevit, but she somehow survived the equally ritual death by drowning after the copulation. The description of the event, given by Gulitza herself, is at the same time both graphic and symbolic. First, there is the pseudo-bordello setting:

> Med Purpurtepper tjeldet
> Var den hvælvede Hal;
> Og Gulvet sammenføiet
> Af sleben Muslingskal.
> De røde Lamper dufted
> Som Rosens første Suk,
> Mens Røgen op sig hvirvled
> Mod Loftets runde Glug. (Winther 1964: 92)

(Draped in purple arras / was the vaulted hall / the floor was joined together / by polished cockleshell. / Scent oozed from scarlet lanterns / like the first sighing of the rose / while smoke was whirling upwards / to the ceiling's rounded hole.)

This is followed by a foreshadowing of things to come in the form of explicit sexual imagery – the wild sea metaphorically penetrating the grotto – as seen by Gulitza:

> Forsigtigt jeg mig listed
> Derhen, og stirred ned.
> Det var et Svælg, et aabent,
> En Afgrund sort og bred;
> Jeg dybt dernede hørte –
> Mens svimlende jeg stod –
> Hvor ind i Grotten bruste
> Den vilde Havets Flod. (Winther 1964: 93)

(I crept with utmost caution / up there and looked straight down. / It was an open chasm / a black and wide abyss; / I heard from down there clearly / while fainting on my feet / the dreadful ocean bursting / into the grotto's mouth.)

And finally, there is the sacrificial intercourse itself:

> Af glødende Læber
> Tillukket blev min Mund, –
> Da vaaned sig og sukked
> Min Sjæl i Hjertets Grund!
> Jeg aned, det var ham
> Med det frygtelige Navn,
> Jeg vidste, det var Guden,
> Der tog mig i Favn. (Winther 1964: 95)

(By burning lips / my mouth was closed / my soul then groaned and sighed / to the bottom of my heart! / I gathered it was him / with the terrifying name / I knew it was the god / who was embracing me.)

No wonder that Rhitra became a dangerous and demonic temptress! Nor is she the only passionate character in the wide-ranging epic, which is generally read as the last echo of the harmonious and idyllic strain of Danish Romanticism, but it is certainly not without its 'romantistiske' dissonances.

The last writer to be dealt with is arguably the foremost erotic Danish poet of the nineteenth century. Emil Aarestrup (1800-56) had a successful career as a physician, so when his first collection of poems *Digte* (1838; Poems) met with little reaction, except for some shocked indignation, he contented himself with writing in private, and his subsequent poems appeared only posthumously in *Efterladte Digte* (1863; Posthumous Poems). Aarestrup describes, in endless variations, the attractions of the female body, sometimes merely through intimations, at other times in much greater detail. This explicitness was too much for his contemporaries and it was only in the twentieth century that he became recognised as a poet of great importance. Aarestrup did not share the religious scruples of many of his fellow writers. His wish to view the erotic as a natural part of human life may of course lead some to place him at the physical extreme of the body/soul divide, but he comes closer to the High Romantic monistic vision than any of his contemporaries, albeit with the balance tipped somewhat in the direction of the bodily aspect.

For the sake of space, let us confine our examples to a few of his justly famous ritornelles (3-lined poems with an a-b-a rhyme scheme):

Frister i Ørken,
O, du har viist mig saa deilige Sager,
At til at modstaa fattes mig Styrken. (Aarestrup III: 139, no. 18)

(Temptress in the desert / Oh, you have shown me so wonderful things / that to resist them I lack the strength.)

If that is rather general in its description, the following is more suggestive:

Den gyldne Fletning,
Der over Skuldren synker ned mod Barmen,
Har lært min Arm sin Slange-Retning. (Aarestrup III: 140, no. 21)

(The golden plait / that sinks down over the shoulder towards the bosom / has taught my arm its snake direction.)

We even get an insight into a doctor's secret thoughts when attending a female patient:

Lægen
Hans blik er naglede til Loftets Planker,
Hans Haand til Ninas Arm, hvor Pulsen banker,
Men under Teppet finder du hans Tanker. (Aarestrup II: 213, no. 150)

(The Doctor: His gaze is fixed on the ceiling beams / his hand on Nina's arm where the pulse is beating / but under the blanket you find his thoughts.)

Nowhere in pre-1870 Danish literature is the erotic side of life portrayed more sensually and with more obvious delight than by Aarestrup. For that reason alone, it is fitting to end this brief survey with him.

References

Andersen, H.C. (2003): *H.C. Andersens samlede værker: Eventyr og Historier I-III*. Det Danske Sprog- og Litteraturselskab. Copenhagen: Gyldendal.

Andersen, H.C. (2003): *Improvisatoren*. In *H.C. Andersens samlede værker IV*, Det Danske Sprog- og Litteraturselskab. Copenhagen: Borgen.

Andersen, H.C. (2003): *Kun en Spillemand*. In *H.C. Andersens samlede værker V*, Det Danske Sprog- og Litteraturselskab. Copenhagen: Gyldendal.

Baggesen, J. (1964): *Labyrinten*. Copenhagen: Gyldendals Bibliotek, Vol. 4.

Blicher, S.S. (1959): *Digte og Noveller*, Vol. I. Copenhagen: Gyldendal.

Ewald, J. (1964): *Philets Forslag og Levnet og Meeninger*. Copenhagen, Gyldendal.

Goethe, J.W. von (1966): *Goethe Werke (Dritter Band) Faust I und II*. Frankfurt am Main: Insel.

Henriksen, A. (1954): *Kierkegaards Romaner*. Copenhagen: Gyldendal/ Nordisk Forlag.

Johansen, J.D. (2003): *Litteratur og begær*. Odense: Syddansk Universitetsforlag.

Kierkegaard, S. (1994): *Enten – Eller*. In *Samlede værker*, Vols. 2/3. Copenhagen: Gyldendal.

Kirk, H. (1964): *Fiskerne*. Copenhagen: Gyldendal.

Kristensen, S.M. (1966): *Den dobbelte Eros*. Copenhagen: Gyldendal.

Lundskær-Nielsen, T. (2007): '"Love is a Many Splendored Thing": On the Treatment of Love in Hans Christian Andersen's Fairy Tales.' In *Scandinavica* 46 (2), pp. 213-35.

Møller, P.S. (1973): *Erotismen. Den romantiske bevægelse i Vesteuropa 1790-1860*. Copenhagen: Munksgaard.

Møller, P.M. (1958): *En dansk Students Eventyr*. Copenhagen: Gad.

Oehlenschläger, A. (1966; 1803): *Digte*. Copenhagen: Gyldendal.

Oehlenschläger, A. (1978): *Aladdin eller den forunderlige Lampe*. Copenhagen: Oehlenschläger Selskabet.

Paludan-Müller, F. (1991): *Danserinden*. Danske Klassikere, Det Danske Sprog- og Litteraturselskab. Copenhagen: Borgen.

Winther, C. (1964): *Hjortens Flugt*. Copenhagen: Gyldendal.

Aarestrup, E. (1922-25): *Samlede Skrifter I-V*. Copenhagen: Henrik Koppel.

Notes

1. See, among other works, Møller Kristensen (1966) and, in a wider European perspective, Møller (1973), as well as more recently Johansen (2003).

2. Shakespeare, *Macbeth*, V.v.24.

3. Goethe, *Faust II*, Act I, p. 140.

4. Although written during the years 1773-77, the autobiographical *Levnet og Meeninger* was not published until 1804-08, which makes Baggesen's travelogue *Labyrinten* (1792-93, The Labyrinth) a wholly original work, probably uninfluenced by Ewald despite the many similarities in style. For both, however, Lawrence Sterne was undoubtedly an important model.

5. My translation here and elsewhere.

6. There are numerous explanations of this concept; a classic one is found in Henriksen (1954: 32-45).

7. A much later example of a similar 'heavenly' intervention is found in Hans Kirk's novel *Fiskerne* (1928; The Fishermen, pp. 104-05) when the holy but sexually troubled bachelor, Anton Knopper, one evening suddenly starts fondling his fiancée, the barmaid Katrine, until, when touching her breast, he catches hold of her silver cross and immediately wants to pray and ask forgiveness, totally oblivious of her wish for him to continue.

8. For a more in-depth study of love in the fairy tales, see my article ' "Love is a

Many Splendored Thing": On the Treatment of Love in Hans Christian Andersen's Fairy Tales,' which also considers some of the so-called 'happy endings' (Lundskær-Nielsen 2007).

9. It should also be noticed that *Enten – Eller* as its motto has two lines from Edward Young's *Night Thoughts* (1741-45): 'Er da Fornuften alene døbt, / ere Lidenskaberne Hedninger?' (Are passions, then, the pagans of the soul / and only Reason baptized?) (*Night Thoughts*, IV.629).

10. This and some of Kierkegaard's other fictional works are sometimes labelled as novels, cf. Henriksen (1954).

Death, Love and Disillusion:
Postmodern Representations of Complicated Lives

Anne-Kari Skardhamar
Høgskolen i Oslo og Akershus

Introduction

The Norwegian author Trude Marstein's novel *Elin og Hans*, a story of love and death, was published in 2002. In the same year the Danish author Helle Helle published a love and death story, *Forestillingen om et ukompliceret liv med en mand* (The idea of an uncomplicated life with a man). The thematic similarity between the two texts invites a comparison, and the fact that Trude Marstein has translated Helle Helle's novel into Norwegian, makes it seem even more relevant to present a comparative analysis of the ideas and discourses of the two novels.

Death – Construction of Events

The story of Trude Marstein's *Elin og Hans* opens on the day after a funeral, five days after the death of the female protagonist. The effect is a shocking start which in traditional crime fiction would have been followed by a murder investigation. However, the novel is not a detective story, at least not in the usual sense. Elin's death is an accident, though the question of responsibility remains to be resolved. The story proceeds with an analepsis, which covers incidents of the married life of Elin and Hans, and then ends approximately where it started.

Similar patterns of circular composition and of retrospective narration are employed in Helle Helle's novel *Forestillingen om et ukompliceret liv med en mand*, which also opens with a death. In the first chapter the male protagonist is found dead in his bed with no indication of the cause of his death. No investigation may be required in this case, as he probably died a natural death. However, the following analepsis, which recounts events in the life of Susanne and Kim during the previous years and ends on the evening before Kim's death, serves as a kind of life and death inquiry.

In the novels of Marstein and Helle the retrospection of the surviving partners illustrates the interdependence of plot and characters. Unexpected death leads to memories of actions and thoughts through which the surviving characters reveal their inner qualities, as they move from seeming happiness to disaster. Causality is implicit rather than explicit, and an analysis of plot and characters has similarities with a crime investigation.

The narration in both novels departs from the chronological order of events. External analepsis, serving as narrative retrospection, is the basic structuring principle in Helle Helle's as well as in Trude Marstein's novel. Within the long analepsis there is also anachrony, as in *Forestillingen om et ukompliceret liv med en mand*, where the narration of the second chapter flashes one month back in time, then another two years back in chapter four and one year forward at the end of chapter six, i.e. one year before the time of the opening chapter. There are similar analeptic variations later in the narrative until it reaches the day before the starting point. The chronology corresponds to fragments of memory and serve to demonstrate how the temperature of the relationship moves up and down, giving a picture of dreams, dissatisfaction and the conflicts of complicated lives. This applies to both of the novels; however, there is a difference of emphasis on the introspective retrospection of the characters.

While *Forestillingen om et ukompliceret liv med en mand* is divided into chapters, and the analepsis starts in chapter two, *Elin og Hans* consists of one long text without any division into sections. All thoughts and actions are rendered by a first-person narrator, who is identical with the male protagonist Hans. On the second page it is made clear to the reader that what has happened draws a sharp line between the present and the past. The rest of the novel is the attempt of Hans to explain the development of his and Elin's marriage, and to answer the question of his innocence or possible guilt. The memories and associations of Hans organize the narrative which stretches from the first time he met Elin when she was twenty-two until the last time he saw her at forty-nine. In Hans' non-stop stream-of-consciousness monologue the chronology is broken by flashes of episodes uncontrollably floating between recent and older events. This makes the character of Hans a challenging object for interpretation.

In both novels repetitions give emphasis to certain details that connect episodes and increase the awareness of the protagonist when he looks back. One example of repetition in Helle Helle's novel is that a brick, which Kim in chapter two intends to use as a doorstop, is mentioned again in the middle of the novel and at the end when Susanne fetches it to keep the door open, and bring the Christmas tree inside, which may mean starting a less complicated life with her partner. Susanne sees his brick and her umbrella as their relationship in a nutshell. Susanne's yoga bag is also a detail which is mentioned several times. The bag connects an episode when she lets her yoga trainer kiss her and her last Christmas shopping in the opening chapter when she by mistake brought her yoga bag instead of her handbag. The example shows Susanne's emotional state, her confusion and her ambivalence about her and Kim's relationship.

Another set of repetitions serves to shed light on causality as regards death and birth. Kim's remark on his breathing problems at night in chapter seven links up with Ester's observation of Kim's loud snoring in chapter nineteen and indicates the solution of the death puzzle. When Susanne finds Kim dead in his bed she simply observes: he failed to breathe.

Pregnancy is highlighted and repeated in connection with Ester, Susanne's colleague, but Ester's expected motherhood also reflects the difference between Kim and Susanne about having children and foreshadows the fact that Susanne may be pregnant at the end of the novel. Susanne's dream of an uncomplicated life with a man includes having children, while Kim in chapter twenty-six declares himself unsuited to being a father. Two pages later Susanne asks why he considers himself unfit and assures him: no, but you will have children, I promise (140). Combining Susanne's statement with her sudden violent attack of hunger in chapter twenty-nine, and the information in chapter fifteen that their sexual activity has been infrequent, but was pleasant some weeks before Christmas, leads to the reader expecting Susanne's pregnancy to be confirmed.

In *Elin og Hans* the most significant repetitions, cigarettes and a green coat, point to Elin's death and reflect her husband's feeling of guilt. Several times during his long monologue he mentions her habit of smoking Barclay cigarettes, and again and again he recalls her last words to him before she left home: 'have you seen my cigarettes?' The new green coat that she was wearing when she was killed is also mentioned a number of times.

Frequently repeated are also Elin's routines and her well-structured everyday life, about which Hans seems to be ambivalent: 'Hun glemte ingenting, overså ingenting (69) (She didn't forget anything, never neglected anything). Hans wished he had said: 'slapp av, Elin, ikke bry deg om det, ta det med ro!' (relax, Elin, don't worry, take it easy). However, he never did, never comforted her when she seemed stressed, never objected to her non-stop efficiency (ibid).

In *Forestillingen om et ukompliceret liv med en mand* the story of Susanne and Kim has a parallell in the story of Ester and Luffe, who more or less invade their lives, as Ester runs away from her husband and temporarily moves in with Susanne and Kim. The parallel story contrasts with the main love story, while it also serves to elucidate aspects of the main characters. Both couples have problems, but while Susanne and Kim stay together until suddenly death does them part, Ester, who is pregnant, faces an open conflict with her unfaithful husband. Ester seems more helpless in all respects than Susanne, and evokes the protective instincts of Kim. The parallel story has a happy ending as Ester gives birth to a daughter and moves back to her husband.

There is only one love story in *Elin og Hans*. Nevertheless, indications of the problems of other couples appear now and then or are presented in fragments, either to reflect or to contrast with the characters, their problems and attitudes. One of these couples, however, advances in the discourse from periphery to the centre of events when their lives are entangled with life and death in the story of Elin and Hans and a triangle is indicated. Elin's colleague Gerhard Svendsen is with her when the accident occurs, and an underplayed relationship between them may have been going on for a while. The presence of Gerhard at the crucial moment prevents Hans from being with Elin when she dies, and he concludes: 'Det var ikke døden som skilte Elin fra meg, det var Gerhard Svendsen' (143) (It was not death that separated Elin from me, it was Gerhard Svendsen).

The disclosure of causality in the chain of events is revealed in what may be called the results of the death investigation, which in its turn is linked to the narrative perspective of the surviving characters. Gradually, the reader realizes the relation between cause and effect as regards Kim's sudden death, and also understands how Hans in a double sense was involved and perhaps responsible for his wife's death.

Love – And the Reliability of the Narrator

Both novels disclose the difficulties of loving and living with another person, and indicate questions like: Why was it so difficult? What went wrong? Possible answers are inseparable from the way the stories are told, who the narrator is, and what the narrator tends to reveal and repress.

Forestillingen om et ukompliceret liv med en mand has an externally positioned anonymous narrator, who does not take part in the fictional universe, nor does he interrupt by comments or explanations. The narrator most of the time delegates the perspective to Susanne who observes and reports what happens without comments, just stating facts and describing in detail movements and objects. Susanne keeps the perspective all through the long analepsis in Helle Helle's novel.

Susanne's and Kim's life has radically changed during the years they have been partners. Kim started as a rather outgoing person who had lots of appointments and came home from work irregularly, while Susanne wanted a closer relationship, and wished he would miss her when she was not at home. Kim's maxim is that they should not possess each other when they moved together. At one point Kim radically changes his life, stops going out and wants peace and quiet, and Susanne realizes that their life together has become close to what she has wanted it to be: they mostly stayed at home (131). As Kim did not tell her much about his past she secretly read his papers, including read letters from his former girl friends, and discovered that his application for the art academy had been rejected, which she pretended not to know. As Kim decided to leave his job and give his writing first priority, the ending of the story seems deeply ironic as fate intervenes and manipulates Kim's dreams of becoming a successful author. Kim ends his artistic career without having started it and without having finished his first book. The contrast between Kim and Susanne is emphasized. While he stays at home all day to write, Susanne works hard as a cleaner at the hospital. She is fed up with a man who does no housework and makes no contribution to their shared economy. On the other hand Kim in a cold voice insists that he is mentally superior to her and calls her empty, pure surface with nothing inside: she shuts out all spirit from this place, he says (110). A more humorous dialogue, though serious enough, takes place when he calls her an idiot and she replies that she sometimes wishes he was not there. He says he could well do without her and asks why she is there. This links up with Susanne's comforting imaginings. Susanne's dissatisfaction with her life or her ambivalence as regards going on with it, becomes clear during the long analepsis with scenes, dialogue and detailed realistic descriptions of things, actions and minor figures in the story.

In Trude Marstein's novel the long stream-of-consciousness

retrospection of Hans reveals his reflections and memories of routines and highlights during a twenty-three-year long childless marriage. So far there is an obvious similarity between the narrative discourses of the two novels. Nevertheless, there is a difference in narrative perspective. From the very first sentence of *Elin og Hans* there is an indication that what the first-person narrator, Hans, thinks, feels and remembers is a question of his interpretation and imagination: 'Som om Elin sto bøyd over meg' (5) (As if Elin was standing bent over me). He remembers details he did not know he remembered nor why he remembers them (7), and he loses the control of his memories when he realizes they are elusive and point in different directions: 'Minnene motsier hverandre' (60) (The memories contradict one another). Memories are never quite reliable, never identical with the situation that is remembered, but more or less fictionalized so that the memory supersedes the original experience: 'Først kommer minnet første gang. Så kommer gjentagelsen, til evig tid, som likevel, sannsynligvis, er mer vesentlig enn selve situasjonen. Det er der verdien kommer inn, det er der man forstår hva som er verdt å huske, eller hva man ikke kan la være å huske' (81) (First the memory comes up the first time. Then the repetition comes, forever, which all the same, probably, is more significant than the situation itself. That is where the value comes into it, where one understands what is worth remembering, or what one cannot help remembering).

The first-person narration of Hans is thus vague and incomplete in the beginning, and like a criminal investigator the reader must add one piece of his memory to the next in order to examine the question of the suspect's guilt. Not until the very last six pages of the novel, when Hans has consumed several glasses of whisky, is he able to remember in detail and reveal the circumstances that led to Elin's death. This serves as his confession although the question of his guilt may not bring him into court, but is for him to judge and come to terms with. It has to do with his love or lack of love for Elin and with his own timidity and feeling of being an outsider. His feeling of guilt for his final deceit, however, makes him expect to be caught.

Disillusion

Through the memories of the surviving partners the novels describe the experiences of two couples, where at least one of the partners keeps dreaming of a better life. There is a striking discrepancy between their dreams and expectations in the beginning of their lives together and the realization of these dreams after some years. The concept of romantic love and the hope of ever realizing it have been abandoned as an illusion. Disillusion is a prominent feeling, and unconscious or explicit thoughts about getting rid of their partners occur in the mind of the focalized characters of both novels.

Susanne comforts herself with three scenarios. One of them is the thought of a life with a man she once knew, a life that would have been uncomplicated and concrete with all the normal things that Kim refuses to have: children, family gatherings, friends visiting and a new lamp over the dining table. She tries to defend herself against these imaginings by the argument that there would have been too little doubt in that kind of life. However, she stays with Kim either because she lacks the courage to leave or because she is too stubborn. Drop your clichés, Kim once said, when she threatened to leave him, 'og det var nok derfor, hun blev' (101) (and that was probably why she stayed). In Susanne's second scenario she is about to write Kim's obituary, and it made her cry as she felt so brave. The problem was which newspaper would want to print Kim's obituary as long as he hadn't even finished his first book. Her third imagining of comfort was how she would arrange and decorate her flat if she lived alone. The innumerable possibilities made her exhausted and ambivalent, and she wondered whether she wanted some restrictions after all.

Susanne's dreams of an uncomplicated life with a man include a proper Christmas celebration with laughter, family, Christmas dinner, decorations and a flat with three rooms en suite. However, Kim is no family man and does not want to celebrate with relatives. Eventually he gives way and reluctantly accepts a real celebration with roast duck, a Christmas tree and Susanne's brother and his wife as guests. However, by an irony of fate he dies just as he is about to behave in a way which Susanne regards as normal. All her dreams come true in an ironic sense: she will have the flat alone, invite her family as she wishes, may have a child, and is free to write Kim's obituary if she likes.

Trude Marstein's figures Elin and Hans start their life together as a happy couple very much in love, according to the recollections of Hans: 'I vår første tid sammen følte jeg virkelig at vi var ett, i så stor grad at jeg kunne bli usikker på hvem som sa hva i en samtale (…) alle Elins tanker og holdninger kunne jeg raskt innlemme i min horisont, dersom de ikke var der fra før.' (14015) (In our first time together I really felt we were one, to the extent that I could be unsure who said what in a conversation

(...) all Elin's thoughts and attitudes I could immediately include in my horizon if they were not there already).

The feeling of two being one does not last for any of them, and when Hans reflects on the part he once played to please Elin, he concludes that he: compromised for years, played Elin's cards, let himself be formed according to Elin's will, and felt ashamed all the time (27). Most of their books had Elin's name in them, and most of the telephone calls were for her (58). In the beginning of their marriage Hans believed that love would lead to knowing her better, but in real life the distance between them increased. When he was still in love with her Hans used to study her face closely, but gradually he ceased to do so and withdrew from her. Just before his fiftieth birthday he explained his attitude: it was not because he was afraid of what he might find, but because he was afraid of what he might not find, or not finding anything at all (60).

Hans had wanted to get closer to Elin, but had been too timid to tackle her strength and what he felt was her dominance. He shows his ambivalence when he both wants to be one with her and nurses his fear of being invaded. Elin's perfect control and her well organized routines give him a safe frame for his life, while her routine life is also a threat, as she seems to be empty and depersonalized and mechanical with no room for him. Hans most likely diagnoses his own situation when he tries to explain the development of marriage to a man he meets at a pub after Elin's funeral. Hans tells him that two people in a marriage rarely develop in the same way, and if so it must be: 'resultat av den enes manipulering av den andre, sier jeg, en indoktrinering av den ene i en erfaringshorisont som var den andres, så å si.' (140) (the result of one of them manipulating the other, I say, an indoctrination of one of them into a horizon of experience that belonged to the other, so to speak).

The marriage of Elin and Hans has for some time been at the point of collapsing when Elin suddenly dies. Elin seems to have initiated an affair with her colleague Gerhard Svensen, though Hans is fairly vague about it. The man first turns up when Elin goes away on a seminar with him for a weekend one year before she dies. One week before the accident Hans reluctantly agrees when Gerhard suggests they bring their wives and go out for a meal together. Hans wonders if Elin ever thought of divorce and remembers a few episodes when she seemed confused, made mistakes in her routine work at home and started to speak about what she missed in their life together. Hans gets quite upset when he remembers these episodes, and this is reflected syntactically in the narrative discourse, with sixteen lines without a full stop. He tries to excuse himself for not having tackled the situation. She would never have been satisfied, no matter what he had said or done, he thinks (71). Gerhard turns up at Elin's funeral, places a personal bouquet without words on the coffin and gives a short memorial speech at the gathering afterwards. However, what moves Gerhard from the periphery to the centre of the story is his presence at the crucial moment in the municipal hall with Elin. Elin knows that Hans knows and the embarrassing triangle situation is the reason why Elin is killed. The causality is clear, the murder investigation may seem ended. Elin did escape, whereas Hans did not. Like the ending of Helle Helle's novel, Trude Marstein's solution is deeply and tragically ironic. That particular day Hans was excited as he was going to see his great work, the new municipal hall finished: the municipal hall was his greatest work to date (38), but his big day became a disaster. Even his success as an architect was undermined, as nobody would be able to think of the architect without remembering how his wife died (21).

Hans expends a lot of energy explaining to himself and his colleagues that the unfinished balcony from which Elin fell was not the responsibility of the architect. The delivery of glass and steel had been delayed, and it should not be his responsibility to secure the door. Even if Hans is right, he cannot expect to be held completely innocent. Besides, as a kind of dramatic irony, the reader knows that Hans has a double responsibility, technically and morally, as he didn't warn Elin when she saw her open the door into nothingness. Hans and Elin exchanged glances, he had seen her potential unfaithfulness, and she had seen him spying, even if he would have claimed his presence was a coincidence. His guilty conscience points to real guilt, not because Hans was the celebrated architect of a building with an unfinished balcony, not because the door to the balcony was not secured - he swears that he did lock it - but because he was too embarrassed when he saw his rival with Elin, Elin's glance when she became aware of his secret presence and his own reluctance to make a fool of himself. Hans should have cried out to warn her when he realized that she was about to step out onto the missing balcony. Her death could have been avoided if he had not been so passive and self-absorbed. Hans also realizes that he should have been with Elin, held her in his arms and gone with her in the ambulance, even if she was dead by then. The doctor stated that she did not die immediately of the damage from the fall, but after some minutes, long enough for Hans to have reached downstairs while she was still alive. Instead he stole away and pretended to be completely ignorant of what had happened. The flaw in his character is his lack of empathy and self-confidence. To protect his timid self, he is not really involved with other people, but is only concerned about his immediate performance and other people's possible impression and interpretation of him.

There is an irony of fate when Hans realizes he does not after all enjoy being alone in the house. He ponders that he thought he had endured one year after the other wanting to be alone, and now finds that he cannot bear being on his own, cannot bear that nothing happens in other parts of the house, that everything is as he left it (41).

The reaction of Hans may mean that he misses Elin, but more likely he dislikes the insecurity of his new position as a widower. According to Hans, his relationship with Elin had long been dead. To convince himself that he is right in this judgment, he argues that aesthetically he was put off by the sight of her varicose veins and the loose skin under her arms, which became more and more unbearable (41). When he watched Elin asleep he saw only what was ungraceful about her, and nothing else. Like Susanne in Helle Helle's novel Hans also goes so far as to wish his partner dead, but unlike Susanne's his fantasies occur in a dream of revenge just after he has felt Elin's reproaching glance: 'jeg forestilte meg et kort øyeblikk at jeg bar henne ut av huset, lempet henne oppi trillebåren og veltet henne ut på komposthaugen' (50) (I imagined for a short moment that I carried her out of the house, lifted her into the wheel barrow and tipped her onto the compost heap).

These thoughts and dreams may serve as a defence for himself in his attempt to be a strong and independent person, and to conceal his ambivalence towards the efficient and focused organizer Elin. Hans tries to defend himself when he feels accused by his guilty conscience. When he is throwing Elin's things away after the funeral he assures himself that he cannot be blamed for anything, and it is possible to think it was all for the best (86). Obviously, he does not succeed very well. He feels guilty for his reaction or lack of reaction in a situation where he is bound to have understood that a reaction would certainly have prevented Elin's death. He reproaches himself indirectly, but argues his own defence beyond moral sense and exposes his weakness and timidity. It seems absurd when he explains his situation as a dilemma: 'Men hva ville skjedd etterpå, etter at jeg hadde hoppet frem bak en brusautomat? Hvordan ville det gått med ekteskapet vårt da?' (123) (But what would have happened afterwards, when I had jumped out from behind a vending machine? What would have happened to our marriage then?) Hans then goes on trying to minimise the import of the accident by listing calamities and crimes in the news. He represses his sorrow and his feeling of guilt by explaining his love for Elin as an illusion belonging to the past. He rejects sorrow by denying the existence of love in his marriage. By concealing his deceit until the last two pages of the novel, he involuntarily exposes his psychological constitution of timidity and alienation. Not until he has been drinking is he able to drop his defensive attitude and reveal in detail what happened when Elin died. He then admits his failure as a husband when he neglected their relationship (146). He stumbles among the graves, thinks of Elin, feels sick and thinks it will soon be over, but he is wrong. Either he is too drunk, or he has reached a point of deeper understanding. His disillusion is ambivalent.

Postmodern Representations

Postmodern, contemporary literature can hardly stir strong feelings. Emotions in the postmodern age are reduced to clichés as in popular music and culture. Instead, minimalism is presented as a mode of experience and realism (Skyum-Nielsen 2000: 63). In Helle's novel emotions are underplayed, but implicit in the way the third-person narrator presents and links her observations. She tries to keep emotions and reflections at a distance also by concentrating on describing practical details. The discourse of Helle Helle's *Forestillingen om et ukompliceret liv med en mand* and Trude Marstein's *Elin og Hans* may be called minimalistic realism as they describe impressions of everyday life, things and actions in minute detail, and an inattentive reader may lose meaningful points.

Irony, which is frequently mentioned as a characteristic feature of contemporary literature, is another discourse strategy for keeping strong feelings at a distance and avoiding clichés. In both novels there is a strong irony of fate as the secret fantasies of the protagonists about getting rid of their partners and being alone, eventually come true, but may prove to have been (to borrow from Shakespeare's words in *The Merchant of Venice*, Act II, Scene VI) 'with more spirit chased than enjoyed.'

Skyum-Nielsen analyses Kjell Askildsen's short stories and highlights as a characteristic feature Askildsen's representation of the distance between man and wife. Love may have been there at the start, but gradually withered, and the characters are stuck together by an untouchable, repressed past. The lack of communication and confidence illustrate their lost ability to imagine themselves in the situations of others (Skyum-Nielsen 2000: 68, 70). In Helle's and Marstein's novels the characters are too self-absorbed to be able or willing to see each other. The surviving protagonists expose their dreams and longing for a closer relationship, but have not given love room to grow and have neglected to develop empathy. There is little interaction between their dreams and reality. Life together has been reduced to everyday routine in *Elin og Hans*, a kind of emotionless, practical security for the male protagonists, but in the long run unsatisfactory for their female partners in both novels.

Empathy is a relevant and significant concept for contemplating life through literature. Ian McEwan asserts that the exercise of the imagination enables, in George Eliot's words, 'the extension of our sympathies,' and that 'the nature of empathy is to see oneself as an other – and the basis for compassion and empathy is the imagination' (Childs 2005: 276).

The two novels both have psychological overtones, but there is a difference in emphasis in the revelation of feelings and inner thoughts of the characters. Emotions are more explicit in the first-person narration of Marstein's novel, though the reliability of the protagonist may be dubious, as he seems to argue in defence of himself and is unwilling to admit or reveal precisely what part he played at the crucial moment of the story. By concealing it until the last two pages of the novel, the first-person narrator involuntarily exposes his timidity and alienation. Per Thomas Andersen analyses the main motifs in *Elin og Hans* and asks whether the novel should be read as a sad story of a traditional marriage which moves from love to boredom, or whether it should be read as the story of a disconnected individual with reduced aptitude for closeness and emotional engagement. Andersen also states that Trude Marstein's stories are challenging as they mobilize the reader's need for self defence. To analyse them becomes a process of self-reflection (Andersen 2003: 148).

When two female authors in the same year thematize love and disillusion in fiction, it may be relevant also to see their texts against the backdrop of feminism. Skyum-Nielsen maintains there is a difference between the feminism of the 1980s which highlighted repression and liberation, dependence and autonomy, and contemporary female writing which thematizes the body as a room, as the very scene of existence (Skyum-Nielsen 2000: 28). The novels of Helle and Marstein are less interested in the body as a context, but they are both interested in existential issues and describe loneliness, emptiness and alienation, a longing for closeness and an uncomplicated life with loving partners. Their stories focus on the difficulties and most likely the impossibility of realizing love. A happy life together turns out to be a (dis)illusion in Trude Marstein's *Elin og Hans* and Helle Helle's *Forestillingen om et ukompliceret liv med en mand*. The two novels express doubt as to whether love only exists as an illusion.

References

Andersen, P.T. (2003): *Tankevaser. Om norsk 1990-tallslitteratur.* Oslo, Universitetsforlaget.

Childs, P. (2005): *Contemporary Novelists. British fiction since 1970.* Hampshire and New York: Palgrave Macmillan.

Helle, H. (2002): *Forestillingen om et ukompliceret liv med en mand.* Copenhagen: Samleren.

Marstein, T. (2002): *Elin og Hans.* Oslo: Forlaget Oktober.

Skyum-Nielsen, E. (2000): *Engle i sneen. Lyrik og prosa i 90erne.* Copenhagen: Gyldendal.

II

Travels

A Comet in a Cultural Constellation:

Hans Christian Andersen and Literary Travel Practice in pre-Twentieth Century Europe

Hans-Christian Andersen

Newcastle Business School, Northumbria University

Movement is in the blood of human beings and stories about journeys take up a considerable part of our histories, mythologies and narratives. Sometimes journeys are a blessing, an escape, at other times a curse, a banishment. Sometimes the journey is a purpose in itself, as in the case of great explorations where the traveller travels in order to be where others did not go before; or as in the case of the great migrations, where tribes move in order to find somewhere else to be. The journey can be a means to an end: the traveller needs get to a destination, but the process of getting there becomes, well, perhaps an Odyssey, a framework for other events that become more important than the arrival.

Not surprisingly, writers have often been preoccupied by travel and the nature and purpose of travel. They do travel, for many reasons, sometimes because they want to travel and write about it. But there are many other reasons of course. Being thoughtful people, writers take the time and effort to explain and rationalise what they are doing and deliver beautiful descriptions in prose and poetry about it and about its power to broaden the mind and change the traveller existentially. The traveller, by travelling, becomes a different person. The writer, by writing, can make this clear.

But writers are special people: they have a gift for seeing and experiencing life and for formulating in writing what they have seen and done. That sets them apart from the great mass of travellers, and today travelling is a mass occupation, a mass business, an industry. In 2006 statistics from the World Tourism Organisation show that 846 million tourist arrivals were recorded worldwide. In that year, 5.9 million holidays were taken by Danes, 6 million by Norwegians, 10 million by Swedes.

Travel is both special and ordinary. It has become part of the normal life experience of modern people: we expect to travel. In our spare time, travel and leisure are inextricably bound together.

We tend to call the ordinary kind 'tourism.' By that we generally refer to a mass-produced travel product, an industrialised leisure experience, often in the shape of a 'package tour,' which the package tourist allegedly consumes in a more or less effortless manner. A huge industry – the world's largest – has developed to supply leisure experiences to this huge market. We also often tend to differentiate that kind of experience from a more 'profound' and conscious experience, undertaken by 'travellers' who may well be tempted to look down on 'tourists,' the mass consumers.

This essay explores how a small number of Scandinavian travellers have used and responded to travel in their writing. It uses 'written records' as the primary source material, in the shape of those authors' travel writings, autobiographical material, correspondence etc. The writers are: Ludvig Holberg (1684-1754); Hans Christian Andersen (1805-1875); Henrik Ibsen (1828-1906); August Strindberg (1849-1912); and Georg Brandes (1842-1927).

These writers obviously span several centuries and therefore also a period when great changes took place in European culture, history and social development. A brief survey of five writers, based in a small selection of their works, cannot hope to reflect changes in travel patterns comprehensively or in detail. However, their lives also span a period when the nature of travel changes significantly, and their experience does reflect that. They illustrate how writers respond to – and use – travel not so much as a special activity as an ordinary activity. They can show how and why they move around in Europe and what that tells us about them as travelling writers; *and* it shows us how travel develops from being a special, elite activity to a much more broadly available – one might use the word 'democratic' – activity.

This essay consequently stresses the continuity rather than distinction between 'travel' and 'tourism.' Indeed, it denies that the distinction makes any sense and insists that it never did make sense. On the other hand, there is, of course, no denying that there are many different kinds of traveller and that some of them – among them professional writers – are able to make travel seem special and to share that sense of the special experience with other people through their writing.

Travel was a central part of Ludvig Holberg's informal education as a prolific author, historian and philosopher. He travelled to France, where he spent a year and a half in Paris, and Germany. He lived in Oxford in 1706-08, doing research at the university for his *Introduction til den europæiske Historie* (Introduction to European History), making a meagre living as a language teacher. He visited Italy and the city that was the destination for all travellers of his age: Rome, once capital of the Roman Empire, whose writings were still extensively used and whose civilisation was central to the Age of the Enlightenment. [1]

It is not surprising that Holberg, a man steeped in European culture, should want to see and be in Europe. Nor does it surprise that he should have passed his experiences down to us in an autobiography written in Latin, although in that respect he also shows himself to belong to a much longer intellectual tradition, stretching back to the Middle Ages.

When Holberg travels in Europe, he is using technology and facilities that had, in many ways, remained unchanged for centuries. We learn from his three-part Latin memoirs (*Tre latinske levnedsbreve,* 1728, 1737, 1743) that there is, indeed, a travel infrastructure in Europe. For the wealthy traveller – say, the English Grand Tourist of the time – it would have included opportunities to buy or rent a carriage and horses and would have involved the use of letters of credit and letters of introduction to the households of local members of the aristocracy, as well as the availability of personal guides and printed travel guides.

But Holberg is often an independent traveller and he financed his first journey by selling all his earthly belongings. Scandinavian literary travellers are often impecunious but Holberg seems to accept this aspect of travelling more readily than many others: if he runs out of money for transport, he walks, even very considerable distances.

He rarely seems to use – or at any rate take the time to write about – the more sophisticated travel facilities of his time. But he does give an insight into a very distinct traveller's Europe in his memoirs: one where bandits and pirates are not just a potential but an actual danger, and also one where a young Holberg resorts to trying to escape from his lodgings without paying his bill. Accommodation is often very primitive and shared with many others and catering services simple and not always appetising.

But despite shortcomings in law and order and in the standard of facilities, there is a travel infrastructure. There is, often but not always, passport control, but Holberg travels to Italy under the name of his Danish friend Mikkel Røg, who lends Holberg his passport when he does not have his own. Passport control and border checks are irregular and, where encountered, can have more to do with charging import duty than regulating the flow of travellers, although on occasion Holberg has to submit himself to thorough investigations of his identity and right to travel.

Europe does have a travel infrastructure in Holberg's time. Europeans travelled to do trade, along the roads and, perhaps even more frequently, along the rivers of the Continent. Holberg avails himself of riverboats towed by men. Over the centuries, Europeans have also travelled for religious reasons, and this means that by the time Holberg arrives there in 1715, a destination such as Rome has been set up to handle large numbers of seasonal visitors. At the great religious festivals – which includes the famous carnival – the Romans would rent accommodation, sometimes their own, to visitors and, as Holberg tells us, touring theatre companies arrive to enhance the festival and make money from it.

Crossing the Alps involves the use of a variety of means of transport, clearly evolved in order to deal with a regular flow of travellers in the summer. Holberg explains:

> Man bestiger Alpene paa mulddyr, derfor en ringe betaling kan lejes ved foden af bjergene; alperyggen er jævn og farbar for firspandsvogne. Da jeg var kommet over højsletten, mødte jeg allevegne folk, der lejer slæder ud; paa dem kan man komme ned paa ganske kort tid. Vi syntes nemlig, vi snarere styrtede end steg ned [...] (Holberg 1971: 199)

> (You climb the Alps on mules which can be hired for a small amount of money at the foot of the mountains; the Alpine heights are level and can be travelled by coach-and-four. Once I have crossed the high plains, I everywhere encountered people who rent out sledges; on those you may descend in very little time. Indeed, we felt as if we were falling rather than descending [...]).

Later on, having missed his river boat, he walks from Lyon to Paris and subsequently makes part of his return to Hamburg on skis.

European travel at Holberg's time is possible, to those with the right papers (their own or otherwise) and the time and other resources, but it is obviously not easy and the traveller needed the right kind of motivation in order to embark on these journeys. In Holberg's case, the motivation was a curiosity to see the world along with a wish to educate himself in the European libraries and by absorbing European culture as he went along. But his traveling often seems improvised, ad hoc, more that of the modern backpacker than the contemporary Grand Tourist: Holberg sees Rome but does not follow the itinerary of the Grand Tour.

He seems to have been aware of the reputation of the Grand Tour, as a supposed educational experience for the young nobleman but one that often descended into a more casual and entertaining extended holiday for the traveller. Perhaps this explains Holberg's skepticism – even cynicism – when advising *against* travel in his Epistola CLXXVII (*Samlede værker* vol 11), where he argues that you can expose young men to proper education at home and that they would be willing to desist from foreign travel if you removed the temptation of plays, operas, spectacle and other visual temptations.

As always with Holberg, given his use of humour and irony, you have to be careful not to give automatic literal credence to what he writes, but what he says here is very similar to the skepticism he expresses in his play *Jean de France* (1868). Travel is not automatically a good thing. Holberg does not suggest that he ever abused the privilege of overseas travel and one can believe that this eighteenth-century ascetic did indeed practice as he preached.

Nevertheless, the developmental benefits of travel were taken for granted and so it is that we find Hans Christian Andersen engaged in educational and cultural travel, from an early point in his career and almost to its very end.

Where Holberg seemed to travel on his own initiative rather than following dominant trends, Andersen's early travel clearly follows an existing pattern. His first journey, to the Harz Mountains in 1830, is clearly a *professional* venture as well as an exciting personal experience. As so often in Andersen's life, he has a purpose with what he does, in this case to write about his journey, and he publishes his first proper travel description, *Skyggebilleder af en Reise til Harzen* (Shadowy images of the Harz Mountains) in 1831, soon after his return.

Andersen is not best known as a writer of travel descriptions but his contribution to the travel genre has very considerable merit. He was not the first Danish travel writer; his work in this genre was preceded by, for example, Peder Paludan's *Beskrivelse over Kalundborg* (Description of the town of Kalundborg, 1788) and Christian Molbech's *Ungdoms Vandringer i mit Fødeland* (Youthful Wanderings in my Native Country, 1811). However, Andersen's travel descriptions, his creative writing based on his travels, as well as his travel journalism, show a writer mastering a range of genres and making Europe accessible through his writing. Mostly he does so by allowing his readers to read about that which they will not be able to see for themselves, because travel was still for the few. In the case of the Blue Grotto on the island of Capri, he pointed the attention of other travellers to an attraction that had been overlooked previously.

Andersen's visits to Rome were particularly important in his life; he visited this city four times between 1833 and 1864. Rome, once primarily a city of Christian pilgrimage, had also long been the ultimate destination of the Grand Tourist as he traveled down through Europe on the trail of the tradition and history of European civilization. In this respect, Andersen followed in the tracks of thousands – in particular young English gentlemen – who had embarked on what had become a standardized educational experience of Europe, culminating in Rome. By the time Hans Christian Andersen first reached the city, in October of 1833, the Grand Tour had become so common that it can rightly be described as 'proto-tourism,' as a systematized and standardized experience, providing a well-established travel and tourism infrastructure throughout Europe for thousands of travellers, moving along well-established trails.

Simply by being in Rome, Andersen became included in a Scandinavian artistic jet-set, gathering in Den skandinaviske Klub, but also a great European artistic tradition. In that sense, the artistic Grand Tour completed his formal education. However, for the student of Scandinavian literary travel the interest obviously does not end here. Andersen is even more interesting for what he, as a writer, *does* with his travel activities.

His first visit is reflected in his great Italian novel from 1835, *Improvisatoren* (The Improvisatore), where he fuses his impressions of Italy with his own life's history to create what is almost his first 'memoirs.' Not only did the novel help establish him on the very important German market, it also shows him creating a narrative about an artist – The Improvisatore – in the same way he was to create the myth about himself in his later, published autobiography. *Improvisatoren* provided Andersen's readers with an imaginative – and imaginary – view of the Italy which most people could then only hope to experience through the written word. It is not just a novel: it also reflects a real Italy which Andersen had seen and this is the work that introduced other travellers to the magic of the Blue Grotto. As is often the case with Andersen, reality and the imaginative are fused and in that respect he exemplifies good travel writing: it shows reality mediated by the writer, and it gives significance to what has been seen in a way that, say, a guidebook could and would not do in the same way.

His second journey – which included a visit to Rome in 1840-41 but also, famously, took him to Greece, Turkey and back through Eastern Europe, resulted in a travel description 'proper': *En digters Bazar* (A Poet's Bazaar, 1842). This counts as a major nineteenth-century contribution to the genre, a colourful and broad introduction to a world both old and new: old, because it had formed part of European history and the shape of European consciousness over centuries; new, in the sense that it was the object of a growing number of travel descriptions of the time. This writing described a Europe that was now becoming much more broadly accessible with the development of modern technology and mass transportation: the steam engine and new, faster and regular connections on land and water. Andersen introduces his Danish readers to the innovative steam train experience in *En digters Bazar*, but he also makes use of steam ships – not so innovative as technology but the reason why Andersen can travel back through Europe along the Danube.

As Andersen travelled through Europe, Thomas Cook 'invented' modern tourism with his pioneering first package tour by train from Leicester to Loughborough on June 9, 1841. The first modern guide books had very recently been published by Friedrich Röhling and Karl Baedeker in Germany, soon followed by John Murray in England. With the modern railways, modern hotels soon followed and as Andersen's travel career developed he increasingly found himself in a very different tourism environment to that which Holberg had encountered. This becomes a motif even in his fairy tales, where we find him moving rapidly from thinking of modern travel as future potential to integrating it in a narrative grounded in the experience of modern travel. In his 1861 tale 'Det nye Aarhundredes Musa' (The Muse of the New Century) he imagines a modern poetic muse as a citizen of a new world where, soon, the Great Wall of China shall fall; the railways of Europe shall reach the closed cultural archives of Asia – two streams of culture shall meet and flow as one (Andersen 2003a: 387). By 1868, in his eulogy to the World Exhibition in Paris, he writes in 'Dryaden: Et Eventyr fra Udstillingstiden i 1867' (The Wood Nymph: a Tale from the Exhibition in 1867): 'We are traveling to the the Paris exhibition. We are there! With speed, with a rush, entirely without witchcraft. We traveled on the wings of speed, at sea and on land. Ours is the land of fairy-tales. We are in the middle of Paris' (Andersen 2003b: 197). By now, in his fairy tales, Andersen was integrating the tourist experience in his work, indicating that the experience was now much more a shared European experience, less and less one enjoyed by the elite only (Andersen 1994: 141).

Andersen absorbs travel and transforms it into writing, sometimes openly creative writing but in many cases also in the shape of explicit travel descriptions. In this respect he is characteristically himself: always working, always writing, in his notebooks, his letters, diaries, his manuscripts. August Strindberg also travelled extensively during his lifetime but in this context he exemplifies a very different approach to travel and travel writing.

Strindberg spent several periods of his life on the European Continent, settling in Berlin and Paris, and in Austria, where he lived with his second wife from 1893 to 1896. As an emigrant, settling abroad with his family – even if only temporarily – he is obviously not so much a tourist or even a traveller but his experience of emigration takes him to new areas of artistic and social experience. One of these was his temporary residence at the Hotel Laurent at Grèz-sur-Loing, where he joined Carl Larsson's artists' colony, expressing his typically austere delight that Larsson has 'förvandlat Grèz från ett sommarnöje till en stadigvarande tillflyktsort, där arbetet kämpar sina tysta stridar mot en idylisk bakgrund' (transformed Grèz from summer pleasantry to a permanent refuge, where labour struggles in silence against an idyllic backdrop), as Strindberg wrote in *Svea* in an 1884 article about Larsson (quoted in Sommar 1995: 16).

That article in itself exemplifies Strindberg's use of travel as a source of journalism which will help him earn a living. His view of travel always seems work-oriented, and indeed sightseeing is clearly not a priority for him: 'Res aldrig ut för att se något; det finns ingenting att se! Ändra bostad får man gärna göra!' (Never journey in order to see something, there's nothing to be seen! By all means, change address!) he writes on September 18, 1883 to his friend Pehr Staaf (quoted in Sommar 1995: 11).

And, indeed, the remarkable contribution which Strindberg makes to nineteenth-century travel literature is businesslike and worthy of an author who takes the same view of the traveling author as Goethe expresses in his *Italian Journey*: the author is not just an observer or even just an author - he is a scientist.

Having failed to persuade his long-suffering Swedish publisher, Karl Otto Bonnier, to let him travel through the Mediterranean on an expedition with Carl Larsson as illustrator, Strindberg conceived another plan to describe the life of the European peasant, to prove how much healthier that life was than life in the modern city. The plan is, partly, to save him from creative writing and in 1886 he sets out on the first leg of the journey to France.

Strindberg, accompanied by the sociologist Gustaf Steffen, was only partly successful as an anthropologist, and the life of the French peasant is not as romantic as Strindberg had imagined. The published outcome of the expedition, *Bland franska bönder* (Among French Peasants, 1886) hardly amounts to the intended grand survey of France. Nevertheless, it shows Strindberg taking an approach typical of his scientific age but perhaps also one that was a throw-back to an earlier Romantic period when it was still possible to believe in the writer as the all-encompassing intellect.

Henrik Ibsen comes to mind when one uses the phrase 'the all-encompassing intellect.' But in his case the author is a man with a truly creative rather than scientific mind, one whose insight, as expressed through his creative works, changes the way his contemporaries think – or, at any rate, presents them with major challenges to the way they think.

To Ibsen, as to Strindberg, the European Continent offered a chance to escape from a restrictive and conservative mother nation, rather than an opportunity to explore travel in and through his writing. That is not to say that the influence of European travel and residence on Ibsen can – or has been – overlooked. Indeed, he spent a very considerable part of his life outside Norway,[2] partly in order to escape from the constraints which a politically and intellectually backward home audience placed on him.

Nordhagen (1981) points out how his residence in Italy influenced Ibsen's *Brand, Peer Gynt* and *Keiser og Galilæer* (Emperor and Galilean) directly but also stresses that Italy and Rome themselves do not appear in his work. Ibsen is not a travel writer and travel is not his project. He is influenced by the European theatre tradition and he, in turn, moves European drama in new directions.

But in this sense, Ibsen also exemplifies that very significant function which travel had for nineteenth-century Scandinavian authors, that of escape to a place that offered peace and the friendship of likeminded artists, allowing the author to develop his art and talent. In a letter to Peter Hansen on October 28, 1870, Ibsen openly – but also humorously – acknowledges the influence of Italy:

> [...] Rom med sin ideale fred, samlivet med den sorgløse kunstnerverden, en tilværelse som ikke kan sammenlignes med noget andet end stemningen fra Shakespeares 'As You Like It' – så har du forudsætningerne for 'Brand.' [...] Efter 'Brand' fulgte 'Peer Gynt' ligesom af sig selv. Den blev skreven i Syditalien, paa Ischia og i Sorrento. Sålangt borte fra den tilkommende læsekreds blir man hensynsløs. [...] Jordbunden har stor indflydelse paa de former, hvorunder indbildningskraften skaber. Kan jeg ikke omtrent som Christoff i Jakob von Tyboe, pege paa 'Brand' og 'Peer Gynt,' og sige: 'Se, dette var en vinrus'? Og er der ikke i 'De unges forbund' noget som minder om Knackwurst og Bier?' (Ibsen 1928-57: 16; see also Nordhagen 1981: 158).

> ([...] Rome with her ideal peacefulness, life in the carefree world of artists, an existence that can only be compared with the

atmosphere of Shakespeare's *As You Like It* – that gives you the foundation for *Brand*. [...] After *Brand, Peer Gynt* followed almost effortlessly. It was written in Southern Italy, on Ischia and in Sorrento. Removed so from your future readership you become reckless. [...] The soil greatly influences the forms in which the imagination works. Might I not, almost like Christoff in *Jacob von Thyboe*, point to *Brand* and *Peer Gynt* and say: 'See, this was a wine rapture. And is there not, in *The League of Youth*, something reminding you of Knackwurst and Beer?')

Like Ibsen, Georg Brandes was equally tempted – even forced – to seek temporary exile in order to escape from his fellow countrymen who failed to appreciate the challenge he presented to their intellectual status quo. Brandes, who is rightly credited with moving Danish literature in the modern Naturalistic period with his *Hovedstrømninger i det 19ende Aarhundredes Litteratur* (Chief Tendencies in Nineteenth-Century Literature, 1871) and whose influence was felt across Europe, knew that travel was necessary as part of one's education. He set out, before giving his epoch-making introductory lecture, on a long European *Entwicklungsreise* in 1870-71, to Paris and London but, primarily, to Italy.

What makes Brandes particularly interesting here is the fact that he sets out on his carefully prepared traditional *Entwicklungsreise*, armed with a copy of Johann Winckelmann's 1764 *Geschichte der Kunst des Alterthums* (History of Art in Antiquity), used by many other previous travellers to help them appreciate classical art. But despite his original traditionalist intentions, Brandes discovers modern French art, argues politics, and speaks critically about the attitudes of his native country with fellow travellers. In Brandes' case, the experience of travel subverts the traditional view of travel. His encounter with the world confirms to him what he is: a modern, international critic and debater. In a sense, the experience of travel becomes a part of Brandes' critical armoury and, as is the case with his critical presentation of the literature of his age, he offers us a mediated view of the relationship between the journey and the individual. Who else, before him, would have suggested, in a way that hardly flatters 'tourism,' that

Snoilsky er som Digter Turist. Hvad han hyppigst har formet til Vers, det er Rejseindtryk fra italien, Spanien, Frankrig, Danmark og Tyskland. Hvad vi med ham først og fremmest oplever er Gondolfarter, Gallerivandringer, Ambassadeballer og Badestedernes fashionable Aftenselskaber; ja selv Sverig synes han at se 'ur waggonsfønstret.' (Brandes 1902: 625)

(As a poet, Snoilsky is a tourist. What he has mostly given shape to in verse is impressions of travel from Italy, Spain, France, Denmark and Germany. What we experience with him is, first and foremost, trips in gondolas, tours of galleries, embassy balls and the fashionable soirées at the spas; indeed, he even seems to view Sweden from the window of the railway carriage.)

As a travel journalist – Brandes wrote extensively about his impressions of the places he visited – he is clearly interested in the broader themes rather than the trivia of travel: history, European art, politics, philosophy, literature. He never misses an opportunity to express his views, his *significant* views. That makes him, perhaps, a less reliable witness to the Europe of his time, as witnessed by the traveller, and more of a cultural critic. That is not to say that we do not hear about his concrete experience of encountering the very uneven standards of service in Europe: he is priceless when he describes being ill in Rome. But cultural, political and philosophical contemporary significance, as seen by and explained by Brandes himself, comes first.

With Brandes, in a sense we come full circle. Like Holberg, he travels to learn. Like Ibsen, he shapes the thinking of his time. Like Andersen, he is a modern man who starts off a traditionalist but becomes a modern man, even if he does so much more radically than Andersen does. Like Strindberg, he needs to get away from his fellow countrymen when they impose their cultural claustrophobia on him.

But no writer turned his travel into art in the way and to the extent we find Andersen doing. If the transformation of travel and tourism into art is the measure of excellence, then he is the writer who excels.

With all the writers dealt with here, it is clear that the continent attracted and influenced: travel was necessary, it formed the artist and the individual. Europe offered a pleasant climate (at least in the south), intellectual inspiration and the friendship of fellow artists, and often an easy life and an attractive holiday atmosphere. They all respond very differently, in ways that reveal their personalities as well as the changing Europe they were visiting. Obviously the change was political, cultural and social: Europe at Holberg's time was entirely different from that which Brandes and Ibsen travel in.

But the change was also related to the changes that were taking place in European infrastructure, and when Brandes ironises over Count Snoilsky's touristic approach to poetry, he can do so because he it is still acceptable to distinguish between superficial tourism and allegedly more profound 'travel' (or, in Strindberg's somewhat unusual case, *exploration*) in western Europe. The writers all made use of the infrastructure that was making Europe a more accessible place for writers to move around in. This in turn allowed them to see Scandinavia not so much as an interesting destination in its own right, but more of a place to start an interesting journey.

References

Andersen, H.C. (1994): 'Hans Christian Andersen – the Journey of his Life.' In D. Blamires (ed.): *Children's Literature*, special issue of *Bulletin of the John Rylands University Library of Manchester*, 76 (3), pp. 127-43.

Andersen, H.C. (2003a): 'Det nye Aarhundredes Musa.' In K.P. Mortensen(ed.): *Andersen: Eventyr og historier. H. C. Andersens samlede værker II*, Copenhagen: Det Danske Sprog- og Litteraturselskab / Gyldendal.

Andersen, H.C. (2003b): 'Dryaden: Et Eventyr fra Udstillingstiden i 1867.' In In K.P. Mortensen(ed.): *Andersen: Eventyr og historier. H. C. Andersens samlede værker II*, Copenhagen: Det Danske Sprog- og Litteraturselskab / Gyldendal.

Andersen, H.C. (2004; 1835): *Improvisatoren*. Edited and with an afterword by Mogens Brønsted. 2nd edition. Copenhagen: Det Danske Sprog- og Litteraturselskab / Borgen.

Andersen, H.C. (2005 [1842]): *En Digters Bazar*. With an afterword by Lars Handesten. Copenhagen: Det Danske Sprog- og Litteraturselskab / Borgen.

Brandes, G. (1902; 1875): 'Carl Snoilsky.' In *Samlede Skrifter*, Vol. 3. Copenhagen: Gyldendalske Boghandels Forlag , F. Hegel og Søn.

Holberg, L. (1971): *Værker i 12 bind. Digteren - Historikeren - Juristen - Vismanden*. Introduced and edited by F. J. Billeskov Jansen. Copenhagen: Rosenkilde og Bagger.

Ibsen, Henrik (1928-57): *Samlede verker: hundreårsutgaven*. Edited by F. Bull, H. Koht, and D.A. Seip. Oslo: Gyldendal.

Nordhagen, P.J. (1981): *Henrik Ibsen i Roma*, 1864-1868. Oslo: J. W. Cappelens Forlag.

Sommar, C.O. (1995): *Strindberg på Resa. August Strindbergs resor i Europa 1883-87 skildrade av honom själv och andra*. Stockholm: Carlson Bokförlag.

Notes

1. Holberg's journeys were: 1704-05 to Amsterdam; 1706-08 to England to study in Oxford; 1708 to Germany as 'Bear Leader' for young Andreas Winding; 1714-16 Holland, France, Italy financed through an award from 'de rosenkrantzske legater.'

2. Italy 1864-68; Dresden 1868-75; Munich 1875-80; Italy 1880-85; Munich 1885-91.

On Forms and Fantasies of Locomotion in Lagerlöf and Andersen

Bjarne Thorup Thomsen
University of Edinburgh

I

Forms and fantasies of locomotion figure frequently and variedly in both Selma Lagerlöf and Hans Christian Andersen. The following takes us on a sketchy tour – twisting and turning at times – through some topographical issues in both writers' works, including a look at some 'travels' undertaken by motifs themselves. The focus is mostly on novels and (other) travel texts.

When Lagerlöf in December 1909 in Stockholm gave her acceptance speech for the Nobel Prize in Literature, her point of departure quite literally was the railway journey that had taken her from Värmland to the capital. In order to stage an encounter with her late father and communicate the news of the prize and her debts of gratitude, she continues by transforming the apparently mundane journey into a space trip:

> Var och en, som har farit på tåget i natt och mörker, vet, att det kan hända, att vagnarna långa stunder glider framåt märkvärdigt stilla utan en skakning. Buller och rassel upphör, och det jämna dånet från hjulen förbyter sig i stillsam och entonig musik. Det är, som om järnvägsvagnarna inte längre fore fram på syllar och skenor, utan glede bort i rymden. Nå, just som jag tänkte på att jag ville råka far, hände något i den vägen. Tåget började ila framåt så ljudlöst och lätt, att jag tyckte, att det omöjligt kunde vara kvar på jorden. Och så började mina tankar leka: "Tänk, om jag nu fore till min gamle far i himmelrik! Jag tycker mig ha hört, att sådant har hänt andra; varför skulle det inte hända mig?" (Lagerlöf 1915: 238f)

(Everyone who has travelled by train in the dark of night knows that it can happen that the carriage, for long periods of time, glides onwards in a strangely silent way without shaking. Thumps and rattlings cease, and the regular noise from the wheels becomes quiet monotonous music. It is as though the train carriages are no longer being carried forward on rails and sleepers, but are gliding off into space. Well, just as I was thinking I might encounter Papa, something just like that happened. The train started to rush forward so noiselessly and smoothly, that I thought it couldn't possibly still be earth-bound. And then my thoughts began to run away with me: 'What if I'm off to see my old Papa in heaven! I think I've heard that such a thing has happened to other people; why shouldn't it happen to me?')[1]

Gesturing towards a text which had been a major contributing factor to the award of the Nobel Prize, this vertical redirection was itself a reworking of the opening chapter, 'Ingmarssönerna' (The Sons of Ingmar), of Lagerlöf's emigration novel *Jerusalem* (1901-02). In this, the thoughts of the protagonist, 'Lill' Ingmar Ingmarson, likewise 'löpte i väg med honom, så att han knappt visste, om han var kvar på jorden' (Lagerlöf 1909a:12f) (ran away with him, so that he hardly knew if he was still on Earth), enabling him to establish a virtual discursive space in which his anxieties can be aired. Incidentally, in a further, transmedial, reworking of the scene in Victor Sjöström's 1919 silent film adaptation of 'Ingmarssönerna' (part I), the protagonist accesses heaven by climbing a giant ladder. This is depicted in a prolonged, stylistically inventive sequence, which combines Biblical iconography with silent cinema's interest in bodily and spatial spectacle. In its ironies and its concretisation of the mobility between spheres it is not unlike the opening of the Nobel speech.

II

Although Ingmar in *Jerusalem* does not take the train to heaven, railway travel performs prominent functions elsewhere in the novel. The motif bridges the seemingly disparate locations of its two volumes, the first focused on the Swedish district of Dalarna, the second set in Palestine. In the conclusion of the first volume the railway is connected with the forces of change and rupture which have descended on the hitherto sheltered and self-sufficient parish. The newly constructed local train station, from which the Swedish emigrants will depart in search of the Holy Land, could be said to provide the first representation of the 'foreign,' alienated condition that they will experience on arrival in Palestine. The over-dimensioned yet empty station environment seems to scar the local landscape that is being abandoned and to function as a primarily prospective place. A few pages into the novel's second volume the railway motif is reactivated, as the disconnect between expectation and experience is played out during the newcomers' train trip from Jaffa to Jerusalem. Partly focalised through the collapsing consciousness of Birger Larsson, a sick and, as it turns out, dying member of the emigrant group, the journey through sacred locations develops into a nightmarish, labyrinthine experience, in which state of mind and topography conflate. The train sequence works to introduce the problem of 'actual' places refuting their Biblical/textual significance, the novel bearing out J. Hillis Miller's argument that the state of homelessness could be seen as corresponding to a crisis in the referential function of language (Hillis-Miller 1995: 11).

In terms of Mikhail Bakhtin's typology of the travel novel in 'Forms of Time and of the Chronotope in the Novel,' *Jerusalem* would seem to belong to the category which contrasts home with 'an alien world separated from one's own native land by sea and distance' (Bakhtin 1996: 245). Apart from the five-line factual summary of the emigrants' itinerary which opens the second volume, the long duration of the journey between north and south disappears, so to speak, in the telling gap between the two volumes. However, as we have seen, the representation of the railway contributes, among several other means, to suggesting a trail of change, modernity and crisis of meaning which cuts across the 'home'-'away' binary.

III

Hans Christian Andersen was no stranger to railway travel and railway tropes either, of course, or to the interlinking of train travel and feelings of flight, for that matter. This is most clearly evidenced by his famous illumination, 'Jernbanen' (The Railway), in *En Digters Bazar* (1842; A Poet's Bazaar), of his own first railway ride, from Magdeburg to Leipzig. Periodising nineteenth-century travel, Roger Cardinal argues that Romantic travel, which tended to be anti-modern, solitary and unregimented, went into decline from the mid-century onwards, when steam-propelled forms of locomotion enforced 'a much higher travel tempo, while also making travel more affordable and thus more democratic' (Cardinal 1997: 148). This, in turn, contributed to creating the conditions for early tourism. While several of these developments are reflected in 'Jernbanen', Andersen's text, however, seems fully capable of locating the Romantic in the railway experience.

'Jernbanen' conveys the commodification of travel, the control of time and space, and also the risks which the train technology brings with it; but more importantly it practises the joy of construction, the thrill of speed and the freedom of space. In part a pedagogical piece, published five years before the first Danish railway line (between Copenhagen and Roskilde) opened in 1847, it begins by building in its reader's mind a model railway. In so doing, it draws on energies similar to those which Fredric Jameson identifies in utopian literature: the pleasures of constructing, of bricolating and cobbling together, and of miniaturisation (Jameson 2004: 35). This latter process is in play when Andersen describes the moment of departure, drawing the toy world, a frequent focus in his fairy tales, into the picture: 'de første Skridt gaaer det sagte, som om en Barnehaand trak den lille Vogn' (Andersen 2006a: 233) ('the first steps are gentle, like a child's hand pulling a little carriage') (Andersen 1987: 7). As the train gathers momentum, the depiction of 'extreme' mobility is facilitated firstly by an emphasis on subjective perception, which dynamises solid structures and challenges notions of unambiguous reality: 'Hvad var det Røde, der som et Lyn foer tæt forbi? Det var en af de Vagthavende, der stod med sin Fane'; 'Marken [er] en piilsnar Strøm'; 'vi foer forbi et Plankeværk, som jeg saae forkortet til en Stang' (Andersen 2006a: 234) ('What was that red thing that went like a streak of lightning close by? It was one of the guards, standing with his flag'; 'The nearest fields go by in an arrow-swift stream'; 'we went by a fence that I saw foreshortened to one plank' (Andersen 1987: 8,10). Secondly, the new travel mode is captured through a range of similes based on alternative, traditional or natural, forms of locomotion. Prominent among these is flying:

> Du seer ud af Vinduet og opdager, at Du jager afsted, som med Heste i Gallop; det gaaer endnu hurtigere, Du synes at flyve, men her er ingen Rysten, intet Lufttryk, intet af hvad du tænkte Dig ubehageligt! (Andersen 2006a: 233)

> (You look out of the window and realize that you are racing away like a horse at the gallop. The speed increases, you appear to be flying, but there is no shaking, no draught, nothing at all unpleasant as you had expected!)

Det er som By ligger tæt ved By; nu kommer een, nu atter een! man kan ret tænke sig Trækfuglenes Flugt, saaledes maa de lade Byerne efter sig. (Andersen 2006a: 234)

(It is as though towns lie close together, now one, now another! This is how towns must appear to birds of passage in flight.) (Andersen 1987: 9)

[…] vi flyve som Skyerne i Storm, som Trækfuglene flyve! (Andersen 2006a: 235)

([…] we fly like clouds before the storm, as birds of passage fly.) (Andersen 1987: 11)

Such similes serve, again, a pedagogical purpose, but they also contribute to the formulation of a compromise between traditional (Romantic) poetic domains and modernity. This quest for compromise informs much of Andersen's travel writing. In 'Jernbanen' it climaxes in an Andersenian happy ending of sorts, when the properties of the machine are poignantly developed from the devilish to the divine.

In *The Railway Journey*, Wolfgang Schivelbusch argues that the emergence of railway travel led initially to a crisis for traditional forms of perception; gradually, however, it became instrumental in developing a new kind of *panoramic* perception, in which machine and mobility are of the essence:

> Panoramic perception, in contrast to traditional perception, no longer belonged to the same space as the perceived objects: the traveler saw the objects, landscapes, etc. *through* the apparatus which moved him through the world. That machine and the motion it created became integrated into his visual perception: thus he could only see things in motion. That mobility of vision [...] became a prerequisite for the 'normality' of panoramic vision. This vision no longer experienced evanescence: evanescent reality had become the new reality. (Schivelbusch 1986: 64)

While, as we saw, dissolution of reality and hence a degree of 'crisis' of perception are evidenced in 'Jernbanen' (but much more so in *Jerusalem's* train sequence), Andersen's text functions first and foremost as an introduction not just to the railway, but to panoramic perception as such. This interest in panoramic vision is shared by Lagerlöf; we shall return to this point below.

IV

An echo of the celebration of the convenience and comfort of railway travel, which is an additional feature of 'Jernbanen,' may be found in Andersen's fourth novel *De to Baronesser* (The Two Baronesses) from 1849. This was his first novelistic attempt after Søren Kierkegaard eleven years earlier in *Af en endnu Levendes Papirer* (From the Papers of Someone Still Alive) had presented his critique of Andersen as a deficient, under-developed novel writer. Arguing that his colleague compensated for a lack of personal development and life philosophy with an excessive and essentially unproductive mobility, Kierkegaard had accused Andersen of being 'overhovedet bedre skikket til at fare afsted i en Diligence og besee Europa, end til at skue ind i Hjerternes Historie' (Kierkegaard 1872: 42) (altogether better equipped to tear around in a stagecoach surveying Europe than to gaze into the history of the human heart). Stagecoaches, carriages and, not least, ships do indeed continue to abound in *De to Baronesser*, although its setting is not broadly European. A state-of-the-realm novel, it explores in its three parts the geographical and socio-cultural diversity of the Danish monarchy in the nineteenth century, including its 'debatable' southern borderlands of Schleswig and Holstein. The novel's desire to delineate the realm not only in 'centre' but also in 'periphery' terms is demonstrated by its middle and most original part. This takes as its destination and main location the outermost limits of the monarchy in the shape of the North Frisian Islands of Halligerne, off the west coast of Schleswig. To reach these the younger of the novel's eponymous heroines and her Holstein foster parents must undertake a taxing horse-driven journey that negotiates all the obstacles, and displays all the diversity, of the Schleswig terrain, from Flensburg in the east to Dagebüll in the west. As they reach the marshland, the narrator provides a vision of the virtues of the infrastructure of the future, as the bumpy roads on the dykes are 'translated' into smooth railways:

> Det flade, grønne Marskland udstrakte sig foran; de lange, stille Canaler vare ved den langvarige Regn gaaede over, og hele Strækninger stode under Vand. [...] Som et Jernbanenet over Sumpe og Enge strækker sig her, med lige Høide, de paa Diger opførte Veie; den Reisende maa ved Synet tænke paa Jernbaner, men med samme skuffede Følelse, som Karavanen i Ørkenen, der ved *fata morgana* seer Søer og Skove, hvor han veed kun er det øde Sand. (Andersen 2004: 377f)

(The flat, green marshland stretched out in front; the long, still canals had burst their banks in the endless rain, and whole stretches stood under water. [...] The roads here, built on dykes of equal height, stretch like a network of railways over swampland and meadow; at the sight, the traveller must think of railways, but with the same sense of disappointment as the caravan in the desert, who, *fata morgana*, sees lakes and woods, where he knows there is but dry sand.)

Thus, one web of traffic lines momentarily morphs into another, while in a parallel movement 'south' is projected onto 'north.' This feeds into a wider agenda of topographical inventiveness in the novel. The favoured field of the experimentation is sea and shipping. The thrust of the imagination is the promotion of the joined-up and hybrid aspects of places, including the porous nature of national boundaries (particular efforts are made to connect Denmark and the British Isles).

V

Surveying the nation, in this case Sweden, remained the key concern in Andersen's subsequent major work, the travel book *I Sverrig* (1851; In Sweden), which bears some interesting resemblances to Lagerlöf's canonical *Nils Holgerssons underbara resa genom Sverige* (1906-07; Nils Holgerssons Wonderful Journey Through Sweden). There is considerable congruence between the texts in terms of their embrace of the Swedish natural-industrial complex. Also, both insist on the role of freedom and imagination in the recording of their journeys by special reference to the motifs of flying and migration.

The panoramic bird's-eye-views, which punctuated the portrayal of train travel in *En Digters Bazar*, are foregrounded in *I Sverrig*. In its prologue, 'Vi reise' (We Travel), the notion of riding on the back of different birds – stork, swallow, gull and swan – works to display the major segments of Sweden, including those not covered in the following, more personalised, travel account. This travel fantasy could be seen, then, as prefiguring the overriding focus employed in that later and most famous illumination of the Swedish terrain, *Nils Holgersson*. Published in the wake of the dissolution of the Swedish-Norwegian union, Lagerlöf's hybrid novel uses the trajectory of the flying flock and the protagonist's panoramic gaze to 'stitch together' the fabric of the Swedish nation. While a direct influence from *I Sverrig* on Lagerlöf's text cannot be established, Gunnar Ahlström demonstrates in his monograph on *Nils Holgersson* entitled *Den underbara resan* (1942; The Wonderful Journey) that an indirect connection is possible through an intermediary Swedish text, 'Det okända paradiset' (1875; The Unknown Paradise) by Richard Gustafsson (Ahlström 1958: 156ff.).

Within Bakhtin's typology of the travel novel, *Nils Holgersson* comes closest to the category which (rather than demonstrating the distance between home and away, like *Jerusalem* ostensibly does) moves along the *road* (in *Nils Holgersson*'s case an airborne version of this) in order to show 'the sociohistorical heterogeneity of one's own country' (Bakhtin 1996: 245). As to the *rail*road, the protagonist's ingenious form of transport leaves little scope for explicit depiction of train travel in *Nils Holgersson*. Railway tracks do, however, cut lines through several of its landscape panoramas. They also figure in the poem by Carl Snoilsky, 'Sveriges karta,' with which the text opens. Like 'Vi reise' in Andersen's survey of Sweden, Snoilsky's poem functions as a prologue which presents a macroscopic picture of Sweden before the narrative proper begins. It introduces *Nils Holgersson*'s main methodology of mapping the nation from the air and could even be read as a fantasy of the book's future function in an educational context. A core idea of the poem is the wanderlust released in the mind of the child as it encounters the map of the nation in a school setting. To the *modern* child – the poem's main concern – the fascination of map, mobility and nation is bound up with the epoch of the railway and its dissolution of distance:

> Nu böjas över kartans blad
> de huvun små i lockig rad,
> som efter oss ta arvet.
> Vad oss synts långt, för dem syns kort,
> och alla avstånd svinna bort
> i järnvägstidevarvet.
>
> De läsa på det svarta nät,
> som korsar älvens blåa fjät
> och genom fjället spränger.
> Lokomotivets gälla sus
> i flodsystemets dova brus
> på kartan in sig mänger.
> (quoted in Lagerlöf 1906: 4)

(Now bent over the map's page
are small heads in a curly row
our inheritors.
What seems far to us, to them seems near,
and all distance melts away
in the age of the railway.
They read on it a black net
criss-crossing the river's blue footsteps
and blasting through the mountain.
The locomotive's shrill whistle
and the river-system's muffled sound
mix on the map.)

In an examination of national ideals in *Nils Holgersson*, Lars Elenius discusses the expansion of the Swedish railway network around the turn of the nineteenth century, highlighting its role not only in the growth of the national economy, but also as a metaphor for national cohesion. He suggests, moreover, that the rapid and complex manoeuvrability of the flying flock in Lagerlöf's novel could read as a parallel to the properties of railway transportation (Elenius 2005: 195). A radicalised version of such affinity between nature and the machine can, finally, be found in Harry Martinson's poetic reflection, 'Vildgåsresan,' on the impact of *Nils Holgersson*. Written in celebration of the Lagerlöf centenary in 1958, the poem turns the protagonist into a pilot and his journey – and the (imagined) mass movement it inspired – into an aviation route:

[Nils Holgersson] blev piloten i vår första flygdröm;
och sträckets väg från Skåne upp till Lappland
var (tecknad som den blev av lärarinnan)
den första flyglinje som världen hade.
Med den flög varje år och var termin
en tallös skara barn på vildgåsvingar.
(Martinson 1958: 11)

([Nils Holgersson] was the pilot in our first dream of flight;
and his path from Scania up to Lapland
was (drawn as the teacher drew it)
the first airline the world ever had.
Along it flew every year and every term
a countless flock of children on wild goose wings)

Thus, on either side of the Modern Breakthrough, there are some notable similarities between Andersen's and Lagerlöf's spatial experimentation in their novel- and travel-writing, as exemplified by the play with forms of locomotion. This experimentation may be seen as part of a wider pattern of resistance against the 'solidity' and seriousness which, e.g., Franco Moretti and Fredric Jameson critique in their understanding of the realist novel (Moretti 2006, Jameson 2006: 112f.). Part of the response in both Andersen and Lagerlöf to the modern condition seems to be to practise freedom of space and explore forms of alterity.

References

Ahlström, G. (1942): *Den underbara resan. En bok om Selma Lagerlöfs Nils Holgersson*. Lund: C. W. K. Gleerups förlag.

Andersen, H.C. (1987): *A Poet's Bazaar. A Journey to Greece, Turkey and up the Danube*, trans. Grace Thornton. New York: Michael Kesend Publishing.

Andersen, H.C. (2004): *De to Baronesser* [1849]. In K.P. Mortensen(ed.), *Andersen. H.C. Andersens samlede værker, Romaner*, vol. II. Copenhagen: Det Danske Sprog- og Litteraturselskab, Gyldendal.

Andersen, H.C. (2006a): *En Digters Bazar* [1842]. In K.P. Mortensen(ed.), *Andersen. H.C. Andersens samlede værker. Rejseskildringer*, vol. I. Copenhagen: Det danske Sprog- og Litteraturselskab, Gyldendal.

Andersen, H.C. (2006b): *I Sverrig* [1851]. In K.P. Mortensen(ed.), *Andersen. H.C. Andersens samlede værker. Rejseskildringer*, vol. II. Copenhagen: Det danske Sprog- og Litteraturselskab, Gyldendal.

Bakhtin, M.M. (1996): 'Forms of Time and of the Chronotope in the Novel'. In M. Holquist (ed.), *The Dialogic Imagination. Four Essays*, Austin: University of Texas Press.

Cardinal, R. (1997): 'Romantic Travel'. In R. Porter (ed.), *Rewriting the Self. Histories from the Renaissance to the Present*. London and New York: Routledge.

Hillis-Miller, J. (1995): *Topographies*. Stanford: Stanford University Press.

Jameson, F. (2004): 'The Politics of Utopia'. In *New Left Review*, 25, pp. 35-54.

Jameson, F. (2006): 'The Experiments of Time: Providence and Realism'. In F. Moretti (ed.), *The Novel*, vol. 2: *Forms and Themes*. Princeton and Oxford: Princeton University Press.

Kierkegaard, S. (1872): *Af en endnu Levendes Papirer. Om Andersen som Romandigter med stadigt Hensyn til hans sidste Værk: 'Kun en Spillemand'* [1838]. Copenhagen: C. A. Reitzels Forlag.

Lagerlöf, S. (1906): *Nils Holgerssons underbara resa genom Sverige* (= *Läseböcker för Sveriges barndomsskolor*, I, A. Dalin and F. Berg (eds.), vol. 1. Stockholm: Albert Bonniers förlag.

Lagerlöf, S. (1907): *Nils Holgerssons underbara resa genom Sverige* (= *Läseböcker för Sveriges barndomsskolor*, I, A. Dalin and F. Berg (eds.), vol. 2. Stockholm: Albert Bonniers förlag.

Lagerlöf, S. (1909a): *Jerusalem*, vol. I: *I Dalarne* [1901]. Stockholm: Albert Bonniers förlag.

Lagerlöf, S. (1909b): *Jerusalem*, vol. II: *I det heliga landet* [1902]. Stockholm: Albert Bonniers förlag.

Lagerlöf, S. (1915): 'Tal vid Nobelfesten 10 december 1909'. In *Troll och Människor*. Stockholm: Albert Bonniers förlag.

Martinson, H. (1958): 'Vildgåsresan', *Lagerlöfstudier*. Malmö: Lagerlöf-sällskapet, Allhems forlag.

Moretti, F. (2006): 'Serious Century'. In F. Moretti (ed.), *The Novel*, vol. 1: *History, Geography and Culture*. Princeton and Oxford: Princeton University Press.

Schivelbusch, W. (1986): *The Railway Journey. The Industrialization of Time and Space in the 19th Century* [1977]. Leamington Spa, Hamburg, New York: Berg.

Note

1. Unless otherwise indicated by in-text reference, translations from Danish and Swedish in this essay are by CCT.

'Ladies and Gentlemen! You are Beings From A World More Advanced than Your Own!'

Civilizing Sublimities in Early Danish Science Fiction

C. Claire Thomson
University College London

I: Three Hundred Tall, Slim, Clean-shaven Men: Science Fiction Comes to the Danish Provinces

On 11 August 1917, several Danish newspapers[1] ran an advertisement seeking extras for the latest project by Nordisk Films Kompagni: *Himmelskibet* (*A Trip to Mars*, dir. Holger-Madsen, 1918).[2] The denizens of the red planet were to be played by three hundred tall, slim, preferably blonde ladies, and three hundred tall, slim, clean-shaven men. The hilarity that these exacting physical criteria immediately inspired in the Copenhagen press transmuted into a sustained fascination with the production process in the weeks that followed. Correspondents pursued the army of Martians from location to location in the provinces, reporting on their costumes (frequently ruined by sudden downpours), their makeshift accommodation, and their tribulations with spiders, lost hats and broken-down trains. Of most interest to the media, however, was the incongruity of ordinary Copenhageners, dressed as Martians, invading small-town Denmark. One lavishly-illustrated feature article in *Dagbladet* (28.8.17) describes the hullaballoo as a chalk mine near the village of Faxe is transformed into the Martian valley where the spaceship is guided in to land by the advanced alien civilisation: local wildlife scatters in the path of the parading aliens, while the townsfolk gather *en masse* to watch the filming. Director Holger-Madsen, meanwhile, has taken up position on a grassy hillock with his megaphone, ordering the crowds of local onlookers to move out of the shot, and coaxing the extras into collective comportment worthy of an alien people much more spiritually advanced than they themselves were.[3] This tableau is absolutely emblematic of the tension at that historical moment between Nordisk Films Kompagni's conception of cinema as a civilising technology – the company's Director General, Ole Olsen, stated often and adamantly that Himmelskibet 'er virkelig en meget alvorlig og moralsk film' (really is a very serious and moral film) (BT, 14.8.17)– and the apparent reluctance of the Danish press and public to take homegrown film seriously as an industry or as an art-form.

The two films which I will discuss in this chapter – *Himmelskibet*, and its precursor *Verdens Undergang* (*The End of the World*, dir. August Blom, 1916) – come right at the end of what is often referred to as the Golden Age of Danish cinema (roughly 1908-1916), and both confirm and complicate the idea that Nordisk lost its international dominance by failing to develop its output from popular melodrama to accomplished art-form (Christensen 1999).[4] The 'perfect storm' of aliens-cum-Copenhageners invading picturesque provincial towns, the spectacle of location shooting, and the bombastic declarations about the film's seriousness and moral mission by Nordisk Film's Director General, Ole Olsen, proved a welcome fillip to public interest in Denmark's film industry, whose fortunes were fluctuating as the First World War raged around the neutral nation (Christensen 1999: 14-15). In this sense, the various newspaper accounts of the location shoots of late summer 1917 have something to tell us about changing conceptions of the role and status of filmmaking amongst Denmark's arbiters of culture, and not least the extent to which cinema was considered a suitable and viable medium for utopian fantasy in the face of wartime deprivation and depravities. I use the world 'depravities' advisedly, as the filmmakers seem to be just as concerned with the evils of drinking, dancing and sex as they are with violence and war. Such debates on the function of film constitute one focus of this essay.

The other focus is the negotiation in *Himmelskibet* and *Verdens Undergang* of the power of technology, particularly technologies of vision, to render the cosmos visible and knowable; but this is in turn underpinned, I will argue, with a more earth(l)y compulsion: mapping the Danish nation socially and geographically. Put differently, although the telescopes of the scientists and the gaze of the common hordes in both films are turned skyward, it is as much the national landscape as the cosmos that is envisioned as embodying the sublime in these films. Holger-Madsen's entreaties to his massed extras to act like creatures from a much more spiritually advanced civilisation unwittingly captures, then, not just the delicious irony of exotic urbanites descending on the provinces in alien garb, but also the social transformation that the director saw cinema as capable of inspiring in humanity as a whole. The ability of film to visualise the sublime – be it a landscape razed by meterorites, the view from a spacecraft, or an alien crowd – is put to work in the service of cinema's civilising mission.

In what follows, the discussion of *Verdens Undergang* and *Himmelskibet* centres on the heavenly bodies that hover in each film: respectively, the comet, and the spacecraft. These objects are the spectacular foci of the films, with telescopes and observatories in both films trained upon them, but they also reflect back the light of events of recent history – the comets of 1910, and wartime developments in aviation – which re-appear here in cinema as the visual ciphers for broader contemporary social anxieties. Furthermore, the comet and the spacecraft necessitate some intriguing experiments and solutions as regards perspective and point-of-view, some of which recall Scott Bukatman's maxim that the aesthetics of science fiction are driven by the desire for 'scopic mastery' (1999: 251) of the sublime. It is certainly possible to trace in these Danish films of the 1910s many of the formal and thematic features of mid- to late-twentieth century science fiction, and the declared intentions of the filmmakers broadly chime with the view established in, for example, Susan Sontag's canonical essay 'The Imagination of Disaster,' of the science fiction film as allegorical and cathartic. While drawing on recent scholarship on science fiction and disaster narratives, I am, however, all too aware that some terms and arguments may be clumsily anachronistic when applied to early and silent cinema. My aim is neither to box *Verdens Undergang* and *Himmelskibet* into the confines of the modern science fiction genre, nor to write them into a teleological history of the genre, but to trace how the films, in their own historical context, achieve their self-declared aim: 'gennem Fantasien at foregribe et af de store Fremtids-Problemer, som før eller senere vil paatvinge sig Menneskeaanden' (Michäelis 1) (to grasp through fantasy the great problems of the future, which sooner or later will impose themselves on the human spirit).

II: *Verdens Undergang*: Comet Fever and National Cartographies

Verdens Undergang is a complex tale, replete with many of the stock motifs of Golden Age Danish cinema. A travelling preacher arrives in a provincial mining town, home to two young women and their mine-owner father. One of the daughters, Dina (Ebba Thomsen) has her head turned by the tycoon Frank Stoll (Olaf Fønss) and elopes with him to Copenhagen. When Stoll discovers from his astronomer friend that a comet is due to strike north-western Europe, he masterminds a run on the stockmarket and flees back to the mining town, hoping to escape the catastrophe by taking his beloved Dina to live below ground in the mine. After a decadent 'last supper' with friends, punctuated by Dina's erotic dance, and an attack by the common people of the village trying to take back what is theirs before the world ends, the couple asphyxiate in the mine, while asteroids rain down, destroying the village. The only survivors are the preacher, Dina's sister Edith (Johanne Fritz-Petersen) and her fiancé Reymers (Alf Blütecher). Throughout the narrative, the comet hovers luminous in the sky.

The premise of *Verdens Undergang*, then, offers up a particularly compelling and photogenic nemesis, and one which, in the 1910s, had been 'tamed' by visual culture, though its effects on the popular imagination were still potent. Astronomers predicted that the Earth would pass through the tail of Halley's comet on 18 May 1910; a lingering meme from the discovery of cyanogen gas in the tail of another comet in 1908 fostered popular suspicion that mass poisoning would come to pass, or that the Earth would be incinerated by hydrogen gas in the tail, or that the calculations were wrong and the comet's head would strike the Earth. Some sealed up their windows; others succumbed to despair and committed suicide (Calder 1980: 24-6). As Calder (26) muses: 'comet fever…remains endemic because nature feeds a human appetite for cheap thrills by tossing in a great comet every ten years or so.'

Pushing the entertainment analogy a little further towards cinema, the cosmos, we might say, regularly lays on a spectacular show of attractions in the night sky. The appearance of a comets is termed an 'apparition' by astronomers, although the Danish astronomer Tycho Brahe established in the mid-sixteenth century that comets were not sublunary phenomena; that is, they were not projected onto the vault of the heavens, but were a long way off in space (Calder 1980: 21). The latest visit of Halley's comet in 1986, in fact, enabled astronomers to establish with more certainty than before that comets are, in a sense, little more or less than the 'dancing seeds' and 'luminous dust' with which cinema is said to work (Deleuze 2005: 201).

In a more concrete sense, however, cometology and film are intertwined in the early twentieth century. The 1910 apparition of Halley's comet was relatively close to Earth, and the photographic plate was an important tool of observation of the comet's dust, gas and spectra; an 'impressive' collection of photographs has been preserved, so good, in fact, that it has recently been re-analysed by computer (Crovisier and Encrenaz 2000: 55-7). The 'flaming sword' that first appears through the iris of an astronomer's telescope, and hovers in the sky throughout *Verdens Undergang*, then, is a special effect tempered by the realism demanded by an audience who had witnessed not one but two comets just six years before, and knew how such objects were discovered and moved.

However, the idea of a space object striking Earth must also have been informed by another, more mysterious because un-photographed, event that reverberated in the popular and scientific imagination of the day: the Tunguska explosion of 1908. Reports from passengers on the Trans-Siberian Express on 30 June 1908 described a fiery blue ball streaking across the sky and deafening bangs. Scientists reached the scene of the blast only in the late 1920s and by 1930 surmised that the explosion was probably caused by the break-up of an asteroid at an altitude of several kilometers, levelling 2000 square feet of forest (Calder 1980: 124-6; Gehrels 1994: 930).

Following Susan Sontag's classic essay 'The Imagination of Disaster,' we might assume, then, that *Verdens Undergang* mitigates 'two equally fearful, but seemingly opposed, destinies: un-remitting banality and inconceivable terror…[Such] films reflect world-wide anxieties, and they serve to allay them' (Sontag 1994: 224-5). The terror that lies behind the visual allegory of the comet is, of course, not the ever-present threat of global nuclear annihilation that haunted Sontag's scifi audiences later in the century (215, 224), but the ongoing Great War, mimicked here by the meteorite bombardment from the sky. Lurking in the theme of working people attacking the rich is perhaps also a sense that a socialist revolution would constitute another kind of cataclysm. Denmark remained a non-belligerent state during the First World War, but while the threat of military attack remained virtual, the hunger for entertainment to off-set wartime deprivations of a more visceral kind was real enough.

The shortages experienced by the population are succinctly summed up by a satirical opinion piece in the newspaper *Politiken* of 7 September 1916, a few months after the première of *Verdens Undergang*. Coincidentally, the notorious Director of Nordisk Films Kompagni, Ole Olsen, shared his name – in any case a very common name – with the General Director of Samvirkende danske Svineslagterier (roughly, the United Danish Pork Butchers). The two Ole Olsens have, says *Politiken*, the task of providing the population with its most beloved and cheapest forms of, respectively, entertainment and food, so that together they represent the maxim *panem et circenses*; however, wails the columnist,

> 'Tilsammen repræsenterer de to Herrer Ole altsaa Princippet *panem et circenses*, Maden og Forlystelserne, men det kniber med den første Del af Programmet....Film har vi nok af, men men hvem kan nyde et Skuespil, naar Maven er tom, og Tarmene knurrer?' (*Politiken* 7.6.19)

> (Together the two Messrs Ole represent, then, the principle *panem et circenses*, food and entertainment, but we're short on the first part of the programme...We have enough films, but who can enjoy a plot, when one's belly is empty and rumbling?)

In this context, then, *Verdens Undergang* needed to offer a diverting light-show, as well as a narrative of redemption, of humankind rising from the ashes of Ragnarok.

It is perhaps not astonishing, given the time lag of six years between the two comet apparitions of 1910 and the première of *Verdens Undergang*, that neither Halley nor the Great Daylight Comet are alluded to in the Danish reviews of the film or related articles. Rather, two themes emerge from the commentaries of the time: firstly, an ambivalence about the relative 'realism' or 'relevance' of the 'novelistic' plot; and secondly, and more interestingly, a general admiration that film technology has developed such that it can represent the cataclysmic events suggested by the ambitious title.

The magazine *Masken*[5] is among several publications to describe *Verdens Undergang* as a 'modern novel,' that is, it is seen to feature a complex plot and an engagement with the social issues of the day. Similarly, the reviewer for *Berlingske Tidende* (3.4.16)[6] praises the well-conceived plot that leads us through the realms of love, stock market speculation and social inequality to natural disaster, but he bemoans some factual slip-ups, such as using a naked flame in a mine-shaft; ultimately, says the reviewer, Nordisk Films Kompagni wins the day with its wonderful technical know-how and the talent of the actors. *Vort Land* (1.4.16) goes so far as to describe the final scene as 'drawn-out...irritating and tiresome.' Similarly, *Børsen*[7] disdains the unlikely plot, but marvels at the 'technical artistry' of the 'impressive sets.'

Many of the reviewers are incredulous that a filmmaker could have the hubris to tackle such an ambitious storyline as the end of the world. The reported popular panic about Halley bringing death and destruction six years previously did not, it seems, strike a nerve; at least, not with the reviewers. Some qualify the film's 'pretentious' (*Børsen* 4.4.16) title[8] by commenting that apparently only part of the world is destroyed (*Vort Land* 1.4.16; *Nationaltidende* 1.4.16). Most reviewers ponder the difficulty for cinema of rendering visible the collision of a comet with the Earth (*Berlingske Tidende* 3.4.16; *Verden og Vi* 14.4.16), and the concomitant 'rain of fire and great flood' (*Politiken*, 2.4.16).[9] Indeed, it is Blom's success in exploiting the potential for spectacle of the said events that seems to impress the reviewers most. In *København* (2.4.16), the film première is said to have given the spectator cause to muse on the 'astonishing' technical possibilities that the film industry now masters. The reviewer for *Vort Land* (1.4.16) reports that there was enthusiastic applause from the full-to-capacity auditorium at the Copenhagen première, despite, he suggests, perhaps a little too much use of smoke and steam in the disaster scenes. The magazine *Masken*[10] lavishes praise on the production values: never before, exclaims the reviewer, not even in the film *Atlantis*,[11] have film technology and crowd scenes resulted in such a triumph as this, a film which features a whole town apparently in ruins! *Verdens Undergang*, he concludes, can hardly be described: it must be seen.

This last reviewer vindicates Sontag's suspicion that 'the thrill of watching all those expensive sets come tumbling down' is indeed common to all periods of cinema (Sontag 1994: 42). The artifice of the destroyed buildings is part of the spectacle. A feature article in the glossy magazine *Verden og Vi* (14.4.16), published two weeks after the première of *Verdens Undergang,* confirms for any viewers still in doubt that the destruction was indeed confined to a film set at Nordisk's Valby studios, and that the house roof from which the heroine is eventually rescued was purpose-built in the middle of a lake. The location for the pre-cataclysm mining town, meanwhile, is named as Höganäs in Sweden, where seven hundred locals had been roped in as extras, many of them milling around the preacher during his sermons, and fleeing in terror as the meteorites rain down. For obvious, financial, reasons, the destruction of Copenhagen or other cities is not portrayed; the stockbroker hero and his cosmopolitan friends meet their end in the provinces. On the other hand, tellingly, the lavish observatory from where the comet had been tracked is amongst the first victims of the meteorites, though we see only an interior shot of the destruction. Nevertheless, the inclusion of this scene in which the telescope and observatory are razed absolutely fulfills Bukatman's observation that sf is often 'rooted in an ambivalent relation to new technologies,' though of course they 'depend upon new technologies for their very effects' (Bukatman 1999: 251).

One important location is not identified in this *Verden og Vi* feature article, however: St Laurentii Church near Skagen, at the northern-most tip of Jutland. This church is commonly known as 'Den tilsandede Kirke' (the sanded-up church). Built in the fourteenth century, it fell victim to the sand dunes of northern Jutland, which have a propensity to creep across the terrain at a fair tack; local lore has it that generations of parishioners dug their way through the sand every Sunday to access the church, until King Christian VII decreed that the building should be decommissioned and torn down, leaving only the original church tower as a marker for passing ships. This architectural curiosity is unmistakably the church tower to which the heroine is drawn at the end of *Verdens Undergang*. As a monument to a human, Christian civilisation now half-buried by the elements, the church tower is – to the modern viewer – reminiscent of the emergence of the Statue of Liberty towards the end of *Planet of the Apes* (Franklin J. Schaffner, US, 1968), or of the various architectural treasures of London and New York that break the surface of the snow or flood-water in posters advertising *The Day After Tomorrow* (Bryant Low, US, 2002). And yet this is no special effect or set; St Laurentii Church had been, quite literally, buried by the sands of time. The same natural force of the creeping sand dunes retains, even today, a distinct national-historical resonance, in that generations of peasant labourers, probably about 100,000 in all, undertook back-breaking work between about 1850 and 1950 to convert the Jutland heath to arable land and to protect it from the encroaching sands (Hedens Opdyrkning I Danmark 1953).Such was the interest in this part of the country that a short documentary film about life on the Jutland heath, made by Nordisk in 1913 and featuring 'pioneers of the heather' was the subject of a press release (1.7.13, 'for various provincial newspapers') and described as one of a series of 'national films from characteristic regions of the country.'

It is hard to believe, all in all, that Copenhagen and provincial audiences of the 1910s would not have been familiar with the church tower and with the natural and national history in which it is – again, quite literally – embedded. The 'two people: a man and a woman' (as the intertitle announces) left alone on the ravaged earth at the end of the film are therefore, for the Danish collective imagination, also in a geo-political sense at the end of the world, standing on the grassy dunes on Grenen (the branch), right at the narrow tip of Denmark, where two seas meet and broil apocalyptically against each other, even when the world is not on the verge of catastrophe. In this way, the *dénouement* of the film – the envisioning of the sublimity of apocalypse – rests on the convergence of land's end and narrative ending, rather than on a special effects spectacular.

In singling out the apparently low-key ending of the film, I want to argue that in the particular historical and geo-physical context of a small, peripheral nation surrounded by belligerent states, a distinct function of the disaster film is to map the cataclysm onto the recognisably national space. In *Verdens Undergang*, this compulsion operates at both narrative and visual levels, such that this film constitutes quite an interesting case study in what Tom Gunning sees as the 'dynamic' relation between narrative and nonnarrative material in the consolidation of classical cinema through the 1910s (Gunning 2004: 43).

The convoluted plot of *Verdens Undergang* involves, as we know, the seduction of a small-town girl into eloping to Copenhagen with a man from 'outside,' much as in the well-known Asta Nielsen vehicle of 1910, *Afgrunden* (*The Abyss*, dir. Urban Gad, Denmark). This facilitates the migration of the action from a rural mining village to the capital city, and back again, a move that situates the protagonists within a national community stretching across a diverse – and at times violently contested – socio-cultural and geographical terrain, but encompassed by the 'homogeneous, empty time,' the time of simultaneity and the novelistic idea of 'meanwhile,' which Anderson (1991: 26) sees as constitutive of the 'classic' nineteenth-century national imagination. The approaching comet, luminous in the night sky, unites the Danes of Copenhagen and Jutland spatio-temporally under the same firmament, as they gaze and point in awe and fear.

Indeed, another Anderson, Hans Christian Andersen, had used the conceit of a comet some decades previously to connect conceptions of linear/historical and cyclical time in one of his tales, 'Kometen' ('The Comet,' first published 1869). The tale opens and closes with passages that describe the same social types star-gazing at two successive apparitions of a comet, while a man's whole life has been lived in between:

> Og Kometen kom, skinnede med sin Ildkjærne og truede med sit Riis; der blev set paa den fra det rige Slot, fra det fattige Huus, fra Stimlen paa Gaden og af den Eensomme, der gik hen over den vejløse Hede; hver havde sin Tanke derved. (Andersen 1989: 921)

> (And the comet came; its fiery core shone and its tail was threatening. It was gazed upon from the wealthy castle, from the pauper's house, by the crowd on the street and by the solitary

walker on the pathless heath; each had their own thoughts about it.)

These passages in Andersen's tale could almost serve as a synopsis for *Verdens Undergang*, were it not for the old man's – or rather his soul's – final departure for 'et videre Rum, end Kometen gjennemflyver' (925) (a greater space than that through which the comet flies). At the very end of the tale, his soul replaces the comet as the object of the gaze, but this time it is the gaze of God, and that of the old man's dear departed ones. The canonical status of Andersen's fairytales – not to mention the publication, in 1905, of the ubiquitous *Jubilee Edition* of his collected tales – makes it a fairly safe bet to posit this literary scenario as an intertext, conscious or not, for *Verdens Undergang*. Likewise, Lorenz Frølich's illustration of the old man leaning back in his chair, watching the comet from his study window, accompanied 'The Comet' in its travels from first publication in 1869 to the *Jubilee Edition*. What is most interesting about this potential intertext is the persistence between one medium and another of the concept of a society united in looking skyward at the visitor from outer space. This chimes with the conceit observed by Bukatman in certain recent scifi films to 'include an explicit and pronounced spectatorial position within the diegesis' (1999: 259). He traces a line from the tiny figures contemplating the sublime landscape or weather in paintings by, for example, Turner, to the appearance (in the work of, especially, the special effects designer Douglas Trumbull) of astronauts or small spacecraft, tiny in the face of the immense, unknowable sublimity of the cosmos or of the alien. For Bukatman, the effect of such a practice is not to 'mediate the experience through the psychology of characters.' Rather, in such scenes, '[f]ictive and theatrical spaces are collapsed, as diegetic and cinematic spectators are, in a metaphorical sense, united' (261).

There is a fascinating contrast in *Verdens Undergang* between three types of diegetic spectators: the professional astronomers, the Copenhagen bankers and sophisticates, and the wordless, milling mining-town peasants. All three groups can be said to join forces with the cinematic audiences in Bukatman's sense; it is the very oscillation between rural and urban, poor and wealthy, diegetic spectators that makes contemplation of the comet a national(ising) experience for the cinematic audience. Once the action returns to the mining village, however, and the meteorites begin to fall, the focus settles on the village as a metonym for the global (or, at least, North-Western European) civilization wiped out by the conflagration. And yet, we find ourselves unmistakably still in the early days of cinema, for the extras recruited in the Swedish village where these scenes were filmed are not all conversant with how to act and move before the camera. There is still a trace here, it seems to me, amongst the Swedish villagers, of the self-consciousness or self-imitation that moving pictures, in Jonathan Auerbach's account (2007: 50-62), compelled their subjects to perform in the first decade of the cinema.[12]

III: *Himmelskibet*: The Gospel of Peace and the Goodness of Technology

Two years later, it is not the end of this world but another world entirely that the Danish provinces are to portray in film. *Himmelskibet* tells the story of the navy hero Avanti Planetaros (Gunnar Tolnæs), whose wanderlust is piqued by his astronomer father, Professor Planetaros (Nicolai Neiiendam). With the help of his friend Dr Krafft (Alf Blütecher) he builds a spacecraft, the *Excelsior*, recruits an international crew, and sets out on an expedition to Mars. There, he finds a technologically and spiritually advanced civilisation which is peaceable, vegetarian, largely celibate, communicates via moving images, and has overcome the fear of death. Avanti falls in love with the beautiful Martian Marya (Lilly Jacobsson), who accompanies him home to Earth to spread her people's message of peace and progress.

That Nordisk was working on a film about Mars was known before the recruitment of the six hundred Martians. The film was of sufficient interest for newspapers, such as *Folkets Avis* (31.7.17) to report that filming had begun. Interest seems to have been piqued by the announcement by Nordisk that this would be the last film project before the company ceased operations for the duration of the war, or until economic conditions improved. Nordisk also publicised the unprecedented production costs of *Himmelskibet*, at least in the Danish context. The cost was reported in a letter of 15.2.18 to the editor of *Berlingske Tidende* as 150,000 Danish kroner.

The mercurial, bombastic General Director of Nordisk Films Kompagni, Ole Olsen, had claimed writing credits on his company's previous *kæmpefilm* (blockbuster), *Pax Æterna* (*Eternal Peace*, dir. Holger-Madsen, Denmark, 1917) an anti-war melodrama, as well as on *Verdens Undergang*,[13] and was now named as co-writer of *Himmelskibet*, alongside the poet Sophus Michäelis. Holger-Madsen (known colloquially as Holger-hyphen-Madsen) was to direct, but Olsen and Michäelis are shown in the opening shot of the credits, discussing their ideas in a comfortable library, their signatures setting the stamp of their authority on what is to follow and lending an air of seriousness to the endeavour. Indeed, the newspaper *Berlingske Tidende* (12.8.17) was quick to temper its light-hearted allusion to the previous day's call for extras by listing the social problems that Olsen and Michäelis intended to tackle in *Himmelskibet*: law, life and death, the unfortunate morals of the day, and over-population.[14] Ole Olsen himself, interviewed in the newspaper *Politiken* (18.2.18) after the film's première, stressed, as he often did, that *Himmelskibet* was *en problemfilm* (a film about social issues), concerned primarily with the problem of justice and the problem of death. Notably, Olsen connects the ambition of *Himmelskibet* to tackle such ethical issues to his own ambition for film as an art and an industry: 'Filmen er nu naaet saa vidt, at vi maa bort fra alt det dagligdags og trivielle. Det er de store tænkere, filmen skal have fat i.' (Film has now developed so far, that we must get away from the everyday and the trivial. It's the great thinkers that cinema must get on board now).

Olsen does not say that *Himmelskibet* is to be an anti-war film as such, though he touts, at every available opportunity, the film's ambition 'at arbejde i det godes tjeneste, at højne og belære, vise de lyse, lykkelige og gode sider ved menneskelivet' (*Ringsted Folketidende* 27.8.17) (to work in the service of good, to elevate and edify, to show the light, happy and good sides of humankind). However, there is no doubt that director Holger-Madsen was, like Olsen, optimistic about the potential of cinema to change minds and win hearts. His discussion of the film *Pax Æterna* a couple of years previously is telling in this regard:

> 'Det er en Fredsfilm – og det i saa meget højere Grad, som vi er ubeskedne nok til at tro, at den endogsaa er istand til at gøre Propaganda for Fredssagen naar den endelig engang kommer frem. Ingen kan...længere være i Tvivl om, at Filmen har en dyb Magt over de store Massers Sind – og hvilket Indtryk tror De ikke, det vil gøre paa alle de Millioner, der engang bliver denne Films Publikum, at se Kærligheden Evangelium – forkyndt paa det hvide Lærred af en skøn Kvinde?...Jeg tror paa denne Film og med denne Tro i mit Hjerte er jeg gaaet [i] Iscenesættelsen af den. –' (BT 6.9.16)

> (It is a peace film – and so much more so in that we are immodest enough to believe that it is also capable of functioning as propaganda for the cause of peace when it is eventually released. No-one can still be in any doubt that film has a profound power over the mind of the great masses – and what kind of impression

do you think it will make on all the millions who will some day be the audiences for this film, when they witness the gospel of love – preached on the big screen by a beautiful woman? I believe in this film, and it was with this belief in my heart that I began to direct it.)

The interviewer, a little sceptical perhaps, goes on to comment that the art form about which the director is so excited was something that fashionable people, just a couple of years before, would dismiss with a shrug of their shoulders. In fact one of the most blatantly didactic elements of *Himmelskibet* is its promotion of the moving image as a civilising tool. The novel use of 'film within film' (*Berlingske Tidende* 12.8.17), which *Pax Æterna* had also featured, was a talking point during the film's production and seems to be associated in the journalists' minds at least with Olsen's civilising mission. An early sequence in *Himmelskibet*, where Avanti Planetaros presents his project to the Scientific Society, shows him lecturing beside a large projection screen, upon which both still diagrams and moving images appear. Indeed, we see the completed spacecraft *Excelsior* for the first time, along with the murmuring and sceptical audience, upon this screen. Avanti is thus a 'visionary' in both senses of the word, and it is hard to miss Olsen's and Holger-Madsen's wish-fulfilment in pitching Avanti and his moving images against the resistance of the audience.

At its première in early 1918, the programme for *Himmelskibet* would state quite unequivocally the scope of its universalist, pacifist message and the ambition of its producers 'to grasp through fantasy one of the great problems of the future' (Michäelis 1918: 1). The pacifist agenda of *Himmelskibet* became apparent at its première not just in the programme and the diegesis but also in the short newsreels selected to accompany it. The reviewer at *Berlingske Tidende* (23.2.18) tells his readers that the audience was, at first, bemused and bored by the first film in the programme, which documented the arrival in Denmark of a Russian prisoner ship. Men on crutches with terrible injuries were shown hobbling to land. Says the reviewer: 'Krigen og Krigens Frugt, stillet op som en grel Modsætning til det Fredens Evangelium, der nu skulde forkyndes' (War, and the fruits of war, presented here as a stark contrast to the gospel of peace which was about to be preached). But most reviews of *Himmelskibet* struck the same chord as those for *Verdens Undergang*: underwhelmed, at times scathing, about the dialogue and story, but impressed by the technical acumen and special effects. The dissonance between the naïve narrative and spectacular images in this film is clear from the audience's (reported) resort to sniggering: even the *Berlingske Tidende* reviewer cited above, so serious about the documentaries on the evening's programme, had to admit that 'Latteren laa og lurede – Gang på Gang brød den frem…' (the laughter lay in wait – again and again it broke out).

Of particular interest to the first Danish reviewers of *Himmelskibet* were the flight through space, the crowd scenes on Mars, the voyage to the Isle of the Dead, and the spacecraft's final descent to Earth through driving rain and lightning. Surprisingly, perhaps, the only direct comment I have been able to find on the look of the spacecraft is in the British press, in *The Times*, which sneers: 'it suspiciously resembles a small dirigible airship, and we were not aware that these were capable of quite such ambitious flights.' (*The Times* 1920: 14). The *Excelsior* does indeed resemble nothing so much as an airship with Wright-flyer-type wings, and definitely does not imitate its rocket-formed precursor in *Voyage dans la Lune* (*A Trip to the Moon*, dir. Méliès, France, 1902). However, it is also recognisably – functionally, symbolically – a spaceship as described in Sobchack's typology of the sf icon, and here I emphasise the expressions in Sobchack's prose which echo Ole Olsen's declared agenda:

> There are those films, for example, which treat the spaceship lovingly, positively, optimistically. There is no doubt as to the *'goodness'* of a technology which can produce such a magnificent toy [...] The ship itself is *'good.'* It is aesthetically beautiful. It is fun to play with. It promises positive adventure, an ecstatic release from the gravitational demands of Earth, and it can remove us from ourselves and the complexity of life on our planet, *taking us to new Edens and regeneration.* (Sobchack 2004: 5, my emphasis)

Central to Sobchack's argument is that the spacecraft in sf is often functionally interchangeable with other forms of fantastical transport; not essential to the genre, as the railroad is to the western, for example (7). In *Himmelskibet*, though, the spacecraft is in a sense comparable to the western's indispensable railroad, in that it conflates a particular kind of movement through space with the notion of historical and ethical progress. Avanti Planetaros' mission is explicitly compared to that of Christopher Columbus early on in the film, when he sits pondering the idea of exploring the universe under an imposing portait of the explorer. The film programme highlights this comparison too:

Paa Trods af sin Samtids Vantro og Spot vovede han en Fart ud i det ukendte og usikre Hav mod en fjern Kyst, en ny Horisont, hvor Menneskeaanden kunde naa skønne og tropiske Riger [...] Saaledes blinker Stjernerne lokkende og forjættende til os gennem Mørket. (Michäelis 1918: 1)

(Despite the scepticism and scorn of his time, he undertook his journey out into the unknown and uncertain ocean towards a far shore, a new horizon, where the human spirit could reach beautiful, tropical realms [...] In the same way, the twinkling stars call to us, enchanting through the darkness.)

In one sense, then, the space mission is mapped onto the familiar story of manifest destiny. On the other, that the film concerns travel to another planet entails the imagining of a very complex geometry, and one which both evokes 'the contemporary fascination with aviation,' as the DVD cover suggests, but also foreshadows much more recent visual conventions of cinematic space travel. It is worth tracing how *Himmelskibet* works with emerging perspectival tropes to '*create* the boundless and infinite stuff of sublime experience, and thus to produce a sense of transcendence beyond human finitudes'that Bukatman (1999: 256, emphasis in original) sees as constitutive of science fiction. A little more cynically, we might also speculate that the film has to work hard to counteract the widespread public knowledge of the entirely prosaic, provincial locations in which the Mars scenes had been shot.

Himmelskibet must first establish the geometry of its journey. Avanti's illustrated lecture at the Scientific Society explains that the mission will be launched at a time when Mars is at its closest orbit to Earth, and the journey is described as taking around six months to reach the red planet. In contrast to Columbus' westward expedition, Avanti's trajectory must first be established as vertical. In fact this work begins from the opening credits of the film, when the main characters are first seen standing on a balcony above the rooftops of Copenhagen, pointing over the city. Attention is paid to characters climbing up into Professor Planetaros' observatory, while Avanti Planetaros' moment of revelation – his realisation that he must lead a trip to Mars – comes in the wake of his becoming a sports pilot and achieving an altitude higher than anyone before him. When his spacecraft is finally ready, it is shown on the brow of a hill, as are the crew preparing for take-off, silhouetted against the dawn in their leather flight suits.[15]

The takeoff of the *Excelsior* is constructed through a series of shots that move through degrees of verticality: first we witness, from above, the racing ground of the runway, then a series of aerial shots of Copenhagen from the point of view of the crew. These are intercut with shots from an observer's point of view of the ship gaining height, and eventually we see the spacecraft disappearing into the clouds through Professor's binoculars. As if to underpin the notion of height further, the rival Professor Dubius (Frederik Jacobsen) is seen on a hilltop, watching the takeoff in envious rage.

Throughout the take-off sequence, and eventually the landing, the film text mimics the perspectives that had wowed Danish society just a year before, when in August 1916 the great *flyver-film* (aviation film) had been shown in the Tivoli pleasure gardens and then on tour in the provinces as part of a donation drive for the Danish airforce. That the thrill and impact of the *flyver-film* consisted in the combination of, on the one hand, the affective response to watching footage from the pilot's eye view and, on the other hand, the recognition of the familiar capital city from the air, is clear from various reviews:

> Det er en helt [illegible] Fornemmelse at se vor By "paa hovedet" fra en 1100 Meters Højde. Man føler sig, som blev man selv tumlet rundt i Luften, og morer sig med at genkende de forskellige Bygninger neden under sig. [...] Alt bliver saa smaat dernede, og Menneskene er bare bitte smaa Prikker. *København* 26.8.16)

> (It is a completely [illegible] feeling to see our town 'on its head' from a height of 1100 metres. You feel as if you yourself are being tumbled around in the air, and it's fun to recognise all the different buildings beneath you [...] Everything looks so small down there, and the people are just tiny little dots.)

> Fra 1000 Meters Højde ser man Kbh i Fugleperspektiv. Det er, som om man selv sad i Flyvemaskinen og gled hen over sin By' (*Dagbladet* 26.8.16)

> (From a height of 1000 metres you see Copenhagen from a bird's eye view. It is as if you yourself were sitting in the aeroplane and gliding over your town...)

> Men interessantest er Fotograferingen under Glideflugt, idet man ser Byen langt nede, dansende som den vildeste Karussel! (*Aarhus Stiftstidende* 27.8.16)

(The most interesting thing is the filming during the flight; you see the town far below, dancing like the wildest carousel!)

In the time between the production of *Verdens Undergang* and that of *Himmelskibet*, then, the Danish cinema-going public has learnt to 'read' aerial perspectives. Concomitantly, they have been exposed to a 'live', aerial map of their national space. Adopting the same perspective on the city allows *Himmelskibet* to squeeze the last vestiges of novelty out of the mediated experience of aviation, but also facilitates a segue into the next two stages of the journey: the spacecraft *Excelsior* must first be imagined as flying through space, that is, in an unfamiliar geometrical context; and it must then enter the atmosphere of Mars and descend, such that the Martian civilisation is understood as both different to, and parallel to, that of Earth – and therefore achievable on Earth.

The sequence in space is remarkably 'readable' for a modern audience. An intertitle announcing that six months have passed is followed by a shot of Earth, and then a shot of the *Excelsior* moving towards the camera. Another shot has the spacecraft pass over the camera, also now conventional in its attempt to position the awe-struck viewer within the film's own artifice (Grant 2004: 21-2), though the sublime that is established here is less the technology of the spaceship, and more the endlessness of the space it must pass through. These exterior shots are intercut with scenes on board, where, the programme tells us, the crew is beginning to feel frustrated and claustrophobic during this 'monotone, ustandselige Flyven gennem det bælgmørke Univers, hvis Stjerner synes at staa lige fjerne og unærmelige' (Michäelis 1918: 3) (monotonous flight through the pitch-black universe, whose stars seem equally far away and unreachable). Tension builds as crew-members turn to drink and foment mutiny.

The human drama on board is resolved by the intervention of the Martians, who decide to bring the spacecraft in to land, increasing its speed tenfold. Interesting here, again, is the switching between perspectives as the two cultures encounter each other for the first time. An intertitle establishes that we are about the see what is happening on Mars; we first see the aliens, splendid in their robes and looking through their telescopes, through a round iris. We then see the *Excelsior* through a *hexagonal* iris, a subtle hint that this is an advanced alien visual technology. And sequences on Mars, while the spacecraft is still approaching, end with the closure of a round iris. The iconography of the telescope, then, is used to establish the distance across which we are witnessing the Martians looking at the incoming humans. A shot of the

Excelsior still in deep space but moving away from us very fast is followed by an intertitle stating that we are now within the atmosphere of Mars, then an aerial shot from the spacecraft, looking down upon grassy planes and some kind of temple. As the *Excelsior* lands, it fills the frame suddenly, moving from right to left, and the 'telescope' optic through which we have witnessed the Martians descending from their temple and rushing to greet the spacecraft has served its purpose: we are now on Mars.

If the Martians are inextricably linked to technologies of vision through our first introduction to them, it is also made clear that their scopic power is vastly superior to ours: they have been watching our planet for thousands of years, it transpires, and have eschewed speech in favour of the universal language of images. When the Earthlings resort to violence and are taken to the cave of judgement, their salvation comes through the Martian Marya's use of moving images on an altar to show Avanti and his friends the violent Martian past that they have now overcome. As in Avanti's lecture, a moving picture show is used as a pedagogic tool. But the moving image as a civilising force is also backed up on Mars by the visualisation, through double exposure, of Avanti's memory of how criminals are treated on Earth, and by a narratorial intervention during the Martians' Dance of Chastity which juxtaposes their behaviour to a series of tableaux of Earthlings dancing, drinking, kissing and tormenting beggars.

Himmelskibet, then, fetishises visual technology in the service of civilisation in two ways. Firstly, moving images are repeatedly portrayed as a tool for education and improvement; the spectacle of 'film within film' is associated both with Avanti's complex and idealistic project, which is later vindicated by its own success, and with the Martians' sophisticated system of social justice. Secondly, the two societies – Earth and Mars – are situated in parallel by the carefully-composed trajectory of the spacecraft, the use of spectacular yet familiar panoramic and vertical perspectives, and the motif of the telescope, a technology shared by Earth and Mars. The commonalities of earthly and martian visual technology – and thus the potential for communication and, ultimately, the potential for achieving the martian utopia on Earth – is, finally, underlined by Dr Krafft's collaboration with his hosts to send a message to his beloved Corona (Zanny Petersen), Planetaros' sister. They send strong beams of light back towards Earth from seven locations on Mars, forming the shape of the constellation Corona; the message is seen by Corona and her father, firmly establishing Earth and Mars within the same spacetime, and establishing the interplanetary potential of 'de levende Billeders umiddelbare Sprog' (Michäelis 1918: 5) (the immediate language of the image).

The return to Earth employs a similar series of images as the departure, but extra tension is added by a violent electrical storm during the descent (mentioned by several reviewers as particularly exciting). Yet again, Professor Dubius clambers up a cliff in his rage, and is struck by lightning. The *Excelsior*, in double exposure, executes a series of manoeuvres, including a nifty right-turn across a cloud-filled frame, as crowds mass and scurry in the city below to welcome it home.

IV: 'Film Has Taught Them That it's Good To Be Clean-Shaven and Nicely Coiffed': Disciplining the Alien Body

We end as we began, then, with a mass of human bodies in a Danish landscape. I would like to linger just a little on the choreography of bodies that people these films; a mass of people caught in the act of being instructed to look and act like people facing the end of the world, or like civilised aliens. As a jumping-off point, we may muse on an extraordinary interview in which Ole Olsen explains the dynamics of cinema's civilising power as beginning from its exposure of Russian peasants and miners to polite bodily practices:

> [F]ilmen har opdraget dem! Filmen har lært dem, hvordan man holder med en Kniv og Gaffel, naar man spiser. Filmen har lært dem, at der er noget der hedder rent Linned, Flipper og Pres i Bukserne. Filmen har lært dem, at det er smukt at være velbarberet og friseret. Og efterhaanden som saa og saa mange tusinde Film har givet dem en vis ydre Fernis af Kultur, har de tillige faaet en længsel efter aandelige Dannelse. (BT 14.7.17)

> (Film has educated them! Film has taught them how one eats with a knife and fork. Film has taught them that there's something called clean linen, collars and a crease in one's trousers. Film has taught them that it's good to be clean-shaven and nicely coiffed. And slowly but surely, as a few thousand films have given them a certain veneer of culture, so too they have developed a longing for a spiritual education.)

Pleasingly, there is a moment in *Himmelskibet* where the common hordes, with or without creases in their trousers, sneak into the picture. One of the crowds featured in the closing scenes on *Himmelskibet* seems to have been a group of locals gathering to watch the location shooting in Faxe; they had arranged themselves so nicely on a grassy slope, a reporter tells us, that Holger-Madsen decided that the shot just had to be used as part of the montage of the spacecraft's homecoming (*Dagbladet* 27.8.17). The onlookers enter into the frame and become the massing, cheering crowds whose presence in the films, as we have observed, constitutes 'an explicit and pronounced spectatorial position within the diegesis' (Bukatman 1999: 259); the crowd on the grassy slope are terrestrial beings caught in the act of learning how to look at science fiction film. It seems also, however, judging from the many reviews of the day that mention *massevirkningsbilleder* (*Aftenbladet* 23.2.18; roughly, mass or crowd scenes) in both films, that the audience is also fascinated by the experience of looking at (and reading about) its collective self in film; that this, too, is a form of spectacle.

Aside from the crowd scenes, as we have seen, most contemporary reviewers marvelled openly at the films' flagrant exhibition of 'spectatorial excess in the form of the *special effect*' (Bukatman 1984: 254, emphasis in original). However, the special effects in the two films tend not to have the effect of 'bringing the narrative to a spectacular halt' (ibid). While the bombardment of the meteorites in *Verdens Undergang* perhaps does bear some trace of the temporality of attractions memorably described by Tom Gunning (2004: 49) as 'an intense interaction between an astonished spectator and the cinematic smack of the instant, the flicker of presence and absence,' it nevertheless builds causally and chronologically towards a cataclysm of destruction. In *Himmelskibet*, meanwhile, the most notable special effects sequence – the flight of the *Excelsior* from Earth to Mars – is intricately composed in the service of constructing a particular space-time continuum.

However, both films feature intriguing sequences which can be said to bring the narrative to a halt in a spectacle of choreography: elaborate set-piece dances which thematise the concerns of the respective film. In *Verdens Undergang*, the climax of the 'last supper' is an erotic dance led by Dina, dressed as a comet, and in *Himmelskibet*, a group of women and children perform the Dance of Chastity. These dance sequences are lengthy, lasting a few minutes each, and a short segment of the latter appears again in a montage of a crewman's memories of his time on Mars.

Marguerite Engberg has written of how kissing, dance scenes, and so on, can be considered a calling card of the Golden Age of Danish cinema (1993: 66). Dina's performance in *Verdens Undergang* does indeed share the erotic movements of, for example, Asta Nielsen's infamous Gaucho Dance in *Afgrunden*. Swathed in luminous veils and a sparkling head-dress of comets' tails, and writhing inexpertly in a clinging gown, she embodies the compelling, blowsy ephemerality of the comets which 'cause astonishment and excitement out of all proportion to their substance' (Calder 1980: 10); of which this film constitutes but one manifestation. The Martians' Dance of Chastity is also about delaying the action, but is more complex: we gaze upon the stately dancers from a respectful distance. They are clad in flowing white dresses and wreathed in flowers. Marya's invitation to Avanti to watch the dance serves to delay his hopes of seducing her. As the programme puts it, 'Hun lærer ham en finere og ædlere Form for Kærlighed end den, jordisk Lidenskab er vant til' (Michäelis 5) (she teaches him a finer and nobler form of love than that to which earthly passions are accustomed). In the end, perhaps Olsen's ambition to civilise the bodies of his spectators runs aground in the attempt, in *Himmelskibet*, to harness the affective power of the cinematic attraction in the service of the rather un-spectacular practices of pacifism, vegetarianism and celibacy.[16]

References

Andersen, H.C. (1989 [1905]): 'Kometen.' *Samlede Eventyr og Historier. Jubilæumsudgave*. Odense: Hans Reitzels forlag, Flensteds forlag.

Anderson, B. (1991): *Imagined Communities: Reflections on the Origin and Spread of Nationalism*. London: Verso.

Anonymous, 'A Trip to Mars.' *The Times*. 6.5.1920, p 14.

Auerbach, J. (2007): *Body Shots: Early Cinema's Incarnations*. Berkeley, LA, London: University of California Press.

Bukatman, S. (1999): 'The Artifical Infinite: On Special Effects and the Sublime.' In A. Kuhn (ed.): *Alien Zone II: The Spaces of Science Fiction Cinema*. London, New York: Verso, pp. 249-75.

Calder, N. (1980): *The Comet is Coming! The Feverish Legacy of Mr Halley*. London: British Broadcasting Corporation.

Christensen, T.C. (1999): 'Nordisk Films Kompagni and the First World War.' In J. Fullerton and J. Olsson (eds.): *Nordic Explorations: Film Before*

1930. London, Paris, Rome, Sydney: John Libbey, pp. 12-18.

Crovisier, J. and T. Encrenaz (2000): *Comet Science: The Study of Remnants from the Birth of the Solar System*. Foreword by Roger Maurice Bonnet. Cambridge: Cambridge University Press.

Deleuze, G. (2005 [1986]). *Cinema 2. The Time-Image*. London: Continuum.

Engberg, M. (1993): 'The Erotic Melodrama in Danish Silent Films 1910-1918.' In *Film History* 5 (1), pp. 63-67.

Gehrels, T. (ed.) (1994): *Hazards due to Comets and Asteroids*. Tucson, London: University of Arizona Press.

Grant, B.K. (2004): '"Sensuous Elaboration": Reason and the Visible in the Science Fiction Film.' In S. Redmond (ed.): *Liquid Metal: The Science Fiction Film Reader*. London and New York: Wallflower Press, pp. 17-23.

Gunning, T. (2004): '"Now You See It, Now You Don't": The Temporality of the Cinema of Attractions.' In L. Grieveson and P. Krämer (eds.): *The Silent Cinema Reader*. London: Routledge, pp. 41-50.

Hedens Opdyrkning i Danmark (1953): *Mindebog udgivet ved Oprettelsen af Kongenshus Mindepark for Hedens Opdyrkere*. Det Danske Hedeselskab.

Michäelis, S. (1918): *Himmelskibet. Filmskuespil i 6 Akter*. (Programme for *Himmelskibet*). Available in pdf format at http://dnfx.dfi.dk/pls/dnf/pwt.page_setup?p_pagename=dnffuldvis&p_parmlist=filmid=5760. Accessed 1.9.08.

Sobchack, V. (2004): 'Images of Wonder: The Look of Science Fiction.' In S. Redmond (ed.): *Liquid Metal: The Science Fiction Film Reader*. London and New York: Wallflower Press, pp. 4-10.

Sontag, S. (1994): 'The Imagination of Disaster.' In: *Against Interpretation*. London: Verso.

Østergård, U. (1996): 'Peasants and Danes: The Danish National Identity and Political Culture.' In G. Eley and G. Suny (eds.): *Becoming National. A Reader*. Oxford: Oxford University Press.

Notes

1. All newspapers quoted in this essay are taken from the Nordisk Films Kompagni special collection at the Danish Film Institute Library. The newspaper clippings are gathered in scrapbooks XIV 32, 33, and 34. In each case, the title of the newspaper and date are given; the vast majority of clippings indicate no author name or page number.

2. The literal translation of 'Himmelskibet' is 'The Sky Ship,' but the film's title for anglophone markets was *A Trip to Mars*. Along with *Verdens Undergang* (The End of The World), *Himmelskibet* was restored and released on DVD in 2006 as a science fiction double bill as part of the Danish Film Institute's Danish Silent Classics series. I shall refer to both films by their original Danish titles throughout this essay, rather than by their unwieldy English titles.

3. This quote, and the exclamation in the title of this chapter, are taken from a report on director Holger-Madsen's address to the assembled extras on location in Faxe. The original (*Dagbladet* 27.8.17) reads: '"Mine damer og herrer! De er væsner fra en anden klode! De er et højtkultiveret folk, der aandeligt står langt over Dem selv....' All English translations in this article are my own, unless otherwise indicated.

4. *Masken* 9.3.16 (the clippings agency has recorded the date as 9 March, but it is almost certainly April, when the film premiered).'Man kan nemlig godt tale om at denne nye Kæmpefilm paa en vis maade er aktuel, skønt Forfatteren side om side med de frygtelige Natur-Begivenheder, vi overværer, har udpønset en ypperlig Intrigue, en moderne Roman med fast Grund i Virkeligheden.

5. *Berlingske* 3.4.16. Paladst. Otto Rung: VU: Der ligger en svimlende dristighed i at skrive en film, som skal svare til titlen VU....Med en stigende spænding og større og større betagethed føres man i de fem saa indholdsrige akter ved hjælp af en godt tænkt handling igennem kærlighedens, børsspekulationens og de sociale modsætningers riger til naturmagternes gigantiske opgør......vanlig rig fantasi og samtidig med en realisme...Men hvem kan beskrive eller "udføre" verdens undergang tilfredstillende? Til trods for den anerkendelse, der maa ydes dette arbejde, kan det ikke forties, at iscenesættelsen af filmen skæmmes af iøjnefaldende urimeligheder, en ferskhed i de indendørs masseoptrin og positive fejl, som f.eks., naar man lader folk færdes i minegange dybt under jorden med tændte stearinlys.....[Nordisk reddes af] den som helhed vidunderlige teknik og skuespillernes dygtighed.'

6. *Børsen* 4.4.16: 'Paladsteater. [...] den noget pretentiøse Titel "Verdens Undergang". Hr. Rungs Fantasi har dog visnok [sic] her spillet ham et Puds. En saa usandsynlig og opskruet Handling maa falde selv den mest nidkære Biograf-

Teatergæst for Brystet; men derfor kan man jo nok beundre Filmens tekniske Kunst, hvis fænomenale Udvikling formår at skabe saa imponerende Scenerier.' ([…] the rather pretentious title The End of the World. Mr Rung's imagination has probably led him up the garden path this time. Such an unlikely and cobbled-together plot must leave even the most inveterate cinema-goer cold; but then one can of course always marvel at the film's technical artistry, whose phenomenal development succeeds in creating such impressive sets.)

7. *Verdens Undergang* is also sometimes referred to by its alternative title of *Flammesværdet* (The Flaming Sword), which is used in the company ledger, but not in any of the Danish reviews of 1916. I have not been able to establish why or when the alternative title emerged, but one might speculate that the incredulous reactions to the bombastic original title may have been one reason.

8. *Politiken* 2.4.16: 'Paladsteatret. "Verdens Undergang": 'Det er ikke nemt i en Film at vise Sammenstødet mellem Jorden og en Komet og Elementernes Rasen. Men Hr. Blom, som har sat Filmen i Scene, har med megen Dygtighed formået at fremstille den voksende Uhyggestemning, Paniken, Ildregnen fra Himlen og den store Oversvømmelse.' (Palace Theatre: The End of the World: It is not easy in a film to show the collision between the Earth and a comet and the raging elements. But Mr Blom, who has directed the film, has very skillfully succeeded in producing the growing sense of unease, the panic, the rain of fire from the skies and the great flood).

9. *Masken* 9.3 (4).16 (see note 10 above): '…kometens sammenstød med jordbanen…ret mesterligt iscenesat…Vel aldrig nogensinde før – ikke engang i Atlantis-filmen – har teknikken og manøvreringen med masserne fejet saadanne triumfer some her…en hel ruin-by. VU kan vanskelig beskrives. Denne kæmpefilm skal ses.'

10. Adapted to film by August Blom from Gerhard Hauptmann's novel in 1913, *Atlantis* has also been restored and is available on DVD from the Danish Film Institute.

11. As late as 1910 in the US, it seems, 'cinematic codes for diegetic narration were still not firmly in place,' as suggested by published advice to actors to ignore the camera (Auerbach 2007: 43). On the other hand, a magazine interview of 1916 with Olaf Fønss, star of *Verdens Undergang*, suggests an appetite amongst the cognoscenti for tips on acting technique: 'But then you need to have film-acting technique in your body, unconsciously. Every feeling, for example, has to be exagerrated, drawn out.' (Original: 'Men desuden skal man jo ubevidst have filmens teknik i kroppen. Alle følelser for eksempel skal forstørres, trækkes ud') (*Verden og Vi*, 14.4.16)

12. *Folkets Avis* (5.4.16) reports with some understatement that other screenwriters were concerned about competition from the General Director, since it was quite certain that he had a good chance of having his scripts accepted; their trade union had written to Olsen to ask him not to sell his scripts to Nordisk at less than the market value.

13. The text of the article actually refers to *tobørnssystemet* (the two-child system).The finished film, and the film programme, make much of the women of Mars giving birth only to two children each, just enough to replace the parents (Michäelis 4). In its review of the film's première, *Aftenbladet* (23.2.18) reports that one of the lines that called forth the loudest peals of laughter was a Mars woman's comment that the two braids in her hair symbolised that she would twice be a mother. This is not made explicit in the currently-available dvd version of the film.

14. It is perhaps not insignificant that the notion of verticality has particular resonance in a country whose national discourse was predicated, in the nineteenth century as well as in chart-topping pop hits of the 1980s, on flatness as an allegory for equality and stability. (See Østergaard 1996)

15. I would like to express my thanks to Christian Hansen, Research Librarian at the Danish Film Institute Library, for going well beyond the call of duty in helping me to access the Nordisk Films Kompagni special collection; to Carol O'Sullivan for useful references on disaster narratives; and to Amanda Doxtater for sharing her knowledge of early Danish cinema and for her hospitality during my stint in the archive.

III

Communities

Women and Ballads:
The Representation of Women in Faroese Ballad Tradition[1]

Malan Marnersdóttir
Fróðskaparsetur Føroya

Introduction

This essay examines the representation of women in the epic ballad 'Brynhildar táttur' of *Sjúrðar kvæði* – one of the famous Faroese epos that is still in use as a dance ballad. In order to contrast the judgments of women in this ballad the essay also examines one woman informant's repertoire. The old Faroese ballads have no known authors, and they are written down from people's singing; each informant was often the source for several ballads and each ballad was found by several informants who produced different versions. The aim of this greeting to Janet Garton is to demonstrate how representations of women in the ballads create and challenge concepts of gender.

Ballad and Dance

In traditional Faroese folk culture, ballads were performed together with the chain-dance (Nolsøe 1988, Luihn 1979: 25ff. Clausen 2010). The ballads were inextricably linked with the dance. The dance is simple, consisting of three steps: two to the left and one to the right.

The performances of dances and ballads are cultural and social events that took place in private homes in the period from Christmas to Lent. People came from other villages to visit during this period of the year, making the event a great opportunity for acquaintances. In the twentieth century, the dancing and ballad singing take place in dance halls organized by dance associations. The original form of the ballads is unknown, as is how exactly they have changed while being handed down from one generation to the next. The actual total repertoire of Faroese ballads is collected in *Corpus Carminum Færoensium* (CCF, 1872-76). This work started at the end of the eighteenth century, and the corpus was published between 1951 and 1972 in six volumes. The work is a source of information about the formation of gender at the time the ballads were collected.

Moreover, Danish ballads became an integrated part of Faroese culture after their introduction in the seventeenth century by the *Hundredevisebogen* (The Book of One Hundred Ballads) by the Danish scholar Anders Sørensen Vedel (1542-1616) (Clausen 2010: 26). By the late nineteenth century Danish ballads had almost excluded the Faroese ballads from the dance.[2] The Danish dance ballads were sung in the same environment as the ballads in Faroese (Nolsøe 1988: 8ff. Luihn 1979: 19, 31), and the dance was the same whether the ballad was in Faroese or Danish. No instrumental music accompanied the dance, which underlines the inseparability of ballad and chain-dance. This unity of ballad and dance is an important element in the construction of the Faroese national culture. In the twentieth century, when the oral culture had been written down for quite some time, and people learned the ballads from books, scholars such as Professor Chr. Matras stated that 'Eingin, sum ikki hevur hesa tríeining í limum og huga, dugir at meta til fullnar okkara kvæði' (Matras 1935: 15) (Nobody who is not aware of this Trinity of voice, text and movement is able to estimate our ballads). He goes as far as to say that contemporary people who only read the ballads without dancing them in their mind do not get much out of them (see also Nolsøe 1988: 6, 20; Hansen 2006: 69).

There were no strict rules concerning the position of men and women in the Faroese chain dance. For instance, you can enter and leave the dance as you please, but it is frowned upon to keep on entering and leaving the chain, because this disturbs the performance. However, it was – and is still to some extent – a custom that if a man is fond of someone he invites her into the ring in front of him, that is, on his left hand side (Luihn 1979: 64).

The lead singer most frequently was a man, but women, too, lead ballads. However, it is said that women have tended to lead shorter ballads (Johansen 1970: 163ff.). More recently, women often lead the dance instruction for children, as K. O. Viderø describes in his own humorous-grotesque way in the novel *Á Suðurlandið* (To the Southern Coast of Iceland, 1990: 8-9). In the dance association of the twenty-first century, women lead the ballad dance almost to the same extent as men.

Women and Oral Poetry

In the community of the epic ballad dance in the Faroes, the performance was simultaneously an event of collective entertainment and contributed to the dissemination of conventions of many kinds, including the meaning of gender. The dance was an opportunity to meet and to initiate relationships. In terms of gender regulation, the ballad singing and the dancing were elements in a formative discourse which repeats stylised actions in time (Butler 2006: 185ff.). The integration of dance, song and ballad can also be seen as an event of negotiation of the sociologist Pierre Bourdieu's schemes of habitus that set the socially accepted gender roles which are constantly reproduced (Bourdieu 2007: 48). In this context I am interested in the ballads as master voices in the attribution of meaning to women's practices. In certain circumstances, the ballads spell out the meaning of specific events and actions of women in the setting. Moreover, activities that are coded specifically as women's activities are made universal by one of the most famous ballads in Faroese oral poetry, *Sjúrðarkvæði* – The Ballads of Sigurd the Dragon Killer. My argument is that the meaning of gender as stated by the great ballads obtained not only in the context of the ballad dance at the time of the collection of ballads in the early nineteenth century. The ballad dancing has also been an institution which formed schemes of habitus and, as such, it explicitly proposes norms for women and men.

The Master Voice of Oral Poetry

Women often play important roles in the old epic ballads, for instance as the object of a man's desire or as a trophy of a battle. In other ballads, women play more active roles in the epic.

The great cycle of epic ballads of champions, Sjúrður the Dragon Killer comprises three main ballads and a number of other ballads with some of the characters in other plots. The first part of *Sjúrðarkvæðini* is 'Regin smiður' (The Blacksmith Regin) in which Sjúrður is born after his father has been killed in a battle. Therefore his first assignment as a young man is to avenge his father with his sword, which Regin the blacksmith has repaired and strengthened. Once done with the revenge, Sjúrður proceeds to kill the great dragon Fafnir and gets hold of the gold the dragon has been keeping. The following two parts, 'Brynhildar táttur' and 'Høgna táttur' (Brynhild's and Høgni's Ballads) are about Sjúrður's women, his tragic death and his wife's cruel vengeance.

Brynhild is the main protagonist in the second part where Sjúrður is about to decide which woman he will give his heart to. Brynhild's father wants her to find a husband but she demands a man of certain qualities. Therefore she has her father surround her castle with fire, which her prospective fiancé has to ride through. As an extra bonus from killing the dragon in the first part of the ballad cycle, Sjúrður was gifted with the ability to understand the birds, and it is from them he learns about Brynhild and her wish to see him. He sets off to her castle, traverses the wall of fire, and finds her asleep, dressed as a Valkyrie. He wakes her by cutting up her coat of mail, she greets him, and they spend some time together. Then he has to leave, as knights like him always must in legends and fairy tales, but before leaving Brynhild warns him against straying too close to other estates. But this is exactly what Sjúrður does: he arrives at Júkagarðar where the châtelaine Grimhild stops him and asks her daughter Guðrun to bring him something special to drink – a drink of oblivion. Sjúrður forgets Brynhild and marries Guðrun. Brynhild and Guðrun meet when bathing in a river and have an argument that ends with Brynhild promising to avenge Sjúrður's betrayal. Brynhild sends her and Sjúrður's daughter Ásla away, and she demands that her new fiancé, who is Guðrun's brother, kill Sjúrður. From then on events escalate. The third part of the *Sjúrðarkvæði* gives an account of Guðrun's revenge, which is even crueller than the intrigue in the first parts. By the end of 'Høgna táttur' (The Høgni Ballad), all her brothers and her sons are killed and she herself is left dying of hunger locked in her castle with her new husband.

There are several versions of each part of the ballad, each of which more or less tells the same story. The whole ring is printed with four line stanzas having the same rhyme and rhythm pattern: second and fourth line rhyme, two stressed syllables in each line. In some parts of the ballad lines and stanzas are repeated, so that two or more stanzas in sequence are anaphoric and identical, except for a few words which stress the content and help the lead singer in the performance of the ballad.

Concerning the attribution of meaning of gender there are some interesting differences between versions. In particular, 'Brynhildar táttur' (The Brynhild Ballad) is interesting from a gender perspective. The responsibility for Sjúrður's death is explained in six stanzas carefully distributed throughout the ballad:

St. 35
Stríða teir í Húnalandi
við útdragin kník,
hevur so mangur edilingur
fyri kvinnur latið lív.

165
Mangur hevur hóttur notið
fyri fagurt vív,
liðið er nú at evstu stund,
Sjúrður missir lív.
166
Mangur hevur hóttur notið
fyri tær fríðu moyar,
nú er liðið at síðstu stund,
Sjúrður hann skal doyggja.
167
Sjúrður var ein avrekskappi,
vá sítt svørð í droyra,
og honum voldu kvinnur deyð,
sum tit skulu fáa at hoyra.
168
Sjúrður varð av lívi tikin
frá tí gullinum reyða,
tað vóru moyar í forðum tíð,
sum voldu mannadeyða.

243
Deyðan tóku teir Sjúrða svein,
bóru inn á skildri,
hevur so mangur latið lív,
helst av kvinnu veldi.
(CCF 1, All)

(35: They fight in Húnaland[3] with their knives. Many noble men have lost their lives for the sake of women.

165: Many men have tolerated beautiful women's threats. Now it has come to the last minutes Sjúrður is going to die.
166: Many have suffered from threats for beautiful maidens. Now it has come to the last times Sjúrður is going to die.
167: Sjúrður was a hero who dipped his sword in blood. Women caused his death as you are going to hear.
168: Sjúrður was deprived of his life away from the red gold. In ancient times maidens caused the death of men.

243: They carried the dead fellow Sjúrður on a shield. Many have lost their life most likely by the power of a woman.)

These stanzas spell out how women cause the death not only of Sjúrður but of many a brave man. There is no moderation or consideration that men ought to be in a position to refuse to do as these women want them to do. An argument against this critique of the ballad could be that if the men did refuse to carry out the women's intrigues there would not be any story to tell. Also, the stanzas display examples of women who caused the death of remarkable men and who in return are made remarkable as well. In Norse mythology there 'was an admiration for women who could behave like men, like Skaði and Guðrun [in 'Grímnismál' and 'Atla kviða' respectively]' (Jesch 1991: 148).

Many ballads contain stanzas like these that moralize over the plot. Such stanzas are equivalent to narrative comments in literary prose up till the end of the nineteenth century when Naturalism put an end to the direct and intrusive authorial voice. It is impossible to say if the commenting stanzas of the ballads are original or not. But they might have been a free area in the ballad where the lead singer or informant could add or omit information on the subject.

In this particular version of *Brynhildar táttur* (the A version) there is a sequence of ten stanzas (st. 247-257) juxtaposing Brynhild's and Guðrun's cruelties with other women in ballads, myths and history who caused the death of great men.

The Brynhild ballad explicitly refers to Guðrun in the Icelandic saga (st. 249) *Laxdala saga*. Guðrun demands her husband Bolli kill her former fiancé Kjartan because he had betrayed her with the daughter of the Norwegian King. This saga also delivers the motif in one of Birita á Mýri's repertoire (we shall return to this in the second part of the article). In another stanza the ballad refers to Ingigerð (st. 250) in 'Torsteins kvæði,' (Torstein's ballad) (CCF 99). In this ballad Magnus, the King of Denmark, proposes to Ingigerð; she gives a spiteful answer which is an insult that Magnus has to avenge, and so Ingigerð kills him by magic. The sequence also refers to Delilah (st. 251) who is a character in 'Samson's ballad' which derives from the bible (CCF 113; Judges, chapter 16). Delilah is the mistress of King Samson whose strength sits in his hair. She cuts his hair in order to help his enemy the Philistine to catch him. The last explicit reference in this sequence of stanzas to women who have caused the death of men is to Ásla Sjúrðardóttir (st. 252-53), and this seems to be a mix of different stories; there is no ballad preserved or stories that I know of where Brynhild and Sjúrður's daughter Ásla causes her husband's or lover's death.

These stanzas about strong women who play important roles in the death of remarkable men in other ballads, myths and stories spell out judgments about women like Brynhild and Guðrun and transform them into universal truths about womankind as such. However, these sequences of stanzas only appear in the very first written record of the ballad, made by J. H. Schrøter in Suðuroy in 1818, for the collection published by H. C. Lyngby in 1822. However, Lyngby omitted the stanzas judging women and the stanzas referring to other fatal female characters in ballads and bible stories – probably because he found these stanzas 'obvious variations and padding' (Lyngby 1980: X). Lyngbye's omission reflects the editor's personal aesthetics, and may also reflect his knowledge of the style in Old Norse and Teutonic poetry which he refers to in the foreword to *Færøiske Qvæder* (1980: VIII).

On the other hand, Schrøter collected the ballad in Suðuroy, where he was the vicar. This means that these sequences must have been active in the living ballad and dance culture in Suðuroy, even though it is not known who his informant was or from which village he or she came (Matras 1951-53: X). All the stanzas in question are included in the A version of the Brynhild ballad in the first volume of CCF where the ballad cycle about Sjúrður opens the book. The position of *Sjúrðarkvæði* (The ballads of Sjúrður) as the most prominent ballads among the entire Faroese ballads is emphasized by the fact that these ballads open the collection of ballads in CCF. The position of the A version at the head of all the versions of 'Brynhildar táttur' charges it with considerable importance, and this is transmitted to the judgments on women. The philological method that informed the work of CCF gave priority to the oldest version, on the assumption that it would be closest to the original.

However, my guess is that the comments about women in some versions of 'Brynhildar táttur' were produced and inserted in the ballad in Suðuroy, at some point between its origins in *Vølsungasaga* and other Old Norse intertexts and the collection of the Faroese ballads in the middle of the nineteenth century. Versions collected later and in other parts of the country neither contain the stanzas about fatal women in general nor the comparison with other fatal women. It is possible that the judgments are a result of changing cultural norms and ideology in the environment and it shows that ballads contributed to the establishing of rules of gender distribution.

The stanzas quoted expressing the ballad's misogynist judgments on Brynhild and Guðrun represent the opinion of the Master Voice of Faroese oral poetry on the subject. Even though the sequences of stanzas about the deadly influence of women are only the choice of Schrøter's anonymous informant, it is interesting to hold it up against one of the woman informants with the vastest repertoire. She, as a matter of fact, lived in Suðuroy.

Women's Choices

Thirty years after Schrøter's collection of the Brynhild ballad in Suðuroy, another very important collector of Faroese ballads, V. U. Hammershaimb, went to Suðuroy in 1848 in order to commit ballads to writing. He had just finished his theology studies, and in 1846 he had constructed the Faroese orthography (Matras 1958). By this time, philology was well developed as a discipline, and researchers were eager to have documentation and precise references to their findings; therefore all the ballads Hammershaimb collected bear the name of the informant. On this trip to Suðuroy he recorded many ballads in writing, including some from women. Many only sang one ballad for him, but three of the women sang several, and their repertoires show the interests of these women. Hammershaimb's collection of ballads is included in CCF.

Of all the informants for the total of 236 ballads in CCF, about one third were women from all parts of the country. The ballads of the women are distributed between the genres in proportion to the size of the genres in general. The biggest genre is the group of heroic ballads, seventeen of which came from women informants. The second genre is ballads of chivalry, fifteen of which came from women. Women were informants for a further fifteen magical ballads, five religious ballads, four humorous ballads, and one historical ballad.

It is difficult to say why there are not more women informants. In Iceland 'sagnadansar,' the oral genre closest to Faroese ballads, were written down as early as the seventeenth century and it was almost only old women who still knew them (Vésteinn Ólason 1979: 18). A few Faroese ballads were written down before 1780 but we do not know much about the informants. J. C. Svabo started his work in the late eighteenth century, but the organized collection of Faroese ballads took place in the nineteenth century. The Faroese ballad collection was doubtless inspired by Romanticism, which means that the status of the genre can have changed compared to the Icelandic situation in the seventeenth century. From being seen as mere old songs, the ballads had become ideological tools on the basis of their status as historic treasures. The romantic interpretation saw them as an expression of the spirit of the people.

Helga Kress has described how poetry is taken over by men when it is written down (Kress 1993: 12ff). From the number of informants alone, it is obvious that men were more important informants than women.

The repertoires of the women informants do not necessarily reflect all the ballads women in general knew. They might have known more ballads than the ones that were written down. In his writings there is no indication that V. U. Hammershaimb took any specific interest in women's repertoire as such.

Birita á Mýri's Choice

The ballads contributed by women informants do not always take a special interest in woman characters, but the majority of their ballads do. Ballads from women informants tell of women who are kidnapped, raped and either forced to love a man or denied the man of their heart; there are strong women and women that carry out special tasks to re-establish the order of things, as in the repertoire of Birita á Mýri. Her official name was Birte Sofie Jacobsdatter (1805-74), and she lived in Vágur in Suðuroy. She was thirteen and thus almost an adult when Schrøter was collecting ballads for Lyngbye. There is no evidence that she met him or took part in his collection, but she may have learned at an early stage that the old ballads were interesting.

Information about Birita á Mýri are from a local village history which says that she was a wise and humorous woman. People said that she could foretell the future. Once Birita and other women from the village were driving the cows back to the village. They came to a hillock which was said to be occupied by supernatural beings, when one of the women got something in her eye. Birita turned around and said 'May something harm you [Ólukka slái tín kjaft]' and asked the other women to go ahead. They saw that Birita was affected by something and as they had entered the village, Birita turned around and said 'Now you can kiss me.' She had seen a wood nymph [huldufólk] throw out the ashes from the fireplace just as she and the other women were about to pass the hillock. In another story about Birita the focus is tea, which was hard to come by in the 1840s. Birita was cooking for a wedding when she got hold of some tea which she put into a pot and cooked. Afterwards she served the tea as a soup that made people say: 'Dejlig suppe, madam Myre' (What a wonderful soup, Mrs. Myre) (Andreasen 1977: 100).

Birita á Mýri informed Hammershaimb about six ballads, two heroic ballads, three ballads of chivalry and one humorous ballad. Her heroic ballads 'Kjartans tættir' (CCF 23A) and 'Einars tættir' (CCF 44B), the songs of Kjartan and Einar, have strong relations to the Icelandic *Laxdæla saga*. 'Kjartan tættir' is about how Kjartan engages Guðrun before leaving for Norway together with his foster brother Bolli. However, Bolli is the first to return back home telling Guðrun that Kjartan is a very good friend of the king's daughter. This makes Guðrun believe that he is engaged to the Norwegian princess. When Kjartan finally returns to Iceland he discovers that Guðrun has married Bolli and he has to find another woman to marry. Guðrun then demands that Bolli fight Kjartan in order to keep her loving him. By doing this she plays the role of the whetter, a role she has in common with other women in Old Norse literature (Jochens 1996: 162ff) e.g. Brynhild in *Sjúrðarkvæði* and *Vølsungasaga*. It does not matter that it was Bolli who lied to her or Kjartan who betrayed her; Guðrun is in a position to claim revenge. Before Kjartan dies he refuses to let his men kill Bolli; that is, he does not want his death to be avenged. This can mean that he acknowledges Guðrun's claim and wants her to live a happy life together with Bolli. In this interpretation, it is the man who represents reconciliation, while Guðrun represents confrontation. Contrary to the Brynhild ballad, 'Kjartans tættir' does not express any explicit judgment of Guðrun's actions.

The other heroic ballad of Birita á Mýri, 'Einars tættir' (The ballad of Einar), is about Einar, who is sent out to fight a troll or ogre. First he has to go to Iceland to ask the famous knight Ílint for help. 'Kjartans tættir' is more interested in love and hatred than 'Einars tættir,' which emphasises men's use of force and great results.

One of Birita á Mýri's ballads is the joking ballad 'Vevpíkan' (CCF 188) (The Weaving Girl), who is invited to a wedding but does not have suitable clothes to wear. She asks people for help but everybody refuses. Instead they ask her to make the clothes herself, but the only result of her efforts is a hat for the cock and a shoe cloth for the hen. Where 'Kjartans tættir' is about the vengefulness of a woman, 'Vevpíkan' indulges in the incompetence of a woman.

There are three ballads of chivalry in Birita á Mýri's repertoire and they all include women in exposed and vulnerable positions. 'Margretu kvæði' (The Ballad of Margreta), relates the story of a woman who, on her way home to visit her father who has put her in a convent, is raped by her brother. It is only after the misdeed that Margreta and the man realise that they are siblings. Margreta returns to the convent and refuses to reveal the identity of the rapist. In return her father sets the convent on fire when he finds out what has happened. The brother is too late to rescue Margreta so they both die.

A special circumstance with 'Margretu kvæði' is that in the dance performance it was most often led by a woman (Nolsøe 1981: 32). One of the variants of the ballad contains an added stanza that tends to deny the cruelty of the father:

> Mangt er sagt um Magnus konga
> ímeðan hann mundi liva
> at hann læt brenna Mariu klostur
> tað finnist ikki skrivað. (Nolsøe 1981: 39)

> (Many things have been told about King Magnus while he was alive but it is not written that he let Maria's convent burn.)

Mortan Nolsøe states that this stanza is meant as a teasing stanza at the end of the dance performance (1981: 44n23). Another interpretation of the added stanza could be that it takes the sting out of the heavy female dominance of the whole performance.

Birita á Mýri has yet another story in her repertoire about force against a woman. 'Pálnir Búgvason' (CCF 156A) is a knight who abducts an engaged woman. The woman offers resistance to Pálnir and warns him about the consequences but once the abduction is complete she adapts herself to the new situation. During the wedding night Pálnir tells his wife that they have conceived twin sons. Soon the bride's father and brothers arrive to avenge the abduction and Pálnir is killed. His wife, the abducted woman, follows the rules for her new role as a widow: she brings up the sons so that they avenge their father. The ballad ends with the boys killing their grandfather. This ballad reveals a taste for complicated family relations that are even more complex in Birita's final ballad.

'Mirmants kvæði,' The Ballad of Mirmant

Birita á Mýri's last ballad recorded is 'Mirmants kvæði' (CCF 109D), which contains several masterful women.

In the initial situation the newlywed and pagan couple the Earl and Countess of Saxland, Hermann and Brita, have no children yet. The Earl dreams that a snake comes out of Brita's breast so when Brita gives birth to the son Mirmant the Earl wants him removed far away, and never to return. Brita arranges that Mirmant spends his childhood with Løðar, the Earl of France and his wife. When he has grown up he returns home for a visit and greets his father with the call to believe in the only true God, the Christian God. His father gets so angry that he takes his sword and brandishes it. Mirmant gets a sword as well and kills his father. To avenge her husband Brita serves Mirmant a drink that is contaminated with leprosy. The ballad explicitly comments on the role of the son and the mother: Mirmant says that it is a small sin to kill a pagan and his mother counters that it is not an act of a son to kill his father. They get even, as Mirmant says that her serving of the contaminated drink is not a maternal act either.

So Mirmant is sick when he returns to his foster father who offers him a seat of honour at the table. His foster mother comments that it is unusual to allow sick men to sit at table. Then Mirmant arranges his fake death and funeral in order to escape to Sicily incognito where he seeks out the king's daughter Sissal, whom he persuades to heal him. Here the father's snake dream reappears as the corporeality of the sickness that Sissal takes out of Mirmant with a fervent kiss:

> Tað var frúgvin Sissal,
> hon andar í hans munn,
> hon myntist við riddaran Mirmant,
> tí henni var svikin kunn.
>
> Við munninum
> hon um høvuðlutin tok:
> 'Halt nú fast um sporlið,
> tað er okkara bót!' (CCF 109, stanza 88-89)

> (Sissal breathed into his mouth/ she kissed Mirmant/ because she knew the deceit.// She took the head of the snake/ with her mouth:/ 'You bite hard on the tail/ that will save us!')

The sensuality of the healing kiss designates the quality of Sissal: she is the good woman who arranges and rearranges what others disrupt. Sissal is Christian and only uses her knowledge whereas the other women use evil magic: Brita, Mirmant's mother, pours infection into his drink, and Katrin, his stepmother, does something similar. In narrative terms such stanzas (CCF 109D, 131) are epic formulas (Holzapfel 1980) which occur in many ballads to indicate supernatural actions most often carried out by women.

As Mirmant has been declared dead he does not identify himself by his real name to Sissal. First he presents himself as Justinus of France, then he is an Earl's son Steffan, and only after the marriage does he tell her his real name. Also in this ballad the man leaves his wife soon after the wedding. When Mirmant arrives at his foster parents the foster father is dead. Katrin the stepmother asks him to stay and sleep with her because Sissal is betraying him with other men during his absence. Mirmant does not trust her, probably because she names Sissal's lover as Steffan, one of the false names Mirmant used while sick. Then Katrin fetches a drink of oblivion and the ballad scene switches to Sissal who gets the message that Mirmant is in danger. She disguises herself as the Earl Herin, collects an army of three hundred men and rides all the way from Sicily to Saxland to challenge Mirmant under the pretext that he has taken his woman. Mirmant knocks down the whole army until only Herin is left. When he rides towards Herin/Sissal, he is not able to move or lift his arms as if they are tied down. His opponent knocks him down from the horse and reveals himself as Sissal.

In the end of Birita á Mýri's version of the ballad, Sissal hits Katrin and buries her alive before Mirmant regains his consciousness. Of the four versions of the ballad, Birita á Mýri's punishment is the cruellest.

Sissal is the hero of the ballad as she rescues Mirmant from leprosy by taking away the snake of his father's dream and discovering his foster mother's incestuous plans. All Mirmant's opponents and all the evil plans against him are destroyed by Sissal's skills. She is the one who establishes a new order, though not without cruelty in the end. However, she is not the only person who is cruel – cruelty is an indispensable part of the ballad environment.

Mirmant's Women

The women of 'Mirmants kvæði' arrange life, and provoke and heal illness and sorcery; the men turn their back on problems like Mirmant's father, or they die like the foster father. Women forge intrigues and reveal them, too, whereas it is the dream of a man that creates the initial conflict in the reigning order of the marriage. Dreams and magical drinks are the means of the intrigues of the mothers, while knowledge and Christianity are the means of the loving Sissal.

The mothers are evil – Mirmant's mother and stepmother are united as wicked women. Mirmant's mother gives him a contaminated drink and the foster mother makes him forget his wife. The two compelling women in the universe of the ballad are the opponents of Sissal, who represents good female power.

Instead of sorcery Sissal dresses like a man and wears weapons in a battle. In medieval societies it was punishable to dress like the opposite sex as well as for women to wear weapons. Lena Norrman suggests that since this is not an offence in the sagas – and neither is it an offence in the ballad – it indicates that maiden warriors belong to a different gender, a gender which is not defined by the binary opposition male/female, but on the basis of the opposition power/powerless (Norrman 2000: 378). All three women in 'Mirmans kvæði,' Brita, Katrin and Sissal are powerful, and the men are relatively powerless. When it comes to family relations, Christianity and sickness, the women have the means that are required to regulate difficult situations.

The distribution of power in Mirmant's ballad also corresponds with Carol Clover's finding that in Old Norse society the important opposition was power-powerless whereas the opposition male-female was far less important. Some men were powerless, which is the case in Mirmant's ballad. Moreover, women could take the place of men in specific situations – for instance pay or receive wergild for manslaughter if there was no son and the woman was unmarried (Clover 1993: 5ff.). Also, 'in the Old Norse saga world "masculinity" was always a plus value, even (or perhaps especially) when enacted by a woman' (Clover 1993: 7), which is an argument for the assertive women in the repertoire of Birita á Mýri. The Mirmant ballad distributes gender in another way than Sjúrðarkvæði, where men are powerful and women as well.

Ballad and Saga

'Mirmants kvæði' is an interpretation and a transposition of the Icelandic romantic saga *Mírmanns saga*, which does not seem to have any foreign model (Jensen 1997). The movement from saga to ballad entails substantial adaptation corresponding to the transposition of a piece of music.

The ballad concentrates the story. Most of the elements in the saga are present but the degree of elaboration varies. The question of Christianity is far more developed in the saga. In the saga the conversion is developed through several parts of the story. Even at home, where Mírmann stays until he is thirteen, he refuses to participate in the worship of the pagan gods – that is, he rejects the 'blót.' It is after this event his father does not acknowledge his son and Mírmann leaves shortly after. His conversion to Chistianity takes place at the home of his foster father, Hlöðvir of France.

When Mírmann's parents hear about his baptism they write a letter to Hlöðvir describing the dishonour his baptism brings on the family 'ættar skò[ó?]m' (Mírmanns saga 1997: 16, 20). They demand that Hlöðvir send Mírmann back home and accuse him of misleading other people's children. Hlöðvir wants to find a means of reconciliation and sends the wisest men in France with Mírmann to convince his parents of the advantages of Christianity. When it is clear that they will not succeed, Mírmann's mother suggests that he meets his father hoping that his mind will change, 'meiri vonn at hans skaplyndi mykiz' (18, 55-56). The depiction of Mírmann's meeting with his father is long, given Mírmann's impressive apologia for Christianity, and the description of the father's sword Ylfingur, which is compared with Roland's sword Dýrumdal in 'Chanson de Roland.' After these preparations the patricide takes place and Mírmann takes over the sword Ylfingur (29, 18). The vast description of his journey from France to Saxland, the meeting with the father and the presentation of his faith in an elaborate speech, and the final fight cover several chapters in the saga (chapter 7-10) whereas in the ballad the events are rendered over ten stanzas.

Despite the fact that Birita á Mýri's version of 'Mirmants kvæði' is rather long (156 stanzas; the longest version has 178 stanzas), it does not relate all the details of the saga. By dint of the abridgement of the saga some parts of the saga are almost omitted, while others have gained importance. In the ballad Mirmant is given his name in a church (st. 11-12) and there is no christening at his stepfather's home. When he returns to visit his parents the ballad does not mention any specific purpose but resorts to a warning frequent in ballads: the foster father tells Mírmann not to drink wine when he comes home or to speak to his father. Instead of an open disagreement on the question of Christianity the father's dream becomes more important at this stage of the process. The ballad implicitly identifies the snake in the Earl's dream with the impression that the unborn son is a threat to him. This permits the father's rejection of the son right from the beginning of the ballad. When his mother asks her husband why he does not want to see his son before his eyes, he answers that the sooner he is moved away the better (CCF 109 D, stanza 14-16). In the ballad Mirmant only stays three months with his parents whereas in the saga Mirmant's father takes an active part in the upbringing of the son, though he and the mother do not agree in all matters.

The ballad and the saga have an exceptional range of assertive women and both texts contain male statements about women. In connection with the death of Hlöðvir's wife, which is not mentioned in the ballad, he wants to make Mírmann his heir. Mírmann is honoured by the offer but rejects it because the king might very well live longer than him. Instead

Mírmann helps Hlöðvir to find a new wife. During their discussions of the matter the saga states that there are not many things that are more difficult to regulate than the form of a woman ('faat se vandara at stilla enn skap *kononnar,' Mírmannn's Saga 1997: 10, 62). This could indicate that the saga supposes that people are made women by training – in other words gender identity is a question about formation. It turns out that King Hlöðvir's new wife – the daughter of king Aðalráði of England – has been badly formed as she very soon tries to seduce Mírmann who does not react to the flirtation (ibid 13, 4ff.).

The ballad does not discuss the shaping of women explicitly but it lets Mirmant reject the foster mother's lies about Cecilia with a statement about women's liability in general:

> Tað var riddarin Mirmant,
> hann kann væl orðum snúgva,
> ongan biður hann kallmannin
> kvinnu orðum trúgva. (CCF 109 D stanza 129)

> (Mirmant knows how to express himself, asking no man to believe women's words.)

In *Mírmanns saga* Katrin forges a real intrigue which includes letters and messages back to Sicily and Mírmann believes her lies about Cecilia's unfaithfulness during his absence. In the ballad Mirmant does not believe Katrin the foster mother's lies about Sissal, therefore she has to find other means. To abridge some of the complications of the saga the ballad turns to stereotyped formulas such as drinks of oblivion. Another famous drink of oblivion is the one mentioned above that Guðrun serves Sjúrður the Dragon Killer in 'Brynhildar táttur.'

Ballad Dance and Gender Performance

The Faroese ballads demonstrate different representations of women. Different ballads also perform different types of gender – neither men nor women are stereotyped if we take the whole ballad corpus into account. However, women are explicitly judged as an entity on an ethical level whereas men always are shown individually or in small groups executing their duties, rights and actions. Hence the ballads challenge and create different gender concepts.

During the performance of ballads certain gender roles are displayed in a way that contributes to the formation of gender. The quality of the assertiveness of the women in 'Mirmants kvæði' is modified by the fact that two of them are wicked and only one is good; she in turn has sensuality on her side.

Breaking traditions and the rules of kinship in the ballad society characterise the ballads of Birita á Mýri. The abducted woman in 'Pálnir Búgvason' adjusts to the rules of the married woman and makes her sons kill their grandfather and her father in revenge for his killing of the father of the boys and her husband. The incest in 'Margretu kvæði' is kept secret so that the father kills his own children. In 'Mirmants kvæði' several rules are broken. First the duty to honour the father, and as Mirmant kills his father, he is not in a position to revenge the death of the father. The incest ban is represented in the stepmother's attempted relationship with him. The son killing the father is a major offence. In the saga it is caused by differences concerning religion but in the ballad it is more like the climax of the father's initial unwillingness to have anything to do with his son.

Birita á Mýri is the informant who has the most extensive repertoire among the female informants. Her ballads are concerned with different situations in women's life primarily linked to the choice of a spouse. Her ballads have long literary roots. This does not need to mean that she and the other informants of the ballad had actually read the saga, but it indicates that the story of the saga was known in society and that the ballad form was able to retain it. In terms of gender schemes Birita á Mýri's ballads describe women in different positions, good and evil and, when she is the victim, the women adjusts to the situation. Seen as a whole her repertoire counters the judgments on women of the Sjúrðar ballads – the women in her ballads do not cause the death of men, the men arrange it themselves. Her ballads do not essentialise women. Her ballads depict specific women who have to arrange vengeance in the ballads such as 'Kjartans tættir' and 'Pálnir Búgvason.'

Birita á Mýri's repertoire also offers alternative distribution of gender based on women's actions in specific environments. Her ballad repertoire negotiates schemes of habitus in so far as it presents other gender roles and thus produces alternatives to women's fatal role in the version of Brynhild ballad practised in Suðuroy in her childhood. Birita á Mýri counters implicitly this Master Voice in the attribution of meaning to women's practices. Moreover, the specific women's activities in Birita á Mýri's ballads are not made universal. On the contrary, her repertoire creates schemes of gender habitus based on specific women's actual performances in different gendered situations of the narratives.

References

Andreasen, P. (1977): *Úr Vágs søgu*. Egið forlag.

Bourdieu, P. (2007): *Den mandlige dominans*. Copenhagen: Tiderne skifter. First published as *La domination masculine*, Seuil 1998.

Butler, J. (2006 [1990]): *Gender Trouble*. London: Routledge.

Clausen, M. (2010): *Vísuløg í Føroyum – Danish Folk Ballads in the Faroes*. Stiðin. Tórshavn.

Clover, C. (1993): 'Regardless of Sex: Men, Women, and Power in Early Northern Europe.' In *Representations*, # 44. The Medieval Academy of America.

Føroya kvæði, Corpus Carminum Færoensium (CCF) (1951-72). Editors: Chr. Matras, N. Nolsøe. Ejnar Munksgaard. København.

Hammershaimb, V.U. (1983): 'Træk af mit livsløb.' *Fra Færøerne: Úr Føroyum*. Dansk-færøsk samfund, pp. 13-66.

Holzapfel, Otto (1980): *Det balladeske. Fortællemåden i den ældre episke folkevise*. Odense: Odense Universitetsforlag.

Jensen, J.L. (1997): 'Introduction to *Mírmanns saga*.' http://nfi.ku.dk/ publikationer/trykte_serier/editiones/mirmanns_saga/ Accessed January 10, 2011.

Jesch, J. (1991): *Women in the Viking Age*. Rochester: The Boydell Press.

Jochens, J. (1996): *Old Norse Images of Women*. Philadelphia: University of Pennsylvania Press.

Johansen, S. (1970): *Á bygd first í tjúgundu øld*. Vágur.

Luihn, A. (1979): *Føroyskur dansur. Studier i sangdanstraisjonen på Færøyene*. Trondheim: Rådet for Folkemusikk og -dans.

Lyngbye, H. Chr. (1980 [1822]): *Færøiske Qvæder om Sigurd Fofnersbane og hans æt*. Collected and Translated by H. C. Lyngbye. With an introduction by P. Müller. Emil Thomsen. Tórshavn.

Matras, C. (1935): *Føroysk bókmentasøga*. Føroya málfelag.

Matras, C. (1951-53): 'Indledning.' 'J. H. Schrøters optegnelser af Sjúrðar kvæði.' In *Færoensia Textus & Investigationes*. Vol. III: IX-LXXV.

Matras, Chr. (1958): 'Sproget.' *Færøenre II*: 71-83, N. Djurhuus (ed.). Dansk-Færøsk Samfund. København.

Mírmanns saga. Ed. Slay, D. 1997. Editiones Arnamagnæanæ. Series A, vol. 17. København: C. A. Reitzels forlag.

Nolsøe, M. (1981): 'Mangt er sagt um Magnus konga.' *Fróðskaparrit*, 28-29. bók, pp. 30-46.

Nolsøe, M. (1988): 'Folkevisa og folkevisemiljøet på Færøyene.' 'Kvæðagreinir.' Ed. Eyðun Andreassen. *Føroyamálsdeild*, Fróðskaparsetur Føroya.

Norrman, L. (2000): 'Woman or Warrior? The Construction of Gender in Old Norse Myth.' 11th International Saga Conference. http://www.arts. usyd.edu.au/departs/medieval/saga/pdf/375-norrman.pdf. Last accessed March 31 2008.

Patursson, J. (1966): *Tættir úr Kirkjubøar søgu*. Felagið Varðin. Tórshavn.

Ólason, V. (1979): *Sagnadansar*, Rannsóknarstofnun í bókmenntafræði, Menningarsjóður.

Viderø, K.O. (1990): *Á Suðurlandið*. Emil Thomsen. Tórshavn.

Notes

1. A version of this essay was first published in *Scandinavica* 49 (2), 2010; it was originally conceived and written for this Festschrift.

2. The farmer, politician and poet Jóannes Patursson (1966: 45) wrote in his memoirs about his childhood in the village Kirkjubøur: 'lítið hevði um tað bilið verið kvøðið av kvæðum í Kirkjubø' (very few ballads in Faroese were sung in Kirkjubø). And he adds that instead, they sang ballads in Danish and his grandmother, who was the chief ballad singer, knew the whole Faroese edition of the Danish balladbook, Danske kæmpe- og Folkeviser, by heart. Tættir úr Kirkjubøar søgu.

3. In Old Norse sources, Hunaland often has a mythological character and can shift between different parts of Europe, depending on what kind of skills the hero is to show. See http://correlator.sandbox.yahoo.net/index.php/people/Hunaland. Accessed September 9 2009.

Gustaf Wasa and *Gustav Vasa:*
Kellgren, Strindberg and a National Icon

Alan Swanson
Rijksuniversiteit Groningen

The life of Gustaf Ericsson Wasa (1496-1560) had enough adventure in it to fill several theatres. Imprisoned by the Danes and escaped therefrom; father beheaded and mother taken prisoner; leader of a revolution; elected as monarch; survivor of several serious revolts; gifted and forceful administrator; and so the list goes on. It is, however, a life we know almost only by official acts. Given Gustaf Wasa's historical importance in Swedish history, it is, perhaps, little wonder that in Sweden he appeared relatively quickly on the stage. It is thought that around 1616, Johan Messenius wrote a play on the subject, whose text is now lost, and Anders Prytz certainly wrote a 'comoedia' about Gustaf in 1621.[1] It is, perhaps, also little wonder that these theatrical representations had a propagandistic edge to them.

Written in the time of the second Gustaf, Prytz' play rehashed the glories of the first's triumphs over the Danish 'tyrant,' Christian II, skating over the fact that his hero had usurped the throne (as had two of Gustaf's sons, including the father of Prytz' current king). Seeing Sweden's (re-) founding father as an underdog striving against great odds, and doing so with the will of the people, seems to have been an implicit necessity in any portrayal of the man and the period. It could probably not have been otherwise, as the play was performed before Gustaf II Adolph in Uppsala, in celebration of Gustaf Wasa's entry into Stockholm a hundred years earlier. In 1621, Sweden was not yet master of the Baltic nor was Gustaf Adolph the 'Lion of the North,' though he had been practising for the role in Russia.

By 1700, theatre in Sweden was dominated by foreign, frequently traveling, troupes, carrying with them, naturally, a non-Swedish repertory. Theatre in Swedish to that point, about which we know little, seems to have been largely limited to the schools and universities.[2] The permanent, largely Swedish-language, mid-century theatre in Stockholm, Swenska Comedien (1737-54), ran a repertory that was heavily influenced by the contemporary Parisian theatre.[3] No Gustaf appears in its play-lists, however, though Alexis Piron's *Gustave* (1733) was having a good run in Paris. Alas, the company ran out of money and steam in 1754 and split into two touring companies.

It remained, then, for a third Gustaf (1746-92), possessed of no Swedish blood whatsoever, to encourage, indeed, to propagate, a new *Swedish* theatre. Beginning with his 1771 inaugural speech as king to the *riksdag*, he consistently emphasized his Swedishness (having, as it happened, been the first Swedish-born monarch since 1720). This policy was reinforced by his insistence upon a Swedish theatre, for which he provided French scenarios to be versified in Swedish by his court poets. An important series of the king's plays were on national (and regal) subjects: *Gustaf Adolphs Ädelmod* (1783; Gustaf Adolph's Nobility), *Gustaf Adolph och Ebba Brahe* (1783/1786; Gustaf Adolph and Ebba Brahe), *Gustaf Wasa* (1786), and *Drottning Christina* (1785/1791; Queen Christina).[4] Dramatic political encomium is still with us, of course, but the blatant service these plays performed as royal propaganda is quite separate from their effectiveness as theatre-pieces. Indeed, in its musical form, with 177 performances to 1900, *Gustaf Wasa* remains the most-performed Swedish opera.[5]

Gustaf III's poet for his dramatic fantasy about the first Gustaf was his slightly younger contemporary, Johan Henric Kellgren (1751-95), who was unquestionably one of the leading *literati* of the day. Poet, playwright, journalist, critic, and one of Gustaf's theatrical censors, Kellgren understood the job he was given.[6] It was probably inevitable that the King's dramatic imagination, and Kellgren's consequent poetic response, would settle upon the ultimate confrontation between Gustaf Wasa and Christian II at the Siege of Stockholm, in 1521. In some ways, this was the defining moment in the creation of modern Sweden.

Kellgren's, and the King's, portrayal of Gustaf Wasa is, not unexpectedly, completely heroic. Gustaf has few doubts; he understands his cause as righteous and ordained, and is given opportunity to evince his inherent nobility and generosity. He is first shown to us in his field tent, the night before the concluding fight, where he displays decisiveness in arranging his order of battle and is given praise and support for his plans.

Gustaf

[...]

fullkommen då det värf, hvartill Er himlen ämnat,
Ett enda anfall än – och Sverge räddas skall.[7]

Sparre

Nej Gustaf, din skall hedern vara
att hafva frälst ditt Land från nöd och slafveri
den första uti stridens fara
skull du och först i segrens ära bli:
[...]
för din förtjenst vi alla vika.[8]

(**Gustaf**

[...]

complete, then, that task for which heaven intended you, only one
more attack – and Sweden will be saved.

Sparre

No, Gustaf, yours shall be the honor of having saved your country
from poverty and slavery. You shall be the first into the battle's
danger and first in victory's glory.
[...]
we all give way to what you deserve.)

And so it goes, leading to the one piece every Swede came to know by
heart, until it was dislodged in the last century by a folk-song:

Ädla skuggor, vördade fäder,
Sverges Hjeltar och Riddersmän!
om ännu dess Sällhet er gläder,
gifven friheten lif igen.
Skola Edra helgade grafvar
trampas af Tyranner och Slafvar?
Nej, må träldomens blotta namn,
Edra vreda vålnader väcka,
och er arm sig hämnande sträcka
ur den eviga nattens famn!

(Noble shadows, honored forefathers,
Sweden's heroes and knights!
If its happiness still pleases you
Give freedom life again.
Ought your holy graves
be trampled by Tyrants and Slaves?

No, may the mere name of servitude
Awaken your angry ghosts,
And stretch your vengeful arm
Out of the hold of eternal night.)

Gustaf's only dilemma in this play is that his mother is in the hands of his enemy, who threatens to kill her in sight of her son. Gustaf is suitably strengthened however by word from his mother that he should persevere, and so he does.

Triumph leads to more praise, of course, and, after his victory and the return of his mother by the equivocal Severin Norby, he has his chance to show mercy, which he does by letting the subsequently captured Danish soldiers go free.

Norbys Vapendragare
Vid åsyn af er sorg och edra dygder rörd,
den ädle Norby sjelf er mor tillbaka sänder –
Gustaf
Hvem? han[?] hvad hör jag? kan det vara,
o himmel på hvad sätt min tacksamhet förklara?
Gån lösen alla fångars band
Och lämnen dem till pris i Sevrin Norbys hand.

(### Norby's Herald
Moved at the sight of your sorrow and your virtue,
The noble Norby himself sends your mother back.
Gustaf
Who? He? What do I hear? Can it be?
O heaven, how shall I make clear my thanks?
Go, loosen the bonds of all prisoners
And return them, to the praise of Sevrin Norby's hand.)

This leads directly into a pageant of further praise, during which our hero is lifted onto a shield and proclaimed king. Following this apotheosis, the original performances concluded with a ballet.

In terms of the sensibility of our own age, accustomed to expecting nuance and fallibility in our protagonists, this Gustaf is completely uninteresting as a stage character. He has one characterization: he is noble and in possession of all – and only – the attributes ideally associated with this state. Johann Gottlieb Naumann's (1742-1801) fine music does little to meliorate this unrelieved stance, and Kellgren's recitatives provide glorious rhetorical periods in which to elaborate the trope (even though Kellgren complained that Naumann seemed always to want cuts in the recitatives, the better to fit into his own musical metrical patterns). The net result is that we, today, do not much care about this Gustaf. It must be strongly emphasized here, however, that this was emphatically *not* the case when this opera opened, when the audience vociferously supported the Swedish side during the great battle-scene in the last act.[9]

Strangely, what is missing from the piece is one aspect of himself that Gustaf III cherished and actively promoted, the view of him as a 'father' to his country. *Gustaf Adolph och Ebba Brahe*, for instance, devotes the entire second act to 'the people,' all of whom frequently let us know that the king is the source of all things good and just. Several Prologues to operas of the period also show us 'the people,' often in appropriate folk costume, celebrating the monarch in similar fashion. This is not obviously the case here, where the individual characters come from the noble classes almost exclusively, and where the soldiers (the people) are only a part of the chorus.

If Gustaf is a cardboard figure, so, similarly, is Gustaf's antagonist, the Danish king. Christian is all things evil, a very incarnation of unreason and injustice, and equally uninteresting as a character. This put a great weight upon Naumann to characterize these two roles musically, something he does not always succeed in doing.

From our modern perspective, the most interesting role, dramatically, in the play is that of the Danish admiral, Severin Norby, also a real person in the middle of things at the time. As Christian's emissary to the Swedish camp, he is given a chance to see both sides, and in choosing a moderate position at the end, he is accorded a humanity denied the two kings. The historic fact that he eventually turned himself into a Baltic pirate and general maritime nuisance was irrelevant to the Gustavian audience.[10]

Gustaf III's and Kellgren's *Gustaf Wasa* was intended as an overtly, heart-on-sleeve, national opera, and it succeeded eminently. In praising the first Gustaf, the third put himself in a position to be identified with him, a rhetorical simile he was not slow to insist upon. But as a dramatic character, even one in an opera, Gustaf Wasa is a personification, not a person. In 'Ädla skuggor,' however, Kellgren and Naumann brought forth a song that was as close as Sweden ever came to a national anthem.

To judge from the repertory lists, it would seem that in Sweden in the nineteenth century, historical plays, especially about its kings and especially about its recent kings, did not make much headway. None of Sweden's regents after Carl XII, for instance, appeared on stage until August Strindberg began his historical dramas, and, even then, the youngest was only Gustaf III.[11]

Gustav Vasa (1899) is one of several plays by Strindberg in which that monarch plays a significant role, the major one being, of course, *Mäster Olof* (1872-75). Though Strindberg, because of his intensive research among documents in order to write *Svenska folket i helg och söcken* (1881-82), probably knew more about Swedish history first-hand than most of his colleagues, he played deliberately fast-and-loose with that history to write his play. He compressed time, introduced anachronisms, and invented characters in order to show us a Gustav in a vice of his own making, a Gustav who was a person, not a personification.[12] *Gustav Vasa* is not, by and large, a celebratory play and certainly not one in the mould of *Gustaf Wasa*. Though it is clear that we are expected to admire the monarch at the end of the play, it is an admiration that we are also expected to see him earn.

Strindberg's Gustav is a powerful man aware of his power and unafraid to use it, cost him what it may. The play opens menacingly as we learn that he has ordered the deaths of friends who have supported him in his early trials but who have now, he thinks, deserted him. In the second act, we come to understand that his relationship to his two eldest sons, especially Erik, the Crown Prince, is fraught, at best, a distance that extends to his wife and mother-in-law, as we discover in the third act. His financial obligation to the Hanseatic League is now over and, so, his relationship with its chief representative in Stockholm, Herman Israel, is now tense. In a parallel instance of father/son disagreement, we learn inferentially that Herman has killed his son for 'betraying' his family by falling in love with a Christian girl. The audience would have known of the death sentence Gustav passed on his secretary, Olaus Petri, but the conflation of historical time does not allow this event to play itself out and we see here only an Olof who is the king's closest advisor.[13]

In the fourth act, we meet a disguised Gustav, wandering the streets of Stockholm with his son, Johan, also disguised, in search of Herman Israel, who, he learns to his deep dismay, has left the country. He is approached by the wife and daughter of one of the Dalacarlian men he has condemned, who thinks he is Herman and begs him to ask the king for her and her mother's share of the family wealth back, but who praises the king, himself. Gustav is suitably humbled and promises help. In the fifth act, Gustav's troubles are seriously mounting, for the Småland rebel, Nils Dacke, has come almost to the gates of Stockholm and the King is about to abdicate and flee, though Olaus Petri tells him to hold fast. The king thinks the Dalecarlians have risen against him, too, and their wooden shoes echoing over the bridge sound to him as a sort of death knell, but their leader, who calls himself Engelbrekt, after an earlier rebel, brings him news that the men from Dalarna will defend the king and put down the rebellion. For some reason, Gustav understands that he has been chastened by God, his sons gather round, his wife and mother-in-law join him, and we have as happy an ending as in an Italian opera. Indeed, in the theatre the short last act is extremely difficult to play, for it can easily verge into the comic.

Strindberg is clear in his attempt here to present us with a Gustav who has more than one characteristic and more than one face. Even Gustav's language varies with respect to whom he is speaking. For instance, at the beginning of Act Three, he almost jokes with his wife:

> **Gustav**
> God morgon, min ros!
> **Dronningen**
> En härlig morgon!
> **Gustav**
> Första vårdagen på en lång vinter.
> **Dronningen**
> Är min konung nådig idag?
> **Gustav**
> Kungens nåd är oberoende av väder och vind! – Fortsätt nu! – Är det Erik det är frågan om?

> (**Gustav**
> Good morgon, my rose!
> **The Queen**
> A beautiful morning!
> **Gustav**
> First Spring day after a long winter
> **The Queen**
> Is my king gracious today?
> **Gustav**
> The king's grace does not depend on the weather and wind? – Go on. – Is it Erik it's a question of?)

This sort of family chat is in contrast to his speech with Barbro, the Dalarna girl whose father he had ordered executed, and who thinks he is Herman Israel:

Gustav

Gån i frid; jag skall tala vid kungen, och rätt skolen I få, ty han vill rätt och gör rätt.

(**Gustav**

Go in peace; I shall speak to the king, and you will have justice, because he wants what is right and does right.)

This is ecclesiastical language, meant to give the greatest assurance to the girl and her widowed mother. One of Strindberg's abiding strengths as a playwright was his ability to use language itself to individualize his characters. To be sure, Kellgren's Gustaf is constrained by the poetic form of his discourse and by the music that must carry it, but that very formality is central to the image to be promoted of one whose life is devoted only to grand and important causes, such as the well-being of Sweden. Strindberg's Gustav is also concerned with the political integrity of Sweden, but we see that concern manifested in a variety of often very human contexts. Strindberg's Gustav has a home life and recognizable family troubles as well as a public persona to deal with.

As with Kellgren, then, Strindberg was responding to current dramatic needs. That something over a century between them made these aims different is only to be expected. The sentimental, realistic, and naturalistic revolutions in theatre of the nineteenth century, to which Strindberg had already contributed, did not, of themselves, of course, impel a different view of the monarch-as-theatrical-character or of how historical plays ought to work. Indeed, they may have generated even greater resistance to the very idea of historical themes as at all relevant to the contemporary theatre. Even Gerhard Hauptmann's controversial *Die Weber* (1892), about the Silesian anti-industrial strikes of the 1840s, was taken originally as a contemporary political and not as an historical play. Strindberg's play does not take that direction, nor does it seem to be apologetic. As with his historical stories, *Svenska öden och äfventyr* (Swedish Destinies and Deeds) and *Nya svenska öden* (New Swedish Destinies) (1884, 1904, 1906), his aim was to give breath to important moments in Sweden's history. In short, we might almost imagine that Strindberg's Gustav actually needs to go to the toilet now and then.

Kellgren and Strindberg share one interesting dramatic technique that is worth noticing. Indeed, it is one they share with Molière and Holberg, as well. Both delay significantly the entrance of the title character. In *Gustaf Wasa*, Gustaf does not appear before the beginning of the second act (of three). In Kellgren's case, the unrelenting evil of Christian in the first act almost forces us to expect the greatest contrast with Gustaf in the second, and we are not disappointed. In Strindberg, he does not appear until the play is half over, at the beginning of the third act (of five), where we, unexpectedly, encounter him in an intimate family context; 'unexpectedly,' because though we have not met him personally in the first two acts, he has been just off-stage the whole time. In the first, he is in a nearby house, passing hard judgment upon those he thinks have betrayed him, but he is ever-present, in the form of his messenger who frequently interrupts the scene before us. In the second, he is the subject of conversation among Prince Erik, Göran Persson, the prince's confidant, Jakob Israel, Herman's son, and Prince Johan, who has come to summon Erik home from the tavern, indeed, to arrest him and Göran if they do not come along. Thus, at a moment in which the fate of the new kingdom may hang in the balance, Gustav is shown as autocratic abroad and inadequately parental at home. Hence, the mild, almost bantering, tone of the opening of the third act creates the jolt of an emotional contrast to what we have hitherto learned of the central character. Thus, rather than confirming our expectations of Gustaf, as Kellgren does, Strindberg confounds them, with yet other views of the character, which he pushes even further in the succeeding act and resolves only in the last. Kellgren's central theme is, ultimately, Sweden, personified in her regent. Strindberg's central theme is Gustav himself, with all his faults and virtues displayed before us.

Icons are, of course, tricky things to manipulate and they are, themselves, also subject to the vagaries of time and taste. The battle-scene in the last act of *Gustaf Wasa*, for instance, so stirring in 1786, was so worn-out by the time of the 1873 performance celebrating the first century of the company that it was largely cut (Nordensvan 1917-18: vol II: 288) . Indeed, except for occasional performances, the opera was rarely given at all after the season of 1822/23. With the exception of *Mäster Olof* and, to some extent, *Erik XIV*, Strindberg's historical plays have suffered a similar fate. Just as Strindberg could imagine another Gustaf from Kellgren, so might (perhaps even, must) we configure the character anew to fit yet another theatrical time.

There are, nonetheless, several things interesting to note about the specific juxtaposition before us. First, both Gustaf III/Kellgren and Strindberg looked into public material – national history, not just something old – to project a figuration of a contemporary image. That Gustaf III/Kellgren's image needed to evince the heroic and Strindberg's the everyday derived from their differing senses of what the theatre was for. Neither was really up-to-date, of course: *Gustaf Wasa*'s form and content creak when compared with Da Ponte's and Mozart's *Le Nozze di Figaro* of the same year, or even with the later *La Clemenza di Tito* (1791), whose old and old-fashioned libretto by Metastasio gave Mozart so much trouble. And Strindberg does not really convince us in the last act that a somewhat bourgeois Gustav has really been adequately chastised to earn his redemption and our admiration.

Second, each text has what we might call a pædagogical edge to it. Gustaf III needed to assert his immanence in the work of Gustaf I at his most glorious moment. The second decade of his absolute reign was deep in economic trouble and the breach between him and the higher nobility caused by his *coup d'état* in 1772 had only widened. He had, on the whole, always had a strong following among ordinary people and this text was a way of reminding the audience of the centrality to Swedish history of monarchs named Gustaf. As the most accessible and broadest form of propaganda at the time, a theatre-piece was an obvious medium to use. Strindberg, like Messenius several centuries earlier, was deeply interested in Swedish history and his *Svenska folket i helg och söcken* really is one of the first modern cultural-historical studies of ordinary Swedish daily life. It is clear that he wanted to de-Romanticise Swedish history, perhaps to bring it in reach of ordinary people, as the historian Anders Fryxell (1795-1881) had done in the forty-six volumes of his *Berätterlser ur svensk historia* (1826-79; Tales from Swedish History). All of Strindberg's historical plays explore the personal side of their leading characters. But the day of the historical play as a genre was over by the time Strindberg wrote *Gustav Vasa*, and he had himself helped to see it off. His historical plays came in the same burst of energy that produced *Brott och brott* (Crime for Crime), *Påsk* (Easter), *Ett drömspel* (A Dream Play) and others that changed forever the way we look at theatre.

Third, these two characters exemplify the change in sensibility of Swedish audiences over the course of something more than a century. An heroic view of Swedish history, especially centered upon its regents, was no longer necessary by the middle of the nineteenth century and, despite the pressing matter of impending Norwegian independence, no longer possible at its end. History was no longer national, but personal.

References

Bonde, C. C. (ed.) (1911): *Duchess Hedvig Elisabeth Charlotta's Dagbok 2*, 2nd ed. Stockholm: Norstedts

Byström, T. (1981): *Svenska komedien 1737-1754*. Stockholm: Norstedts.

Klemming, G.E. (1863-79): *Sveriges dramatiska litteratur*. Stockholm: Norstedts.

Nordensvan, G. (1917-18): *Svensk teater*, 2 vols. Stockholm: Bonniers.

Peterson, A. (1929): *Studier i svenska skoldramat*. Göteborg: Wettergren och Kerber

Strindberg, A. (1999): 'Öppna brev till Intima Teatern.' In A. Strindberg, *Teater och Intima teatern*, August Strindbergs Samlade Verk 64, P. Stam (ed.). Stockholm: Norstedts.

Notes

1. See G.E. Klemming (1863-79: 21-22). Klemming speculates that Messenius may have incorporated his earlier work into his later play, *Gustaf I* (1642).

2. See Peterson (1929: 35-72), and Kurt Johannesson (2007: 81-101). There was certainly some church drama, as well: Klemming (1863-79: 1-6) gives the entire text of a Swedish-language religious play from the latter half of the fifteenth century.

3. Its repertory is given in Byström (1981).

4. I omit *Siri Brahe och Johan Gyllenstjerna* (1788), where Prince Gustaf Adolph makes a guest appearance.

5. A calamitous and tendentious 1991 revival has probably scotched for a long time any possibility of hearing Naumann's wonderful music for Kellgren's fluid poetry, but there is a studio recording of that performance (Virgin Classics VCD 5 45148 2 1).

6. That he also regarded his dramatic work as worthy is shown by his inclusion of all but his first text, *Proserpin* (1781), in the first of the three volumes of his *Samlade skrifter* (1796).

7. Kellgren's *Samlade skrifter* and the text gathered into *Kongl. svenska theatern VII* both have a considerably longer recitative here.

8. The text versions here are based on the Score, Ms. Statens musikbibliotek KTA Operor G1.

9. Among other reports, see Duchess Hedvig Elisabeth Charlotta's *Dagbok 2* (Bonde 1911: 108-9).

10. In the original printed libretto, Kellgren provided historical notes for the main characters and mentioned there that Norby ended up badly.

11. I take this from the list in Nordensvan (1917-18, vol II: 489-99).

12. Ten years after he had written *Gustav Vasa*, Strindberg wrote that, in order to be able to be able to deal with the legend that Gustav Vasa was, he had had to shrink his narrative to one episode in his reign and chose the period of Nils Dacke's rebellion (1542): 'Denna förtvivlans tid ger bäst tilfälle skildra den stora människan Gustav Vasa med alla hans mänskliga svagheter.' (Strindberg 1999: 201)(This confusing time offers the best opportunity for portraying Gustav Vasa the person, with all his human weaknesses.)

13. In fact, there is also disagreement, of an intellectual nature, between Olof and his son, Reginald, who is about to go off to study at Wittenberg. It is interesting to see the very different portrayal of Olaus in this play compared with that in *Mäster Olof*, almost thirty years earlier.

Nameless Communities:
The Representation of the Town of ... in
Den Fallna (1848) by Wendela

Elettra Carbone
University College London

In his *Imagined Cities* Robert Alter argues that the urban environment is the ideal setting for novels. As Alter puts it, 'it makes perfect sense that novels' – 'the modern literary genre par excellence' whose readership was predominantly bourgeois – should focus on a town or a city, 'the principal theatre of bourgeois life and also the form of collective existence that undergoes the most spectacular, dynamic growth throughout the modern period' (Alter 2005: ix). Yet, what happens when the name of the town represented in a novel is omitted and when this town is not really represented as a physical space? How can a space without a name and without a specific topographical configuration even be called a space? This is what I will explore in this essay analysing the Finland-Swedish novel *Den Fallna* (1848)[1] by Wendela demonstrating how a space – in this case more specifically a town – can be defined and represented through what Michel De Certeau would call 'everyday practices.' In other words, space is created in this novel through the actions of the people that live in it. By walking in the nameless streets of this anonymous town, by dwelling in their homes or moving from one home to the other, the inhabitants of the anonymous town create the town as well as the network of relations at the basis of any community (de Certeau 1984: 91-110).

Den Fallna is a fairly unknown Finland-Swedish novel. Little is also known of the author of this novel, Wendla Randelin (1823-1906), who used the pseudonymous Wendela. Positively reviewed when it was first published in 1848, *Den Fallna* remained forgotten until 1999, when Kati Launis published a Finnish translation of the novel under the title of *Elisabet*, from the name of the female protagonist (Mazzarella 2005). In this novel Randelin portrays the life of a bourgeois woman, dividing her life between taking care of her young family, attending fancy balls and listening to the latest gossip. In her back cover text, Launis defines *Den Fallna* as 'unoduksiin jäänyt rakkausromaani viime vuosisadalta' (a forgotten love novel from the last century), and goes on to explain in her preface that Randelin herself tried to minimise the importance of her own work in the hope of avoiding harsh criticism (Launis 1999: 5). The central topic of the novel is, however, far from being frivolous. There is no doubt that Randelin – like other Finnish women writers of the 1840s – was deeply influenced by the Finland-Swedish writer Fredrika Bremer (1801-1865), the author of the first middle-class realistic novels in Sweden challenging the contemporary male-dominated society (Algulin 1989: 98-102; Grönstrand 2008). *Den Fallna* is a novel about adultery where Randelin shows how the harmony of a perfectly happy bourgeois family, the Lindmark family, can be destroyed due to the workings of what the narrator calls 'den onda genius' (an evil genius) (Randelin 1848: 72). The Lindmarks and their home are carefully placed within a bigger context, namely that of the Finnish town in which they live and which remains unnamed throughout the whole novel.

How is this anonymous town represented? What about its inhabitants, its community? What is the effect of the three dots used to replace the name of the town? What treatment do other places receive in the novel? Is there a world beyond Finland in the novel and, if yes, is this all made of anonymous spaces?

Marriage and Adultery

Wendla Randelin was the daughter of a parish priest. She studied for some time in Turku, before getting married to Uusikaupunki's city mayor Pehr Gustaf Randelin (1808-1858). *Den Fallna*, the only novel she ever published, was her debut work in 1848 and was followed by the short story 'Maria' in 1853. Between 1854 and 1866 Randelin also wrote for the Finnish children's magazine *Eos*. When her husband died in 1858, she faced economic and social difficulties as she had to raise twelve children on her own. Her economic situation improved when she started receiving the Finnish widow and orphan's pension in 1859 and when she inherited an estate from an old uncle in 1864.

Den Fallna is the story of a love triangle between the beautiful Elisabeth, her fair husband Leonhard and his dark and mysterious friend Rudolph. The story is seasoned with all the necessary ingredients: love, passion, betrayals, gossip, small-town mentality and characters dying of love. The plot of this novel is, on the whole, quite complicated. When Rudolph Berg, the new mayor and a good friend of Leonhard's, arrives, Elisabeth has been happily married for six years and enjoys a comfortable life together with her husband and three children. As romantic feelings become more and more evident between Elisabeth and Rudolph, the couple becomes the talk of the town. When Leonhard, otherwise reluctant to listen to the gossip, finds out that his wife is in love with Rudolph, he leaves for Brazil. Left alone, Elisabeth refuses to give in to Rudolph's advances. She will never divorce her husband and enter a relationship with another man, unless it is he who asks for the end of their marriage. Rudolph's and Elisabeth's love comes however to a sudden end when, as Elisabeth takes part in a ball with Rudolph, two of her children die. The triangle even becomes a 'quadrangle' when Ferdinand, Elisabeth's cousin, who is hopelessly in love with her, helps and supports her and her daughter Helena until her reunion with Leonhard.

Despite casting a critical light on aspects of the society of the time and, in particular, on the position of women, in *Den Fallna* Randelin does not really attempt to question the principles of a patriarchal society. Debates about the institution of marriage became topical in Finland between 1840s and 1850s. For those who, like the Finnish philosopher and statesman Johan Vilhelm Snellman (1806-1881), were championing the national cause, the function of the traditional family was of crucial importance. Women had a duty to preserve the stability of society by maintaining their place in the home (Melby 2006: 52-53). Throughout the novel the narrator invites the reader to refrain from condemning or judging the characters but to reflect on the motivations behind their actions. At the same time, the narrator appears to be supportive of the rules and codes of behaviour imposed by society on men and women, as she emphasises that those attempting to subvert these canons will be struck down by punishment, either divine or social. References to the compliance to strict moral codes in this novel are in line with the revivalist movement which, dissatisfied with the standards of morality of the Church of Finland, contributed to spread pietism in Finland. The revivalists, led in particular by a peasant from Savo called Paavo Ruotsalainen (1777-1862), gained a substantial number of followers, especially from the countryside, but also from some elites and small communities (Lovery 2006: 64).

In the novel, the woman protagonist is ultimately punished by Fate for not having conformed to her role of wife and mother. Having left her home and sick child in order to attend a social gathering with Rudolph,

Elisabeth receives the news that something terrible has happened at the same moment as she is engaging in a conversation with Rudolph about divorce. When Ferdinand walks in to take her home, where two of her children lie dead, Elisabeth has just given into the idea of divorcing Leonhard:

> Rudolph såg hennes strid; den gladde honom. Med melodisk lockande stämma talade han om sin kärlek, om den sällhet, som skulle bli båda deras lott och sade sluteligen: 'Bäfva ej för svärigheterna, som denna skiljsmessa skulle medföra: burna af oss båda, bli de icke tunga. Säg blott ja, och jag skall bestyra om allt.' Elisabeth var besegrad. Hon sjönk till hans bröst och hennes läppar öppnade sig för alt framhviska det förrädiska ordet, då i detsamma en sträng röst yttrade: «Elisabeth!». (Randelin 1848: 160-1)

> (Rudolph saw her battle; it pleased him. With alluring melodic voice, he spoke of his love, of how happy they would both be and finally said: 'Don't fear the difficulties that will be caused by this divorce: if we both bear these, they won't be heavy. Say only yes, and I will take care of everything.'
> Elisabeth was defeated. She sank to his chest and her lips opened to whisper the treacherous word, when at that instant a stern voice said: «Elisabeth!».)

Despite references to Elisabeth's punishment, the novel remains ambiguous when it comes to treating gender issues. As Grönstrand effectively puts it, at the time when it was written *Den Fallna* 'was read as a declaration of the strength of the family and the institution of marriage,' while today it 'is widely regarded as one of the early novels dealing with eroticism and female adultery' (Grönstrand 2008: 50). The key to understanding this ambiguity is in the representation of a set of 'communities' and of the main characters' relationship and interaction with them. The anonymous town in which *Den Fallna* is set is shaped into a well-defined space not through a detailed physical representation of streets, houses and cityscapes, but through references to groups of people forming at least three partially intersecting communities: the nation in which the nameless town is located, the town itself and the world outside this town and nation.

Constructing National and Local Communities

There is no doubt that the novel is set in Finland not only because towards the end Finland is defined by one of the characters as the beloved home country, but also because there are several references throughout the text to Finnish culture and literature. In particular the characters are represented singing lyrical songs by the Finnish national poet Johan Ludvig Runeberg (1804-1877), who incidentally is also the author of the Finnish national anthem 'Vårt land' which was performed for the first time in 1848, the same year as *Den Fallna* was published (Randelin 1848: 17, 88). On the whole the mentions of Runeberg and of the love for the home country are in line with the national romantic movement of the time. Finland had been a Grand Duchy and part of the Russian Empire since 1809 and it was struggling to affirm its national identity. In particular, Johan Ludvig Runeberg, who was one of the so-called Turku Romantics, was trying to create with his poems a Finnish national consciousness (Branch 1998: 3-7; Laitinen 1998: 51-63).

Although we know for sure that the novel is set in Finland, the name of the town where the narration takes place is never mentioned and is always substituted by three dots. The narrator thus talks about the 'de snöbetäckta, smala gatorna i …' (Randelin 1848: 5; the snow-covered, narrow streets in …), Leonhard's 'ankomst till …' (ibid 30, arrival in) and of 'en osynlig magt som drog honom [Ferdinand] till …' (ibid 163, an invisible power which drew him [Ferdinand] to …). The three dots give the novel an aura of mystery and authenticity. Whether or not the three dots disguise the name of Randelin's birthplace, Huittinen, or the place she moved to once she got married, Uusikaupunki, is not important. What is interesting, on the other hand, is to analyse the effect created by the omission of the town's name. Through the use of the three dots the reader is induced to believe that the narrator is trying to protect the anonymity of a 'real' town and, inevitably, is tempted to keep looking for clues that could somehow disclose the identity of this location. This same principle of omission is applied when it comes to the personal names of some of the characters. The main characters are all given a name and a surname (Leonhard and Elisabeth's surname is Lindmark and Rudolph's whole name is Rudolph Berg). However, most of the other personal names are reduced to an initial, in a way similar to that employed by Fredrika Bremer in her novel *Familien H-----* (1828-1831). The families hosting the balls where Elisabeth and Rudolph meet are the 'R..s' and the 'Y..s' (ibid 77, 101). The identity of these families that are clearly part of the well-to-do society of the town is protected. The crowd of people gossiping about Elisabeth and Rudolph is also made of letters of the alphabet rather than names but in this case the use of 'fru A.,' 'fru B.,' 'fru C.' and 'fru D.' seems to have nothing to do with an attempt to hide their identity: the name of these individuals is not important, they are a group and they express the views and thoughts of the society of which Elisabeth, Rudolph and Leonhard are part (ibid 82-3).

This crowd of initials makes up the society of the town. They are all members of the growing wealthy middle class living in the urban environment. In the 1840s Finland's economy was still overwhelmingly based on agriculture. In 1811 only 40,800 people lived in cities, Turku being the largest city with 10,000 inhabitants (Wuorinen 1965: 181, 187, 193). Yet, during the first half of the nineteenth century Finland witnessed the growth of a wealthy middle class which was profiting from the slow industrialisation of the country – particularly the forestry, textile and metal working industries – and from the development of trade (Singleton 1998: 82-89). In *Den Fallna* the wealthy bourgeoisie partake in balls and promenades and follow a strict division of gender roles: husbands, all wealthy tradesmen and landowners, are the family breadwinners, while wives take care of the household and of the children. In the novel the society of this town is always paired with the adjective 'goda' (good) (Randelin 1848: 38, 56, 74, 134, 152), and whenever the 'good' people of … gather they engage in the latest gossip. The word 'rykte' (rumour) recurs every time the narrator reports dialogues among people of the town's high society:

> 'Ja, tyvärr är det så!' sade fru C. med en suck, 'och hvad värre är ändå …… men man skall ej sätta tro till alla rykten.'
> 'Rykten, hvad är det för rykten?' frågade med största ifver alla fruarna på engång.
> 'Kors vet ni inte det?' sade den tillfrågade helt stolt öfver att vara ensam egarinna af den stora hemligheten.
> 'Nej, nej! Ack berätta för all del söta Marie!' bädo alla. (ibid 82-3)

> ('Yes, unfortunately,' said Mrs. C., with a sigh, 'and what's even worse is …… but you shouldn't believe all the rumours.'
> 'Rumours, what rumours?' asked with utmost excitement all the ladies at once.
> 'Gosh, don't you know that?' said the respondent quite proud of being the only owner of the great secret.
> 'No, no! Ah, tell us by all means sweet Marie!' begged everyone)

...'s society is one where everybody knows everything about everybody. The town's good society seems to notice that Elisabeth has feelings for Rudolph even before Elisabeth herself has realised this. When Elisabeth actually falls in love with Rudolph she becomes the topic of conversation of all good men and women. The only one who seems not to notice that Elisabeth is in love with Rudolph is her husband Leonhard and, for this reason, some good members of society see it as their duty to inform the clueless husband.

The town where the novel is set is the only one that remains completely anonymous. The other towns and cities in Finland are generally mentioned using the capital initial followed by two dots. In certain cases it is not really possible to deduce the name of the location, while in other cases it is possible to make an informed guess (given the context provided in the novel, it is possible to imagine that H.. stands for Helsinki and V.. stands for Vyborg). Overall it seems that for the narrator it is less important to protect the anonymity of cities that in the novel remain only places and are not represented in fullness together with their local societies. Interestingly there is even a Finnish city that is openly mentioned throughout the novel, Åbo (Turku). Åbo is the city where Elisabeth's cousin Ferdinand is appointed as parish priest, but also the city from where Rudolph starts his last journey that brings him away from his beloved Finland.

Beyond Finland

Although most of the novel is set in Finland, there is a world outside this country: Italy and Brazil. This outside world, away from the eyes of Finnish society, is represented as healing and liberating. The Italian section of the novel is only over twenty pages long and is divided into three short chapters, namely 'The dying man,' 'Meeting with the grave,' 'Both letters.' At a first glance Italy might well appear as an exotic intermezzo. Yet the Italian section is much more than a final extravaganza before the novel draws to its conclusion. All the conflicts which have arisen in the course of the novel are solved on Italian ground.

It is difficult to establish what exactly inspired Randelin to include Italy in her novel. Unlike Bremer, who undertook a long journey to Rome, Palestine and Greece from 1860 to 1862 in order to discover – as many others had done before her – the roots of western culture and later wrote a collection of her travel impressions under the title *Life in the Ancient World* (*Livet i gamla världen*, 1862), Randelin never travelled to Italy and the short section in *Den Fallna* is all she wrote about this country. At the same time, the travelling tradition to Italy was certainly part of the cultural context in which she lived. Although very short, the Italian section in *Den Fallna* is not only of extreme significance within the plot of the novel, but it also condenses some of the features that are typical of the movement generally referred to in Swedish as *Italiaromantiken*, a term that refers to the general attitude of members of Nordic cultural circles towards Italy between the end of the eighteenth and the first half of the nineteenth century, but which continued to play a significant role throughout the century (Lagerroth 1966: 189).

The Italian journey is introduced quite abruptly and, as the novel so far has been set in Finland, it comes as a surprise. The first time the reader is warned that a change of setting is likely is at the end of the chapter 'The last meeting,' when Elisabeth and Rudolph meet for the very last time and Rudolph announces that he is going to leave Finland:

> Aldrig skall jag mera störa din frid, ty jag går nu bort för att i ett fremmade land, under en varmare, skönnare himmel, söka mig en graf, der jag i lugn får hvila ut från alla strider och qval. (ibid 201)

> (I will never again disturb your peace, as I am now leaving for a foreign country with a warmer and more beautiful sky in order to find myself a grave, where I will be able to find rest away from all the strife and sufferings.)

Rudolph is represented as he melancholically leaves Finland by boat: he will travel to Sweden and then to the South (ibid 203). The journey to the southern countries – we have in fact not yet been told that the final destination is Italy – is ambiguously referred to as a journey to a new life as well as a journey to death. Rudolph's friend, Verner – who is accompanying him on this journey – is convinced that Rudolph's health will benefit from the Southern climate:

> Du reser ju nu ut för att söka ny helsa i ett mildare klimat och säkert återvänder du helt frisk derifrån efter ett par månader, eller ett år (ibid 204).

> (You are now travelling to find new (or renewed) health in an milder climate and you will certainly come back from there completely recovered after a couple of months or a year.)

Verner thus believes that the journey to the South will have a therapeutic function, as Rudolph will recover from his illnesses and return healthy once again. This is, however, not what Rudolph seems to have in mind. To leave Finland is for Rudolph a great sorrow as he is sure that he will never recover and therefore never set foot in his beloved home country again. Italy is the destination of a self-inflicted exile. Feeling guilty of the pain he has caused to Elisabeth, Rudolph pays the ultimate price. He has imposed on himself what he considers one of the greatest punishments, namely to die abroad. His journey ends at the first stage of the journey and he is not able to continue further south to Rome, Naples and Palermo as his friend encourages him to do. Although conscious of his condition, almost with panic he realises that his life is over:

> Ja jag vill utan blygsel bekänna [...] att jeg längtar bort, bort till mitt kära hem, till det älskade Finland. Nu är det för sent, nu får jag ej mera, ty mina krafter äro slut, jag skulle ej nå hemmet, utan skulle duka under på vägen, och detta ställe är så godt som något annat också. (ibid 212)

> (Yes, with no shame I will admit [...] that I am longing for my dear home, for my beloved Finland. Now it is too late, I will never get it back, as my strength is spent, I would never be able to reach my home now, but I would only die along the way, so this place is as good as any other.)

Particularly interesting is the location where the Italian section is set, one that today is not part of Italy any more. Rudolph and Verner's journey to Italy does not go any further than Nice, their first destination, a city which remained Italian until 1860. Being part of the country that the narrator defines as 'herrlig och mild' (ibid 206, lovely and mild), Nice is immediately characterised by many of the typical Italian elements: the blue sky, the smell of oranges, the never-ending spring. Nothing is said of the local population. The narrator merely refers to a number of foreigners promenading along the streets, an army of people from England, France, Spain, Germany and the Nordic countries trying to recover from their illnesses.

As the narrator puts it, '[e]n osynlig ande för oss nu bort till en fjerran strand' (ibid, 'an invisible spirit has now brought us to a shore far away'), but for what reason? Is it only to punish Rudolph or – to be more precise – to demonstrate his repentance? Is it to enjoy, though only for a very short while, Italy's warm climate, orange-perfumed air and beauty? Why has the reader been brought to a country that the narrator herself – as she admits – has never seen but only dreamt about? After Rudolph's death, the Italian *intermezzo* seems to be coming to an end without having brought any particular development to the plot, but at the beginning of its second chapter Italy works its magic. For no clear reason, Leonhard, who is back from Brazil, stumbles by chance on Rudolph's grave in Nice. Here he meets Verner, who gives him two letters that will make him return to Finland and reunite him with his wife and daughter. Italy has fulfilled its mission: this country has solved the conflicts that triggered most of the events in the plot, thus bringing the novel to its happy ending.

While Italy heals, Brazil liberates. Not much is said about Brazil in the novel and yet this country becomes of crucial importance. Brazil is not only the place where Leonhard travels to when he finds out about his wife's affair. It is also the place where Leonhard and Elisabeth emigrate to at the end of the novel. Brazil is represented as an oasis of freedom and happiness. The positive representation of this country is hardly surprising if one considers this in relation to the novel's historical context. Between 1822 – the year of Brazil's independence from Portugal – and 1870 over 350,000 Europeans emigrated to Brazil hoping to settle and become small farmers and landowners (Lesser 2013). Brazil is the country where Elisabeth, metaphorically speaking, can stand up again after having fallen. This is the country where she can live happily ever after with her family. As the narrator concludes, nobody ever heard back from the Lindmark family after they left for Brazil, but people in Finland continued to feel sorry for Leonhard and to condemn Elisabeth for her behaviour (ibid 238).

Punishment or Freedom?

The construction of the anonymous town in which the story of Leonhard, Elisabeth and Rudolph's love triangle unravels does not have much to do with the construction of the town as a physical urban space, but of the town as a community of people. All the reader needs to know in terms of the physical space is that the novel is set in a place that has the essential elements that we would expect to find in a urban environment, namely streets, buildings, parks. On the other hand, in *Den Fallna* the narrator goes to great lengths to represent this 'imagined community,' where members of the community, despite not necessarily meeting their fellow members, are aware of their communion on a local and national level (Anderson 1983: 6). The narrator creates a network of relations among the inhabitants of this town and, in particular, among members of the middle class. People belonging to the working class, such as maids, are only briefly mentioned as part of the bourgeois world. The mechanisms driving this community where everybody knows everything about everybody become the focus of the whole narration, to the extent that by the end of the novel, the reader almost forgets that this town has no name. The name is not important but the community is. Overall, no negative remark is made about the society of this anonymous Finnish town. At the same time, the fact that all the characters involved in the adultery affair have to move away from Finland in order to regain their freedom and peace is indicative of how oppressive this kind of society can be for the individual. Rudolph has to look for a peaceful grave in Italy, while Leonhard and Elisabeth have to emigrate overseas. Furthermore, the narrator insists so much on the fact that the people of this town are good, honest, beautiful and gracious that the reader cannot help but wonder whether there is a hint of irony in her comments. On the one hand, by omitting their names the narrator wants the reader to believe that she is protecting their identity. On the other hand, by the end of the novel, we find out that all the people that are mentioned with their full names do not need to be protected any more: Rudolph and Ferdinand are dead and Leonhard and Elisabeth are in Brazil.

The anonymous town is only a fraction of the bigger community constituted by Finland. References to other Finnish cities as well as to the common cultural elements that make Finland a nation are used to remind the reader of the wider context.

There is, finally, one other community that emerges in this novel. It is the one made of those that leave their town or their country. They are still part of their community of origin, but, at the same time, they detach themselves from it, creating a community of their own. All the Northerners we meet in Italy have one thing in common: their desire to renew their life. They are all in search of something that they think their home country cannot offer them. Yet, while most of the foreigners in Nice will head home in the end, Elisabeth and Leonhard make a much more radical decision. If they want to try to reconstruct their life together, their only option is to leave their hometown for ever. Only in Brazil, away from the eyes and norms of their fellow citizens, will they be able to start afresh. Two different attitudes towards the idea of 'leaving' the community of origin become clear in the end. If we follow Rudolph's reasoning, leaving Finland, the home country, should be interpreted as the Lindmarks' greatest punishment, but if we believe Leonhard's final statement, leaving Finland is the family's last hope to find a new freedom and rise again after having fallen.

References

Alter, R. (2005): *Imagined Cities: Urban Experience and the Language of the Novel.* New Haven: Yale University Press.

Algulin, I. (1989): *A History of Swedish Literature.* Stockholm: The Swedish Institute.

Anderson, B. (1983): *Imagined Communities.* London: Verso.

Branch, M. (1998): 'Finnish Oral Poetry, Kalevala, and Kanteletar.' In G.C. Schoolfield (ed.), *A History of Finland's Literature.* Lincoln: University of Nebraska Press, pp. 3-33.

Grönstrand, H. (2008): 'In Fredrika Bremer's Footsteps: Early Women Authors and the Rise of the Novel Genre in Finland.' In *NORA - Nordic Journal of Feminist and Gender Research*, 16 (1), pp. 46-57.

Lagerroth, U.-B. (1966): 'BENGT LEWAN: Drömmen om Italien. Italien i svenska resenärers skildringar från Atterbom till Snoilsky.' In *Samlaren* 87, pp. 189-195.

Laitinen, K. (1998): 'New Beginnings, Latin and Finnish.' In G.C. Schoolfield (ed.), *A History of Finland's Literature.* Lincoln: University of Nebraska Press, pp. 34-63.

Launis, K. (1999): 'Esipuhe.' In Wendela, *Elisabet*, Kati Launis (trans.). WSYO: Helsinki, pp. 5-7.

Lesser, J. (2013): *Immigration, Ethnicity, and National Identity in Brazil, 1808 to the Present.* Cambridge *et alia*: Cambridge University Press.

Lovery, J.E. (2006): *The History of Finland.* Westport: Greenwood Press.

Mazzarella, M. (2005): 'Kvinnorna som vägrade vara milda.' *SvD*, August 16 2005. http://www.svd.se/kulturnoje/understrecket/kvinnorna-som-vagrade-vara-milda_447799.svd. Accessed August 21, 2013.

Melby, K. *et alii* (2006): *Inte ett ord om kärlek. Äktenskap och politik i Norden ca. 1850-1930.* Stockholm et alia: Makadam Förlag.

Wendela (Wendla Randelin) (1848): *Den fallna.* Åbo: J. W. Lilljas förlag.

Wendela (Wendla Randelin) (1999): *Elisabet*, Kati Launis (trans.). Helsinki: WSYO.

Wuorinen, J.H. (1965): *A History of Finland*. New York: Published for American-Scandinavian Foundation by Columbia University Press.

Note

1. A special thank you goes to the UCL Interlibrary Loan Services for their assistance in my search for a copy of this novel. Thank you also to my father, Modestino Carbone, for his help in translating relevant Finnish sources.

Texts for Change:
Constructing Feminine Citizenship

Helena Forsås-Scott
University College London & University of Edinburgh

To change discursive practice, it has been pointed out, 'is to change the world' (Frazer and Lacey 1993: 210). The potential of texts in the contexts of the relations of power that determine, at any one time, dominant and alternative discourses, is no doubt both obvious and important to the British academic who is female; whose research is in a field such as the Scandinavian one, inevitably marginal in an English-language context; who translates from Norwegian; who over a number of years has edited a leading scholarly journal in the field; and who has co-founded a small publishing venture, also centring on texts from and about the Scandinavian countries, and who is still very much involved in running it. This text is for her.

The potential of texts would have been no less important to the women who launched the Women Citizens' College at Fogelstad in Sweden in 1925, just a few years after the introduction of female suffrage, and then ran it during the early years of the welfare state, throughout the Second World War and on until the closure of the College in 1954, at a time when a notion such as women's citizenship – not to mention feminism – had become largely invisible in the Social Democratic welfare state. Not only did the five women who launched the Women Citizens' College themselves publish articles and books, with Elin Wägner being a leading journalist and novelist: in 1923 they had founded the radical weekly *Tidevarvet* (1923-36), a prerequisite of the Women Citizens' College according to Honorine Hermelin, Director of the College throughout its lifespan (Hermelin 1969: 30). Fogelstad's course participants learned about books and study skills, making good use of the College library (Eskilsson 1991: 162-64; Lindberg 2000: 170), but the focus during the weeks they spent at the College was on lectures, many of which were given by leading intellectuals of the period; on the writing of essays and minutes; and on participation in debates and discussions. Hanna Valtasaari from Rymättylä in Finland, who took part in three courses between 1938 and 1945, has highlighted the importance of the contact established between the course participants (*kursdeltagare* was the word used for teachers as well as students at Fogelstad), taking her starting-point in the first-name terms which in Sweden at the time signalled a comparatively close and relaxed relationship:

> Att alla människor borde kunna vara du med varandra så som man var på Fogelstad, det känns för mig självklart. Men hur fjärran man är från det i verkligheten! Denna verkliga demokrati var kraftströmmen i samvaron på Fogelstad, från de gemensamma måltiderna ute på fältet eller inne i tältet, till vandringarna på dagen, samkvämen på aftnarna och diskussionerna i de enskilda rummen långt in på nätterna. (Valtasaari 1956: 175-76)

> (To me it is obvious that all human beings should be able to be on first-name terms, as they were at Fogelstad. But how distant this goal is in real life! This real democracy was the power current when we were together at Fogelstad, from the joint meals out in the open or in the marquee, to the walks during the day, the social gatherings in the evening and the discussions late into the night in the course participants' rooms.)[1]

The potential of texts is fundamental to my study of the prolific output of Elin Wägner in its economic, political, social and cultural contexts, *Re-Writing the Script: Gender and Community in Elin Wägner* (2009). Here *Tidevarvet* and the Women Citizens' College are explored in Part II, 'New Communities: A New Society? 1922-47,' in the context of an alternative discourse on citizenship but – for reasons of space – without the back-up of the kind of detailed analyses of texts that characterise the sections on the work of Wägner. I now want to take this opportunity to analyse the constructions of feminine citizenship in three texts about Fogelstad and, in so doing, reaffirm the key role of texts. I am also challenging the claim about the members of the Fogelstad group made by a recent writer, Ulrika Knutson, that 'det är via deras personligheter vi har störst behållning av deras verk' (Knutson 2004: 13) (it is via their personalities that we get the most out of their work). However fascinating the personalities, the vagueness of the phrase 'ha behållning av' is troublesome; and the notion of getting the most out of something surely includes, in this context, learning about how it functioned and what it achieved, which means learning from relevant texts. My chosen texts, interestingly, all foreground the uniqueness of Fogelstad in terms of language. As in *Re-Writing the Script*, my analyses have been inspired by Chris Weedon's work on feminist poststructuralism and Mieke Bal's on narratology (see Forsås-Scott 2009: 16-23). As in my study of Wägner, I am focusing on the subject positions constructed in the texts, but in this essay, then, along with their relations to and implications for feminine citizenship. But before we move on to my chosen texts I shall provide a brief outline of the background and contribution of the College, and of some relevant theorisation of feminine citizenship.

The Women Citizens' College was founded by five members of the National Association of Liberal Women (*Frisinnade Kvinnors Riksförbund*) to provide women in Sweden – who had been able to vote for the first time in parliamentary elections in 1921 – with the knowledge, skills and confidence to function as fully-fledged citizens. The College was non-political and independent, and the courses centred on social studies – including history – and psychology and aimed, in a much-quoted phrase, to strengthen the connections between 'handens, hjärnans och hjärtats arbete' (anon. 1925: 1) (the work of the hand, the brain and the heart). The College soon became a meeting-place for intellectuals, politicians, authors, journalists, actors, artists, musicians and composers, all of whom, as course particpants, gave lectures and/or took part in discussions and other activities. It has been estimated that around 2,000 women, coming from all walks of life and increasingly also from the other Nordic countries and sometimes from further afield, attended courses at Fogelstad; and while many of them arrived with experience of working in trades unions, local authorities and local politics, others began to work in these areas following their spell at Fogelstad (Lindberg 2000: 173). Out of the 70 women elected to the Swedish *riksdag* between 1922 and 1954, no fewer than 14 were members of *Fogelstadförbundet* (Larson 1985: 232-33), the association of former course participants that was established in 1925 and continued to function until 1981 (Clayhills 1991: 119).

A key insight gained at Fogelstad, according to a course participant attending the summer course in 1938, was that 'samhället och världen behöver kvinnans intresse och insats, liksom kvinnan för egen del behöver vidga sin horisont för allt mänskligt i vår värld' (Hermelin, C. 1956: 120) (society and the world need the involvement and contributions of women, just as women need to widen their horizons to encompass all that is human in our world). This ran counter to the dominant discourse on feminine citizenship in Sweden at the time which constructed feminine citizenship within the context of marriage (see Forsås-Scott 2009: 213-23, 234-35). As the political scientist Carole Pateman has pointed out, the marriage contract is fundamental to women's oppression, subjecting the individual woman to her husband's control (Pateman 1997: 187-88). In light of the Social Democratic project launched in Sweden with the election victory in 1932, and more especially in light of the measures developed from 1934 onwards to tackle the decline in the birthrate, Pateman's analysis, as I have argued, can usefully be combined with that of Jean Bethke Elshtain who, in the summary of Birthe Siim, interprets 'the family, women's responsibility "as mothers" and their preoccupation with "immediate concerns"' not as a barrier to women's political participation but rather as the basis of their political role (Siim 2000: 34). Clearly neither marriage nor motherhood underpin the construction of feminine citizenship that emerges in the material from Fogelstad. I have suggested that the Australian ecofeminist Val Plumwood's concept of 'self-in-relationship,' which 'includes respect, benevolence, care, friendship and solidarity' (Plumwood 1993: 155), can provide a basis for reading feminine citizenship at Fogelstad (Forsås-Scott 2009: 235). The analyses that follow will test this claim on three texts about the Women Citizens' College.

My first text is a three-page leaflet, *Kvinnliga medborgarskolan vid Fogelstad* (The Women Citizens' College at Fogelstad), published in 1939 and written '[a]v rektor Honorine Hermelin' (Hermelin, H. 1939: 1) (by Honorine Hermelin, Director). A pamphlet designed to attract new course participants, the text, illustrated by a postcard of the College, foregrounds an institution which has been teaching citizenship to women throughout 14 years and 45 courses (not counting the continuation courses for members of *Fogelstadförbundet*) and whose aims are summarised in the opening quotation from the first prospectus which includes the well-known phrase about the importance of the connections between the work of the hand, the brain and the heart. Narrated in the third person, the first section is factual, setting out the history of the College, details of the pioneering course offered in 1922, *urkursen*, and information about the current range of courses and the syllabus. This section is complemented by the concluding paragraphs, also in the third person, with details about fees, scholarships and the managing committee. But the formality of the opening and the conclusion is in sharp contrast to the central section, which makes up about a third of the total text. Here the narrator switches to first-person narrative as she tries to summarise her experiences from 45 courses, and the narrative becomes both tentative, with words and phrases such as *kanske* (perhaps) and *jag tror* (I think), and enhanced by metaphors. It is no coincidence that the pivotal moment during each course is referred to in terms of language: 'den punkt, då av en kurs blivit en enhet, då undret skett och en ny harmoni framgått ur en mångfald av olikheter, då en ny insikt med *ett nytt levande språk* blivit till' (Hermelin, H., 1939: 2; my italics) (the point when a course has developed into a whole, when the miracle has happened and a new harmony has been created from a multitude of differences, when a new insight with *a new living language* has been born). Emerging as a subject, the narrator is not the authority we might expect in a text labelled as authored by the College Director but a course participant among others, crucially dependent on the members of the group. '[W]e must understand the self as *essentially* related and interdependent,' according to Plumwood, drawing here on the work of Jessica Benjamin, 'and the development of self as taking place through involvement and interaction with the other' (Plumwood 1993: 153; italics original). Referring to the role of that which is uniquely individual for the creation of a new community, the narrator in the Fogelstad prospectus continues in terms that foreground the tentative, the spoken delivery:

> Och det är detta, det har Medborgarskolan lärt mig, som är den punkt eller det djup, där själva medborgarskapet har sin rot, där den enskilda människan blir medveten om sitt egna, levande politiska ansvar och därför verkligen blir vågsam nog att ute i det praktiska livet ge sig i kast med samhälleliga uppgifter. (Hermelin, H. 1939: 2)

> (And it's this, I've learnt from the Citizens' College, that is the point or the depth where the citizenship as such is rooted, where the individual human being becomes aware of her own living political responsibility and so actually becomes brave enough to tackle societal tasks in real life.)

However brief, Hermelin's text points the way towards a construction of feminine citizenship very different from that of the dominant discourse, and Plumwood's concept of 'self-in-relationship' is clearly highly relevant to the alternative emerging here.

Can we expect an equally bold – or perhaps even bolder – construction of feminine citizenship in my second text, a reportage by Elin Wägner entitled 'Gruppens ande. På Medborgarskolan vid Fogelstad' (The Group Spirit: At the Citizens' College at Fogelstad), written ten years prior to Hermelin's pamphlet and published in *Tidevarvet* on 6 July 1929? Wägner was reporting on the continuation course and the annual meeting of *Fogelstadförbundet*; but arguably the more open-ended and dialogical genre of the essay is as relevant a genre categorisation here as that of the reportage.

Wägner was just over half-way through her writing career when she wrote 'Gruppens ande,' and Birgitta Wistrand has singled out this text as defining the themes that 'framstår som avgörande' (stand out as decisive) for the remainder of her output. However, just one page into her three-page summary of the text Wistrand undermines her reading by pinpointing as one of Wägner's 'grundteser' (fundamental theses), foregrounded in the text, that of 'att inte arbeta efter ett fast ideal' (Wistrand 2006: 156-57) (not to work according to a predetermined ideal). As I have shown repeatedly (Forsås-Scott 2003, 2007, 2009), Wägner's texts are first and foremost exploratory, testing positions rather than defining and idealising them, and the dialogic form of many of them ensures that the narratee, 'the receiver of the narrated text' (Bal 1999: 63), becomes prominently involved in their innovative projects. Wägner's texts cannot all be labelled feminist, but I would argue that a considerable number of them illustrate the potential of the feminist text as outlined by Elizabeth Grosz: such a text 'must [...] help, in whatever way, to facilitate the production of new and perhaps unknown, unthought discursive spaces – new styles, modes of analysis and argument, new genres and forms – that contest the limits and constraints currently at work in the regulation of textual production and reception' (Grosz 1995: 23).

'Gruppens ande' sets out the context provided by the College, before going on to survey the issues discussed during the course and at the annual meeting, and to provide a close-up of a debate on heredity. The text is narrated partly in the third person but mostly in the first person plural: the pronoun *vi* (we) predominates. And in common with Hermelin's text it turns language into a central metaphor: 'Det är gruppens andes språk vi alla lärt oss att tala och hjälpt till att bilda' (Wägner 1929: 1; 1999: 115) (It is the language of the group spirit that we have all learnt to speak and helped develop). In Wägner's text, however, the centrality of language hinges on a paradox, as the narrative raises the possibility of it being nothing but a failed attempt to capture the group spirit – 'ty vad vore det för ande, som läte sig plockas in i en låda av ord?' (Wägner 1929: 1; 1999: 114) (what kind of spirit would allow itself to be shut into a box made of words?). Words are not sufficient and yet the narrative continues, its prominently tentative quality and the questions, including an entire paragraph consisting of questions one third of the way into the text, irresistibly engaging the narratee. This text represents a considerable development of the participation characteristic of the middle section of that of Hermelin, and despite the fact that Elin Wägner's name appeared immediately under the title of her text – which took up the three central columns at the top of the front page of *Tidevarvet* – the subject that emerges is by no means that of the experienced journalist and major novelist. There is no *jag* (I) in this text; instead the subject constructed in the markedly tentative narrative of 'Gruppens ande' is a collective *vi* (we) which extends not just to the participants at the annual meeting and the continuation course but also to the narratee.

The effect of this sense of community and its implications for the construction of feminine citizenship are illustrated by a summary of the debate on heredity versus the environment. A (male) scientist had argued that the social and political structure in late-1920s Sweden was the product of hereditary factors: 'De skikt som nu är ovanpå och ledande är det tillfölje sina förnämliga arvsfaktorer' (Wägner 1929: 4; 1999: 117) (The strata that are currently on top and in charge are so as a result of their superior hereditary qualities). In the debate the argument is quickly demolished with reference to a combination of modern psychology and life experience, but then the discussion is radically expanded as the course participants proceed to redefine the concept of *miljö* (environment) beyond childhood experiences, education and the influence of peers and teachers:

> Man vill söka få in däri hela den värld, den tysta och osynliga miljö som påverkar oss rakt genom huden, i vilken vårt väsens finaste trådar är nedsänkta, den gemensamma mänsklighetens själ, detta som färgar oss liksom ljuset färgar klorofyllen i växtens blad. Det var vissheten om den livliga växelverkan mellan personligheten och det omgivande universum, som gjorde det omöjligt att binda oss vid någon av de motsatta teorierna[.] (Wägner 1929: 4; 1999: 118)

> (We wanted to include the entire world, the silent and invisible environment that is affecting us through our skin, in which

the thinnest threads of our being are immersed, the soul of all humankind, that which colours us just as light colours the chlorophyll in the leaves of the plant. It was this certainty of the lively interdependence between the individual and the surrounding universe that made it impossible to restrict ourselves to either of the opposing theories).

Dating as it does from 1929, this analysis is strikingly bold and perceptive. The role for the key concepts of Western culture of what Plumwood terms the 'line of fracture between reason and nature' and its gendered implications have been extensively investigated since around 1980, with major contributions from Carolyn Merchant (*The Death of Nature: Women, Ecology, and the Scientific Revolution*, 1980) and Genevieve Lloyd (*The Man of Reason: 'Male' and 'Female' in Western Philosophy*, 1984), with all three theorists highlighting the significance of power. Men as well as women, Plumwood has argued, 'must challenge the dualised conception of *human* identity and develop an alternative culture which fully recognises human identity as continuous with, not alien from, nature' (Plumwood 1993: 36; italics original). However, while investigating the reason - nature dualism in greater depth than Hermelin's much shorter text, that of Wägner, by definition, can do little more than flag up the fact that a different kind of society must result from this alternative citizenship: the new social order 'måste läras och levas fram' (Wägner 1929: 4; 1999: 116) (must develop through life and experience). In Wägner's text the prominence of the narratee has paved the way for her involvement and thus, arguably, for a kind of narrative version of the *kamratsamhälle* (society of comrades) (Wägner 1929: 4; 1999: 116), a term that perhaps – however tentatively – conveys something of the project the course participants have been working towards.

My final text is considerably longer than the previous ones, 42 pages of what might be labelled an autobiographical fragment, 'En tjuguårings möte med Fogelstadskolan' (A twenty-year-old encounters the College at Fogelstad), written by Ragna Kellgren (1913-1994) who took part in the summer course in 1934 and became an active member of *Fogelstadförbundet*. Kellgren went on to publish poetry and prose fiction and also edited a volume about *Tidevarvet*. The text I am going to discuss appeared in her volume, *Klasslöst. Tre veckor i nutid och forntid vid Fogelstad kvinnliga medborgarskola* (1973; Free from Class(es): Three Weeks in the Present and Past at the Women Citizens' College at Fogelstad). There is nothing to confirm that 'En tjuguårings möte' was actually written during the summer course in 1934 although the text, as I shall show, does foreground on-the-spot immediacy; in contrast the 'Efterskrift' (Afterword), four and a half pages, would seem to have been written in 1972 (Kellgren 1973: 245). To my knowledge, Kellgren's text has not been analysed before; indeed, there does not seem to be any published work on any of Kellgren's texts.

In 'En tjuguårings möte,' the narrator points out, the course participants are fictitious characters: the exception, she claims, is the narrative 'I' (Kellgren 1973: 205n1). But this is a narrative 'I' in a context where it soon becomes apparent that '"själva levandet", "det praktiska levandet", [...] inte fanns färdigt varje morgon som ett plagg att klä på sig' (Kellgren 1973: 211) ('actual living,' 'practical living,' [...] was not ready and waiting every morning like a garment to be put on), and where the construction of subjectivity is consequently foregrounded. My analysis will draw on Susan Stanford Friedman's distinctions between male and female autobiographies that enabled Friedman to define women's autobiographies in terms of 'relationality,' and more specifically in terms of a set of concepts that Georges Gusdorf in his seminal work on autobiography in the 1950s had dismissed from autobiographical selves: identification, interdependence, and community (Friedman 1998: 75). My focus will be on how Kellgren's text uses language to construct identification, interdependence, and community, and thus on the kind of feminine citizenship that emerges in this text constructing a narrative 'I' participating in a course on women's citizenship at a time when the 'I' herself is on the verge of the age of majority, 21.

We have seen how both Hermelin's and Wägner's texts use the metaphor of 'a new language' to convey the impact and potential of the community of course participants. Kellgren's text, by contrast, *is* the new language. With its profusion of direct speech, frequent use of ellipsis and only occasional overviews, it seems to have the effect of plunging us straight into life at Fogelstad. During the festivities on the final evening, the character called Honorine Hermelin explicitly confirms the creative role of the interdependence of speaker and audience (Kellgren 1973: 233), but the interdependence of the individual course participant and the community has effectively been foregrounded throughout as fundamental to the '"kokprocess" på olikheter' (Kellgren 1973: 240) (process of 'boiling' differences together) which the narrative 'I' can finally survey, which she realises has brought her into a 'förut okänd form av vid gemenskap' (ibid) (previously unknown form of extensive community), and whose plans for humankind and society do not fit within the 'föreskrivna, handlagda, uppritade och färdiga system inom vilket männen är fulländade, färdiga – bundna' (Kellgren 1973: 241) (prescribed, managed, marked out and finalised system within which the men are perfect, complete – confined).

Intense sense impressions are central to Kellgren's text. One passage details the leftovers on the dinner table: 'Förbluffad blev jag stående och betraktade vad som låg på faten, rättare den tavla jag såg: självlysande ryggraden och huvudet av en fisk, blomkålsstjälkar, ett par gröna blad, urkavd ost, koppen med lindblomste ur den gamla kopparkannan' (Kellgren 1973: 217) (Astonished, I remained and looked at what was on the plates, or rather at the painting I was seeing: the luminous backbone and head of a fish, cauliflower stalks, a couple of green leaves, the remains of a piece of cheese, the cup of limeflower tea from the old copper kettle). Plumwood has contrasted the 'self-enclosed world of meaningless and silent objects [that] exclusionary, monological and commodity thinking creates' with '[a] world perceived in communicative and narrative terms' (Plumwood 2002: 230); and it is significant that the Fogelstad world represented in Kellgren's text repeatedly emphasises the role of the present and the moment, taking us straight into what one of the course participants refers to as 'det stiglösa, lödiga nuet' (Kellgren 1973: 233) (the uncharted, consummate present) of new possibilities. But if there are conspicuous pointers here towards what Plumwood has termed 'the relational self' and thus towards a feminine citizenship very different from that of the dominant discourse, Kellgren's text arguably takes us a crucial step further in its representation of the atmosphere at Fogelstad:

> I den upphörde att finnas – till min förvåning – något avgränsat andligt och något avgränsat materiellt. Brödet lyste. Marken var något lika fint som själen. En människas själ lyste genom kroppen, en helhet tillsammans. Blommorna levde som aldrig förr jag sett. Också tingen hade liv. Av allt levande syntes ingen, och inget, på en trappform högre - lägre – sådan var den fulla dagern. (Kellgren 1973: 213)

> (In this – to my astonishment – the boundary between the spiritual and the material ceased to exist. The bread was shining. The ground was as exquisite as the soul. The soul of the human being was shining through the body, the two fusing into an entity. The flowers were alive as I had never seen them before. The objects,

too, were alive. Nobody and no living being appeared as if on a ladder higher – lower – such was the full light of day.)

What Kellgren's text represents here in fact goes well beyond the kind of feminine citizenship that was defined in the publicity for Fogelstad or has been located in the texts analysed above: pointing straight into the environmental crisis of the twenty-first century, Kellgren's text constructs what Plumwood (and others) have termed 'an ecological self', a self 'in non-instrumental relationship to nature' (Plumwood 1993: 154), and thus adds a new strand to the alternative discourse on citizenship that we have been tracing here.

The ways in which texts construct meanings and subject positions for the reader, Chris Weedon has emphasised, have political implications that do not just apply to the historical context but also to the present (Weedon 1997: 162). The Social Democratic construction of feminine citizenship, launched in 1928 and determined by the framework of the concept of *folkhemmet* (the home of the people) (see Forsås-Scott 2009: 213-14) with its emphasis on the housewife and mother, differed sharply from the alternative construction that emerges in these three texts about Fogelstad. The 'self-in-relationship' points the way towards a society quite unlike the capitalist welfare state taking shape in Sweden, instead signalling, in Kellgren's text, towards what Plumwood has termed 'the rationality of the mutual self' which, she has explained, 'could begin to treasure the incomparable riches of diversity in the world's cultural and biological life, and to participate with earth others in the great dialogues of the community of life' (Plumwood 1993: 196).

What, then, do these texts about Fogelstad mean in the present? Lena Eskilsson, an intellectual historian who has written the only doctoral dissertation specifically about the College, ends up effectively dismissing what she terms 'Fogelstadidealen', the ideals developed and fostered at Fogelstad, as 'en liten slingrande stig som snart glömdes bort och växte igen' (Eskilsson 1991: 211) (a narrow winding path that soon became forgotten and overgrown). It is true that the Women Citizens' College, along with *Tidevarvet*, were neglected in the history of the women's movement in Sweden that Lydia Wahlström published in 1933 (*Den svenska kvinnorörelsen. Historisk översikt*) (Manns 2003: 162), and also that surprisingly little research has been done on the College despite the wide range of archive material available, especially in KvinnSam at Göteborg University Library. Developing the argument from Manns, Ebba Witt-Brattström and Lena Lennerhed have claimed that the history of Fogelstad was effectively written with Elin Wägner's proto-ecofeminist pamphlet *Väckarklocka* (1941; Alarm Clock) (Witt-Brattström and Lennerhed 2003: 8); and as I have demonstrated, the narration of this text certainly helps foreground the construction of an alternative community (Forsås-Scott 2009: 297-316). What is remarkable is the extent to which the construction of an alternative feminine citizenship, so prominent in the three very much shorter texts analysed above, similarly points the way towards a radically different community – and now does so with all the more urgency in a world facing far-reaching environmental changes with possibly devastating consequences. The Women Citizens' College at Fogelstad may have closed down well over half a century ago, but the texts associated with the project certainly have not lost their potential for change.

References

Anon. (1925): 'Kvinnliga medborgarskolan i Fogelstad.' In *Tidevarvet*, 21 Feb.: 1.

Bal, M. (1999; 1997): *Narratology: Introduction to the Theory of Narrative*. 2nd ed. Toronto, Buffalo, London: University of Toronto Press.

Clayhills, H. (1991): *Kvinnohistorisk uppslagsbok*. Stockholm: Rabén & Sjögren.

Eskilsson, L. (1991): *Drömmen om kamratsamhället. Kvinnliga medborgarskolan på Fogelstad 1925-35*. Stockholm: Carlssons.

Forsås-Scott, H. (2003): '"Tänk själv, säger denna bok." Om Elin Wägners *Väckarklocka'*. In Witt-Brattström, E. and L. Lennerhed (eds): *Kvinnorna skall göra det! Den kvinnliga medborgarskolan vid Fogelstad – som idé, text och historia*. Huddinge: Södertörns högskola, Samtidshistoriska institutet, pp. 23-48.

Forsås-Scott, H. (2007): 'Förord.' In E. Wägner, *Väckarklocka*. Stockholm: Albert Bonniers förlag, pp. 5-26.

Forsås-Scott, H. (2009): *Re-Writing the Script: Gender and Community in Elin Wägner*. London: Norvik Press.

Frazer, E. and Nicola L. (1993): *The Politics of Community: A Feminist Critique of the Liberal-Communitarian Debate*. Toronto, Buffalo: University of Toronto Press.

Friedman, S.S. (1998): 'Women's Autobiographical Selves: Theory and Practice.' In S. Smith and J. Watson (eds), *Women, Autobiography, Theory: A Reader*. Madison: University of Wisconsin Press, pp. 72-82.

Grosz, E. (1995): *Space, Time, and Perversion: Essays on the Politics of Bodies*. New York and London: Routledge.

Hermelin, C. (1956): 'Varför kom du till Fogelstad?' In E. Björkman-Goldschmidt (ed.), *Fogelstad. Berättelsen om en skola*. Stockholm: P.A. Norstedt & Söners förlag, pp. 112-122.

Hermelin, H. (1939): *Kvinnliga medborgarskolan vid Fogelstad*. Stockholm: Saxon & Lindströms tryckeri.

Hermelin, H. (1956): 'På avsiktsfri mark.' Orig. publ. 1935. In E. Björkman-Goldschmidt (ed.), *Fogelstad. Berättelsen om en skola*. Stockholm: P.A. Norstedt & Söners förlag, pp. 202-204.

Hermelin, Honorine (1969): *Från Ulfåsa till Fogelstad. Samlade fragment*. Stockholm: Natur & Kultur.

Kellgren, Ragna (1973): 'En tjuguårings möte med Fogelstadskolan.' In R. Kellgren, *Klasslöst. Tre veckor i nutid och forntid vid Fogelstad Kvinnliga Medborgarskola. Ur kursprotokoll och egen erfarenhet*. Julita: Kvinnliga medborgarskolan vid Fogelstad, pp. 203-247.

Knutson, U. (2004): *Kvinnor på gränsen till genombrott. Grupporträtt av Tidevarvets kvinnor*. Stockholm: Albert Bonniers förlag.

Larson, M. (1985): *De arbetade för fred. Kvinnoföreningar i Sverige med fred på sitt program 1898-1940*. Stockholm: Författares bokmaskin.

Lindberg, B. (2000): *Kvinnor – vakna, våga! En studie kring pedagogen och samhällsvisionären Honorine Hermelin Grønbech*. Lund: University of Lund, Dept. of Education.

Manns, U. (2003): 'Så skriver vi historia. Den svenska kvinnorörelsen ur ett historiografiskt perspektiv.' In Witt-Brattström, E. and L. Lennerhed (eds): *Kvinnorna skall göra det! Den kvinnliga medborgarskolan vid Fogelstad – som idé, text och historia*. Huddinge: Södertörns högskola, Samtidshistoriska institutet, pp. 143-74.

Pateman, C. (1997; 1988): *The Sexual Contract*. Cambridge: Polity Press.

Plumwood, V. (1993): *Feminism and the Mastery of Nature*. London and New York: Routledge.

Plumwood, V. (2002): *Environmental Culture: The Ecological Crisis of Reason*. London and New York: Routledge.

Siim, B. (2000): *Gender and Citizenship: Politics and Agency in France, Britain and Denmark*. Cambridge: Cambridge University Press.

Valtasaari, H. (1956):'Fogelstad och jag själv.' In Björkman-Goldschmidt, E. (ed.): *Fogelstad. Berättelsen om en skola*. Stockholm: P.A. Norstedt & Söners förlag, pp. 175-177.

Weedon, C. (1997): *Feminist Practice and Poststructuralist Theory*. 2nd ed. Oxford and Cambridge, MA: Blackwell.

Wistrand, B. (2006): *Elin Wägner i 1920-talet. Rörelseintellektuell och internationalist*. Uppsala: University of Uppsala, Dept. of Literature.

Witt-Brattström, E. and L. Lennerhed (2003): 'Förord.' In Witt-Brattström, E. and L. Lennerhed (eds): *Kvinnorna skall göra det! Den kvinnliga medborgarskolan vid Fogelstad – som idé, text och historia*. Huddinge: Södertörns högskola, Samtidshistoriska institutet, pp. 4-8.

Wägner, E. (1929):'Gruppens ande. På Medborgarskolan vid Fogelstad.' *Tidevarvet*, 6 July, 1, 4. Reprinted in Wägner, Elin (1999): *Vad tänker du, mänsklighet? Texter om feminism, fred och miljö*, ed. H. Forsås-Scott. Stockholm: Norstedts, pp. 114-119.

Note

1. All translations are my own (HFS).

Love, Exile, Loss and Liberation:
Two Swedish Writers of Iranian Background

Ingeborg Kongslien
Universitetet i Oslo

Migrants turned writers in Sweden and other Nordic countries during the last four decades have slowly acquired recognition, concurrent with public discourse on migrant and multicultural issues and with the growth – quantitatively and qualitatively – in the literary output of this new literary tradition. They write from a position between places, histories and cultural practices, and their language of stories and poems is a second language. In Azade Seyhan's words in the introduction to *Writing Outside the Nation*: 'Modern narratives of migrancy, exile, and displacement have generated new epistemologies of bilingualism, language change, and translation' (Seyhan 2002: 20). These are texts by translingual writers, i.e. those writing in a different language than their mother tongue or first language, and thus they belong to a growing international literary phenomenon in an age marked by migration and globalization. Parallels are many in American literature, for example Julia Alvarez (background: Dominican Republic) and Bharati Mukherjee (background: India), in British literature, Buchi Emecheta (background: Nigeria), and in German literature, Emilie Özdamar (background: Turkey), to name just a few women who are translingual writers. Writers of what can be named second or third generation, but who feature their migrant background and bicultural stance, are abundant, in American literature and British literature in particular, for example Zadie Smith of Jamaican background, but increasingly also on the international scene.

The Women and a New Language

Within this new Scandinavian tradition, two Swedish writers of Iranian background have established themselves in Swedish literature during the last decade and a half. They are women, novelists Fateme Behros and Azar Mahloujian – the latter also a writer of essays and travel journals. Fateme Behros has been quite successful in gaining a readership in Sweden, and with three novels to her name written within a paradigm of contemporary realistic feminist writings, she has given voice to the exile and migrant experiences.[1] Azar Mahloujian's three novels also deal with topics of cultural encounters; moreover, her travel report from present day Iran and her presentation of the Parsees in India in the historical context dating back to the seventh and eighth century add considerable dimensions to her reflections on exile and identity.[2]

The novels by Behros and Mahloujian are representations of exile and identity negotiations, of translingual imagination and repositioning, from women's point of view. The poet Jila Mossaed, also with Iranian background, can serve well as an appropriate point of departure, with her positive and forceful attitude towards her new language and accepting it as a creative challenge:

> Lär mig ordens rötter/låt mig leka med dina ord/låt mig skapa/nya konstiga meningar med dem/låt mig ge orden/nya färger/nya dimensioner/låna mig ditt språk/dina substantiv/låt mig ta dem med på en äventyrlig resa. (Mossaed 1997: 69)[3]

> (Teach me the origins of the words/let me play with your words/ let me create/new and strange meanings with them/let me give the words/new colours/new dimensions/lend me your language/ your nouns/let me take them on an adventurous journey).

These writers adopted Swedish as their literary language after a little over a decade in their new homeland. This is of course in order to reach the general literary public, but also testifies to their facing the challenge of mastering a second language to express the dislocation and relocation experience. In a study of transcultural American autobiographies, Aneta Pavlenko concludes that writing in a second language becomes 'the locus of self-translation' and that such narratives represent 'ideal discursive spaces for repositioning' and for 'negotiation of identity' (Pavlenko 2001: 324, 339). Although Pavlenko's focus is autobiographies, I think her perspectives are valid for this poetic and fictional material as well. Mahloujian's first book was labled 'an autobiographical novel,' and Behros' second book has a peritext stating that 'the characters do not exist in real life and the names are fictitious,' but hopefully, in spite of that, readers will be able to recognize both themselves and others.

This does not mean that I suggest reading these novels in a reductionist manner, just as testimonies from writers with foreign-sounding names and migrant experiences, but within the context of translingualism and transculturalism to acknowledge their particular epistemologies and discursive spaces.

The most comprehensive study of Swedish writings by authors of migrant backgrounds is done by Lars Wendelius (2002). Regarding women writers, he states that the material he has studied shows a 'pendling mellan betoning av migrationsprocessens destruktiva och emancipatoriska verkningar för kvinnornas vidkomande' (Wendelius 2002: 139) (wavering between stressing the migration process' destructive and emancipatory effects regarding women). He also refers to and makes a comparison with Scandinavian-American literature's depiction of women which to a large extent showed them as suffering from homesickness and problems of adjustment.[4] The Iranian women turned Swedish writers that are in focus here, from a presumably traditional and patriarchal society and entering into a liberal western society like Sweden, depict in their texts the process of migration and exile, of cultural encounters and identity formation, of new lives and liberation.

Two Stories of Flight and Exile

The respective debut novels of Behros and Mahloujian, *Som ödet vill* (1997) and *De sönderrivna bilderna* (1995), both describe situations of political oppression and persecution as backgrounds for migration from Iran. Behros' tale is a broad realistic novel about a family with three children, while Mahloujian's book, as mentioned, presented as 'an autobiographical novel' and originally for safety's sake published under a pseudonym, consists of short chapters depicting the flight of a single woman, as well as incorporating the narrator's reflections of a more essayistic character. Both texts vividly portray strenuous physical and emotional encounters, including delays in transition countries on their way to Sweden. Both books clearly display a double perspective or double consciousness, thematically as well as structurally. Both narratives convincingly unfold processes of dislocation and relocation.

Behros' novel has a prologue, a peritext, naming it 'en sann historia' (a true story), 'upplevt' (experienced), 'sett eller hört' (seen or heard), but 'ändrade och färgade [...] innan jag berättade ur mina minnens skattkammare' (changed and colored [...] before I narrated out of the treasure throve of my memories) (Behros 1997: 7). The prologue is set in italics; one can ask whether it is the author or the narrator that speaks. Close to three quarters of the novel details the dramatic journey over the border through the mountains between Iran and Turkey and a prolonged stay in Istanbul prior to arriving in Sweden where 'vi drack te och firade. [...] det smakade fridom' (261) (we drank tea and celebrated. [...] it tasted [of] freedom). But freedom is soon mixed with sorrows – family disintegration, loneliness, the couple drifting apart and the children drifting into the Swedish society, language change and problematic behaviour. In spite of this, the third person narrator and protagonist pushes ahead, gets her 'kemtvätt' (dry cleaning), her small business up and running. She is temporarily set back by the news of the assassination of prime minister Olof Palme, experiencing a strong feeling of sorrow and abandonment:

> Någon hade skutit Palme. [...] Jag hade förlorat min beskyddare och var nu både faderlös och hjälplös. [...] Han hade lämnat mig, oss och Sverige, vi bar på samma sorg. (338)

> (Someone had shot Palme. [...] I had lost my protector and was now both fatherless and helpless. [...] He had left me, us and Sweden, we were burdened with the same grief.)[5]

This political appropriation of Palme sees him as a guarantee of freedom and human rights, and thereby for the immigrant's existence and new life in Sweden. The disintegration of her family makes her lonely and unhappy, but her work and the prospect that her best friend will come from Iran and visit her, as well as the arrival of the Scandinavian spring, give her some hope. Hearing the Swedish national anthem, she sings along, but is still not quite sure if she wants to affirm the lines that say 'Jag vill leva, jag vill dö i Norden' (357) (I want to live, I want to die in the North); it is like choosing one child over the other, the narrator states, and concludes that, so far, she will leave that decision to fate. How such a development proceeds is the theme of Behros' next novel.

Mahloujian's book *De sönderrivna bilderna* consists of 40 short chapters, distinctly divided up in two equal parts. An introductory page, apparently written many years later, indicates that the news that a young man from her past has died during a flight is the immediate impetus for the writing project. The first main part is a chronological and day to day account, sometimes hour to hour, of the narrator's flight from Iran, over the mountains, freezing cold and dangerous, to Turkey. The detailed descriptions of her fellow travelers as well as helpers, of landscapes and events along the way, told in the present tense, lends a mode of desperation as well as suspense to the presentation. A short stay in Istanbul and three desperate months in Belgrade, with many attempts at finding a country that will receive this refugee, finally end with a happy arrival in Sweden, where even the police shake hands with you! The second half of the book recounts the narrator's first years in Sweden, alternating with chapters about her past life in Iran. Of a more essayistic nature, these chapters show her eager attempts at getting ahead in the new society, as well as some critical observations of it, for example of not being looked upon as a free and independent woman because of being from the Middle East, and of how adapting to Swedish ways changes her.

A few years later, both of these writers published novels that depicted women's lives in Sweden – integration processes, identity negotiations and new attachments. Fateme Behros' *Fångarnas kör* and Azar Mahloujian's *Älskar du någon annan?*, published 2001 and 2002 respectively, were for each writer her second book and for both, a step away from the strong autobiographical attachments of their first books, although their new texts are still inspired by their double perspectives and their narratives are discursive spaces for repositioning and for negotiation of identity, to use Pavlenko's characteristics quoted earlier.

To Find Your Space and Your Voice

In *Fångarnas kör*, an introductory chapter has the first person narrator and protagonist Shabtab experiencing a nightmare about being dragged down and obliterated. The phone calls her back from her sleep, but only to an unpleasant proposition from a male, fellow Iranian who looks upon her as a fallen women since she has changed from a traditional to a 'modern' woman during her years in Sweden. Reflecting on her dream and how to interpret it, whether to ask for help from Freud or her paternal grandmother, she soon discards Freud since he is a European and she longs for her dead grandmother who would have properly understood the Muslim woman. This opening of the novel underscores two important aspects of it: the Iranian-Swedish in-between position of Shabtab and the double consciousness inherent in her development depicted in the narrative, that is, from adhering to the traditional Muslim values of her background to adopting the liberty that is offered to her and that is even necessary in order to find her place in the Swedish context. Her grandmother states what is best for a woman: 'Så, en vacker dag kommer han. En ung ryttare på en hvit häst [...]. [...] Gud äskar kvinnor som lyder sina män.' (Behros 2001: 16) (Then, one day he comes. A young rider on a white horse [...]. [...] God loves women that obey their men.) In her new, Western context, it does not quite work that way, which is actually what this narrative is about. But, her grandmother also says that a woman has strength and needs knowledge to use it, which turns out to be the case as well.

Shabtab leaves Iran for Sweden to enter into an arranged marriage with an Iranian man who has already settled there. The backdrop is the political upheavals, one brother was killed opposing the shah, the other brother is totally supporting the present mullah's regime. Her husband is not quite as young or as good looking as she had hoped for, but she is reasonably content and throws herself into learning Swedish and adapting to her new life. But her man turns out to be wholly traditional, in spite of his years in Sweden: 'Kvinnan i mitt liv måste hålla sig innför min kultur. Hon skall lyda mig.' (123) (My women must adhere to my culture. She will obey me.) They drift apart; she goes out one night on her own and is attacked and raped which leads her to attempting suicide and slipping into insanity, and a long period of recovery has her reconsidering her entire existence. Being in a group with a few other women, also hurt and suppressed in different ways, she is slowly able to return to life. For all of them, it is about women's honour and women's restricted space. Throughout, she continues school and gets ahead in knowledge of both language and society. She reflects:

> Många invandrarkvinnor, [...] var här ofta mycket duktigare än sina män. De lärde sig språket bättre och anpassade sig fortare till det svenska samhället.Varför? Det visste jag inte. Kanhända at de hade fått status. De hade fått det som deras män nyss hade förlorat. (212)

> (Many immigrant women, [...] were often much more clever than their men here. They learned the language better and adapted more quickly to Swedish society. Why? I didn't know. Maybe they had obtained status. They had obtained that which their men had just lost.)

This type of essayistic reflection is quite frequent in the book, summing up what the narrative discourses have mediated, as is the case here. Sometimes this comes at the expense of the aesthetics of the literary text, sometimes it strengthens the political aspect.

The second stage of Shabtab's life has her venturing out into society more, with mixed results. She takes pride in being a good student and mastering the language. She notices differences in ways of talking and reacts to that:

> Det ar rolig att se svenskarnas min när de hörde två invandrare som talade med varandra. «Kommer du i morgon till mig?» «Får se, jag vet inte. Jag kanskje inte hinner!» «Du måste komma! Annars dödar jeg dig!» «Nei, snälla du! Döda mig inte! Ja älskar ju dig!" " Okej jag kommer, bara du lovar att inte jobba för mycket.» (226)

> (It was fun to see how Swedes reacted when they heard two immigrants talking to each other. "Will you come and see me tomorrow?" "We'll see, I'm not sure maybe I don't have the time!" "You have to come! If not, I'll kill you!" Oh no, please! Don't kill me! I love you!" "Ok, I'll come, just promise me that you don't work too hard".

She goes to the library, reads Swedish books, and attends appearances by Swedish authors. She tries hard to find a room for herself within the urban space of Uppsala, and one day she even finds love in the person of the Swedish Hans. For a short period, she experiences a relationship of both emotional and intellectual fulfillment, as well as equality, being a free and modern woman. But with that new status, she has to face all aspects of it. Hans avoids taking responsibility when she gets pregnant and forces her to terminate the pregnancy, and eventually ventures back to his ex-wife and children. This time, although unhappy, the protagonist takes charge and arranges a skillful seduction scene, but at its height, leaves the man high and dry; she humiliates him instead of being humiliated. After this, she devotes herself to her studies, to her women friends, and to finding her feet.

Throughout the narrative, the telling of her Swedish story is continuously in a double perspective with her Iranian past, through communication with her family, and when that is broken because of her walking away from her marriage, through remembering and thus communicating with many of her now deceased grandmother's views and sayings about life and love. Edward Said, well known for his seminal work *Orientalism* (1978), has written a lot about exile, and his use of the term 'contrapuntal' focuses on this double perspective in multicultural literature: 'Thus both the old and the new environments are vivid, actual, occurring together contrapuntally' (Said 2000: 186). In Behros' novel, the Iranian elements form 'a voice' within the basically Swedish discourse, and this voice is important in the identity negotiations of the main character's gradual integration into the new society, while all the way retaining a double vision. And this is Shabtab's position when she is about to enter into her third relation to a man, this time to Ramin, a minor character who has surfaced a few times throughout the text. He is characterized as 'trevlig' (nice), coming from the same area back home and is 'lika gammal som jag' (233) (the same age as me). The happy ending that is indicated seems to rest on equality and on balanced positions between the old and the new homeland for both; neither was part of the earlier relationships.

An interesting narrative self-reflection occurs towards the end of the book: 'Ibland när jag satt ensam och skärskådade mitt eget liv, verkade det som om jag läste en bok' (316) (Sometimes, when I sat alone and thought through my life, it was as if I was reading a book). And when Shabtab now has been able to reposition herself, she feels empowered to give voice to both herself and others who have been oppressed and restricted: 'Jag skall skriva en bok. [...] Den skall heta 'Fångarnas kör' [...] (338) (I will write a book. [...] It will be titled 'The prisoners' choir' [...]). The reference to Verdi's opera is clear, but from the context, it seems that it is the voices of the vulnerable women, Shabtab and the other immigrant women around her, that she will give voice to. Moreover, the idea to use a narrative to understand the story of your life is frequently featured in multicultural literature, both in fiction and autobiographical writings. It is found with several Scandinavian writers of migrant backgrounds, as well as with many contemporary American writers of what Pavlenko calls 'crosscultural autobiographies' as mentioned above. For example, Eva Hoffman (1999: 10) talks about exile experiences as 'a powerful narrative shaper.'

In this story of exile and integration, of loss and liberation, the individual seems to be able to claim her new space through the narrative. And in addition to the political appropriation found in Behros' earlier book, in the name of Olof Palme, in this book there is a cultural appropriation. The female protagonist, an immigrant to Sweden in the 1980s, feels a kinship with Kristina, the emigrant from Sweden depicted by Vilhelm Moberg, who becomes a farm wife in pioneering Minnesota in the 1850s and 1860s: 'Jag var djupt tagen av denne kvinnas [Kristina från Duvemåla] upplevelser i et främmande land. Vi delade saknad och längtan. (341) (I was deeply moved by this woman's experiences in a foreign country. We shared loss and longing.) Behros here equates her female protagonist with a character from one of Swedish literature's canonical works, anchored in Swedish history, also mediated in the modern form of a musical.[6] Towards the end, Shabtab also listens to a modern Swedish pop singer, Eva Dahlgren (332). All of these references underscore her attachment to her new existence, and from this position, she is able to reconnect with her Iranian past, talking to her mother on the phone and sipping her tea.

Love, Loss and the Double Perspective

Azar Mahloujians *Älskar du någon annan?* (2002) is a tightly structured narrative with a third person narrator telling a bitter-sweet love story anchored in Iran in the years leading up to the fall of the shah in the late 1970s, and this story is then framed by and interspersed with the tale of the random reconnection of the two main characters in Sweden in the early 1990s.[7] The novel consists of seventeen chapters. In alternate chapters the setting is Teheran, constituting about three-quarters of the text; in alternate chapters, including the frame, the setting is Stockholm. Thus, a double perspective is its basic structure.

The contemporary Swedish setting has Shamsi, the female protagonist and a refugee form Iran, now employed as an interpreter for the Swedish authorities when interviewing asylum seekers to Sweden, suddenly faced with her former husband as one of the new arrivals. The challenge is to balance professional duties with her emotional reaction when confronted with the past. The main part of the novel depicts their student days, their love story and its demise under political oppression, interspersed with short chapters depicting their few days together after more than a decade. A leitmotif is a popular song, 'Mara Bebus,' used by the male protagonist at important or happy moments. It first occurs at their initial meeting at the university in Teheran, then called 'en bekänt melodi' (22) (a well known melody), secondly when they are planning to get married (103), and thirdly when the two of them are on their way to Mandela's lecture in Stockholm. The origin of the song text is explained as written by an intern in the shah's prison the night before his execution, becoming a 'kampsång' after his death, 'en mycket romantisk kampsång' (119) (a very romantic battle song). Finally, it is in evidence during their lovers' reunion, functioning as their goodbye at the end of the novel, where we also learn some of the text: "'Jag är din gäst i natt/Jag stannar hos dig/tills du läggar dina läppar på mina läppar'" (184) (I am your guest tonight/I stay with you/until you put your lips to my lips). It indicates the book's love theme, but love does not last, it is 'a guest,' as the narrative shows.

Their student days are dominated by very strict control by the authorities, represented by the secret police, Savak. Shamsi, a good student and young woman has been part of some quite minor student opposition with demands for a bit more independence than is tolerated, so she has become 'känd' (known or noticed) and thus brought in and interrogated by the police about her own activities and those of her friends. There are leftist thoughts among the students, and the regime's suppression gets increasingly stronger. Mixed with the political theme is that of gender, as indicated in the police officer's statement: "'Det finns två typer av flickor, de som är vackra och de som studerar vid universitetet," sade han [...]' (59) (There are two types of girls, those who are pretty and those who study at the university, he said). And when she is released, her mother's greatest concern is not the political trouble her daughter is in, but whether her honor has been violated: "'Har de rört dig?" "Jag kom ut som jag kom in." [...] För modern [...], trösta sig med at katastrofen inte var större [...].' (66) ('Did they touch you?' 'I came out as I went in.' For the mother [...] take comfort in the fact that the catastrophe was not greater). But Shamsi's life has changed, some of her friends get arrested and the police spread the word that she is a 'bad girl.' She and Nadar, an oppositional student, leftist and anti-royalist, find each other and challenge the moral codes, but do get married to avoid that being used politically. Their married life is under a lot of pressure; she works as a teacher while he is in and out of prison and of the military, and so distrust destroys their relationship, summed up in his question: "'Älskar du någon annan?'" (Do you love someone else?), cf. the title of the novel. It ends in divorce, Shamsi is criticized for abandoning a political refugee, and suspicion is directed at her in those heated times leading up to the Islamic revolution. Issues of politics and gender are intertwined in this narrative of love, loss and exile.

When the former lovers meet again in Stockholm, not much is revealed about their lives in the decade that has passed. She has re-established her life and is now a professional and part of the Swedish asylum apparatus, he is a recently arrived exile who has had new experiences of imprisonment, ironically under the new regime who took over from the one he earlier opposed. Their brief encounter is bitter- sweet since their reunion is simultaneously another departure, though this time around more mellow and less bitter. The picture of the woman in exile is one who has rebuilt her life in Sweden, the depiction of which is very much anchored in the urban space of the capital with numerous references to streets, places, institutions.

Concluding Remarks

Unlike Behros' narrative whose main focus is on the process of integration and search for love and happiness in the new country, the perspective in Mahloujian's tale is more on how political oppression in general and of women and love relationships in particular is destructive and results in exile from the old country. Each has a double perspective, thematically and structurally, that is key to the narratives presented here. Behros' first person narrator continuously refers to and interacts with her Iranian past, while Mahloujian's third person narrator continuously contrasts the Iranian main story with the Swedish frame narrative.

Behros and Mahloujian belong to the group of migrants turned writers who have introduced new perspectives into Swedish life and letters. They write in Swedish and are thus part of the national literature, they are translingual writers and thus their texts reflect two contexts. They write 'contrapuntally,' they write 'outside the nation,' and they write in a second language, which can mean both 'self-translation' and 'repositioning.' Their stories are new national narratives.[8] And these oeuvres are Swedish examples of a cosmopolitical and transnational literature.

References

Behros, F. (1997): *Som ödet vill*. Stockholm: Natur och Kultur.

Behros, F. (2001): *Fångernes kör*. Stockholm: Natur och Kultur.

Hoffman, E. (1999): 'The New Nomads.' In A. Aciman (ed.): *Letters of Transit. Reflections on Exile, Identity, Language, and Loss*. New York: New York Public Library.

Hoffman, E. (2008; 1989): *Lost in Translation. A Life in a New Language*. London: Vintage.

Mahloujian, A. (1995): *De sönderrivna bilderna*. Stockholm: Bonner Alba.

Mahloujian, A. (2002): *Älskar du någon annan?* Stockholm: Atlas.

Mossaed, J. (1997): *Månen och den eviga kon*. Stockholm: Ordfront.

Olsson, B. and I. Algulin (eds.) (2009): *Litteraturens historia i Sverige* (5th edition), Stockholm: Norstedts.

Pavlenko, A. (2001): "'In the world of the tradition, I was unimagined:" Negotiation of identities in cross-cultural autobiographies.' *International Journal of Bilingualism* 5 (3), pp. 317-344.

Said, E.W. (2000): *Reflections on Exile and Other Essays*. Cambridge, Mass.: Harvard University Press.

Seyhan, A. (2002): *Writing Outside the Nation*. Princeton and Oxford: Princeton University Press.

Wendelius, L. (2002): *Den dubbla identiteten. Immigrant- och minoritetslitteratur på svenska 1970-2000*. Uppsala: Centrum för multietnisk forskning, Uppsala Universitet.

Notes

1. Fateme Behros was born in Iran in 1944, came to Sweden in 1983 and died in 2009. Her three novels are *Som ödet vill* (1997, As Fate Decrees), *Fångarnas kör* (2001, The Prisoners' Choir), and *I skuggan av Sitare* (2004, In the shadow of Sitare).

2. Azar Mahloujian was born in Iran in 1949 and came to Sweden in 1982. Her first book, *De sönderrivna bilderna* (1995, published in English as *The Torn Pictures* in 2005), characterized as an autobiographical novel, was first published under the pseudonym 'Nahid,' but later reissued under her own name. Her other novels are *Älskar du någon annan?* (2002, Are you in love with someone else?) and *Møter dig i Larnaca* (2011, Meet You in Larnaca). *Tilbaka till Iran* (2004, Back to Iran) is a report on her visit to Iran after two decades of absence, and *Vi lyser som guld* (2006, We Shine like Gold) is a story of exile dating back 1200 years, namely that of the Persian Zoroastrians that moved to India and of their (the Parsees') existence there today.

3. Translations from the Swedish are my own (IK).

4. It could be noted that the vast majority of these writers were male, and furthermore, they wrote in their respective Scandinavian immigrant languages.

5. Prime minister Olof Palme was shot to death in the evening of February 28, 1986. This was a traumatic event for most Swedes. His social democratic politics marked the Swedish welfare state, and in his international engagement, he opposed dictators of many stripes and supported oppressed peoples. Cf. Wendelius (2002: 73-74), who discusses several such references to Palme in writings by immigrants.

6. The woman in Moberg's epic that the woman in Behros' novel associates herself with is referred to as Kristina from Duvemåla, which is actually the correct name from the novel, but this is not how she is mainly referred to there. The reference though is identical with the title of the musical by Benny Andersson and Björn Ulvaeus (ex Abba), whose libretto builds on Moberg's novel. The musical ran in the 1990s and was popular both in Sweden and abroad, and gave Moberg's characters and work new actuality.

7. The story is generally anchored in known political realities, and in addition, a few specific events are mentioned to further contextualize the narrative. These include the demonstration in Teheran to support the taking of American hostages in November, 1979 (174-76), and in the contemporary Swedish part, Nelson Mandela's visit to Stockholm, Sweden in 1990 (121-22).

8. The Swedish histories of literature are not up to par as evidenced in the latest (5th) edition of *Litteraturens historia i Sverige* (Olsson and Algulin 2009). One page out of 640 (the same as ChickLlit in Swedish), under the title 'Exilens erfarenheter' (Experiences of exile) is devoted to 'migrant' or 'translingual' literature. The new and vibrant multicultural literature, with the hugely successful Jonas Hassen Khemiri at its centre, is not much better off with less than five pages in the same literary history.

IV

Textualities

Story and Situation:
Sebald Compared to Conrad

Jakob Lothe
Universitetet i Oslo

By story we mean at least two things. First, a story is often used synonymously with narrative. Second, inspired by narrative theory, we can consider story as a chronologically ordered summary of the action or plot of a fictional or non-fictional narrative. This second sense of story – story as summary or paraphrase, corresponding to Gérard Genette's definition of *récit* – is often contrasted with discourse, i.e. the narrative presentation of the story. Broadly, the distinction between story and discourse is critically useful. Still, like many terminological distinctions, this one too is often less obvious in practical criticism than it appears to be in narrative theory. For instance, even though the narrative situation of a literary text tends to disappear in a story version of that text, it can be important both for the narrative discourse and for the plot. There is a strong sense in which the narrative situation is located at the crossroads of story and discourse. Seen thus, the narrative situation in a short story or novel is related to Mikhail M. Bakhtin's notion of the chronotope or the chronotopic motif, marking a zone of narrative formation and transition in which the literary dimensions of time and space are curiously compressed, and which for that reason becomes significant both structurally and thematically (Bakhtin 1982: 248). This is certainly the case in several of the texts by W. G. Sebald, not least the novel *Austerlitz* (2001). It is also the case in several of the major novels by Joseph Conrad, including *Heart of Darkness* (1899), *Lord Jim* (1900), and *Under Western Eyes* (1911). In this essay I will consider the main narrative situations in *Heart of Darkness* and *Austerlitz*, arguing that these situations not only introduce key elements of narrative structure but also shape significant thematic patterns. One premise for my argument is that the way in which the narrative situations simultaneously depend on and highlight what Bakhtin calls 'the chronotope of the threshold' (Bakhtin 1982: 248, original emphasis), serving to emphasize the problems of identity and identity formation. In the narrative situations under consideration here, we can see how both Conrad and Sebald establish a basis for constituting, exploring, questioning, and possibly reconstituting human identity, thus forming, to borrow a phrase from Terence Cave's discussion of fictional identities, 'a locus of tension and unease' (Cave 1995: 118, original emphasis).

As many readers will know, *Heart of Darkness* begins thus:

> The *Nellie*, a cruising yawl, swung to her anchor without a flutter of the sails and was at rest. The flood had made, the wind was nearly calm, and being bound down the river the only thing for it was to come to and wait for the turn of the tide.
>
> The Sea-reach of the Thames stretched before us like the beginning of an interminable waterway. In the offing the sea and the sky were welded together without a joint and in the luminous space the tanned sails of the barges drifting up with the tide seems to stand still in clusters of canvas, sharply peaked with gleams of varnished sprits. A haze rested on the low shores that ran out to sea in vanishing flatness. The air was dark above Gravesend, and farther back still seemed condensed into a mournful gloom brooding motionless over the biggest, and the greatest, town on earth. [...]
>
> The sun set; the dusk fell on the stream, and lights began to appear along the shore. The Chapman lighthouse, a three-legged thing erect on a mud-flat, shone strongly. Lights of ships moved in the fairway – a great stir of lights going up and going down. And farther west on the upper reaches the place of the monstrous town was still marked ominously on the sky, a brooding gloom in sunshine, a lurid glare under the stars.
>
> 'And this also,' said Marlow suddenly, 'has been one of the dark places of the earth.' (Conrad 2006: 3-5)

This opening consists of two beginnings. However, both of them are inseparable from the narrative situation, and one important constituent element of this narrative situation is the chronotope of the threshold. In this chronotope, as in related ones such as the staircase, the front hall and the corridor – and, in our texts, the *Nellie* and the railway station of Antwerp – 'time is essentially instantaneous; it is as if it has no duration and falls out of the normal course of biographical time' (Bakhtin 1982: 248).[1]

Let us first briefly consider the first beginning, which consists of the whole quotation except Marlow's opening remark. The pronoun 'us' refers to the five characters aboard the *Nellie*. One of them is Marlow, who is to perform crucial functions in the story both as narrator and as character. However, it is significant that not Marlow but an anonymous first-person narrator is narrating here. This frame narrator introduces us both to the narrative situation and to Marlow as the main narrator. When Marlow is introduced and begins to tell his story, the frame narrator's function becomes more complex, since he also becomes a narratee in the group Marlow addresses (cf. Lothe 1989: 22-28). To put this another way: in accordance with the narrative conventions employed, once Marlow has started telling his story the frame narrator functions first as a narratee, and then as a first-person narrator relaying Marlow's story to us as readers. The phrase 'narrative convention' is necessary because the time of traditional, simple narratives is over in *Heart of Darkness*. At first sight, the novella's narrative situation seems to resemble what Wolfgang Kayser in his still valuable *Das sprachliche Kunstwerk* calls 'die epische Ursituation' (Kayser 1971: 349) – the epic 'proto-situation' in which a narrator tells a group of listeners something that he or she has experienced. The resemblance is nonetheless superficial – not only because the concept of the epic proto-situation excludes the device of the frame narrator but, more importantly, because in *Heart of Darkness* both the act of narration, its motivations, and its thematic implications are much more fragile and problematic than in the epic proto-situation. The reader's impression of the narrative situation's fragility is highly significant thematically, related as it is to the difficulties and challenges of sustained, meaningful narrative communication in the modern era.

Reading and re-reading the beginning of *Heart of Darkness*, we increasingly appreciate the way in which the narrative situation's fragility is balanced by constituent elements of narrative. Here as in the main narrative situation of *Austerlitz*, a narrator tells an engrossing story to a listener. In both narratives, attention is focused on the narrator, who performs a key function in imparting the story to his listener or listeners. In the classic frame narrative, the frame narrator tends to be the most authoritative and knowledgeable of the narrators. This is not so in *Heart of Darkness*, nor is it the case in *Austerlitz*. For although the frame narrator passes on Marlow's story, and although it is important that he appears to be reliable (an impression formed, interestingly, not least by his relative naïveté), his insights prove to be distinctly inferior to Marlow's. We note his use of the superlative when describing London: for the frame narrator, the capital of the British Empire is not only 'the largest' but also 'the greatest' town on earth. Moreover, having finished his introductory description, he goes on to ask: 'What greatness had not floated on the ebb of that river into the mystery of an unknown earth? . . . The dreams of men, the seed of commonwealths, the germs of empires' (5, original ellipsis). Considered in isolation from its context, the answer to the rhetorical question sounds like a piece of imperialist rhetoric. The frame narrator has just been referring to explorers such as Sir Francis Drake and Sir John Franklin – 'the great knights-errant of the sea' (4). As Anthony Fothergill has noted, such references 'imply a certain sort of reader, one whose competence enables the correct decoding of the historical referents and more importantly one who endorses the positive judgments made on these "heroic" figures' (Fothergill 1989: 15). References and allusions of this kind remind us of the connections between Marlow's audience, of which the frame narrator is a member, and Conrad's readers, on whose interest and goodwill he was utterly dependent as an author. We must not forget that, at the time he was writing *Heart of Darkness*, Conrad was still attempting to establish himself as a writer of fiction in his third language. Considering the fact that *Heart of Darkness* appeared in *Blackwood's Magazine*, February-April 1899, surrounded by various pieces that are not only patriotic but even in part jingoistic, the novella's critique of imperialism is all the more striking.

Even though the narrative's second beginning is contrasted with the first, they are both part of the novella's narrative situation, and they both constitute the basis for the following story. Compare Marlow's first words: '"And this also," said Marlow suddenly, "has been one of the dark places of the earth"' (5). This narrative variation is one of the most effective in all of Conrad's fiction – possibly in English literature overall. The frame narrator's reference to London's 'greatness' increases the impact and suggestiveness of Marlow's first words. Exposing the frame narrator's relative naïveté and limited insight, Marlow's remark prefigures the sombre implications of the tale he is about to tell. The comment anticipates his later reflections on the arrival of the Romans in Britain, 'nineteen hundred years ago – the other day. . . .' (5, original ellipsis). For the Romans, Marlow plausibly goes on to suggest, Britain must have seemed an inhospitable wilderness 'at the very end of the world' (6). Moreover, it is indicative of the extraordinary narrative economy of *Heart of Darkness* that Marlow's opening words are also a prolepsis of 'darkness,' the text's central metaphor which (like ivory) becomes a powerful symbol. Although the Romans 'were men enough to face the darkness [...] They were conquerors, and for that you want only brute force – nothing to boast of, when you have it, since your strength is just an accident arising from the weakness of others' (7). Obviously referring to the Romans, this generalizing statement also includes a proleptic reference to the narrative Marlow is starting. Suggesting that Marlow's level of insight is superior to that of the frame narrator, these brief observations also indicate some key characteristics of Marlow's first-person narrative: a reflective rhetoric designed to impress and persuade, a blend of personal and intellectual curiosity, and a tendency to generalize on the basis of individual experience. Yet although Marlow is clearly the more important narrator in *Heart of Darkness*, the effect of his narration is inseparable from, and depends in large part on, the function of the frame narrator. In this text there is a close connection between the stasis of the narrative situation and the movement, including travel, of the story told by Marlow. As Susan Jones has shown, in *Heart of Darkness* 'movement and stillness, the use of active gestures and silent poses operate not just as isolated descriptive moments, but form part of a complex relationship between physical and narrative movement that contributes in significant ways to the author's predominantly skeptical mediation of the story' (Jones 2008: 101).

The use of a narrator is a defining feature of narrative fiction. It is a distancing device, and in *Heart of Darkness* Conrad accentuates this distancing process by using two narrators rather than one. At the same time, the novella is also a good example of a fictional text in which distancing devices paradoxically increase the reader's attention and interest. Conrad effectively exploits the conventional or common character of the frame narrator to make Marlow's story more plausible. The frame narrative manipulates the reader into a position resembling that of the frame narrator as narratee, a position distinguished by a meditative and broadly sympathetic response to the disillusioned insights of Marlow's story. This effect is particularly evident in the novella's last paragraph. Uttered by the frame narrator, its two last words – 'immense darkness' (77) – echo the numerous references to 'darkness' throughout. Repetition plays a key role here, not least in transforming the darkness metaphor into a symbol.

The frame narrator and Marlow are key narrators, two indispensable narrative instruments that Conrad uses in order to construct *Heart of Darkness* as a piece of prose fiction. As Wayne Booth reminds us in *The Rhetoric of Fiction*, one of the strongest conventions of fiction is that as readers we trust the narrator, until or unless the narrative discourse signals that he or she is unreliable (Booth 1983: 4). Since, at least according to some critics, Marlow's reliability is questionable, it becomes crucially important to trust the frame narrator. His conventionality, which is linked to his sense of identity as a British citizen, makes it easier for us to do so. As the frame narrator becomes intrigued by Marlow's story, this facet of his identity contributes to the tale's peculiarly tentacular effect – the narratees are also British (cf. Watts 1977: 22-47). As a corollary, this passage brings out the affinity between Marlow's motivation to narrate and the narratees' (including the frame narrator's) motivation to listen, indeed to remain listening for a long while. 'It is plausible to assume,' notes Ross Chambers in Story and Situation,

> that at bottom the narrator's motivation is like that of the narratee and rests on the assumption of exchanging a gain for a loss. Where the narratee offers attention in exchange for information, the narrator sacrifices the information for some form of attention. Consequently, there is a sense in which the maintenance of narrative authority implies an act of seduction, and a certain transfer of interest (on the narratee's part) from the information content to the narrating instance itself. (Chambers 1984: 51)

This observation is illuminating if related to *Heart of Darkness*, and it equally applies to the main narrative situation of Sebald's *Austerlitz*. In *Heart of Darkness* as in *Austerlitz*, there is a productive correlation between Marlow's and Austerlitz's first-person narration, which takes the form of an ordering and existentially motivated re-experience, and those of the frame narrators, which proceed from an unexpected involvement and surprising understanding. In both novels, the frame narrator's insight appears to increase as a result of the impressionist narrative he himself transmits, thus suggesting that in these texts not just the plots but also the narrative presentations of them are unusually unstable. And in both cases, much of the effect depends on the frame narrator's combined function as narrator and narratee.

Moreover, the relationship between author and narrator is particularly interesting in these two narratives. Marlow is not Conrad, nor is the Marlow of *Heart of Darkness* identical with that of *Lord Jim* (or Austerlitz of *Austerlitz* with Sebald). And yet Marlow can represent Conrad more adequately, and in more nuanced fashion, than any other narrator in the author's service. One reason why is that although Marlow's identity and point of orientation are clearly British, these facets of his fictional identity are blended with those of other European nations and traditions. As Zdzisław Najder observes in his masterly biography of Conrad, Marlow was the embodiment of everything Conrad would wish to be if he were to become completely anglicized. However, Najder adds that

> since that was not the case, and since he did not quite share his hero's point of view, there was no need to identify himself with Marlow, either emotionally or intellectually. Thanks to Marlow's duality, Conrad could feel solidarity with, and a sense of belonging to, England by proxy, at the same time maintaining a distance such as one has toward a creation of one's imagination. Thus, Conrad, although he did not permanently resolve his search for a consistent consciousness of self-identity, found an integrating point of view that enabled him, at last, to break out of the worst crisis of his writing career. (Najder 1983: 231)

In the critical context of this essay, I link 'Marlow's duality' to the ways in which his narrative acts are both aided and problematized by a series of fragmented narratives incorporated into his own. In Conrad's fiction, identity-formation and identity-positioning are closely related to variants of narrative distance and perspective.

A similar point can be made about Sebald, whose last book, published in 2001 and entitled *Austerlitz*, is a curiously unclassifiable narrative which – combining the genres of the novel, the memoir, the fragment, and travel writing – tells, or rather attempts to tell, the story of Austerlitz. As several critics have observed and as few readers fail to notice, there are important thematic links between this generically unstable text by Sebald and the novella which Conrad wrote almost exactly a hundred years earlier. The main reason why *Heart of Darkness* is one of the strongest intertexts in *Austerlitz*, however, is that these thematic connections, which include variants on a search for European origin and identity formation, are supported by structural and narrative ones. I have already mentioned that Sebald uses a frame narrator, as does Conrad in both *Heart of Darkness* and *Lord Jim*. In common with Conrad, Sebald makes his frame narrator meet a character who also becomes a narrator – and whose story, imparted to the frame narrator as narratee, is then passed on by him to the reader.

In several ways Conrad and Sebald are of course very different writers. Yet Sebald is a particularly interesting example of an author who, searching for his own identity as a German and a European at the turn of the twenty-first century, looks to Conrad for inspiration – partly perhaps because of a sense of similar destiny, revolving (in both cases) round an uneasy combination of voluntary and involuntary exile (cf. Brooke-Rose 1996: 291). In his wonderful essay on Conrad in the essay collection *The*

Rings of Saturn (Sebald 2002: 103-134), Sebald stresses the importance of Conrad's Polish background. Thus Sebald is an illustrative example not only of Conrad's continuing significance for contemporary writers but also of how, as Ian Watt puts it in his Epilogue to *Conrad in the Nineteenth Century*, 'Conrad may be said to have inherited much of his modernity - perhaps his post-modernity – from his Polish past' (Watt 1980: 359).

Austerlitz begins thus:

> In the second half of the 1960s I travelled repeatedly from England to Belgium, partly for study purposes, partly for other reasons which were never entirely clear to me, staying sometimes for just one or two days, sometimes for several weeks. On one of these Belgian excursions which, as it seemed to me, took me further and further abroad, I came on a glorious early summer's day to the city of Antwerp, known to me previously only by name. Even on my arrival, as the train rolled slowly over the viaduct with its curious pointed turrets on both sides and into the dark station concourse, I had begun to feel unwell, and this sense of indisposition persisted for the whole of my visit to Belgium on that occasion. (Sebald 2002: 1)

On a first reading, we perhaps think that the first-person narrator, the 'I' who travels 'repeatedly from England to Belgium,' is identical with Austerlitz. Yet although, as it turns out, there is a peculiarly strong resemblance between the first-person narrator and the novel's main character – who also, as the case of *Heart of Darkness*, becomes the main narrator – this beginning is actually a frame narrative whose function is to establish a narrative situation in which the two can meet, and in which Austerlitz can talk.

With regard to the narrative and thematic fabric of *Austerlitz*, the gains of employing a frame narrator are considerable, and they strikingly resemble the effects of Conrad's use of the same narrative device. In both narratives, the main narrator is introduced by a frame narrator, who then becomes a keenly interested listener or narratee. Moreover, in *Austerlitz* as in *Heart of Darkness*, the frame narrator's relative conventionality renders him more reliable, thus making it easier for us to believe Austerlitz's extraordinary story, which the frame narrator reports to us as readers. This narrative strategy creates a tentacular effect: we are drawn into the narrative in a manner comparable to the way in which the frame narrator is irresistibly attracted to Austerlitz's account. I have already referred to Ross Chambers's observation that, at a deep and frequently unthematized level, the narrator's motivation to narrate is complemented by the narratee's readiness to listen, and that, for both parties, possibilities of gain as well as risks of loss are involved. The narrative situations in *Austerlitz* offer ample illustrations of this important point. For example, by telling fragments of his story Austerlitz risks confirming his sense of loss and estrangement, yet his narration may enable him to negotiate than loss. By listening the narratee risks losing, or being drawn out of, a comfortable position of ignorance, yet the fact that he not only listens but also retells what Austerlitz has told him suggests a learning process, and thus the possibility of gaining essential knowledge.

One notable difference between the two narratives, and also between their basic narrative situations, concerns the original way in which Sebald incorporates black and white photographs into the verbal narrative of *Austerlitz*. Even though both the frame narrator and Austerlitz are presented as fictional characters, the pictures which Austerlitz takes – and at least some of which, the reader assumes, are presented in the book – seem to refer to the same physical reality as those included in, for instance, the collection of essays entitled *Luftkrieg und Literatur*. And yet we read the pictures in *Austerlitz* differently: it is as though they simultaneously oppose and are coloured by the fictional verbal discourse in which they are embedded, and from which Sebald makes it exceedingly difficult to disentangle them.

This point is closely linked to the first, and perhaps the most important narrative situation in the novel. It occurs in the 'Salle des pas perdus, as it is called, in Antwerp Centraal Station [...] constructed under the patronage of King Leopold II' (4), who at the end of the nineteenth century claimed all of Belgian Congo, 76 times the size of Belgium and the location of the plot of Heart of Darkness, as his personal property. Austerlitz is introduced thus:

> One of the people waiting in the *Salle des pas perdus* was Austerlitz, a man who then, in 1967, appeared almost youthful, with fair, curiously wavy hair of a kind I had seen elsewhere only on the German hero Siegfried in Fritz Lang's *Nibelungen* film. That day in Antwerp, as on all our later meetings, Austerlitz wore heavy walking boots and workman's trousers made of faded blue calico, together with a tailor-made but long outdated suit jacket. Apart from these externals he also differed from the other travellers in being the only one who was not staring apathetically into space, but instead was occupied in making notes and sketches obviously relating to the room where we were both sitting [...] Once Austerlitz took a camera out of his rucksack, an old Ensign with telescopic bellows, and took several pictures of the mirrors, which

were now quite dark, but so far I have been unable to find them among the many hundreds of pictures, most of them unsorted, that he entrusted to me soon after we met again in the winter of 1996' [...] (6–7)

If *Austerlitz*'s narrative is relayed to the reader via the frame narrator, so are the pictures, including one of a building (which could be the Centraal Station) positioned close to the quoted passage. Once the frame narrator approaches Austerlitz the latter almost immediately starts talking, thus establishing a narrative situation in which, as in *Heart of Darkness*, the frame narrator becomes a narratee. Their first conversation takes place in the railway station, 'in the restaurant facing the waiting-room on the other side of the great domed hall' (8). They meet again several times, and Austerlitz refers to these meetings as 'our Antwerp conversations' (8).

The narrative situation of *Heart of Darkness* includes the spatial environment of the *Nellie*, that is the site of Marlow narration as well as that of the frame narrator's and the other sailors' listening act. Significantly, the threshold of the boat simultaneously constitutes and characterizes not only that of the act of narration but also that of the narrative – Marlow's story – because it was literally a boat that took Marlow out to the Congo and back to Europe. Similarly, in *Austerlitz* the railway station assumes the form of a threshold: a public space distinguished by restless movement, it is also a hall in which the frame narrator's meeting with Austerlitz immediately, apparently irresistibly, blends into a narrative situation in which the former is captivated by the latter's narrative. In an insightful comment on *Heart of Darkness*, Tzvetan Todorov (1978) has said of Marlow's narration that it spirals towards a thematic core or centre which, however, turns out to be empty. There is a sense in which this description applies to *Austerlitz*'s narration too, since both the verbal narrative and the textual images seem to be gravitating towards a nightmarish vacuity. In *Heart of Darkness*, this empty centre becomes indistinguishable from the protagonist. Compare Kurtz's two powerful exclamations: the handwritten 'Exterminate all the brutes!' (50) and the spoken 'The horror! The horror!' (69). In *Austerlitz*, the empty centre, repeatedly hinted at but never expressed directly, is a narrative and thematic element as well as a historical event: Auschwitz – both as the destination of countless deportations and as a symbol of the Holocaust (cf. Lothe 2008: 117-119). While Austerlitz, a Czech Jew, escaped from the Nazis in the summer of 1939, his father, Maximilian, fled to France. His mother, Agáta, remained in the Czech Republic together with Věra, a non-Jewish friend of the family. As Austerlitz's search for his parents now, many years later, take him 'further and further east and further and further back in time' (262-63), his conversations with Věra, with whom he resumes contact, make him believe that his mother was interned in the ghetto of Terzín in late 1942 (281), and then deported to Theresienstadt in the autumn of 1944. His father, he thinks, was possibly deported from another threshold: Gare d'Austerlitz, the train station in Paris whose name is identical with his own, and which is represented visually at the end of *Austerlitz*. One particularly important paragraph here establishes a link to the main narrative situation presented at the beginning of the novel:

> Curiously enough, said Austerlitz, a few hours after our last meeting, when he had come back from the Bibliothèque Nationale and changed trains at the Gare d'Austerlitz, he had felt a premonition that he was coming closer to his father. As I might know, he said, part of the railway network had been paralyzed by a strike last Wednesday, and in the unusual silence which, as a consequence, had descended on the Gare d'Austerlitz, an idea came to him of his father's leaving Paris from this station, close as it was to his flat in the rue Barrault, soon after the Germans entered the city. (404-405)

'I imagined,' says Austerlitz to the frame narrator serving as his narratee at the Gare d'Austerlitz, 'that I saw him leaning out of the window of his compartment as the train left [...]' (406-407). As Austerlitz connects this railway station with his father, it becomes a catalyst of his memories. And as the threshold of the novel's beginning is extended to include the ending as well, there is a strong sense in which both the main narrator, the frame narrator and the reader return to the point where he or she began narrating, listening, reading, or remembering. Thus the importance of the narrative situation is reaffirmed and further strengthened, as is the interplay of situation and story.

References

Aristotle (1995): *Poetics*. Edited and translated by Stephen Halliwell. Cambridge, Mass.: Harvard University Press.

Bakhtin, M.M. (1982): *The Dialogic Imagination. Four Essays*. Edited by Michael Holquist. Translated by Caryl Emerson and Michael Holquist. Austin: University of Texas Press.

Booth, W.C. (1983): *The Rhetoric of Fiction*. Second edition. Chicago: The University of Chicago Press.

Brooke-Rose, C. (1996): 'Exsul.' In *Poetics Today*, 17(3), pp. 289-303.

Cave, T. (1995): 'Fictional Identities.' In H. Harris (ed.) *Identity: Essays Based on Herbert Spencer Lectures Given in the University of Oxford*. Oxford: Clarendon Press.

Chambers, R. (1984): *Story and Situation: Narrative Seduction and the Power of Fiction*. Manchester: Manchester University Press.

Conrad, J. (2006 [1899]): *Heart of Darkness*. P.B. Armstrong (ed.). New York: Norton.

Fothergill, A. (1989): *Heart of Darkness*. London: Open University Press.

Genette, G. (1980): *Narrative Discourse*. Oxford: Blackwell. First published as 'Discours du récit: essai de méthode'. In *Figures III*. Paris: Seuil, 1972, pp. 67–227.

Jones, S. (2008): '"She walked with measured steps": Physical and Narrative Movement in *Heart of Darkness'*. In J. Lothe, J. Hawthorn & J. Phelan (eds.): *Joseph Conrad: Voice, Sequence, History, Genre*. Columbus: The Ohio State University Press, 2008, pp. 100–117.

Kayser, W. (1971): *Das sprachlice Kunstwerk. Eine Einführung in die Literaturwissenshaft*. Bern. Francke Verlag.

Lothe, J. (1989): *Conrad's Narrative Method*. Oxford: Clarendon Press.

Lothe, J. (2008): 'Narrative, Genre, Memory: The Title of W. G. Sebald's Novel *Austerlitz'*. In M. Jansson, J. Kantola, J. Lothe, and H. Riikonen (eds.): *Comparative Approaches to Nordic and European Modernisms*. Helsinki: Gaudeamus Helskinki University Press, pp. 110–127.

Najder, Z. (1983): *Joseph Conrad: A Chronicle*. Cambridge: Cambridge University Press.

Riikonen, H.K. (2002): 'Halls, Corridors and Staircases: Chronotopic Motifs in James Joyce's *A Portrait of the Artist as a Young Man'*. In B. Tysdahl, M. Jansson, J. Lothe and S.K. Povlsen (eds.), *English and Nordic Modernisms*. Norwich: Norvik Press, pp. 239-252.

Sebald, W.G. (1999): *Luftkrieg und Literatur*. München: Carl Hanser Verlag.

Sebald, W.G. (2002): *The Rings of Saturn*. Trans. Michael Hulse. London: Vintage. First published in German 1995 by Vito von Eichborn Verlag, München.

Sebald, W.G. (2002): *Austerlitz*. Trans. Anthea Bell. London: Penguin. First published in German 2001 by Carl Hanser Verlag, München.

Todorov, T. (1978): 'Connaissance du vide: *Coeur des ténèbres*.' In *Les Genres du discours*. Paris: Seuil.

Watt, I. (1980): *Conrad in the Nineteenth Century*. London: Chatto & Windus.

Watts, C. (1977): *Conrad's 'Heart of Darkness': A Critical and Contextual Discussion*. Milan: Mursia.

Note

1. A good discussion of Bakhtin's concept of the chronotopic motif is given by Hannu Riikonen in *English and Nordic Modernisms* (2002). With a view to the editing and production of this book, as well as the accompanying volumes *Anglo-Scandinavian Cross-Currents* (1999) and *European and Nordic Modernisms* (2004), Janet Garton's encouragement was of inestimable value. On the behalf of the editors I thank Janet Garton for her interest and support. More broadly, we also express our gratitude to Professor Garton for her significant contributions to the study of Anglo-Scandinavian and Scandinavian literature.

1,000,000 Stories and 99 Lyrical Forms

Gitte Mose
Universitetet i Oslo

Do-It-Yourself! Choose 6 numbers among 000.000 to 999.999 and combine your own story! You may use a 10-sided-die, your retirement date, your birthday, your favourite numbers, suggestions from friends, anything – to create a story!

This is what a reader must do to read *En million historier* (One Million Stories) created by Peter Adolphsen. The thin grey booklet is found inside a sheer plastic zip lock bag, which also contains the 10-sided die, some postcards, a sheet of stickers identical to that of the cover of the booklet carrying a title, a name, a publishing house, and several pictograms in black and white.

Inside the reader finds 14 pages, including title- and colophon-pages, a 'Brugsanvisning' (Instruction), 9 pages from page 0 to 8 cut into 6 strips of 2 lines, and an uncut page 9. The back cover carries more pictograms and the following text:

> Skal elefantpasseren, lastbilchaufføren, eller måske den fulde bankmand flyve, kravle eller forvilde sig op på en trampolin, ned på knæ eller rundt i landskabet? Frem i skoene? Og skal han kysse malkepigen, kvæle rengøringskonen eller smile fjoget til nabotøsen? Eller?
> Der er en million forskellige historier at kombinere frem. Med en historie i minuttet giver det stof til 694 døgns uafbrudt læsning. (*Samleren* n.d.)

> (Is the elephant keeper, the truck-driver or maybe the drunken banker going to fly, crawl or stray up onto a trampoline, or down on his knees or round about in the landscape/the countryside? Forward in his shoes? And is he going to kiss the milkmaid, strangle the cleaning lady or smile idiotically to the girl next door?

Or?
There are one million stories to be combined. Making one story per minute you get enough material for 694 days of uninterrupted reading.) [1]

And most certainly! Just as the Instruction informs us, the reader can choose between 10 different beginnings, which each have 10 possible continuations, which each can be followed by 10 different sections and so on. Going through the strips the reader may combine one single story of 6x2 lines out of the 10 to the power of 6 (=1 million) possibilities in the book. 10 pages = 60 tiny text-bites = 1 million stories, which not many readers will ever read[2] (whereas one may read the 10 'pages' and afterwards combine from one's own memory).

One may recall the technique from the continuous folded drawings or, as we are told in the Introduction, 'head-body-and-leg-picture books' from our childhood. Adolphsen, however, attributes his literary inspiration to Raymond Queneau, whose work *Cent mille milliards de poèmes* (A Hundred Thousand Billion Poems, 1961) contains 10 sonnets (also) cut into strips and resulting in 1,000 billion poems – which would take about 200 million years to read. Together with François Le Lionnais, Queneau in 1961 formed Oulipo (Ouvroir de littérature potentielle or Workshop for Potential Literature), a loose gathering of (mainly) French-speaking writers and mathematicians.[3] Among its members were Italo Calvino and Georges Perec; the latter wrote the lipogrammatic novel *La disparition* (A Void, 1969) entirely without the letter e, and *La vie mode d'emploi* (Life: A User's Manual, 1978). Oulipo's program was to investigate what happens to literature when subjected to formal rules like constrained writing techniques. By forcing the script – and the reader – through a playful and investigating reading process, we enter a kind of story-making-machine that provokes our reading habits and literary expectations.

In a way one could argue that Adolphsen already 'joined' this community through his first two books and the stories 'Beretning om sproget gitii' (Account of the Gitii Language) from *Små historier* (Tiny Stories) and 'Luboslav Hacek' from *Små historier 2* (Tiny Stories 2). With *En million historier* he also enters a Danish tradition from the 1960s, including two works by Vagn Steen *Riv selv: en kalender med digte + digte* (Tear it Yourself: a Calendar including Poems + Poems, 1965) and *Skriv selv / En kalender fuld af muligheder* (Write it yourself / A Calendar Full of Possibilities, 1965); *Dage med Diam* (Days with Diam, 1969) by Svend Åge Madsen; and more recent works like Morten Søkilde's double-book *Pan* and *Landskaber* (Landscapes, 2007), a cycle of sonnets with lines consisting of 36 signs, only using the vowels e and a; and Mikkel Thykier's bag of loose leaves *Struktur. 16 objekter* (Structure. 16 Objects, 2003). According to the 'foreword' in the bag, this work is a homage to Peter Louis-Jensen who made the sculpture *Struktur* in 1966 (see Anonym 2003). It consisted of 16 boxes without lids, which were to be moved around in the city on a truck. The intention was to create a particular communication between the sculpture and the public, who would see the box(es) in different places. Space between the boxes and around the boxes thereby became as important as the form.

Quite apparently all these works share a need for active and playful readers and 'users' who do not mind having a bit of fun and their reading habits challenged, even by nonsense and absurdity.

310808

And indeed: Some of the combinations of *En million historier* do turn out absurd and nonsensical, others make perfectly good sense. But let us try to make a story based on a special date:

> **3** En fuld mand stod i en bank. På ét ben. Manden, Henning, arbejdede i banken og skulle bevise for sin mistænksomme chef, at han var ædru. Det gik sådan okay, fordi / **1** han havde spist en svampekompot i Quito, Equador. Der skete en tømmermandseftermiddag hos nogle flossede typer, han havde mødt på rejsen. Han længtes efter / **0** en frugt. Af en sær slags. Men så huskede han, at al frugt rådner. Alt styrer mod sin opløsning, selv elefanter. Ingen hukommelse standser døden, end ikke med hjælp fra / **8** terpentin. Opløsning var den eneste måde, hvis man ville opnå at træde tilbage i økosystemernes store pulje. 'Døden er meningen med livet,' hviskede han og svajede / **0** over en trillebør. Det måtte være Katrine, indbegrebet af distraktion, der havde glemt den. Han snurrede rundt og råbte: 'Hvis ikke din ordenssans ligger i Sibirien, så er jeg / **8** en tyk bog af alverdens kloge hoveder.' Han tog hende i favnen og stod helt stille til deres hjerter havde fundet same rytme. Så rev hun sig løs med et: 'Din klammerik!'

> (**3** A drunkard was standing inside a bank. On one leg. The man, Henning, worked in the bank and was going to prove to his suspicious boss that he was sober. It turned out more or less okay, because / **1** he had eaten a mushroom stew in Quito, Ecuador. It happened one hung-over afternoon with some shifty characters

he had met on the trip. He was longing for / **0** a fruit. A special kind of fruit. But then he remembered that all fruits rot. Everything steers towards its dissolution, even elephants. No memory stops death, not even by using / **8** turpentine. Dissolution was the only way, if one wanted to re-enter the big pool of eco-systems. 'Death is the meaning of life,' he whispered and staggered / **0** over a wheelbarrow. Katrine, the essence of forgetfulness, must have forgotten it. He spun around and cried, 'If your sense of order isn't somewhere in Siberia then I am / **8** a thick book of/by all the clever heads in the world.' He took her into his arms, stood absolutely motionless until their hearts had found the same rhythm. Then she tore herself loose with a 'You pervert!')

Despite some obvious absurdities in this particular story, we recognize a beginning, a main-character, a conflict, a climax and an ending – the basics of a story. This pattern or common plot of the different combinations of the strips display a peculiar meeting between two people, whose names start by He... (males) and Ka... (females), who may or may not be in love. Some stories end in a kiss, some in a sudden awakening and some in a strangling. The scene(s) seem to be set in the countryside, in a zoo, in foreign countries, in Copenhagen, in a bank, on a motorway, in a balloon, early morning, during the day, late at night. Smells and sounds connected to the scenes, genitals of human beings and animals, sense and sensibility, masculinity and femininity, bodily fluids and emissions, artists, bankers, farmers, milkmaids, cleaning ladies, questions of life and death, Nietzsche and Kaiser Franz are among the ingredients.

The stories very often seem to be open-ended and are terminated by question marks rather than answers. Have we read a love story or a crime story, is the woman a femme fatale or a housewife? What does Katrine's exclamation signify? Has Henning the world-traveller and banker, while undertaking his existential contemplations, actually been searching for his beloved, Katrine? Does it matter if we find out?

Perhaps this is indeed why the critic Lars Bukdahl has termed Adolphsen's (and Bukdahl's own) favourite genre, that is, short short fiction, a kind of 'revenge' on the novel (see, for example, Bukdahl's discussion of generational cycles in *Generationsmaskinen*, 2004). This may be tied to an early statement by Peter Adolphsen, where he stated that he did not see his first book (and nor, perhaps, *Små historier 2*) as a collection of short short stories, but rather as a 'totalroman' (aggregate novel). The ambition was to test - and one may say in accordance with Oulipo's programme – to show a multiplicity of co-ordinated epic possibilities.

Put differently, it was 'to present the non-specific about human beings in an encyclopaedic way and in a form which regarded text by text was aesthetically perfect and compact' (Skyum-Nielsen 2000).

As idea and project, this encyclopaedic view may also be applied to Adolphsen's two compressed, philosophical and 'natural scientific' novels *Brummstein* (2003) and *Machine* (2006) in 68 and 71 pages respectively. Their contents are also temporally compressed: 55 million years, spanning the smallest and the greatest things. In *Brummstein* the main 'character' is a chipped-off piece of humming stone from the formation of the Alps. In *Machine* we follow a heart from a drowned pre-historic miniature horse transformed into a drop of oil, and eventually gasoline. Both novels are set against the backdrop of the world's *historier* (this word in the title of both Adolphsen's early collections encompasses both 'histories' and 'stories' in Danish), and simultaneously about the basic elements of existence and how they are related through continuous transformations.

En million historier is clearly a prolongation of these earlier works by once again exploring the basic elements of classic prose fiction – this time in a compact conceptual book-object.

'FIRST THE KING DIED AND THEN THE QUEEN DIED'

Some of Peter Adolphsen's stories from *Små historier* and *Små historier 2* are discussed in my paper 'Flashes: Danish Short Short Fiction at the Turn of the Twentieth Century.' Among the sources was Norwegian author Jan Kjærstad's essay 'Et plot som aldrig tar slutt' (A plot that never ends) (Kjærstad 1989), which is written in the form of a lexicon. The entries were: FIRST THE KING DIED AND THEN THE QUEEN DIED FROM CHAOS, a 'revised' version of E. M. Forster's formula for a plotted story based on principles of cause and effect (see Forster 1968: 35, 93). Plot seen as a way of structuring the world – and the reader reading for the plot (see Brooks 1984), can no longer be regarded as a valid answer to the modernist wish to order chaos, but rather as a process of 'creating' a new kind of order *through* and *by* chaos. Kjærstad, who is influenced by Niels Bohr's quantum mechanics amongst other things, here places 'chaos' instead of 'grief' as the driving mechanism of the plot, to create a kind of polyphonic plot. He thus calls for the development of new novel-forms, whose purpose and goal is reflection, transgressing reality and mental borders.

This could be said to be in accordance with sociologist Anthony Giddens' term 'late modernity'[4] and Kjærstad's view of modern man's identity as manifold, as a spectrum of possibilities. Contrary to postmodernism the strategies of the late modern age centre on counteracting the disintegration of the central values of existence through reflection, and organising the fragmented into a temporary totality. Giddens (1991) is particularly preoccupied with the individual's potential to realize him- or herself in this provisional totality, and the individual's ability to establish a 'momentary continuity' which can be revised continuously as a result of reflection and subjective analysis.

To Kjærstad this is the 'unsolvable' plot: Man is not fragmented but 'coheres' in different ways than through a centre, and all human beings could be said to present individual plots, which could for example be represented as one million in a tiny booklet! I would argue that this is what Adolphsen perhaps also tries to describe and act on through his playful yet serious investigation of and occupation with space and time, form and content; he investigates the the roots and the basics of minimal story-telling.

Katalognien – 99 Lyrical Forms

This strange word and term refers to Peter Adolphsen's next work. It was first made public on December 30, 2007 when the newspaper Politiken published a rather wild, absurd and nonsensical versified short story or poem 'Duerne flyver højt over byen' (The Pigeons Fly High over the City) signed by Peter Adolphsen and somebody called Ejler Nyhavn. The short story is about the escapades of the two gentlemen one new year's night in Copenhagen.

This text is one of 99 examples of lyrical forms which the duo published under the title *Katalognien* (a word combining catalogue + a suffix indicating a country!) in 2009. So once again we may return to Oulipo and Raymond Queneau, and this time to his *Exercises de Style* (1981) (*Exercises in Style*) telling the story of a man seeing the same stranger twice in one day. This very short story is told in in 99 different ways, demonstrating the tremendous variety of styles in which storytelling can take place.

But who is Ejler Nyhavn? Apparently he has only published one work, *Sofa-ode-strofer* [Stanzas of a sofa-ode], which Peter Adolphsen found in a box outside a second-hand bookshop. Being very impressed by the book, he started looking for Ejler Nyhavn, finding the bibulous loner in a tiny, chaotic and dirty room, filled with empty bottles. They became friends and on November 28, 2007 Adolphsen helped Ejler Nyhavn to set up his Facebook-profile on the Internet where he then published some of his poems.[5] They have since worked together on *Katalognien*.

On January 10, 2008 the newspaper *Information* used Ejler Nyhavn to present what was then a new trend among Danish writers who have signed up to Facebook, thereby forming a new literary network serving both as a social meeting place and a showcase. *Information* also introduced the enigmatic Ejler Nyhavn (whose last name, by the way, is a well-known locality filled with bars in Copenhagen), as an example of an experiment with new literary forms and identities. The personal 'wall' on Nyhavn's Facebook naturally filled up with questions about his identity, and as time went by Nyhavn was 'found' by his old grammar-school teacher, a childhood friend, his daughter – who is another Danish writer, etc. Ejler Nyhavn quickly collected around 350 'friends,' among them several renowned Danish writers, and of course Peter Adolphsen who seems to know him intimately but categorically denies that he himself is Ejler Nyhavn. He does, however, offer this comment:

> Ejler Nyhavn-universet er en form for interaktiv litterær installation [...] [Hans] profil [...] er et kontinuerligt og foranderligt kunstværk, hvor alle kan byde ind og skrive på 'the wall' og dermed blive en del af foretagendet. Og det gør folk. Der har selvfølgelig været indlæg af blandet kvalitet, men generelt er niveauet højt, og folk følger stilen.' (Sørensen 2008)

> (The Ejler Nyhavn-universe is a sort of interactive literary installation [...] [His] profile [...] is a continuous and dynamic work of art, where everybody may join in and write on 'the wall' to become part of the enterprise. And people do that. Of course there have been contributions of a mixed quality, but generally they are of a high standard and people stick to the style.)

So Ejler Nyhavn does exist *qua* his existence on Facebook. Like Adolphsen's print-based projects, he exists as a 'continuous and dynamic work of art.' This brings us back to what seems to be Peter Adolphsen's continual project to probe language and story-telling. His credo (openly 'stolen' from the Danish poet Per Højholt) that art is made from art – not from life! – depends for its expression this time on the interactive participation of his readers, who must accept being creative in handling 'momentary continuities' through choice and chance – both when meeting Ejler Nyhavn and reading *En million historier*.

References

Adolphsen, P. (1996): *Små historier*. Copenhagen: Samleren.

Adolphsen, P. (2000): *Små historier 2*. Copenhagen: Samleren.

Adolphsen, P. (2003): *Brummstein*. Copenhagen: Samleren.

Adolphsen, P. (2006): *Machine*. Copenhagen: Samleren.

Adolphsen, P. (2007): *En million historier*. Copenhagen: Samleren.

Anonym (2003): 'Teksteksempel. Uddrag fra struktur. 16 objekter forarbejder til Peter Louis-Jensen.' *Sentura: Magasin for litteratur og levende billeder*. http://www.sentura.dk/struktur_digt.html. Accessed July 25, 2013.

Brooks, P. (1984): *Reading for the Plot. Design and Intention in Narrative*. London: Vintage Books.

Bukdahl, L. (2004): *Generationsmaskinen. Dansk litteratur som yngst 1990-2004*. Copenhagen: Borgen.

Forster, E.M. (1968): *Aspects of the Novel*. London: Penguin.

Giddens, A. (1991): *Modernity and Self-Identity*. London: Polity Press.

Kjærstad, J. (1989): 'Et plot som aldrig tar slutt.' In *Menneskets matrise. Litteratur i 80-årene*. Oslo: Achehoug, pp. 239-66.

Mose, G. (2002): 'Flashes: Danish Short Short Fiction at the Turn of the Twentieth Century.' In J. Garton and M. Robinson (eds.), *On the Threshold. New Studies in Nordic Literature*. Norwich: Norvik Press. This paper originated as a plenary lecture at the IASS-conference in Norwich 2000, chaired by Janet Garton.

Samleren (n.d.): 'En million historier.' http://www.rosinante.dk/Books/9788763806565.aspx. Accessed July 25, 2013.

Skyum-Nielsen, E. (2000): 'Ved fiktionens rødder.' *Information*, April 11, 2000. http://www.information.dk/42353. Accessed July 25, 2013.

Sørensen, R.B. (2008): 'Mød Ejler Nyhavn og alle hans mange venner.' *Information*, January 10, 2008. http://www.information.dk/152926. Accessed July 25, 2013.

Notes

1. All English translations are by the author (GM), unless otherwise indicated.

2. Additionally the reader may go to the Internet, where she'll find Peter Adolphsen helping her 'handling' the book at http://www.youtube.com/watch?v=ie2iU8sHAtY. She may also find a 'clicking' demonstration at http://enmillionhistorier.dk/ and the author reading the resulting story!

3. The year before Oulipo had functioned as a subcommittee of the Collège de Pataphysique entitled *Séminaire de littérature expérimentale.*

4. The need and wish to create relations and networks can be connected to the characteristics of late modernity analysed in Giddens 1991. Giddens does not operate directly with breaks in modernity. Instead he talks about the late modern age co-existing with the post-modern and modern, and views all of modernity as a coherent period from industrialism till today. But the main characteristics of late modernity is reflexivity and focus on a scepticism towards a certain epistemological foundation of knowledge which, on the contrary, has to be revised continuously. The late modern age is regarded as relational in contrast to the post-modern rejection of all relations and connections and a belief in emancipation in the fragmentation and undermining of meaning and identity.

5. www.facebook.com/people/Ejler_Nyhavn/779083193. The profile has since been removed.

Death in Rødby:
The 'Obituary' Poetics of Helle Helle[1]

Dag Heede
Syddansk Universitet

> 'På en uge var der fire der døde, sådan var det hernede'
> (In one week four people died, that is how it was down here)
> (Helle 2005: 5)

A Minimalist Realist

Helle Helle (born 1965) is often classified as a 'minimalist realist' writer, typical of the 1990s. She studied at the Forfatterskolen in Copenhagen, a writers' school, and her first book, *Eksempel på liv* (Example of life) saw her assigned to the slightly derogatory category of 'Rittersport-generationen' (The Ritter Sport Generation) that produces small, chunky prose texts in the shape of the eponymous German chocolate bar: 'quadratisch, praktisch, gut' (square, practical, good).[2] Her subsequent books meanwhile have taken a turn away from the main focus on language itself to simple, yet sophisticated, depictions of everyday scenes in the lives of everyday people.

Her aim is to study and experiment with how much can be left unsaid without the text becoming meaningless in the name of minimalism, echoing writers like Ernest Hemingway and Raymond Carver. Very little happens, it seems, and most things are left unsaid. But between the lines Helle manages to capture tensions and undercurrents of human interaction and communication.[3]

Her first book is thus atypical in its often surreal and absurd sketches; it takes words literally in an examination of language expressed in seemingly tautological subtitles, such as 'Names or what they are called,' 'Words or what they are saying,' 'Age or how old they are.' Helle was also immediately included in the young generation of so-called female 'anorexic' writers, who supposedly dared only nibble at reality only to immediately expel it.[4] These include writers like Solvej Balle, Kirsten Hammann, Christine Hesselholdt and Merete Pryds Helle. *Eksempel på liv* actually starts with a recurring character called 'Marianne' violently vomiting. But out of her stomach there comes not food, but letters! More than four times the alphabet. A writer thus comes into being through incomplete or interrupted digestion (echoing the enigmatically 'raw' and unmediated character of the prose) and texts are produced by vomiting. This is a move typical of the down-to-earth Helle, who would rather write about breathing and air than about spirituality and creativity. And always in a strangely fascinating, captivating, hypnotizing, even anaesthetizing language, with the stylistic mastery of a sleepwalker and a pronounced paradoxical tendency to pre-reflexive superficiality.[5] Furthermore the vomiting can reflect the strange, almost involuntary production of the text, a text that the narrator seems to avoid ownership of, and that is almost understood as an abject part of the narrating (mostly female) voice.

Obituary Poetics

Most Helle-scholars[6] have focused on the minimalist style of her writing and the sophisticated narrative techniques. Her texts have been compared to an iceberg, where only one seventh is above the surface with the rest hidden beneath the sea – or between the lines – at depths only hinted at. Critics have rightly underlined how little the reader is actually told.[7] This essay will, instead, focus mainly on the thematics of Helle's work and play the different books out against one another. Agreeing with the often-stated observation that the texts are full of gaps that it is up to the reader to fill in, I will experiment with placing the different texts on top of one another and let them in part fill in each other's gaps. The goal is not a complete picture or a finished jigsaw puzzle,[8] but a reading to see, how, where and if the different texts can, if not complement, then certainly comment on, each other. Thus collapsing Helle's two collections of short stories and three novels I will play with the intratextual possibilities of the work.

The second approach I will take, connected with the first move, is a claim that the common denominator of all of Helle's writing is an obsession with death.[9] This theme, whether explicit or implied, resolved or repressed, manifest or latent, subdued or pronounced, outspoken or taboo, penetrates her books on many levels, not just thematically,[10] but also, even more fundamentally, as a unique kind of 'obituary poetics.' Helle acts as a kind of queer, inverse Scheherazade, not postponing death by writing, nor claiming death as an authenticating truth. Instead, death is presented as the very reason for writing, the engendering of the word just like in *Eksempel på liv* the vomiting was the woman's access to creativity (she experiences a strange pride when looking at the letters she has expelled from her body).

Death, then, becomes vital to the production of stories, texts, and letters. The writing could be one on a tombstone, a strange 'epitaphic' creativity that sometimes takes the form of a grief process as in *Hus og hjem* (1999; House and Home). Or it can be explicitly named at the very beginning, as in the intriguing opening of *Rødby-Puttgarden* (2005) quoted as the motto of this essay, or in the first chapter of *Forestillingen om et ukompliceret liv med en mand* (2002; Imagining an Uncomplicated Life with a Man), where the protagonist finds her partner dead in bed. In *Forestillingen…* his death, of course, colours the whole narrative, which relates the events of the previous two years leading up to the death. The reader, thus, reads the whole text, so to speak, through the corpse of the deceased Kim, or – if one prefers – over his dead body.[11]

Coming Up For Air: *Forestillingen om et ukompliceret liv med en mand*

The gender of the corpse is not always relevant in Helle's work, but in this case, it clearly is. Kim's death is not directly caused by his partner Susanne, but probably by the sleep apnoea that is hinted at on several occasions in the novel: his snoring is unusually loud. Ester, the third party in this little chamber play, notices this condition and warns of the danger: 'Det kan godt være farligt, sagde Ester, men ingenting kunne have interesseret Susanne mindre i det øjeblik, for hun var ved at finde tøj frem, som ville egne sig til at lave yoga i' (Helle 2002: 105) (It could be dangerous, Ester said, but nothing could have interested Susanne less at that moment, for she was busy finding clothes she could wear to do yoga in). The yoga, in an indirect way so typical of Helle, is stated as somehow the cause of Kim's death and it plays a pivotal role in Susanne's exit from the relationship. Not only does she have an 'almost-affair' with the yoga teacher, Dennis (thus echoing Anne's flirt with Jens in *Hus og hjem*), but while grocery shopping on the day of Kim's death, she has mistakenly brought her yoga bag instead of her handbag with her purse. Yoga is, of course, all about breathing, which is what Kim early on has complained about not doing in his sleep (Helle 2002: 35).

Air is in an enigmatic way a 'weapon' of the constant, partly unspoken war that dominates the destructive and unhappy relationship between Susanne and Kim, neither of whom is presented as a particularly sympathetic character. Their 'gender war' is therefore without clear villains or victims; the two are both suffering in the relationship, but seemingly unable to end it, stuck as they are in destructive patterns that have resulted in an increasing degree of social isolation. When Kim leaves Susanne on one occasion, his explanation is a need for a 'change of air' (ibid). Coming back, he suffocates!

Air epitomizes their conflict in a very matter-of-fact way, typical of Helle's down-to-earth acts of symbolization. Susanne has had a period as a student (we are not told her subject) but works as a professional cleaner, first in a hospital, later on with private clients. She is obsessed with cleanliness and order. One winter a hidden and subsequently forgotten bottle of cologne behind a book causes a persistent smell: this makes Susanne regularly air out the house, to the dismay of Kim. The partner is becoming more and more of a recluse, as he works at home on a novel that is never to be completed. 'Du lukker al ånd ud af det her sted' (110) (You're letting all the spirit out of the place) Kim reproaches her, using his linguistic superiority against Susanne, the Danish word *ånd* meaning both 'spirit' and 'breath.'

Ester, Susanne's former coworker, moves in with the couple, as she is pregnant with the child of her unfaithful lover, Luffe, whom she has left. She not only takes up a lot of space in the cramped apartment, she contributes in the 'air war' by regularly letting out some very non-silent emissions.[12] Susanne and Kim, thus, are literally fighting over and for air. They seem to have only a limited amount of creativity available in their common space and somehow Kim is using it all up. For Susanne to write, it seems, Kim must suffocate.

Life, Death and Language

Apart from air, language is a key element in Susanne and Kim's war. When she threatens to leave him, he uses language to stop her: 'En gang havde hun sagt: "Kim, jeg går fra dig, for jeg ved ikke, om jeg elsker dig".

"Hold op med dine klicheer", havde han sagt, og det var nok derfor, hun blev'" (Helle 2002: 101) (Once she had said: 'Kim, I am leaving you, because I don't know if I love you.' 'Stop your clichés,' he had said, and that was probably why she stayed). And Kim says at an early stage of their relationship: 'Kom igen, når du får et sprog' (45) (Come back when you get yourself a language). Perhaps the novel itself can be seen as Susanne's deadly return with a language.

Getting a language is a crucial task, not only for Susanne, but also for other female protagonists like Anne, who in *Hus og hjem* can finally put the tragic facts of her parents' deaths into words; and certainly for Jane in *Rødby-Puttgarden*, where language is the way to break the generational patterns of her grandmother, mother, sister and – perhaps – niece.

However, acquiring a language does not come as easily to any of these women as Marianne's vomiting does to her. It may require the death of a beloved or near one. Helle's narrators and protagonists literally walk over corpses and these corpses create, perhaps, the very material from which the texts stem. The corpse is thus somehow a blank page, on which the narratives become engendered just as, in so many of the texts, the birth of a baby is followed by, or accompanied by, the death of an adult. The cycles of life and death discreetly structure all three novels. The deaths give room for not only unborn babies, but also unwritten texts.

The Creativity of Death

Death thus seems the enigmatic prerequisite or condition for the telling of tales. The whole story of *Forestillingen om et ukompliceret liv med en mand* not only starts with the death of Kim, but seems to be occasioned by his dead body, if not actually written on it. Susanne's access to writing, language, and even reflection is blocked fundamentally by Kim: her first act of writing, when she passes Ester her phone number, is, significantly, not with pencil, but using her eyeliner on a scrap of paper (Helle 2002: 50).[13] Her only acts of writing with pen and paper appear on the occasion of her frustration with and anger at Kim (114). This is what drives her to write and put the problems of the relationship down on paper. The animosity she feels for the partner is the driving force of her textual creativity.

Of extreme importance in this respect is Susanne's enigmatic desire to write Kim's obituary, or to give an impressive speech at his funeral (101). This description can perhaps be read not only as an expression of

Susanne's latent wish to kill Kim (since she seems unable to leave him and be herself), but also at a metapoetic level as a summing up of the whole novel. Although not written in the first person, the book itself can perhaps be read as the description of one woman's long battle to come into linguistic and textual existence, a female, minimalist and everyday version of the Wordsworthian 'Prelude,' which is at the same time an epitaph for Kim: and perhaps an ironic comment on the novel that Kim never managed to write, or at least publish. In a morbid way, he does produce a book, but at the cost of his life. He cannot create art, but occasions it, a move familiar to many ill-fated female muses (Bronfen 1992). Ironically, Susanne is frustrated in her morbid fantasy about the obituary by the fact that Kim has published nothing. Therefore, no newspaper would be willing to publish her text on him.

Funeral Speeches

Like so many of Helle's works this novel is narrated exactly at the moment between a person's death and his or her funeral, thus situating the text at the transition between corpse and embalmment. *Rødby-Puttgarden*, too, stops exactly at the point where four people have died and just before the two of them, Martin and Mr. Lund, are to be buried. This makes the texts somehow into burial speeches, which indeed is the title of one of the very enigmatic short stories from the volume *Biler og dyr*: 'Tale ved bisættelsen' (Speech at the Funeral), a text so elliptic that it is barely comprehensible without intertextual reference to Helle's other texts.

A pregnant woman, wife and mother, seems to have a bad conscience about her dream about suddenly finding an extra room in her crowded house and now she feels remorse. However, reading the short text 'on top of' or 'next to' the three novels, the reader can from the enigmatic title of the short story guess at a (car?) accident, in which perhaps the husband and the two children died. Is the text expressing the woman's remorse for at times having wished her family dead?[14] On its own it leaves us guessing: read in the light of the novels, it functions almost as a poetics of the whole of Helle's oeuvre. Like Susanne, who in the end has lots of space, having got rid of both Kim, Ester (and Ester's baby), this nameless woman certainly now seems to have the whole house to herself.

In any case, according to its title, this intriguing short story is situated exactly at the point of narration of both *Rødby-Puttgarden* and *Forestillingen om et ukompliceret liv med en mand*: the period between death and burial. *Hus og hjem* only partly diverges from this chronology, for it could be argued that this text, also, is a very belated 'burial speech.' Anne has suffered years of repression and never worked through the pain stemming from the loss of both her parents within a couple of months, when she was a teenager. The mother died of cancer, the father in a car accident with suicidal overtones. Only the return to her 'home' town, which is also the site of the parents' deaths (and their graves), and conversations with the local pastor and with her old school friends result in the happy resolution at the end of the novel. Anne can finally face the grave site that she is showing her friend's baby son: 'Her bor min mor og min far. De bor nede i den jord, siger jeg og ser på bogstaverne i gravstenen, navnene og årstallet[…]'(Helle 1999: 209) (My mum and dad live here. They live down in that earth, I say and I look at the letters on the tombstone, the names and the year […]).

The letters on the tombstone might also refer to the letters of the novel itself and, perhaps, the process of writing altogether, which is conjured in the very first sentence: 'Jeg har været her i fem dage, og det er mit femte brev til Anders' (5) (I have been here five days, and this is my fifth letter to Anders). The deixical 'this,' of course, refers to the apparently daily letter to Anders, but perhaps, also, to the novel itself, which tells of Anne's fundamental feelings of loss, estrangement and paradoxical homelessness in her old 'home' town: and also of her attraction to the neighbouring pastor with whom she spends a lot of time in a communication that mixes flirtation with confessions of an almost therapeutic nature. Perhaps at one level, Anders is really the hidden addressee of the whole text that is both confession of a secret passion and a cathartic narrative of parental loss and orphanhood. In that way this novel is a mirror image of *Forestillingen om et ukompliceret liv med en mand*, which was mainly generated by Susanne's hatred for Kim. *Hus og hjem* is, rather, a declaration of love, and perhaps even one long proposal letter to Anders, whom she seems to marry in the end.

The Broken Frame

Hus og hjem is divided into three parts, and further subdivided into twenty-three chapters. The three parts are headed March (1-15), June (15-20) and September (21-23), thus representing the seasons (early) spring, (early) summer and (early) autumn. One season, of course, is missing: winter. This seasonal structure is discreetly echoed by the text itself, as Anne explains the decoration of the living room:

> [...] og jeg hænger tre af Anders' små billeder op på væggen ud mod entreen. De forestiller Frederiksberg Have på forskellige årstider: vinteren mangler, fordi det billede gik i stykker under forrige flytning, og vi har aldrig fået skiftet rammen ud' (Helle 1999: 114)

> ([...] and I hang three of Anders' small pictures up in the front hall. They depict Frederiksberg Gardens in different seasons: the winter is missing, because that picture broke during the previous move, and we never managed to change the frame).

The broken frame echoes the partial 'frame' of the whole text, and the missing winter points to and highlights the general repression of death, grief and mourning that dominates both Anne's life and her narrative, to the point of immobilization.[15] The missing grief process can explain her bizarre passivity, apparent laziness and total lack of academic and professional ambition: '- Jeg ved egentlig slet ikke, om jeg gider bruge den uddannelse' (17) (I just don't know if I can be bothered to use that education), Anne states, as her female friends inquire about her job plans.

The novel relates the christening of Anita's baby, but omits both the death of Anita's father and his funeral. So the 'holes' or gaps in the narrative, once again, exclude actual death and burial, which of course only make these themes all the more dominant and significant. Death is never more present in Helle's work than when it appears to be absent. It is the almost invisible frame that surrounds the seemingly open and 'unfinished' texts.

Death Pays a Visit: Still Life With Pheasant

This is certainly the case with a short story like 'Fasaner' (Pheasants), which introduces the volume *Rester* (Remains). It is one of Helle's most read and studied texts, already a classic in Danish secondary schools. The short, highly suggestive text depicts a scene rather than an 'event': a former resident, Richard, visits his old apartment now occupied by a single woman, the enigmatic narrator, whose name we are not told, and whose reported age (thirty-two) we are told is not quite the truth. Contrary to gender clichés this woman probably is not trying to pass as younger, but as older, as she appears, somehow, afraid of the intruder who does not seem to take no for an answer.[16] If the woman were still in her twenties, she would be the same age as the majority of Helle's female protagonists, of which she is the prototype: passive, defensive, introverted and overly protective of her social façade.

The narrative describes the seemingly non-eventful (non-)meeting, lasting less than an hour. It abounds with 'half hearted' symbols, i.e. suggestive objects that might or might not mean more or something other than what they describe.[17] The forty-one-year-old Richard who comes to pick up some forgotten objects from his past – some remains, echoing the title of the collection – can, in view of the general death symbolism, be read as a figural *memento mori*, and the little text as a genre painting in the tradition of the still life. Death is thus here not only the frame, but also 'genre' of this text. The pheasant itself is, of course a (if not the) classic item of the *nature morte* painting.

The half-burnt candle is another key item, symbolizing the passage of time and the ephemerality of life. This candle indeed does play an important role at two points in the text. Richard needs light in the basement and asks the narrator to accompany him with a candle and matches.[18] She exchanges the potentially dangerous candle for her bicycle lamp. Later Richard successfully demonstrates how the draft from the window can extinguish the candle, once again pointing to death.

Richard is an eerie visitor on many levels. He represents, of course, the imminent danger of rape and murder: a single woman living on her own in an old, run-down house with a plumbing company as her only downstairs neighbour, which is, naturally, unmanned after working hours. This is probably why the woman almost spontaneously lies about expecting dinner guests in a minute (and about her age). But apart from such immediate threats, the figure of Richard also points to mortality and death in a number of other uncanny ways.

A Memento Mori

With his intimate knowledge of the apartment, Richard reminds the narrator that her home is fundamentally just part of a house and has not been 'hers' in the past. She is at some level herself a 'visitor,' or an intruder, in the apartment. Richard does not really respect the privacy of the narrator, but enters not only her toilet in the basement, but also her bedroom and asks even to look into her bedroom closet.[19] He also lifts the lid of her cooking pot, where the small amount of food perhaps exposes the narrator's lie about the expected guests.

The house could, perhaps, be seen as a human body, with the toilet and shower cabin in the basement, the plumbing as a symbolic digestive system on the ground floor, and the upper body as the narrator's apartment and 'face' on the first floor. In that case Richard's invasion takes almost the character of a rape (oral and anal/vaginal), where he intrudes into both the bottom and the top levels. The house also mirrors, perhaps, the Freudian model of the personality with the super-ego, ego and id (a favourite model of Danish high school readings of the text), which certainly can be at least partly substantiated by the painting from Richard's past that he is now hoping to find.

The narrator had it hanging on her bedroom wall, but quickly hides it under her bed before Richard's entrance. It can easily be read as a description of the unconscious: 'og så forestillede det som sagt en solsikke med rødderne i havet og en hel masse små fisk, der nærmest blev kvalt i rodnettet' (11) (and then as said it depicted a sunflower with its roots in the ocean and a lot of small fish that were almost suffocating in the root system). The narrator's handing over of the painting is certainly giving back Richard a part of his past, as it is a gift from his youth. He got it on his twenty-first birthday from his brother, who had bought it in Berlin, but then dropped it and had to buy a new frame for it.[20] So the painting, Richard states, has a history of its own, which it certainly has, by also secretly hanging on the narrator's bedroom wall without its (former) owner's knowledge. Perhaps the painting could tell stories from that room like Scheherazade's bedroom tales…

The painting in the text might also discreetly refer to the text itself as a still life painting, just like the missing winter photograph of *Hus og hjem* points to the overall structure of the novel. Richard's multilayered painting, of course, mirrors the narrator's multilayered house with the basement underground, the water installation on the ground, and the 'flower' of the female narrator on top, who likes the summer and the open air: 'Jeg siger at det her hus vist altid har været lidt i uorden. Men at huslejen stadig er billig, og her er også rart om sommeren, når vinduerne kan stå åbne, og det er varmt udenfor' (8) (I say that this house has apparently always been somehow out of order…But that the rent is still cheap, and that it is nice in the summer, when the windows can be open, and it is warm outside). Furthermore, the many references to paintings with broken frames point, on a more general level, to the metapoetics of all of Helle's writing that never seems 'completed' or 'framed,' but always open for the reader to 'finish,' or 're-frame' (or perhaps 'digest').[21] Finally,

Richard[22] is a reminder of mortality to the point of becoming a symbol of death in his general appearance. His visit in wet clothes on a rainy autumn evening, his unsettling, yet polite manner, his inquisitiveness about the narrator's age, and his knowledge of the apartment can all point to death, as do the objects that populate the title of this short text. The third sentence introduces an obvious sign of mortality (and miscommunication): 'en opblødt avis ligger på trappestenen' (7) (there is a soggy newspaper on the doorstep).

At the end of the scene (and of the story), the newspaper has been replaced by the title object (but in the singular): a pheasant cock. Like the wet newspaper, it is at the point of destruction and seems to represent death in more than one way: 'På trappetrinet ligger en fasan, dyngvåd. Som om den er druknet efter sin død. Dens fjer er brune og grønne' (13) (On the doorstep there is a pheasant, soaked. As if it drowned after its death. Its feathers are brown and green). 'Death' is thus not only the seventh last word of the text, but penetrates the whole text on the thematic, symbolic and narrative levels. The enigmatic text is perhaps a still life rendered in words, where the description of the literal painting (and the inflammable paint cans in the basement) discreetly points to its general ekphrastic character, a word painting as suggestive as any painted *memento mori*.

Rødby-Puttgarden: **Portrait of the Artist as a Young Woman**

Still life dominated by death could also sum up the existence of the narrator in one of Helle's most recent[23] novels, the prize-winning *Rødby-Puttgarden*.[24] An unresolved grief process once again apparently paralyzes a young version of the typical Helle-heroine, Jane, an unambitious working-class girl. Her mother died suddenly while Jane was finishing her A-levels. Instead of processing the loss, Jane started an education as a therapist in another town. After eighteen months[25] she inexplicably collapses with uncontrollable shaking. The breakdown can probably be seen as a belated response to the death of the mother with the ironic twist of a student of physical therapy having no insight into the psychosomatic reactions of her own body. The collapse leads her to move back in with her sister, a single mother, and her baby daughter, Ditte. Tine gets Jane a job in the local ferry perfumery where she herself worked until the birth of the baby. Later both sisters become colleagues.

The three create a rather strange family, where Tine and Jane take turns mothering Ditte, but Tine also mothers Jane the way she always seems to have done, since their own single mother reproduced the pattern of her mother, procreating without stable male partners. *Rødby-Puttgarden* is very much a description of generations of women without men, a pattern that is revealed to the reader at an early stage, but only to the strangely passive narrator in an epiphanic realization at the very end of the text:

> 'Det var mig der var Tine.
> Det var mig, der var vores mor.
> Det er rigtigt nok. Der var ikke andre'
> (175)

> (It was me who was Tine.
> It was me who was our Mum.
> It is quite true. There were no others).

The text in one sentence changes into the present tense, indirectly claiming the truth of the fiction and pointing only here to a present, from which the story is narrated. Unlike Susanne, and partly unlike Anne, this novel contains a number of hints that this narrator is on her way to become a writer. *Rødby-Puttgarden* in that respect is also a 'Portrait of the Artist as a young Woman.'[26] These hints are spaced throughout the novel. Jane is a good student and Tine, herself not interested at school, always made sure that the younger sister completed her homework. The mother insists that Jane's bookish abilities stem from her, not Jane's dyslexic father. And Jane herself expresses a sense of words. She is, almost to the point of idiosyncrasy, sensitive to the language mistakes of her surroundings; the attractive Tim loses part of his appeal when he cannot decline the word 'kilometer' (60). But Jane's feeling for language dates back much further to her childhood investigations in dictionaries to check out unusual and poetic words (88). Her narration is not described as a sudden vomiting but as the result of a bookish yearning that goes many years back.

Charon's Boat to Hades

> '– Og de ventede til de døde, og de ventede til de døde'
> (*Rødby-Puttgarden*: 38)
> (– And they waited 'till they died, and they waited 'till they died).

Death, of course, penetrates this zombie-like story of repetitions and monotonous everyday routines that seem to echo the timetable of the ferries between Northern Germany and Southern Denmark, both poor and marginal areas. The major change for the women workers on the ferry is to turn night into day and in that way use the night shifts to bring necessary variation into one's life.

The big incident to shake up Jane's somnambulant existence is, of course, the many deaths, especially the sudden death on water, a major accident one foggy night, where a tanker hits the ferry, causing a hole in the side of the ship. One of the shop assistants is sucked to her death in the icy water.[27] The news of the disaster reaches Jane the following morning. She has been interrupted in her sexual encounter with a married Danish electrician at a building site near Hamburg. The man had to rush home to his wife, who has suddenly fallen ill, leaving Jane without clothes or money to make her way home on a later ferry.

Chance thus dictates that Jane is not working on the ferry on that disastrous night, but Tine is. However, an earlier description of a typical night shift suggests that Jane could easily have been the victim. An introductory emergency lesson leaves all participants uninterested and the uneventful night shifts typically develop into cosy, shared meals. The fatal accident took place on Easter Friday making it almost (one night removed) into a sort of secular Last Supper, a Christian symbolism that is always present (but always somehow remote) in Helle's writing. Perhaps Marie Svendsen's death functions somehow as a late wake-up call for the comatose Jane, a reminder that life can never be taken for granted and must not be wasted.[28]

Rødby-Puttgarden is also, thus, a kind of obituary, developed on the occasion of the four people who have just died, but are not yet buried within the scope of the narrated time, as Jane is left in the rocking chair immediately before the funeral services of Mr. Lund, Bo's father, and Martin, a former school friend who has committed suicide. Is the whole novel then Jane's 'burial speech'?

Writing as Matricide

The text also involves the corpse of the dead mother, whose death is somehow connected to Jane's development as a writer. Although Jane's mother claims to be the source and origin of the girl's linguistic talent, she certainly is also a barrier to the daughter's access to language.

Although it can be argued that the whole novel, narrated in the first person singular, is certainly to be ascribed to Jane (especially the part that narrates the background, upbringing and youth of Jane's mother, 'Vores mor' (Our mother)), she does without a doubt write one, unusual, 'poetic' phrase. During her crisis in Hamburg, when she realizes that she is nothing more than a casual lover for the married Aksel,[29] she has a breakdown that is also somehow a breakthrough to language. This key scene is also a linguistic epiphany:

> Jeg følte mig bedøvet og lettet. Jeg låste mig ind på værelset og fandt blokken og en kuglepen i skrivebordsskuffen, skrev det ned: 'bedøvet og lettet.' Det var første gang, jeg skrev på den måde. Jeg kiggede på ordene, de sagde mig ikke noget som helst. Det var næsten, som om jeg kunne høre vores mors stemme, 'Nu skaber du dig. (160)

> (I felt anaesthetised and relieved. I locked myself into the room and found the pad and a biro in the desk drawer, wrote it down: 'anesthetized and relieved.' It was the first time that I wrote in this way. I looked at the words, they meant nothing to me at all. It was almost as if I could hear our mum's voice: 'Now you are making a scene').

The scene might somehow mirror the very first page of Helle's work, where Marianne vomits the alphabet, but it is now invested with violence. There is an uncanny parallel to Susanne whose passage to writing is occasioned by Kim's corpse and her fantasies of writing his obituary and Jane's having to deaden her mother's voice to become a writer and, perhaps, an individual. Thus, if we go back to the mother's sudden death, it is significant that on that very day, Jane has her final exams – in Danish written composition. Jane's access to language certainly has matricidal overtones.

Writing in Helle's universe is perhaps a painful transport over dead bodies and an enigmatic inscribing of tomb stones. Deaths, funerals, mourning and grief constitute not just large parts of the explicit themes of Helle's writing and an even larger part of the blank spaces of the unwritten. Death seems to define the very poetics of the text, both the beginning, the ending and its very condition of existence. The canvas and the frame.

References

Aabenhus, J., A.N.B. Albertsen and P.K. Hansen (eds.) (2011): *Hvor lidt der skal til. En bog om Helle Helles forfatterskab*. Odense: University Press of Southern Denmark

Ariès, P. (1974): *Western Attitudes towards Death: From the Middle Ages to the Present*. Translated by P.M. Ranum. Baltimore: The Johns Hopkins University Press.

Bronfen, E. (1992): *Over her Dead Body. Death, Femininity and the Aesthetic*. Manchester: Manchester University Press.

Bruun Jensen, J. (1998): 'I virkelighedens tyste billede. Helle Helle og Simon Fruelund over for minimalismen, de litterære kategorier og deres egne form.' *Litteraturmagasinet Standart*, vol. 2, pp. 18-19.

Engberg, C. (2005): 'Hverdagen kort fortalt. Realismens genkomst i Helle Helles kortprosa.' In T. Ørum, M. Ping Huang and C. Engberg (eds.): *En tradition af opbrud. Avantgardernes tradition og poetik*. Copenhagen: Forlaget Spring, 275-284.

Gemzøe, A. (1998): 'Et ikke-mødes kronotop. Tid og rum i Helle Helles "Fasaner" (1996).' In *Edda. Nordisk tidsskrift for litteraturforskning* 4, 357-368.

Goffman, E. (1959): *The Presentation of Self in Everyday Life*. New York: Doubleday Anchor Books.

Gorer, G. (1965): *Death, Grief and Mourning in Contemporary Britain*. London: Cresset Press.

Gubar, S. (1982): '"The Blank Page" and Issues of Female Creativity.' In E. Abel (ed.): *Writing and Sexual Difference*. Brighton: Harvester.

Hansen, P.K. (2000): 'Helle Helle.' In *Danske digtere i det 20. århundrede*, Vol. III. Copenhagen: Gad, pp. 499-503.

Helle, H. (1993): *Eksempel på liv*. Copenhagen: Lindhardt og Ringhof.

Helle, H. (1996): *Rester*. Copenhagen: Samleren.

Helle H. (1999): *Hus og hjem*. Copenhagen: Samleren.

Helle, H. (2000): *Biler og dyr*. Copenhagen: Samleren.

Helle, H. (2002): *Forestillingen om et ukompliceret liv med en mand*. Copenhagen: Samleren.

Helle H. (2005): *Rødby/Puttgarden*. Copenhagen: Samleren.

Knudsen, B.T. (2002): 'Teksten på overfladen. Interview med Helle Helle.' In B.M. Thomsen and B.T. Knudsen (eds.), *Virkelighedshunger. Nyrealismen i visuel optik*; Copenhagen: Tiderne Skifter.

Notes

1. This chapter was first published in *Scandinavica* 49 (1), pp. 47-64.

2. One reviewer, Hans Andersen, in the newspaper *Jyllandsposten*, remarked about her first book: 'Hun hedder Helle Helle. Hun kan skrive skrive. Men hun har ikke noget at skrive skrive om' ('Her name is Helle Helle. She can write write. But she does not have anything to write write about').

3. Of her first novel, *Hus og hjem*, reviewer Lars Bukdahl remarked in *Weekendavisen*: 'Der sker ikke en skid, men det er denne ikke-skid, der sker og sker, der er interessant' (Not a shit happens, but it is this non-shit that keeps happening that is interesting). *Hus og hjem* in some ways resembles the classical *livre sur rien* (book about nothing), Gustave Flaubert's *Madame Bovary*, but in Helle's novel the protagonist's extramarital affair is never consummated and she does not die in the end. So even less 'happens' in Helle's version of the life of an idle woman in the provinces.

4. See Anker Gemzøe's characterization: 'Stilen signaliserer en bestræbelse på at holde ned, holde under kontrol, inddæmme, en dybtliggende frygt for at lade stå til, give efter for impulser' (Gemzøe 1996: 192) (The style signals an endeavour to hold down, keep under control, hold in, a deep-lying fear of letting be, giving in to impulses).

5. Charlotte Engberg characterizes the writing as an antipsychological, 'slice-of-life' technique: 'Teksterne dyrker overfladens evne til både at skabe stemning og distance, de er både forlokkende hverdagsligt pragmatiske og "frastødende"

tomme og overfladiske' (Engberg 2005: 278) (The texts cultivate the ability of the surface to both create atmosphere and distance. They are both enchantingly common-or-garden pragmatic and 'repulsively' empty and superficial).

6. In 2011 the first monograph on Helle's oevre *Hvor lidt der skal til* (Aabenhus et al) was published.

7. Helle has stated that she tries to capture her characters before any reflection has begun: '…personerne er midt i begivenhederne. Tingene ramler imod dem, punktum og så er det slut. Det vil sige, at hvad der måtte ligge af refleksion, ligger efter selve novellen, eller den ligger hos læseren som en eftertanke' (Bruun Jensen 1998: 5) (…the characters are in the midst of the events. The things run right into them, full stop, and that is it. That means that any possible reflection happens after the short story itself, or it happens with the reader as an afterthought).

8. With an atypically obvious symbolism in *Hus og hjem* the narrator, Anne, with the help of the local pastor, Jens, pieces together her past in a narrative that is conducted while the two assemble a complex jigsaw puzzle.

9. Helle in this way confronts one of the key taboos of modern Western civilization, which according to French historian Philippe Ariès is a main problem of our culture and society: 'In our day, in approximately a third of a century, we have witnessed a brutal revolution in traditional ideas and feelings… It is really an absolutely unheard-of phenomenon. Death, so omnipresent in the past that it was familiar, would be effaced, would disappear. It would become shameful and forbidden' (Ariès 1974: 87). British anthropologist Geoffrey Gorer (1965) suggests that the present secret fascination with death as a forbidden topic resembles the Victorian obsession with sexuality.

10. Not only the three novels, but also a large number of the short stories, deal explicitly with death: 'Indsamling' (Collection), 'Min tante døde' (My Aunt Died), 'Tilflyttere' (Immigrants), 'Tale ved bisættelsen' (Speech at the Funeral) and 'En lille tur' (A short trip) from *Biler og dyr* (Cars and Animals) and 'Rester' (Remnants) and 'Der er ikke noget nyt' (There's Nothing New) from *Rester* (Remnants) all deal explicitly with death. However, death also plays a central, if more implicit role in many, if not all of the other short stories like for instance 'Fasaner' (Pheasants).

11. Helle suggests an interesting connection between female creativity and (male) corpses and, as such, a mirror image of the many examples that Elisabeth Bronfen supplies in *Over her dead Body*, where the deaths of beautiful women, in morbid and fetishist ways, engender male works of art.

12. In the terms of Erving Goffman (1959) it is interesting to note how the pregnant Ester interrupts both the 'front' and 'back regions' of Susanne and Kim's

home 'stage.' First she sleeps on the couch in the living room, but in the end she breaks her arm and must use their bed, thus forcing the couple's back stage region to the front of the apartment, as the two now have to sleep on the living room sofa.

13. Susanne's act of expression thus reiterates the concepts of Susan Gubar (1982) in '"The Blank Page" and the Issues of Female Creativity,' where she states that women have been excluded from painting – other than their faces.

14. The burial speech points, of course, to Susanne's central fantasy of giving a touching speech at Kim's funeral and also to her ambivalent dream of how she would decorate her home if she were on her own (Helle 2002: 114).

15. The theme of the immobile woman is further developed in the ironically titled short story, 'Mobil' (in *Rester*), where the passive housewife does nothing substantial to save her imperiled husband who calls her on his mobile after he has had an accident in his car in an icy winter night.

16. On the communication between the man and the woman, see Gemzøe.

17. Helle in personal communication has stated that she had to use the pheasant, because the partridge is already too heavily loaded with symbolism in Danish literature. Danish post-war writer Martin A. Hansen used it for the title story of a famous volume, 'Agerhønen' ('The partridge'). The snipe he used as a key symbol in the novel *Løgneren* (The Liar).

18. Gemzøe reads wedding symbolism into this offer, which the narrator declines.

19. Again in the terms of Erving Goffman (1959) he does not keep himself to the 'front stage' of the apartment – entrée and living room – but invades the person's 'back stage': her bedroom, her basement and her toilet. Wanting to open her bedroom closet seems almost a sexual invasion.

20. Like the winter photograph of Anne's partner, this painting, too, had a broken frame.

21. See also Engberg's observation: 'Fortællingerne slutter, men de bliver ikke rundet af' (Engberg 2005: 27) (The stories end, but they are not completed).

22. Perhaps the man's name is not really Richard. Perhaps he, too, like the narrator, lies.

23. In April 2008, Helle published a new novel: *Nede hos hundene* (Down with

the dogs).

24. The untranslatable title describes the most important ferry route connecting Copenhagen to the continent via Germany, an equivalent of the former Dover-Calais ferry.

25. Eighteen months is not a very long time compared to the years it seemed to take Anne in *Hus og hjem* to deal with her parents' deaths. That a death trauma can take even longer is suggested by the case of Jane and Tine's mentally disabled friend, Bo, a man in his thirties still living with his parents. Bo was permanently damaged at the age of twelve, when he encountered the body of the neighbour's daughter, who had hanged herself in the garage.

26. I do not hereby mean to imply that the novel must be read biographically, although there are a number of characteristics shared by Jane, Tine and Helle Helle: all are born and raised in Rødbyhavn. Helle's mother worked at the perfumery on the Rødby-Puttgarden-ferries like Jane and Tine. Susanne and Anne also come from the island of Lolland, where Rødby is situated.

27. The text refers to an actual accident where two ferry workers died. An urban legend has it that one of the victims died because her colleague had to let go of her hand.

28. This Easter death with its possible theme of substitutional suffering and sacrifice of course invests the disaster with a discreet Christian symbolism. But as always in Helle's work the symbols seem enigmatically 'half-hearted.'

29. I am not implying that the enigmatically numb Jane herself is in love with Aksel. Throughout most of the narrative, the narrator puts a clear distance to the man, even robbing him of his proper name, and using 'Abel,' the nickname Tine has made up for him. The name refers to a Danish nursery rhyme, thus highlighting Jane's infantile perception of the world (including men).

V

Bodies

Sexual Perversity in Christiania:
Fri Kærlighet and 'Decadence' in Ibsen's Drama

Errol Durbach
University of British Columbia

I

The phrase 'fri kærlighet' – free love – is first uttered in tones of reprehension and distaste by Rektor Kroll, that arch-conservative of the evangelical right, in Ibsen's *Rosmersholm* (1886). Rejecting Rosmer's claim for a moral system rooted in human nature rather than dogma, he defines his brother-in-law's relation with Rebecca West as a symptom of left-wing moral decay:

> KROLL. I didn't know until last night that it was a question of an apostate and … an emancipated woman living under one roof.
> ROSMER. Ah…! So you don't think there is any sense of virtue to be found among free-thinkers? Doesn't it strike you they might have a natural instinct for morality?
> KROLL. I don't place much reliance on any kind of morality that is not rooted in the faith of the Church.
> ROSMER. And you include Rebecca and me in that too? My relations with Rebecca … !
> KROLL. I cannot bring myself, merely on your account, to abandon my view that there is no tremendous gulf between free-thinking and … hm!
> ROSMER. And what?
> KROLL. … and free-love, if you must have it. (VI, 327)[1]

Many of the elements of 'decadence' cohere in Kroll's accusation against these two moral degenerates: the 'new' or emancipated woman and her male counterpart – the apostate who has abandoned ethics for an adulterous alternative. 'In the conservative mind,' writes Elaine Showalter, 'the two were firmly linked as a couple sharing many attributes. Both were challenging the institution of marriage and blurring the borders between the sexes.' (Showalter 1990: 169). Kroll's harangue has as its primary motive, indeed, the attempt to get Rosmer to legitimize his anomalous relation with a woman whose role in his house can be defined only as mistress, and whose very presence compromises Rosmer's integrity as a representative of the political right. It also compromises his usefulness to the liberal faction: Mortensgård, the left-leaning journalist, is no less embarrassed by Rosmer's transgression of the boundaries of free thought. And even the servant, Mrs. Helseth, shares their view of the decadent couple, her last comment – as the curtain falls – bristling with the indignation of outraged moral rectitude: 'Gud forlade de syndige mennesker! Slår de ikke armene om hinanden!' (VI, 92) ('God forgive the sinful creatures! Putting their arms around each other!') (VI, 381).

'Fri kærlighed' is perhaps the more conventional definition of Decadence in the late nineteenth century – 'the pejorative label,' as Elaine Showalter puts it, 'applied by the bourgeoisie to everything that seemed unnatural, artificial and perverse' (1990: 169), the precursor to cultural degeneration and decay. In one sense, of course, Ibsen endorses this point of view. Free love, in the world of the play, is Rebecca's justification for killing anyone who stands in the way of her passion for Rosmer, and free-thinking gives Dr. West the license (if we agree with Freud) to have sex with his daughter. But Kroll and Mortensgård and Mrs. Helseth are manifestly wrong in their bourgeois assumptions about Rosmer and Rebecca. What is even more perverse about their relationship is not its flouting of social morality, but its extreme sexual asceticism – a reticence on Rosmer's part that we now recognize as a severe form of emotional repression, and on Rebecca's a determined sublimation of sexual desire into forms of exalted cultural aspiration. The only time they actually touch in the play is during that split second on the bridge, before they hurl themselves into the millrace. Sexual perversity in Ibsen extends the definition of decadence into Showalter's other realm of the senses – what she refers to as 'a post-Darwinian aesthetic movement that crossed European boundaries' (169) and displaced the biological and sexual body with erotic fantasy and artifice. The casualty of this form of decadence was inevitably the woman – her body sexually neutralized, vilified or transformed into a myth of spiritual purity. 'Women,' writes Showalter, 'reappear as objects of value in decadent writing only when they are desexualized through maternity or thoroughly aestheticized, stylized, and turned into icons or fetishes.' (170) And these two aspects of Decadence – the bourgeois condemnation of moral decay, and the asexual deflection of the body's desire into aesthetic fantasy – exist in Ibsen as the poles of a dialectic, points of tension in his analysis of the sexual malaise of the late nineteenth century.

II

Krafft-Ebing's study of sexual disorders, the *Psychopathia Sexualis,* appeared in the same year as *Rosmersholm* – 1886 – and it is not surprising to find him making the same rough distinction between these two forms of Decadence: the binaries, as he calls them, of 'perversion' and 'perversity.' Although his primary concern is with homosexual behaviour, he makes a clear general distinction between the reality of a sexual act between same-sex partners ('perversion') and the indulgence of desire in unrequited feelings ('perversity'). 'The determining factor here is the demonstration of perverse feeling for the same sex; not the proof of sexual acts with the same sex. These two phenomena must not be confounded with each other; perversity must not be taken for perversion' (quoted in Stor 1998: 15, original emphasis). This same tension exists in Ibsen's early plays – in *Peer Gynt,* for example, where Peer's conspicuous consumption of sex, in acts of bridal rape and casual copulation with cowgirls and troll-princesses and houris, exist in stark juxtaposition to his fantasies of Solveig's immaculate purity and his determination not to soil her with troll-dirt. And in Ibsen's last play, *When We Dead Awaken*, this same structural pattern is emphasized in the stagecraft: Maja and Ulfheim descending the mountain towards the valley of their carnality, while Rubek and Irene strive ever upwards to a realm of discarnate bliss where sex is sublimated into spiritual essence. Two forms of decadence: 'perversion' and 'perversity.' It is the latter, however, that becomes increasingly more compelling as Ibsen's comment on the post-Romantic world of the late nineteenth-century; and I want to look at a few selected examples of this aspect of perversity in his dramatization of tragically dysfunctional sexual relationships.

The sex in *A Doll's House* can hardly be described as tragically dysfunctional; and Torvald's fantasies, unlike those of the protagonists of the late plays, do not function as a displacement of or barrier to real sex. But, as an early example of perversity, the play is an intriguing *entrée* into the bedrooms of Christiania. Take, for example, the Helmers' return from the party in Act III – Torvald sexually excited by the tarantella, and Nora bracing herself for death. His sexual overtures are an embarrassing amalgam of marital possessiveness and extra-marital fantasy: on the one hand a claim on Nora's loveliness as his by right – 'mine and mine alone, completely and utterly mine' (V, 269), and on the other a vision of defloration as a stimulant to love-making – 'I pretend that you are my young bride, that we are just leaving our wedding, that I am taking you to our new home for the first time…' (V, 270) His erotic dialogue may be unexceptional, but there is nevertheless a decadent edge to his preferences – especially to the stimulant of Nora's dressing up in the costume of a Neapolitan fisher-girl and her titillating performance in the tarantella that sets his blood on fire (V, 270). What is disconcerting about the sexuality is the form that his fantasies take: what Elaine Showalter calls a 'decadent aesthetic' (1990: 170) that turns experience into artifice and the woman into a mechanism, a doll like Hoffman's Olympia or a Stepford wife. But there is also another less obviously decadent element in Nora's fantastic identity as the *Capri*-cious fisher-girl: the crossing of class boundaries and the importation of a proletarian identity into a middle-class environment. The sexual anarchy of decadence, as Showalter points out, also involves this peculiar form of transgression – the celebration of 'romantic alliances between the classes, with both men and women turning to working-class lovers for a passion and tenderness missing in their own class surroundings.' (170) Strindberg's *Miss Julie* will, of course, emphasize this aspect of his protagonist's erotic desire and its tragic consequences. *A Doll's House* merely hints at a form of sexual preference, on the edge of dysfunction that will develop into full-blown decadence in the late drama with its fantasies of sexual avoidance, and its elaborate aesthetics of sublimation and repression.

Rosmersholm, as I have suggested here and elsewhere (Durbach 1977, Durbach 2006), is the *locus classicus* for a decadent/psychiatric discourse in Ibsen. Indeed, Freud's famous analysis of the play has its origins in the displacement of reality into the wish-dream of sex; and he treats the play as a canonical text in the diagnosis of a working-class variant of the Oedipus complex. What intrigues him is the daydream of the household servant or companion who, like Rebecca West, fantasizes the 'disappearance' of the wife or her displacement in the bed of the master of the house. '*Rosmersholm,*' he claims, 'is the greatest work of art of the class that treats of this common phantasy in girls' (Freud 1970: 399). In the context of the play's decadent psychology, this is a disappointingly reductive reading of Rebecca's tragic experience; and although Freud goes on to develop his thesis that 'she stood under the domination of the Oedipus complex, even though she did not know that this universal fantasy had in her case become a reality' (398), *Rosmersholm* remains a far more complex example than he admits of a variant of *psychopathia sexualis*. The dialectics of decadence – sexual perversion and sexual perversity – are the central organizing themes of the play; and what I want to pursue, briefly, is the desexualization of Rebecca, the 'aestheticization' of desire, and the shared fantasies of sexual avoidance that make *Rosmersholm* a decadent masterpiece of the 1880s.

One way of understanding Rebecca is to suggest that she has internalized the processes of perversion and perversity, and transformed herself from one pole of the decadent dialectic into the other. Less abstractly stated, Rebecca's experience of sex as an uncontrollable erotic force – 'et vildt, ubetvingeligt begær' (VI, 81) – has driven her to the devious soul-murder (Strindberg's term) of Rosmer's wife, deluding herself into the belief that her motives have been ideological rather than sexual in the execution of her rival. Sex and perversion are synonymous in this act – as they are, indeed, in the sexual abuse that she has experienced (if Freud is correct) in her father's bed. But the Rebecca we see as the curtain rises on *Rosmersholm* is a woman whose erotic energies have been 'ennobled' into a desexualized form of *agape* – as if the self-deluding ideological purpose that drove her to eliminate Beata has now displaced the reality of desire. She has, in a sense, elevated her love for Rosmer into a fantasy of transcendence, a myth of desire drained of passion and transformed into pure spiritual essence – 'den store, forsagende kærlighet, som nøjer sig med samlivet, slig, som der har været imellem os to' (VI, 82). ('Love as that great desire for self-renunciation that contents itself just with the way of life that we have shared together.' IV, 82). Ibsen, as in all his dialectical structures, invests even this kind of perversity with a loveliness that contradicts the negative implications of such renunciation. The fantasy may be desexualized and a denial of the reality of desire, but it is also enveloped in a spiritual peacefulness that is compelling – however inadequate it may be as compensation for the passion lost in the transformation.

The trouble with the new life is that it can never rid itself entirely of the old perversion – not only in the sense that Beata's death cannot be dismissed without penalty, but also in Rebecca's subconscious awareness of a sexual taint that compromises her relationship with Rosmer. (Freud's psychoanalytical discussion of the incest theme remains insistent.) But Rebecca's devastating threnody of loss in her confessional speeches has little to do with the consequences of perversion. Their theme is the tragedy of perversity itself – the self-deceiving fantasies that structure

Rosmer's repression of a guilt-laden sexuality, and her own sense of the consequences of sexual sublimation, her 'deflection of sexual instinctual forces to higher cultural aims.' (Gay 1988: 164)

Rebecca's analysis of the sublimating process lies at the very heart of the play's experience and articulates her tragedy of human incompletion, trapped between the antinomies of perverse pleasure and social conditioning:

> Det er Rosmer-slætens livssyn, – eller *dit* livsynn I alle fald, – som har smittet min vilje […] Og gjort den syg. Trælbundet den under love, som før ikke gjaldt for mig. Du, – samlivet med dig, – har adlet mit sind – […] Det rosmerske livssyn adler. Men – men, – men – […] men det dræber lykken, du. (VII, 83)

> (It is the Rosmer philosophy of life ... or in any case *your* philosophy ... that has infected my will. […] And made it sick. Made it a slave to laws that had meant nothing to me before. You ... being together with you ... has given me some nobility of mind ... […] The Rosmer philosophy of life ennobles all right. But ... but ... but... […] But it kills happiness.) (VI, 371)

'Ennobled' is the key term in her summing up of the situation – an idea possibly borrowed by Freud and his Viennese colleagues in their search for a new language in which to describe the psychic life. 'Adler' in Ibsen's *Riksmål* reverberates as 'adelt' in the German translation of the play – the term used by Freud and Otto Rank to describe their theory of anarchic sexual energy deflected into elevated spiritual purpose. 'Ennoblement' and 'sublimation' are not merely cognate terms. They are, as Otto Rank's translator indicates, synonymous. "Veredelt," he writes, 'has been rendered 'sublimated,' even though a more literal English version would be 'ennobled,' which might better suggest the highly positive sense Rank clearly associated with the German word.' (Richter 1992: xxxix).

For Rank, ennoblement, sublimation, and repression were indeed the index of a civilizing process and the measure of social evolution – in much the same sense that Freud, later, was to define the rewards of Civilization as compensation for the deprivations, the *Unglücklichkeit*, of human discontent. Ibsen, as I have suggested, offers a partial endorsement of the cultural loveliness of ennoblement. But the dialectic within the dialectic forces an acknowledgement of the perversity and loss that are inseparable from the sublimation demanded by the civilizing process; and Rebecca is forced to mediate between sensations of ennobling beauty and the ravages that sublimation imposes upon the erotic life.

There is an intense physical anguish in her lament for the desexualized body, for 'perversity' in *Rosmersholm* ultimately lies in this substitution of nobility for happiness:

> Rosmersholm has broken me. [...] Completely and utterly broken me. When I first came here I had some spirit; I wasn't afraid to do things. Now I feel crushed by a tradition quite foreign to me. I feel after this as though I hadn't any courage left for anything. (VI, 367)

> Rosmersholm has paralysed me. My will-power has been sapped, my spirit crippled. Once I dared tackle anything that came my way; now that time is gone. I have lost the power to act, Johannes. (370)

> It is the Rosmer philosophy of life ... or in any case your philosophy... that has infected my will. [...] And made it sick. (371)

Knækket, bøjet ind, magtstjålet, stækket, forkludret, smittet (VII, 79-83): Rebecca's experience of irreparable damage is both sexual and metaphysical – a sense of psychic enervation for which 'Rosmersholm' is both the cause and the metaphor. As an emblem of decadence in its post-Darwinian aesthetic mode, 'Rosmersholm' traces the transformation of unfettered *Eros* into a form of selfless *Agape*, perversion into perversity, and a wild and murderous sexual energy into the sublime fantasy of the Third Empire.

The dream of the Third Empire, in Ibsen, is that elusive quest for perfection that resolves the unresolvable dialectic and offers a way out of tragic contradiction and the destructive operation of binary forces. In *Rosmerholm* it takes the form of a new political dispensation, a demi-Paradise of spiritual perfection before the intrusion of the serpent into the garden. To sustain the fantasy, Rebecca and Rosmer must of necessity maintain that asexual and ascetic fiction that Kroll regards with incredulity, but that slowly over time erodes the reality of their sexual attraction for each other. Rebecca, as I have suggested, *sublimates* erotic energy as if to deny the perversion – Beata's soul-murder – that compromises the spiritual perfection of the Third Empire fantasy she shares with Rosmer. And Rosmer *represses* any possibility of desire for Rebecca lest its conscious revelation incriminate him in the death of his wife and so destroy the innocence and the purity of his fantasy Kingdom. Trapped between the reality of a perverse desire and the perversity of a fantasy that has sapped them dry of passion, Ibsen's 'lovers' can find no exit from the destructive nexus of decadent antinomies. And yet – and this is the crux of the play, and the occasion of much critical disagreement, as comprehensively summarized by Wells (2006) – there does seem to be a way out of the dialectic and a minor triumph over Decadence and its denaturing aesthetic.

To the extent that Rebecca is able to deal with perversion, she embarks on a process of atonement that assuages the guilt of Beata's murder and frees her to reestablish her relationship with Rosmer as his legitimate wife. Accepting the ethic that requires justice for crimes committed, she consigns herself to death – rediscovering the will and a paradoxical sense of joy that Rosmersholm, in the final analysis, has *not* been able to kill in her. To make the fantasy Kingdom a reality, she will enact – as proof – her newly recovered sense of healing integrity and so exculpate the perversion that has enthralled her. What she cannot escape is the perversion of sexual abuse in her relationship with her father; but the fear of reenacting the Oedipal trauma in her relationship with Rosmer is no longer the barrier, as Freud argues, to her marriage. The greater deterrence is Rosmer's own repressed guilt and the hopelessness of his ever recovering the passion sacrificed to his Third Empire fantasy. And yet he too is able to step out of the dialectic, dispel the emasculating fears of perversion by stepping onto the bridge from which his wife had flung herself into the millrace and committing himself to Rebecca's fate – even if it means dying with her. The play ends with an act of human atonement – not some abstract fantasy of sexual transcendence, but an affirmation of love as a sacrament and a physical embrace that restores passion, however momentarily, to a relationship that experiences it for the first time as an erotic impulse. Free of the perversity of sublimation, Rebecca and Rosmer finally become lovers – a triumph compromised by the necessity of death that valorizes their action, but not, surely, by the pusillanimity of bourgeois attitudes that still insist on reading their love as perversion. Mrs. Helseth, piously calling on God to forgive the adulterous couple, has the last word in the play – Ibsen's challenge to the audience to dismiss this temptation to misrepresent the resolution that they have just witnessed.

III

The play that serves most usefully as a coda to this discussion of perversity in Ibsen's late drama is *Little Eyolf* (1894), his image of the 'aestheticization' of incest and his most notable contribution to *Das Inzest-Motiv* in post-Romantic drama. Not surprisingly, the play insinuates itself into Freud's therapeutic case-histories – he can safely assume, for instance, that the 'Rat Man' will have seen the play and understood its symbolism[2] – but it was his disciple, Otto Rank, who shifted discussion of *Little Eyolf* from psychoanalytical diagnosis to a paradigm of the *Zeitgeist* and a significant document in the evolution of Modernity. For Rank, the play is a turning point in the 'progress of sexual repression' in the psychic life of the nineteenth century and an index, therefore, 'of general cultural progress.' (Rank 1992: 230). His thesis – clearly at odds with Ibsen's view of repression as a debilitating fantasy – is that the measure of civilization is the extent to which incestuous impulses find expression not in a perverse reality, but in the subliminal intimations of perversity. Ibsen's play, he argues, in the obscurity of its style, represses the very perversion it purports to deal with, and so shifts the treatment of incest from the realism of its treatment in Romantic drama to the decorous defense mechanisms of Modernity. There is, he suggests, a certain 'delicacy' (330) in Ibsen's dramatization of incest – even if neurotic discontent is the result. 'In lieu of incestuous acts,' he writes, '[...] we find reserved affections, unpronounced relationships, or differences of opinion, debates, and conflicts of will. The characters are doomed not by some external, powerful fate but by their own sufferings – by their neurosis.' (542) Ibsen's view of these reserved affections and ineffable relationships in *Little Eyolf* is considerably less tolerant of their neurotic delicacy. Such perversity is treated as a violation of every aspect of 'Human Responsibility' – the great theme of Allmers' unwritten thesis – responsibility to his child, to his desexualized wife, and above all to his erotically desired 'sister' who (in Showalter's description of decadence) is aestheticized, stylized and turned into a pseudo-religious icon of the spiritual life.

What Otto Rank calls the *Geschwister-Komplex*, brother-sister incest, lies at the very heart of *Little Eyolf*, not as a pathological syndrome but as an elaborate fantasy of sexual evasion and a rejection of all forms of biology that define the mortal condition. In the place of process – time, mutability, change and death – Ibsen's protagonist substitutes the perversities of a complex and artificial defense against Nature, his own particular *A Rebours*, which cancels all human connections in the quest for an antidote to the decay of the body and the senseless determinism of the post-Darwinian world. Allmers is a self-styled philosopher whose marriage to a wealthy wife has provided the leisure to indulge his existential musing, and also to provide support for his 'sister' – the object of his sexual desire who renders him incapable of any love not sheltered by incestuous prohibition. The quotation marks around Asta's 'sisterly' relationship are intended to anticipate the revelation in Act II that she is an illegitimate child, no blood relation whatsoever to her 'brother', and therefore free of the *Geschwister-Komplex* that might have made her sexually ineligible. Coming half-way through *Little Eyolf*, this revelation enables us to see both the structural contents of Allmers' fantasy, its source in his sexual anxiety, and the consequences of its cancellation. It is this decadent aesthetic, not his philosophical inquiry, that is his most notable contribution to the *Weltanschauung* of the 1890s: a channeling of natural process, faith, and love through the distortions of temperament into fantastic redefinitions of traditional value. In their simplest formulation, what Allmers' fantasies create is a decadence that uncouples Eros and Thanatos in a perversity of sexless, immutable, and inhuman existence outside of time (see Durbach 1982: 104-127).

Mortal fear in *Little Eyolf* is manifest in the recurrent idea of *forvandlingens lov* – the law of change and the implicit immanence of death; and because sex and the body are subject to this inevitability, Allmers experiences desire as a form of dread – a compulsion that (like the Rat Wife and her dog) fascinates and horrifies, as ineluctable as the undertow and to be resisted by whatever symbolic means are to hand. His impossible fantasies are those of imperishable bliss that defies the mortality of the body while affirming desire, that acknowledge the irresistible while denying the dread of imperfection and death; and it is in his incestuous love for his 'sister' that Allmers locates this mythic icon. She becomes his Big Eyolf, the pseudo-religious corollary to the poor crippled boy who is cast as the spiritual child of his incestuous family structure; and just as he immortalizes little Eyolf as consummation and apotheosis, so he invests Asta with transcendental intimations of a sexual/sexless principle of salvation – love eternally available because exempt from the laws of mutability:

> ALLMERS. And it's you, Asta, I want to come home to again [...] my dear, dear sister. I must come back to you. Home to you so that I can be cleansed and purified from living with ...
> ASTA [*disturbed*]. Alfred ... this is a sin against Rita!
> ALLMERS: Yes, I have sinned against her. But not in this. Oh, think back, Asta! Think how we used to live together? Wasn't it like one high holiday from beginning to end? [...] Because the love between brother and sister ... [...] That is the one relationship that is not subject to the law of change. (VIII, 86)

What, one wonders, does he concede as the 'sin' against his wife? The text is fairly obscure, as Rank would have it, on the nature of his offence, but hints and suggestions of the perverse are legion. Has he married Rita to protect himself against his desire for his 'sister'? Does he fantasize the 'sister' in the arms of the wife, even calling out Alma's name at the moment of orgasm (Kerans 1965)? Has he even slept with Rita since the accident, during their lovemaking many years ago, when the child tumbled off the table? The psychopathologies of everyday life are legion, and Allmers seeks to perpetuate them in his relationship with Asta even after her revelation that they are neither kith nor kin:

> ALLMERS. But what change does that make to our relationship? None at all.
> ASTA. It changes everything, Alfred. Our relationship is not that of brother and sister.
> ALLMERS. Maybe not. But is equally sacred. Will always be sacred.
> ASTA. Remember ... it is subject to the law of change ... as you said a moment ago. (VIII, 87)

Both 'Eyolfs' are dead – his twin 'defences against the inroads of passion' (McFarlane 1977: 23) – and Allmers is left to cope with the cancellation of all his evasionary techniques for denying responsible commitment to other human beings. Asta, freed at last by a beneficent law of change from the stultifying sexlessness of the *Geschwister-Komplex*, finds no sense of reciprocal release in Allmers' inability to accommodate himself to her sexual eligibility. All that remains is for her to step outside of the fantasy that negates her as a sexual being – a fantasy that has endured ever since childhood, with her dressing up in boys' clothes and her assumption of the role of 'Eyolf' as further protection against the inroads of desire. The only antidote to perversity is to relinquish it, and Asta saves herself by leaving her brother for Borghejm – in many ways a poor second choice for the man she loves, but at least someone free of the nexus of the incest-myth.

The last act of the play tests the Allmers' capacity for dealing with perversity and, like Rosmer and Rebecca, they are driven to confront the cosmic emptiness of a life without illusion, cut off from the consolations of faith, and incapable of finding easy answers in human love. One solution, of course, is to make 'human responsibility' viable as committed action instead of another escapist ploy, and to acknowledge the creative possibility of *forvandlingens lov*. 'Perhaps,' Allmers tentatively suggests, 'the law of change might nevertheless hold us together.' (VIII, 99) There is a dying fall to the play's dénouement, a deeply moving attempt – as in the last few moments of Albee's *Who's Afraid of Virginia Woolf?* – to survive the insulating shelter of perversity. Like George and Martha, they have to relinquish destructive fantasy to dynamic process and death, and find in agonizing change the possibility of recovery and renewal. Can mortal sexuality replace the stasis of transcendental fantasy? Can the meaning of 'Eyolf' shift from an evasion of responsibility to an ethical involvement with the wellbeing of the quayside waifs? As always in Ibsen, there is no unequivocal answer to the human problem. But decadence and perversity in *Little Eyolf* are complicated by the pathetic dignity of Rita and Allmers' attempt to rediscover the reality of human values under the great stillness that envelops them. Somewhere between the alluring region of the stars and the destructive undertow of the sea, there remains the tentative hope that Ibsen's pair may overcome their fear of living life without illusions and finally confront the challenges of modernity.

References

Durbach, E. (1977): 'Ibsen, Rank, and Freud: Rosmersholm and the discourse of Viennese Psychiatry.' In *Scandinavian-Canadian Studies / Études scandinaves au Canada*, 10, pp. 35-52.

Durbach, E.(1982): *'Ibsen the Romantic': Analogues of Paradise in the Later Plays*. London: Macmillan.

Durbach, E. (2006): "Fra det ubevidste Sjæleliv': Ibsen's Existential Poetry.' In *Scandinavica*, 45 (2), pp. 145-162.

Freud, S. (1955 [1909]): 'Notes Upon a Case of Obsessional Neurosis.' In *The Standard Edition of the Complete Psychological Works of Sigmund Freud*, translated and edited by J. Strachey, vol. X. London: Hogarth Press.

Freud, S. (1970 [1916]): 'Some Character-Types Met With in Psycho-analytic Work.' Re-printed in J.W. McFarlane (ed.): *Henrik Ibsen: A Critical Anthology*, Harmondsworth Penguin. Originally published in English in *The Standard Edition of the Complete Psychological Works of Sigmund Freud*, translated and edited by J. Strachey, vol. XIV. London: Hogarth Press, 1957.

Gay, P. (1988): *Freud: A Life for Our Time*. New York: Norton.

Kerans, J. (1965): 'Kindermord and Will in *Little Eyolf*.' In T. Bogard and W. Oliver (eds.), *Modern Drama: Essays in Criticism*. London: Oxford University Press.

Ibsen, H. (1914): *Samlede Værker*. Kristiania: Gyldendal.

Ibsen, H. (1960-1977): *The Oxford Ibsen*. Edited by J. McFarlane. London: Oxford University Press.

McFarlane, J.W. (1977): 'Introduction.' In *The Oxford Ibsen*, vol. VIII. Edited by J. McFarlane. London: Oxford University Press.

Showalter, E. (1990): *Sexual Anarchy: Gender and Culture at the Fin de Siècle*. Harmondsworth: Penguin.

Stor, M. (1998): 'Transformations: Subjects, Categories and Cures in Krafft-Ebing's Sexology.' In Bland, L. and L. Doan (eds.), *Sexology in Culture: Labeling Bodies and Desires*. Chicago: University of Chicago Press.

Rank, O. (1992 [1912]): *The Incest Theme in Literature and Legend: Fundamentals of a Psychology of Literary Creation*. Translated by G. Richter. Baltimore: Johns Hopkins University Press. First published 1912 as *Das Inzest-Motiv in Dichtung und Sage: Grundzuge einer Psychologie des dichterischen Schaffens*.

Richter, G. (1992): 'Introduction.' In O. Rank, *The Incest Theme in Literature and Legend: Fundamentals of a Psychology of Literary Creation*. Translated by G. Richter. Baltimore: Johns Hopkins University Press.

Wells, M. (2006): '*Rosmersholm* – An Ibsenian Tragedy?' *Scandinavica*, 45 (2), pp. 163-188.

Notes

1. Ibsen, Henrik, 'Rosmersholm'. Translations derive from the *Oxford Ibsen*, ed. James McFarlane (London: OUP), with volume and page number in parentheses. References to Ibsen's original derive from *Samlede Værker* (Kristiania: Gyldendal, 1914), with volume and page number in parentheses.

2. 'One day the Rat-Wife in *Little Eyolf* came up in the analysis, and it became impossible to escape the inference that in many of the shapes assumed by his obsessional deliria rats had another meaning still – namely, that of children.' (Freud 1955: 215).

Reading Dance: Dance-scenes in Scandinavian Literature before 1900

Annegret Heitmann
Ludwig-Maximilians-Universität München

Why should dancing not have a place in the serious genre of the *Festschrift*, whose aim it is to celebrate the academic achievements of an esteemed colleague?[1] For dance is associated with joy, energy and vitality, all of which seem perfectly appropriate to a salutation of this kind – even if its other connotations, of expressivity, physicality and rapid movement, seem quite foreign to the usual modes of academic celebration. On the other hand dance is an expressive mode with a variety of characteristics and connotations, by no means inferior in its suggestivity to other art-forms, and which for that reason has become a recognised subject of scholarly analysis.[2] Reference to dance in the medium of literature is of particular interest, as well as a challenge, to a textual reading, because – and this is my main point – the intermediality involved often implies a self-reflexive gesture. By quoting the medium of dance in a literary text, its medial alterity brings about a reflection of its own mediality; its aesthetic means can be designed to incorporate or mirror characteristics of a particular dance or of dance in general. This paper takes a closer look at three Scandinavian texts from the turn of the nineteenth and twentieth centuries, in order to explore the significance of dance in literature both as a theme of some cultural importance as well as a poetological reference in this sense.

Dance is an extremely adaptable and differentiated, but also transhistorical and transcultural, form of human expression and social interaction. The study of dance(s), or its description in a literary text, gives us an insight into particular cultural and socio-historical periods and shifts.

An example might be the transition around 1800 from the highly formal, indeed geometrical, minuet of the sixteenth and seventeenth centuries to the waltz, a dance for couples that implies a quite different concept of space and subjectivity (Klein 1992: 98ff). If we visualise these two forms of dance, it is not difficult to understand that dance not only expresses changing attitudes towards the body but also allows insights into gender relations. Dancing in couples, as well as ballet (whose earliest forms developed around 1500), has a marked erotic component; the almost weightless ballerina in the Romantic ballet corporealises a certain ideal of femininity.[3] The history of dance can also, however, provide information about religious beliefs and practices – we have only to think of the hostility to dance of a particular strand of Christian moral teaching, or the belief that dancers might become possessed – and about social norms and hierarchies as well as power relations. Increasing disciplinary regulation of the body is manifested in changing dancing conventions. A text can thus present dance as a social praxis,[4] it can add information about the social setting, the relationship of the characters, and conceptions of gender and the body. Moreover, it may also attempt a formal representation of a particular dance aesthetic, or it may quote or refer to the aesthetics of dance as a medium in a more general way. The dancing body stages a script; it represents a sign-system of 'Körperbilder und Raumfiguren' (Brandstetter 1995: 16).

The challenge here lies in exploring the relationship between language and the non-linguistic medium of dance. It poses a particular methodological problem, for two reasons. First, dance is not a pure or single medium but an inherently complex portmanteau phenomenon: 'Strukturell fügen sich Körper / Bewegung, Zeit / Musik, Raum (von Bühne und Körper), Beziehungen der Tänzer, bearbeitete Sujets und anklingende Assoziationen zu einem theatralen Setting aus Licht, Ton, Requisite und Objekten zusammen.' (Huschka 2002: 25). To a lesser degree the same is true of non-art dance: it is by definition a complex medial expression of bodily movements in space and time. Second, temporality and the non-linguistic mode are two of its most basic characteristics. Dance consists of a series of 'unrepeatable moments' and has an inherent resistance to documentation and fixation (Brandstetter 1995: 15). Recording a choreography in notation, its transcription, is notoriously difficult; it is indeed virtually impossible to render fluid, aerial, fleeting and transitory movements in any fixed form. But this difficulty, this 'Hiatus zwischen Tanzen und Schreiben,' should not tempt us to think of dance as a pre-linguistic medium (Huschka 2002: 20). Its wealth of connotations and sheer range of expression speak against any such assumption, as do the literary texts that have taken up the challenge of turning dance into language. These have added a further level to the Mallarmean idea that dance is an *écriture corporelle*, whereby the text itself mirrors or replicates such 'writing' of the body (Brandstetter 1995: 21). This effort to create a corporeal script and a corresponding reading became particularly marked at the crisis-ridden time around 1900, when a fundamental distrust of the communicative and expressive abilities of language and its conventions led to a quest for alternative modes of perception and expression, for new communicative signifiers, a drive in which the signifying potential of dance played an important role. 'Free dance' became an important discourse accompanying the crisis of perception and of language around 1900 (Brandstetter 1995: 19).[5] Moreover, when the 'free dance' movement emerged in the early twentieth century, it was associated with change, with fleetingness and fortuity, all of which were also thought of as characteristic of modernity (35). As Gabriele Brandstetter observes, 'Der Tanz verkörpert ein Grundmuster der Ästhetik der Moderne,' inasmuch as it is an art-form, 'die das neue technische Zeitalter als eine durch Bewegung definierte Epoche zu reflektieren such[t]' (ibid).

***

It is thus no coincidence that we find several examples in Scandinavian literature around 1900 of attempts to engage with dance as a medium and as a mode of cultural expression.[6] The most prominent dancer in all Scandinavian literature is probably Nora Helmer in Henrik Ibsen's drama *Et Dukkehjem* (1879; *A Doll's House*). Although a dance is only performed on-stage very briefly, the tarantella is generally believed to be a crucial scene for the understanding of one of Ibsen´s best-known dramas. Along with the debt-bond to Krogstad, Nora´s dance can be understood as a second key sign in the play, and its multiple layers of significance have evoked a number of controversial interpretations (Haakonsen 1948). It runs through the play as Nora's personal sign, is alluded to several times, and twice performed – once on-stage (in the rehearsal in Act Two) and once off-stage in Act Three. The tarantella, which Nora performs in costume and with a tambourine, is a South Italian peasant dance and thus connotes the southern temperament and Mediterranean *joie de vivre*. For Helmer it evokes memories of their young married love and his naive, eroticised view of their marriage.

The symbolic value traditionally accorded to the dance is however not quite so clear-cut. On the one hand the very name links it with the tarantula, whose bite is painful and (according to one interpretation) induces a frenetic dance of death, so-called tarantism; on the other, it was considered a dance of courtship, whose steps expressed love and sexual desire. Both of these conflicting ascriptions – fear of imminent death and eroticism – play an important roll in Nora's performance. Ibsen happens to mention the source of his information about the tarantella in one of his letters, namely a novella entitled *Den lykkelige Familie* (1869, The Happy Family) by the contemporary Danish writer Vilhelm Bergsøe, a friend of his with whom he had spent time in Italy.[7] The narrator of Bergsøe's novella describes a walk over the hills on the island of Ischia to witness a locally-famous performance of the tarantella in a remote farm. Already in Bergsøe's narrative the tarantella is given a dual significance, being performed twice: once (by an old married couple) as a love-dance, and then (by a young pair of siblings) as a saucy parody (Bergsøe 1907: 83-9). Knowing Ibsen's interest in the polyvalence of signs, we may well conclude that he was not so much interested in the simple folkloric implications of the dance, but that it was this ambiguity and subversive potential that attracted and challenged him.

As a dramatist he will also have been intrigued by the medial shift involved in the brief foregrounding of dance in the drama in place of the dominant medium of language. This shift is made significant by the iconic and indexical meanings of dance, which have to do with the illusion of expressivity, the 'transitorische Einmaligkeit' of rhythmic motion, and the guidance of the gaze (Brandstetter 1995: 24). What makes dance dance is its materiality, its sequencing, the spatial movement, its transitoriness. So when Nora dances she moves 'voldsomt' (Ibsen 1933: 334: wildly, violently), 'med stigende villhet' (334; more and more wildly), and as Helmer later observes, her dance is 'vel megen naturlighed' (343; all too natural).[8] The different perceptions – Nora's own, that of the on-stage voyeurs,[9] as well as that of the audience – are a function of the different possible relations between iconic and symbolic understanding: movement, expressivity, memoria, sexuality and fear are aligned in a variety of permutations. The dizzy whirling of the dance, which characterises her tarantella performance, corresponds to a spiralling of the semiotic process, which proceeds from the folkloristic quotation through the husband's querulous attempts at restraint and Rank's voyeuristic gaze to Nora's own ambivalence between desperation and self-liberation.[10] No clear and definite meaning can be deduced from the semiotic structure of the spiralling dance. Just as she forges her father's signature on the bond, Nora here, too, tries to manipulate a sign for her own ends: her wild, ecstatic motion can be understood as an anticipation of those movements, especially the spiral twist, that shortly afterwards, in the form of avant-garde 'free dance,' would become famous as a counter to the rigidities of the corporal *tenue* associated with the repressive norms of society (Brandstetter 1995: 29-31). The connotation of Nora's wild dance, a conventional set of signs re-interpreted, is thus partly an attempt at self-liberation. Yet in the context of the drama this expropriation of a cultural pattern – an equivalent to what Judith Butler (1993) calls 're-signification' – affords neither freedom nor political self-determination. On the contrary, Nora's ecstasy simply increases her husband's compulsion to own and control her. He insists on 'kunstens fordringer' (Ibsen 1933: 343) (the demands of art) and the cultural norms, and tolerates Nora's wild excess only because of her success.

Not merely in the matter of dance but all through the play Nora's behaviour, often considered ambivalent (Østerud 1993: 175-7), is characterised by expropriation and re-signification. She accepts her song-bird role to satisfy Helmer, she plays the spendthrift in order to get hold of as much money as possible to pay off her debt, she acts the vamp to entrance Rank. She commands the entire register of helplessness, charm, naiveté and seduction. In playing the squirrel, she plagiarises from her own natural spontaneity and the supposed 'nature of woman.' But the advantage that accrues from all this re-signification is limited; she fails to break out of the ascriptive circle. Several critics have commented on the 'masquerade of femininity' (Selboe 1997; Langås 2004), the constant playing within the play, and recognised its self-reflexive character. In this light, the end of the drama cannot be read as an affirmation of emancipation, as which it has often been misunderstood. If we look closely at the implications of the re-signification process being staged in this central scene, with its ambivalence between self-liberation and existential angst, and its evocation of erotic power-fantasies, we receive a rather different impression. Helmer's last line is a helpless question, which is answered only by the slamming of the front-door downstairs, both of them implying a fundamental scepticism about language as an expression of truth. It is obvious that the slamming signifies Nora's abandonment of the doll's house, but it also signals a move into the unknown, which picks up the non-linguistic a-topia of the dance[11] and affirms once again the play's 'pronouncedly gestural [mode]' (McFarlane 1989: 245). The question about 'woman's place,' which Derrida (1986) raises in connection with the choreography of dance, is not only confronted by the impossible future of women in the doll's house, but also shown, through the combination of the linguistic scepticism and the a-topia of dance, to be unanswerable.

That means that the speculation about where Nora goes, which has engaged audiences and critics ever since, is in vain. It should come as no surprise to find that Ibsen himself, when asked the same question, simply replied that he had no idea: she could just as well return home as become an itinerant circus-artiste.[12] Here again he alludes to a-topia. It is not for nothing that the last sign in the play is a doubling of contradictory signs: a question and an exclamation mark instead of a statement. Ibsen provides a provocative ending, a dilemma. However, the play's carefully-worked out structure implies a disillusioning conclusion: the whirling motion of the dance can be understood as a poetological signal for the hopeless striving for fixed meanings and ready solutions (Langås 2004: 127). As in many of Ibsen's dramas, the text provides a parallel story in the Linde-Krogstad couple, which in almost every detail complements – or rather inverts – that of the Helmers. Mrs. Linde actually makes the sacrifice that Nora aims for: the crook Krogstad forgives, which the coward Helmer cannot. Nora is now going where Kristine has come from, both topographically and metaphorically; the one puts on her outdoor clothes, the other removes them (Selboe 1997). Already in 1879, Nora's supposedly liberating emancipation is undermined by disillusioning re-significations: leaving the doll's house equals a-topia.

***

Written almost ten years after Ibsen´s play, Amalie Skram's novel *Lucie* also thematises woman's place in society, gender and power relations and it also does so by alluding to the theme of dance. Here again dancing is dominant neither structurally nor thematically, but its associations do focus the novel's potential conflict at the charged meeting-point of social and sexual difference. The subject is mentioned several times in an apparently casual fashion; Lucie herself is shown dancing on three occasions. In the very first scene, where she is introduced not as his wife but still as Gerner's lover, she skips and dances happily through the apartment: 'Tralalalalalalalalala, hun danset reinlendertrin over gulvet inn i soveværelset' (Skram 1888/1911: 204) (Tralalalalalalalalala, she danced the steps of an écossaise along the floor into the bedroom). Singing and movement seem to convey innocent joy. She looks into the mirror to see a young woman happy and apparently at ease in her body, so that one's first reaction is to see dance here as an expression of pure uninhibitedness, as a token of the true, original nature of woman. But we know from other works by Amalie Skram that this apparently uncomplicated relationship between outer and inner self of women is indeed a complicated and critical one (Langås 2004: 188-213).

Her husband Gerner, who never dances, and who systematically represses Lucie with his everlasting rules and precepts, offers a complete contrast, which leads her to the regretful conclusion: 'Tenk, jeg har ikke fått mig en eneste svingom siden jeg giftet mig' (Skram 1888/1911: 94) (Imagine, I haven't shaken a leg since I got married). Lucie occasionally tries to escape this oppressive joylessness by visiting her friends from Tivoli-times, and not least to get in 'en ortli' polkett' (67) (a decent polka) or a gay waltz. Different attitudes towards dance thus seem to encapsulate the contrast between the natural (with its feminine connotations) and its repression by the male as well as the social difference between bourgeois and proletarian. 'Splittelsen,' Unni Langås concludes in relation to Skram´s presentation of the body in *Fru Inés* (1891), 'avslører i siste instans en kultur som ikke er i stand til å ivareta menneskenes behov som kjønnede subjekter' (The split reveals a culture which is not capable of looking after the needs of human beings as gendered subjects), and she notes a 'misforhold' (disturbed relationship) between bodies, roles and expectations (Langås 2004: 213).

This critical conception of the subject is also brought about by the topic of dance in *Lucie*. The text soon gives the lie to any simple dichotomy of natural femininity and male repression. The social contrast is complicated by Mrs. Reinertson, who also loves a dance, and the various balls thrown by the middle-class. The association between dancing, flirting and physical contact comes out not just in Lucie's visits to her old proletarian haunts but also in her dance with Knut Reinertson at a perfectly respectable venue. Her seduction by the attractive Reinertson negates the gender dichotomy too, which at first seemed to suggest that femininity equals naturalness and being uncomplicated. The masked ball, and Reinertson's calculated flirting, link dance with pretence and deception too. Lucie is deceived as she dances: body language offers no fail-safe access to truth. The very fact that all the dancers are masked, that is, appear in other personae, suggests a divorce between appearance and reality; Reinertson's patent manipulation of Lucie discredits the idea that expression in dance is somehow direct and unfalsified. It not only is subject to different social and gender norms but provides the perfect screen for projecting all manner of fantasies.

The meeting-point of these projections is the socially-accepted double morality, conveyed in the novel by Gerner's marriage to a former Tivoli-girl. The Kristiania Tivoli, a smaller version of the famous fun-park in Copenhagen, had always to struggle against its rather doubtful reputation (Melvold, n.d.). Despite repeated attempts to make it attractive to the middle-class as well, the park continued to be mainly associated with the dance-evenings patronised by 'berygtede Kvinder' (ibid) (disreputable women). Gerner's reluctance to dance has, no doubt, its roots in this association between Lucie and Tivoli. It is a reminder of his own double morality, since he got to know Lucie as a dancer and prostitute, presumably in Tivoli itself. He projects onto dance in general his own experience of it as the prelude to sex with prostitutes, and his fear that Lucie's past occupation may somehow be inherent in her. Lucie too associates dance not simply with physical movement but primarily with a whole gamut of ideas: first of all her belief in the power of her own beauty, as we see from the way in the very first scene that she keeps looking at herself in the mirror; then her memories of her own earlier innocence, which of course totally ignore the darker aspects of her previous life; and finally her escape into fantasy-worlds, which allows her to believe that Reinertson might love her. All this turns dance into a world of appearances, a screen for projections – a *tabula rasa* able to accommodate almost any sort of notion or fancy: the fear of defeat vis-à-vis faith in one's own strength, morality, immorality, double morality, feminine authenticity, and male deceit. The physical symptoms – the racing pulse, the sweating, the redness of face – are only partly due to the activity itself; the feeling of weightlessness, of floating in the air, that Lucie experiences when she dances with Reinertson, is a result of her wilful obliviousness towards her real surroundings; her breathlessness and the thumping of her heart have less to do with exertion than with her excitement at hoping for a new liaison. Skram's skilfully nuanced descriptions of her protagonists' physical subjectivity allows us to glimpse their psyche through and beyond the dramatic instant (Hjort-Vetlesen 1993: 462). There is therefore no need for long descriptions of the dancing – in *Lucie* they are indeed relatively brief. Skram's method of 'writing dance' is a matter rather of suggesting the medium's manifold potentialities for conveying not only the figures' emotional state but also a whole range of social connotations and contemporary conflicts of value. So much for natural spontaneity, then: a woman dancing is more of a palimpsest.

***

In Herman Bang's story *Irene Holm*, first published a couple of years after

Skram's novel, dance is the main theme, however. The text is about dance as an artistic medium (the ballet of the Royal Theatre) which is contrasted with its opposite, in this case a village dancing-school. The two worlds are linked by the protagonist Irene Holm and the disaster that brought her from the Copenhagen stage to this dismal provincial village. The former ballet student is forced to earn her living as a dancing instructor for the young people of the village, who have no interest in what she has to offer them, while she continues to mourn her failure in the capital many years ago. The climax of the text is a ball held to mark the end of the course, where she allows herself to be talked into performing her supposed show-piece, which turns into an involuntary parody of her artistic ambitions and exposes her pretensions for what they are. The forty-year-old spinster lifts her skirts and starts dancing a tarantella from 'La grande Napolitaine.' Without realising it, she finds herself dancing the part of the doomed Fenella, the solo she aimed for in vain all those years ago. At the high point of ecstasy, of intended release, her illusions and her hopelessness are all too plainly expressed. The connotations of the medium of dance, energy, agility, grace and joy, are utterly unsuited to Irene Holm. This realisation is anticipated in the story's very first sentence:

> Det blev læst op en Søndag efter Gudstjenesten, af Sognefogdens Søn, ved Stævningsstenen udenfor Kirken: at Frøken Irene Holm, Danserinde fra det kongelige Teater, den første November i Kroen vilde aabne sine Kursus i Holdning, Dans og Bevægelse, saavel for Børn som for Viderekomne, Damer og Herrer – saafremt et tilstrækkeligt Antal Deltagere tegnedes. Prisen fem Kroner for hvert Barn, for Søskende Moderation. (Bang 2006: 576)

> One Sunday after the service the son of the chairman of the village council read out an announcement at the usual spot in front of the church: Miss Irene Holm, dancer at the Royal Theatre, will give courses in deportment, dance and movement, for children and adults, beginners and advanced, ladies and gentlemen, from the first of November in the village inn – provided that a sufficient number are registered. Cost: five Kr. per child. Rebate for siblings.

Anyone familiar with Bang will recognise that this sentence, simply on account of its length and complexity, is unusual for his style. Yet it contains and anticipates the story's central problem and conflict. As a whole, it makes an announcement about a future venture, dance lessons, that would normally be intended to provide pleasure and distraction. But what the tone of the announcement actually conveys is routine, repetitiveness, convention – it suggests an utter lack of joy, amply confirmed as the story unfolds. The announcement is in fact Janus-faced: it looks forward to something that is going to take place, but also looks back, in mentioning that Irene Holm is a 'Danserinde fra det kongelige Teater.' Such a claim belongs at best to the past, but is in fact a *suggestio falsi*, if not an outright lie, for the former ballet student never actually attained the status of a member of the corps de ballet. In this mix of pasts and futures, of promise, convention and illusion, the present never actually occurs; the story's first sentence actually does not, as we are used to and might expect from Bang's impressionist prose, toss us *in medias res*.

The rhetoric and the medial status of this first sentence make the same point. It is not merely an announcement, it is a proclamation, almost a prophesy. What is going to happen is written down and read out in public by an official crier at a recognised spot, near the church, immediately after the Sunday service. This fusion of announcement and prophesy ironises the message; the intervention of the crier makes it an indirect, mediated communication. This indirect status is also perceptible in the choice of language: the communication is verbose, complicated by subordination; the syntax is halting and employs (in the Danish) two passive forms and a conditional clause. Provisos are expressed, terms and conditions set out, the dominant concern is with formalities – all this is conveyed by the lexis and the tone.

This insistence on the mediality and obliqueness of the communication anticipates the theme of the story, which is basically about the intermediality of dance as a kinetic medium. Dance has again several layers of signification here. In the first place, it represents the protagonist's purpose in life – her livelihood as a teacher of dance, and her shattered dream of becoming a member of the corps de ballet in the Royal Theatre. Secondly, it is something to be taught to the young people of the village: they are to learn not merely specific dance-steps but also middle-class style and comportment. Thirdly, once Irene Holm takes on the role of Fenella, it constitutes the story's climax, for she involuntarily becomes a tragicomic figure, a pathetic caricature of the acclaimed solo dancer.

Once again the plethora of signs in the course of the story attests to the effectiveness and power of dance as a medium of communication. In this case too, the story is based upon the assumption that as an artistic medium it is characterised especially by expressivity and delicacy, by a rapidity of movement that commands both space and the instant. Even in ordinary life, the movement of dance is generally experienced as liberating and pleasurable rhythm – dance is connected with celebrations, beauty, grace, sexual pursuit and *joie de vivre*. But all this forms the illusory sub-text for Irene Holm's efforts. In her world, dance is bound up with exercises and discipline, disappointment and tragedy – she remembers the criticisms of the ballet-master, whose directions and authority she attempts to pass on to the village youth: 'En – to – tre – Battement ...' (Bang 2006: 578) (one, two, three, battement ...). But the rhythm is overwhelmed by her memories of past humiliations and her failed career, the ballet-master's mortifying disparagement: "'Holm har ingen Élan ... Holm har ingen Élan ...'" (581) (Holm has no *élan* ... Holm has no *élan*). Her dreams of making a career have given way to resigned retrospection, grace to absurdity. Her solo performance in the village inn turns into a fiasco, because she loses herself totally in the music and the illusion, and in doing so forgets both rules and poise: 'Hun saae ikke Tilskuernes Ansigter mer – hun aabnede Munden – smilede, viste alle sine Tænder (nogle græsselige Tænder), hun vinkede, agerede, – vidste, følte kun "Soloen"' (586) (she was no longer aware of the faces in the audience – she opened her mouth – smiled, showed all her teeth (horrible teeth), she waved, danced – experienced, felt only the 'solo'). But this undisciplined self-surrender is totally inappropriate to the art form of dance, whose essence is the subordination of dynamic to rules and the artificial staging of purely illusory effortlessness. In Irene Holm's case, the two basic constituents of expressive dance have lost touch with one another: all she can do is to impart the dead husk of rules and drill, so her teaching is perfectly adequate for the young people of the village.

The mediated form of the announcement that begins the story thus anticipates what dance signifies for the protagonist and for the text as a whole: not fluid movement but jerkiness, not immediacy but an illusion-filled attachment to the past, not graceful poise but convention and *tenue* ('Holdning'). Nothing here corresponds to the true requirements of dance, spontaneity and expressivity. The calculated failure of the beginning to toss us *in medias res* signals that the expected fluid grace will be suffocated by convention, that the freedom aspired to through dance is an illusion. Directing our attention initially to the crier's proclamation and its carefully staged mediality is not only a hint at the significance that mediality will bear in the text, but also that we will find mediation and mediocrity instead of immediacy.

***

These three texts, appearing in Norway and Denmark between 1879 and 1890, belong to different genres and their protagonists could hardly be more different in character. What connects them is that their common theme of dance has to be understood in its complex relation to social, psychological and gender issues, and reveals the interdependence of these contexts. In all three cases dance is primarily associated with femininity and is thought to signify the attempt at self-emancipation – gainsay the rules, dance oppression or fear away; or: just for once to dance the solo! But since in each case the aim of finding authenticity, recognition and freedom fails, there is no indication that the point here should be to celebrate the victory of non-verbal immediacy over the conventions and norms of the culture. On the contrary, at the level of the dancing protagonists, the writing of the body is no match for modernity's discourse of crisis; they cannot dance themselves out of their respective situations of crisis and despair. Dancing is shown not to be an alternative, but an integral part of the crisis of culture. On the other hand, the authors who chose to use dance as a means of expression were able to exploit its plethora of signs: they could make use of its signifying potential in order to reveal significative vacancies at the level of their protagonists. To that end they made a point of transferring some of the medial characteristics of dance into their texts: perpetual gyration, which serves to convey the unlimitable process of semiosis and undecidability of truths and values; the multiplicity of possible connotations, which may serve as metaphors for projections and semanticise the complex inter-relationship of inner and outer self, of body and psyche; or the pairing of effortlessness and drill, whose divorce turns dance into farce and exhibits a rigid medial structure free of its supposed message of grace and lightness, and shows a sign-system in a completely arbitrary relation to the message it conventionally conveys. The writing of the body follows a script no less complex than language – the a-topia of dance seems to convey ideally the uncertain position of women around 1900.

References

Bang, H. (2006; 1890): 'Irene Holm'. In *Under Aaget* (København), reprinted in H. Bang, *Noveller*. København: Gyldendal.

Bergsøe, V. (1907): 'Den lykkelige Familie'. In *Gengangerfortællinger. Poetiske skrifter*, vol. VI. København/Kristiania: Gyldendalske boghandel, nordisk forlag, pp. 60-109.

Brandstetter, G. (1995): *Tanz-Lektüren. Körperbilder und Raumfiguren der Avantgarde*. Frankfurt a.M.: Fischer Taschenbuch Verlag.

Brandstetter, G. (1997): 'Choreographie und Memoria. Konzepte des Gedächtnisses von Bewegung in der Renaissance und im 20. Jahrhundert'. In C. Öhlschläger and B. Wiens (eds.), *Körper – Gedächtnis – Schrift. Der Körper als Medium kultureller Erinnerung*. Berlin: Erich Schmidt, pp. 196-218.

Butler, J. (1993): *Bodies that Matter. On the Discursive Limits of ‚Sex.'* New York: Routledge.

Derrida, J. (1986): 'Choreographies, The Ear of the Other'. In Christie McDonald (ed.) *Otobiography, Transference, Translation*. London: Schocken Books, pp. 163-186.

Foster, S.L. (1986): *Reading Dance: Bodies and Subjects in Contemporary American Dance*. Berkeley and Los Angeles: University of California Press.

Haakonsen, D. (1948): 'Tarantella-motivet i *Et dukkehjem*', In *Edda* 48, pp. 263-275.

Hjort-Vetlesen, I.-L. (1993): 'Lidenskabelig naturalisme. Om Amalie Skram,'. In E. Møller Jensen (ed.), *Nordisk kvindelitteraturhistorie*, 2: *Faderhuset*. Copenhagen: Rosinante, pp. 456-467.

Huschka, S. (2002): *Moderner Tanz. Stile, Konzepte, Utopien*. Reinbek bei Hamburg: Rowohlt Taschenbuch Verlag.

Ibsen, H. (1933; 1879): *Et dukkehjem*. In F. Bull, H. Koht and D.S. Arup (eds.), *Samlede Verker*. 21 vols. Oslo: Gyldendal, 1928-57, vol. 8.

Klein, G. (1992): *Frauen Körper Tanz. Eine Zivilisationsgeschichte des Tanzes*. Weinheim and Berlin: Quadriga.

Langås, U. (2004): *Kroppens betydning i norsk litteratur. 1800-1900*. Bergen: Fagbokforlaget.

McFarlane, J.W. (1989): *Ibsen & Meaning. Studies, Essays and Prefaces 1953-87*. Norwich: Norvik Press.

Melvold, E.O. (n.d.): 'Fra Klingenberg til Tivoli.' http://www.ude.oslo.no/Oslo-patriot/index.html. Accessed August 28, 2013.

Østerud, E. (1993): 'Ibsens italienske karneval. Visualitet og teatralitet i *Et dukkehjem*'. In *Agora*, 2-3, pp. 162-186.

Paulsen, J. (1900-03): *Erindringer*. 3 vols. København: Gyldendal.

Selboe, T. (1997): 'Maskerade – kvinnelighet – frihet. Perspektiver på Henrik Ibsens *Et dukkehjem*'. In *Edda* 97, pp. 88-98.

Skram, A. (1911; 1888) *Lucie*. In *Samlede Verker. Mindeudgave*. Kristiania/Kjöbenhavn: Gyldendalske Boghandel, Nordisk Forlag, pp. 201-314.

Notes

1. Though not a *pas de deux*, this article is a joint gift to a former UEA-colleague from the author AH and Richard Gordon who translated the German text into English. All translations from Scandinavian languages in this paper are my own (AH). As the addressee is a specialist not only of Scandinavian literature, but also holds a degree in German, I have retained a few citations from secondary material in that language.

2. E.g. Klein 1992; Foster 1986 (my main title is taken from this latter book).

3. In Scandinavian literature, we may think of e.g. August Strindberg's *Fröken Julie*, 1888 or C.J.L. Almqvist's *Drottningens Juvelsmykke*, 1834.

4. E.g. Ludvig Holberg's *Jean de France*, 1723.

5. Brandstetter talks about a 'Begleitdiskurs.'

6. Apart from the texts discussed in this essay, I should at least mention August Strindberg's work, particularly of course his play *Dödsdansen* (1901). Alexander Kielland, Selma Lagerlöf, Gustaf Fröding, Stella Kleve, Victoria Bendictsson and many others invoke the expressivity of dance in their texts.

7. See Vilhelm Bergsøe, *Den lykkelige Familie*, in *Gengangerfortællinger*, which in turn is included in his *Poetiske skrifter*, vol. VI (København/Kristiania 1907: 60-109).

8. The Eng. tr. of James McFarlane has 'perhaps rather realistic' here (World's

Classics ed. p.67), which fails to catch the implication of wild (female) nature suggested by Ibsen.

9. On voyeurism in *Et Dukkehjem*, see Østerud 1993.

10. Haakonsen (1948: 269-271), whose essay on the tarantella-motif is always cited, fails to differentiate between fear, madness and self-release. He does mention Bergsøe as the source but admits in a footnote that he is not familiar with the novella. Langås (2004: 126) refers to Madame de Staël's novel *Corinne* as a possible source.

11. See Derrida (1986: 168). I owe this reference to Brandstetter (1997: 215f).

12. See John Paulsen, *Erindringer*. 3 vols. (København 1900-1903), at vol. 2, 130.

Arne Garborg and Knut Hamsun at Vika and Karl Johan:
Scenes of Prostitution in *Mannfolk* and *Sult*

Jan Sjåvik
University of Washington

A topic of great interest to the Norwegian naturalists, prostitution received considerable attention in the literature of the 1880s as a social phenomenon, as a matter of personal tragedy, and as a lens through which one could more clearly discern some of the essential features of middle-class marriage. Rather than offering a wide-angle view of the topic, however, this essay will focus on Arne Garborg's representation of prostitution, and particularly on a scene that takes place in Vika – the red light district of Christiania – in the evening of May 17, 1880 and that is depicted in Garborg's novel *Mannfolk* (Menfolk, 1886). I will then examine a similar scene, with Karl Johan Street as its setting, found in Knut Hamsun's novel *Sult* (1890; tr. *Hunger,* 1899), with a view to uncovering some of the differences between Garborg's and Hamsun's treatment of the subject. The differences thus established will, in turn, help illuminate the contrast between Garborg's naturalism and Hamsun's modernism. Hamsun's depiction of the unconscious as a force in the life of a writer will be further discussed through a reading of a scene in the fourth part of *Sult*, in which the narrator's landlady prostitutes herself with one of her lodgers while observed by her husband – and the narrator – through a keyhole. This scene serves as a key, as it were, that unlocks Hamsun's view of the relationship between writing and sexuality. Throughout this analysis, Garborg's naturalistic view of sexuality serves as a contrast to Hamsun's emphasis on its personal and artistic dimensions.

As I argued in my book *Arne Garborgs Kristiania-romaner* (Sjåvik 1985), Garborg has a clear view of the economic dimensions of love and marriage. This perspective is in accord with naturalism's focus on the relationship between cause and effect, as socio-economic conditions in Norway in the 1880s are seen as inevitably leading to multiple forms of dysfunction in the relationships between women and men. Two of Garborg's essays from the second half of the 1880s bear the titles 'Ægteskab istedetfor prostitution' (Marriage instead of Prostitution) and 'Fri skilsmisse' (Available Divorce), and while these titles truly speak volumes about the general tenor of his concerns, the introduction to the latter offers a succinct summary of Garborg's views:

> Ved vor norske kjærlighedsdiskussion er at bemærke, at man ikke er nået så langt som til kjærlighed.
> Det er usædeligheden, man holder på med. Denne kjærlighedens udartning, som samfundet gjennem sin ægteskabsordning, sin økonomiske ordning og sit opdragelsessystem stadig påny fremkalder og gir næring, opfattes som et fænomen for sig, og vore doctores, barberer og signekjællinger lægger råd op om, hvordan man skal kunne fjerne denne sygdom uden først at fjerne dens årsager. (Garborg 1950: II, 76)

> (It should be noted regarding our Norwegian debate about love, that one has not gotten to the love.
> People keep concerning themselves with immorality. This perversion of love, which society repeatedly calls forth and nourishes through its system of marriage, its economic system, and its educational system, is perceived as a separate phenomenon, and our doctors, barbers, and wise women counsel with each other about how this illness may be removed without getting rid of its causes.)

The touch of both moralizing and optimism found in this statement shows that Garborg was hardly a consistent naturalist, but rather a writer who found naturalist esthetics suitable for his own brand of literary social criticism. Garborg's main point was precisely that perverted love could only be done away with through a radical reformation of social norms, but he also found it necessary to accurately describe this kind of immorality in order to motivate his audience to work for the social and economic reformation that he deemed necessary.

It is well known that those who Garborg criticized in 'Fri skilsmisse' did not like the idea of having to pay the price necessary to get rid of what Garborg identifies as immorality. In *Kolbotnbrev og andre Skildringar* (1890; Letters from Kolbotn and other Depictions) Garborg mentions that 'Oftedølene' – the followers of the low-church Stavanger preacher Lars Oftedal – were tickled to hear that he, the author of 'den svinske Bog' (the swinish book) *Mannfolk*, had been fired from his government job

(Garborg 1891: 109). Garborg also realized, however, that the leadership in Johan Sverdrup's Liberal Party had, in essence, decided to sacrifice him in order to not lose the support of the Oftedal faction.

The scene from *Mannfolk* that will be analyzed here should be read with this social, political, and historical background in mind. Even though the action in *Mannfolk* takes place during the year 1879-1880, the novel was published in 1886, and there is no question that it reflects Garborg's sober appraisal of the possibility of social change in Norway subsequent to the disappointment provided by Sverdrup's lack of progressivism after his great victory in 1884. It can be argued that Garborg's negative assessment of the relationship between men and women is of a piece with his general disappointment in Sverdrup's politics, and that Garborg tries to show how insufficiently ambitious public policy negatively affects even the most intimate aspects of people's lives.

The setting of Garborg's narrative in *Mannfolk* is 'restaurasjonen i studentersamfundet' (Garborg 1990: 279) (the restaurant at the student society), where current political and social issues are being subjected to a debate fueled by copious amounts of beer and toddy. A number of characters are introduced, but gradually the omniscient narration changes to personal narration from the point of view of Gabriel Gram, who is one of the book's central characters. Gram's later search for a prostitute is motivated by his excessive drinking, which destroys his inhibitions:

> I den stundi sovna minnet for Gabriel Gram; minnet og umtanken.
> Berre ein litin flekk i heilen hans vakte enno.
> På den flekken steig det fram eit bilæte; eit lite ljost, koselegt rom
> med raude veggir, og i det romet ei gjente i kvit nattbunad. [...]
> Som ein ring i eit tryne drog det fagre bilæte 'n av stad; trygg som
> ein svevngangar tok han vegen nedyvi til Vika. (Garborg 1990:
> 291)

> (At that moment Gabriel Gram's memory fell asleep, his memory
> and his inhibitions. Only a small spot in his brain was still awake.
> On that spot appeared an image, a small, cozy room with red walls,
> and in the room a girl dressed for bed, wearing white. [...]
> The beautiful image pulled him along like the ring in the snout of
> a pig, and he took off down toward Vika, as safe as a sleepwalker.)

One wonders if this may not be the very passage that caused the conservatives to consider *Mannfolk* a *svinsk* book. At any rate, the ring in the pig snout is a quintessential naturalist image in that it underscores the animal nature of man, a favorite motif of the naturalists.

Gram discovers that business is brisk at Vika: 'I alle vindaugo var ljos; alle stadir var det mannfolk. Han banka stundom, men fekk alltid same svaret: 'ikke alene." (There was light in every window, and men were everywhere. From time to time he knocked on a door, but always got the same answer: 'Not alone.') His reply, 'So dra til helvite' (Garborg 1990: 291) (Then go to Hell), is characteristic of the dehumanizing nature of the situation. Wandering from house to house, however, he begins to sober up:

> Det livna so smått i hovudet på Gram. Den vakne flekken vart større og større [...] alle desse ægtemennar og festemennar, som snikte seg um her på forbodne stadir med halen millom knei; aldri i verdi ville han vera i deira skinn. (Garborg 1990: 292)

> (Slowly Gram's head began to wake up. The spot that was awake became larger and larger [...] all these husbands and engaged men who were slinking around here in forbidden places with their tails between their legs; never in the world would he want to be in their skins.)

Garborg is known to have disliked dogs, and his canine image does not speak well for the male visitors at Vika. But the accent is not on individual responsibility, as it is social and economic conditions that turn men into pigs and dogs, and these conditions are not likely to change in the absence of the political will demanded by Garborg's radicalism but denied by such men of compromise as Johan Sverdrup.

* * *

The first scene from Hamsun's *Sult* that will be discussed here is found in the book's third part, in which the narrator is living well because a friend has given him some money. He is, however, significantly weakened physically, having lost much of his hair and being bothered by headaches and nervousness. While in this condition, he notices that a heavily veiled lady has been watching for him three evenings in a row by a lamp post outside his quarters. Preoccupied with thoughts about this lady but penniless and desperate with hunger, he spends his time walking around town:

Jeg gik rundt Slottet tre, fire ganger, tok derpå den bestemmelse å vende hjem, gjorde endnu en liten avstikker ind i parken og gik endelig tilbake nedover Karl Johan.

Klokken var omtrent elleve. Gaten var temmelig mørk og det vandret mennesker omkring overalt, stille par og larmende klynger om hverandre. Den store stund var indtrådt, parringstiden når den hemmelige færdsel foregår og de glade æventyr begynner. Raslende pikeskjørter, en og anden kort, sanselig latter, bølgende bryster, hæftige, pæsende åndedrag [...] Hele gaten var en sump som hete dunster steg op av.

Jeg forfarer uvilkårlig mine lommer efter to kroner. Den lidenskap som dirrer i hver av de forbigåendes bevægelser, selve gaslykternes dunkle lys, den stille, svangre nat, altsammen har begyndt å angripe mig, denne luft som er fyldt av hvisken, omfavnelser, skjælvende tilståelser, halvt uttalte ord, små hvin; endel katter elsker [...] Og jeg hadde ikke to kroner. [...] Hvilken ydmygelse, hvilken vanære! (Hamsun 2006, 81)

(I walked around the Castle three or four times, then decided to go back home, took yet a small side trip into the park and finally walked down Karl Johan Street.

It was about eleven o'clock. The street was quite dark and people were walking around everywhere, quiet couples intermingled with noisy groups. The great moment had come, mating season when the secret traffic is taking place and the happy adventures begin. Rustling girls' skirts, now and then a burst of brief, sensual laughter, billowing breasts, excited, heavy breathing [...] The whole street was like a swamp from which hot fumes arose.

Spontaneously I search my pockets for two crowns. The passion that vibrates in the movements of each passer-by, the dim light from the street lamps, the quite, pregnant night, everything has begun attacking me, this air that is full of whispering, embraces, trembling admissions, halfway spoken words, tiny squeals; some cats are making love [...] And I had not two crowns. [...] What humiliation, what disgrace!)

Much like the scene in Garborg's *Mannfolk* discussed above, Hamsun's scene is focalized through his protagonist, but Hamsun's animal imagery has a radically different function from that of Garborg. Gabriel Gram is drawn to Vika like a pig with a ring in its nose and observes the scene there, gradually coming back to full consciousness, while it is the already existing hypersensitivity of Hamsun's protagonist that causes him to notice the cats as well as to sense the ubiquitous passion of the pregnant night.

In order to get a sense of how to analyze this scene, however, it is necessary to return to the first part of *Sult*, in which Hamsun offers an important lesson in how to read his own particular type of writing. The narrator is pestering two ladies as they are walking along Karl Johan in broad daylight:

> Da jeg kom ned i Slotsbakken indhentet jeg to damer [...] Idet jeg passerte dem streifet jeg den enes ærme, jeg så op, hun hadde et fyldig, litt blekt ansigt. Med ett blusser hun og blir forunderlig vakker [...] skulde det være fordi jeg hadde berørt hendes arm? Det høye bryst bølger hæftig nogen ganger [...]. (Hamsun 2006, 15)

> (When I came down to the slope below the Castle, I caught up with two ladies [...] As I passed them I brushed up against the sleeve of one of them, I looked up, she had a full and slightly pale face. All of a sudden she blushes and becomes strangely beautiful [...] could it be because I had touched her arm? Her high breast billows excitedly a few times.)

The narrator is 'i et pirrelig lune' (in an excitable mood) and is gripped by 'en sælsom lyst til å gjøre denne dame rædd, følge efter hende og fortrædige hende på en eller anden måte' (a strange wish to frighten this lady, follow her and annoy her somehow or other) (Hamsun 2006: 15). So, he walks past her again, turns around, and says: 'De mister Deres bok, frøken' (Hamsun 2006: 16) (You are losing your book, Miss).

It is not only the narrator's desire to annoy that is strange, but also the way he goes about doing it. Why does he claim that the lady has lost her book? Why not some other object? The answer may be provided half a page later, when the narrator repeats the statement to the lady, but after we have learned that the lady had just passed 'Paschas boklade' (Pascha's book store) (Hamsun 2006: 16). It seems plausible that the reader is expected to understand that the narrator has unconsciously chosen to claim that the lady has lost her book because he has unconsciously noticed that she is following a trajectory that would take her past a book store. This reading is in line with the theory of literary creativity that Hamsun expressed in his essay 'Fra det ubevidste Sjæleliv' (From the Unconscious Life of the Mind, 1890). Hamsun's reader is expected to decode the unconscious motivations of his protagonist according to the clues left in the text by the author. Since this reading lesson is presented by Hamsun close to the beginning of *Sult*, it makes sense to assume that it is intended to set the tone for the reader's interaction with the entire novel.

If we look for unconscious motivation in the Karl Johan scene found in part three of *Sult*, we first notice that there is a physical link between this scene and the pestering incident. Both scenes take place at Karl Johan. There is a causal connection as well, for the narrator believes that the lady that appears by the street lamp next to his quarters is, in fact, the same woman whom he had tormented earlier, and to whom he had given the name Ylajali, 'et navn med en glidende, nervøs lyd' (Hamsun 2006: 16) (a name with a gliding, nervous sound). It is after seeing her by the street lamp three times that he finds himself drawn to Karl Johan late in the evening, and his three or four trips around *Slottet* are no doubt calculated, albeit unconsciously, to delay his walk down the street to the appropriate time. The same is true for his detour into the park.

Since it is the triple sighting of the veiled Ylajali that has motivated the narrator to be at Karl Johan during 'parringstiden' (mating season), it may be worth looking at what kind of unconscious material may be contained in this name. Consisting of seven letters, it contains both the formally female name 'Yla' and the male name 'Ali'. The palatal semivowel 'j', which joins the two parts of the word, is phonetically a glide, and does much to bring about the *glidende* sound of the name. It also joins the two parts of the word into a kind of couple. Furthermore, 'Yla' is virtually an anagram of 'Ali', particularly when one remembers that 'i' and 'y' are phonetically rather similar in Norwegian. Thus 'Yla' and 'Ali' come very close to being mirror images of each other, albeit with a slight difference, as, for example, the Arabic numerals 6 and 9, which figure prominently later in Hamsun's text. The name 'Ylajali' may also be read as containing such common Norwegian words as 'la', 'ja', and 'li'. Their significance, if any, may be uncertain, so I will here simply limit myself to pointing out that the affirmative 'ja' is surely the answer the narrator would like to receive to the most pertinent questions he might want to ask Ylajali.

There is little question, though, that the narrator within his heart of hearts knows that he is poorly equipped to participate in what he terms 'den hemmelige ferdsel' (the secret traffic). Not only does he lack the requisite two *kroner* with which to pay a streetwalker, but his prolonged starvation has made him impotent as well. This is shown by his scorn for those whom he sees: '[. . .] jeg trak sint på akslerne og så ringeagtende på dem efterhvert som de passerte, par for par' (Hamsun 2006: 81) (I angrily shrugged my shoulders and looked derisively at them when they passed, couple after couple). He even puts the salve of religion on his wounded pride: 'Jeg løftet mit hode og følte med mig selv velsignelsen av å kunne bevare min sti ren' (Hamsun 2006: 81) (I lifted my head and felt within myself the blessing of being able to keep my path pure).

The narrator's invocation of religion is a manifestation of gross hypocrisy, and so is his subsequent act of impersonating a pastor when he addresses a prostitute, asking her if it is appropriate for her to be out so late. When the woman interprets his question as a veiled invitation, he is forced to confess that he has no money, after which the woman says:'Ja gå så pokker ivold med Dem!' (Hamsun 2006: 82) (Then go to the Devil!). This phrase is reminiscent of Gabriel Gram's 'So dra til helvite' (Garborg 1990: 291) (Then go to Hell), spoken in a similar situation.

When the girl next offers her services free of charge, the narrator is left with no means of concealing his impotency. Believing him to be on his way to someone else, the girl puts the narrator in a position where he simply has to lie out of shame: 'Forresten var mit navn det og det, pastor den og den. Godnat! Gå hen og synd ikke mere!' (Hamsun 2006: 83) (By the way, my name was such-and-such, pastor so-and-so. Go thy way and sin no more!). But the narrator cannot but be aware of his own utter misery, which manifests itself in all areas of his life, including his health, his position as an aspiring writer, and his relationship to women. The link between his starved condition, his impotence, and his inability to succeed as a writer is surely implicitly present throughout the text, starting with his initial desire to annoy Ylajali rather than pursue her romantically.

I have elsewhere discussed the relationship between male sexuality and creative literary power in Hamsun's novel *Pan* (1894; tr. 1920) (see Sjåvik 2004: 96-118). While drawing on the work of Sandra Gilbert and Susan Gubar, I pointed out that they have demonstrated, as Hazard Adams and Leroy Searle have succinctly put it, 'how the most intimate representation of a writer's creative power has been systematically treated as phallic and patriarchal' (Adams and Searle 1986: 485). The narrator in *Pan* is in thrall to this masculinist myth of artistic creativity, and clearly so is the narrator in *Sult*. This is shown not only by his veiled references to his sexual impotency but also by two instances of mutilation of limbs and by a perverse focus on the sexuality of other characters.

There are two acts of physical mutilation in *Sult*, and both of them may be read as instances of symbolic castration. The narrator bites his own finger until it bleeds, and later his foot is run over by a cartwheel. Both of these acts are reminiscent of Glahn's shooting of his left foot in *Pan*. Of even greater significance, however, is an event that takes place after the narrator has again encountered Ylajali and has made arrangements to meet her later. While waiting for the appointed time, he drinks too much and steals a taxi ride:

> Vi kommer forbi en politibetjent og jeg lægger mærke til at han har numer 69. Dette tal træffer mig så grusomt nøie, står med en gang som en splint i min hjærne. 69, nøiaktig 69, jeg skulde ikke glemme det! (Hamsun 2006: 99)

> (We pass a police officer and I immediately notice that he has number 69. This number hits me in a cruel way and stands immediately like a splinter in my brain. 69, exactly 69, I would not forget it!)

What kind of unconscious material would the author of both 'Fra det ubevidste Sjæleliv' and *Sult* wish us to assign to the narrator's observation of the number 69? As readers we are enjoined to look for 'de hemmelige Bevægelser, som bedrives upaagtet paa de afsides Steder i Sjælen' (the secret movements that take place unnoticed in the out-of-the-way places in the soul) and to look at 'det delikate Fantasiliv' (the delicate life of the imagination) with a magnifying glass (Hamsun 1994: 17). Would it, from this perspective, be unreasonable to interpret the number 69 as gesturing at a form of sexual expression that would be consistent with the narrator's impotence? And since the number on the police officer's badge is so strongly identified with a different human being, it might be equally reasonable to think that the narrator is projecting his own infirmity onto the police officer.

The narrator's preoccupation with the sexuality of other people, as well as the connection between sex and writing, becomes a major theme in the fourth part of *Sult*, after his miserable failure during the tryst with Ylajali at the end of part three, when the narrator deliberately misreads Ylajali's encouragement to hurry up – she says that the family's servant girl will be returning soon – as an invitation to leave. During the time covered by part four, the narrator lives at a cheap pension and is working on 'et en akts drama, "Korsets tegn", æmne fra middelalderen' (a drama in one act, 'The Sign of the Cross', with its topic from the Middle Ages) which has as its main character 'en herlig, fanatisk skjøge som hadde syndet i templet' (a glorious, fanatical harlot who has sinned in the temple) (Hamsun 2006: 128). Hounded by his landlady because he has run out of money, he is sitting outside on a bench, struggling to formulate a line spoken by a monk and a speech by a judge condemning the woman. When he returns to his lodgings, however, he catches the landlady's husband spying on his wife through a keyhole:

> Jeg blev stående aldeles stille indenfor. Like foran mig, bare i to skridts avstand, stod værten selv, uten hat og uten frak, og kikket ind gjennem nøkkelhullet til familjens egen stue. [...] Han stod og lo.
> Kom hit! sa han hviskende.
> Jeg nærmet mig på tærne.
> Se her! sa han og lo med en stille, hidsig latter. Kik ind! Hihi! Der ligger de! Se på gammeln! Kan De se gammeln?
> Inde i sengen, ret under Kristus i oljetryk og like mot mig, så jeg to skikkelser, værtinden og den fremmede styrmand [...] Og i sengen ved den andre væggen sat hendes far, den lamme olding, og så på [...]
> Jeg vendte mig mot min vært. [...]
> Så De gammeln? hvisket han. Å Gud, så De gammeln? Han sitter og ser på! Og han la sig igjen ind til nøkkelhullet. (Hamsun 2006: 139)

> (I stood completely quiet inside. Right in front of me, only two steps ahead, stood the host himself, without hat and coat, and peeped through the keyhole into the family's own living room. [...] He stood and laughed.
> Come here! he whispered.
> I approached on the tips of my toes. [...]
> Look here! he said and laughed quietly and excitedly. Look inside! Hihi! There they lie! Look at the old man! Can you see the old man?
> In the bed, right below the glossy print of Christ and straight ahead of me, I saw two people, the landlady and the strange mate [...] And in the bed by the other wall sat her father, the paralyzed old man, and watched [...]
> I turned toward my host. [...]
> Did you see the old man? he whispered. Oh God, did you see the old man? He is sitting there watching! And he again squeezed himself against the keyhole.)

There are three levels of voyeurism in this scene. The old man is watching his daughter copulate in a bed placed below a glossy picture of Christ, her husband is watching his father-in-law observing the scene, and the narrator is looking at all of them. There are at least two and probably three impotent men present, each of them substituting the observation of sex for the act itself. It is thus likely that they are enjoying a degree of pornographic satisfaction.

The narrator is unable to make progress on his writing project, however, especially when he hears a little noise 'fra stuen indenfor' (Hamsun 2006: 140) (from the room inside). His concentration improves when he further identifies with the sailor by going into the man's room in order to write there:

> Nu gik det i flere minutter aldeles utmærket. Replik efter replik opstod fuldt færdig i mit hode og jeg skrev uavbrutt. Jeg fylder den ene siden efter den andre [...] klynker sagte av henrykkelse [...] Den eneste lyd jeg hører i denne stund er min egen glade klynking. (Hamsun 2006, 141)

> Now things went really well for several minutes. Line after line arose completely finished in my head and I wrote without a break. I fill one page after another [...] whimper slowly with rapture [...] The only sound I hear at this moment is my own happy whimpering.)

There can be little doubt that this writerly *jouissance* is brought about by both the narrator's observation of and identification with the sailor. Furthermore, the centerpiece of his drama, the idea of a woman sinning in the temple, has clearly been inspired by the narrator's earlier unconscious observation that his landlady's bed is situated below a picture of Christ and the likelihood that her many children have not been fathered by her rather passive husband. The idea that sex is intimately connected with writing is present even in the choice of wording in the text, but at the same time it seems likely that the narrator's second-hand sex can only result in second-rate writing. It is, in fact, shortly after this creative rush that he comes to terms with the inevitable, hires on to a ship and leaves town, presumably in order to regain all aspects of his health.

* * *

Hamsun's depiction of prostitution is notable for its complete lack of social criticism. In contrast to the statements about social ills made by Garborg both in his essays and in his fictional works, Hamsun's main point seems to be that his narrator is strongly preoccupied with sex on the subconscious level, and that this preoccupation shows up in his erratic behavior vis-à-vis women of various social classes, from prostitutes to middle-class ladies. There is nothing new in the observation that this focus on the unconscious life of the soul is an important feature of Hamsun's modernism, of course, but it may have been worth our while to examine in some detail how Hamsun's text contains traces of the unconscious mental activity of his narrator, as well as how these traces enable readers to reconstruct the strange workings of the narrator's mind.

Hamsun's text is sufficiently rich and complex that a detailed and painstaking analysis may help show the extent to which his individualist aesthetic ideology manifests itself in his work, even on the lexical level. This is particularly the case with the connection between creativity and male sexual potency, which is an underlying theme throughout Sult. While actual hunger for food, as portrayed by such naturalistic writers as Garborg is motivated by the need for physical survival, Hamsun's hunger is both physical and metaphorical, that is, it is also an expression of the desire to create. While the relationship between creativity and sexuality may be simply viewed as a story that male writers tell themselves in order to further their work, perhaps by gaining increased access to the resources of their subconscious minds, it is a story that has left tangible marks on the pages of *Sult*. This type of trace is unthinkable in the work of a writer such as Garborg, whose focus is social and political rather than directed at the most secret mental locations and operations.

References

Adams, H. and L. Searle (eds.) (1986): *Critical Theory since 1965*. Tallahassee: Florida State University Press.

Garborg, A. (1891): *Kolbotnbrev og andre Skildringar*. 2nd edition. Bergen: Mons Litleré.

Garborg, A. (1990 [1886]): *Mannfolk*. In A. Garborg, *Bondestudentar – Mannfolk – Hjå ho mor*. Oslo: Aschehoug.

Garborg, A. (1950): *Tankar og utsyn. Artiklar*. 2 vols. Oslo: Aschehoug.

Hamsun, K. (1994 [1890]): 'Fra det ubevidste Sjæleliv.' In *Fra det ubevidste Sjæleliv. Artikler om litteratur*. Oslo: Gyldendal.

Hamsun, K. (2006 [1890]): *Sult*. In *Hamsuns beste. Ungdomsverker*. Oslo: Gyldendal.

Sjåvik, J. (1985): *Arne Garborgs Kristiania-romaner: En beretterteknisk studie*. Oslo: Aschehoug.

Sjåvik, J. (2004): *Reading for the Truth: Rhetorical Constructions in Norwegian Fiction*. Christchurch, New Zealand: Cybereditions.

Horse Riding and Female Physical Freedom in Victoria Benedictsson's *Pengar*

Sarah Death
Independent Scholar and Translator

When Janet Garton and her fellow founders of Norvik Press drew up their initial wish list of Scandinavian classics deserving translation into English, Victoria Benedictsson's novel *Pengar* (1885) was one of the titles on it. Norvik Press eventually published *Pengar* in English as *Money* in 1999, and the translation has enjoyed steady sales since then, to the extent that a revised edition was published, again by Norvik Press, in 2011. Benedictsson's works, particularly her plays, are currently enjoying something of a renaissance in Sweden, alongside the work of other female dramatists of the 1880s such as Anne Charlotte Leffler and Alfhild Agrell. Her play *Final* was staged at the Royal Dramatic Theatre in Stockholm in the autumn of 2007. Benedictsson's reputation as a dramatist has also reached London: her *Enchantment* had a run at the National Theatre in its 2007 summer/autumn season. This was an English version of the play *Den bergtagna*, left as a draft by Benedictsson on her death and completed by her friend and writer colleague Axel Lundegård.

Pengar is a novel, but it is a consciously structured work with all the dramatic impact of a play – or a film, given the prominence of horseriding scenes. This is how Selma Berg, the novel's central character, is first seen by the man she will eventually marry:

> Men ingen hade nämnt ett ord om att det fanns en ung flicka i huset, och han blev så överraskad när hon öppnade dörren och kom in, blossande röd och varm, med ett par skridskor vårdslöst kastade över armen, så att de skramlade för vart steg hon gick. Håret var hoptovat av värmen, klänningslivet draget i olag av den häftiga rörelsen, och hon måste blinka mot ljuset för att kunna se. (Benedictsson 1950: 112)[1]

(But no one had said a word about there being a young girl in the house and he was taken by surprise when she opened the door and came in, flushed and warm, with a pair of skates thrown carelessly over her arm which clattered with every step she took. Her hair was matted with the warmth, the bodice of her dress disordered by the vigorous exercise, and she was blinking in the light.) (Benedictsson 1999: 49)

Her uncle's visitor, the wealthy, solid, eminently eligible Squire Kristerson, is struck by her freshness and unabashed exuberance. He finds himself abandoning his rational plans to marry for money and, against his own better judgement, soon desires only Selma. She is just sixteen years old; he is almost three times her age. The age gap is bad enough, but the gulf between them in terms of energy and enthusiasms will prove even more destructive.

Victoria Benedictsson (1850-88), who came from the southern Swedish province of Skåne and wrote under the male pseudonym Ernst Ahlgren, is today considered one of the leading writers of the 1880s and the so-called Modern Breakthrough. She wrote two novels of which *Pengar* (1885) was the first, as well as many short stories, several plays and a remarkable, multi-volume diary *Stora boken* (The Big Book). *Pengar*, as its title indicates, is an indictment of a society in which young women were little more than commodities to be bought and sold in the marriage trade. As a story of a woman's rebellion against the stultifying conventions of late nineteenth-century society, *Pengar* has long been compared to Henrik Ibsen's *A Doll's House*, and seen as belonging to the often autobiographical 'indignation literature' produced by writers, especially women, of the period. Feminist scholars have in recent years taken a more text-centred approach and revealed the novel's far more complex construction: for example how it underlines the power imbalance between the sexes by use of; narrative technique, shifting focalisation and use of light and dark; the deep undertow of ambivalence and tension regarding gender and self-image; and the importance of the relationship between language and the human body in *Pengar* (see Forsås-Scott 2005; Leffler 2005; Holm 2003; Sjöblad and Witt-Brattström 1993; Witt-Brattström 1993).

One very important aspect of Benedictsson's development of her main character Selma is the focus in the novel on female physical freedom or the constraints placed on it. Horseriding is a central motif here; it is the most physical but by no means the only outlet for Selma's youthful energy, which fate does not allow her to channel in otherwise natural directions for a young woman.

On the first page, the reader meets a teenage Selma who is lanky, boyish and not entirely at ease in her own growing body: 'gången hade icke en stadsdams trippande behag, snarare en halvvuxen pojkes slängande fasoner' (65) (her gait had nothing of the mincing charm of a lady from town, but rather the gangling action of an adolescent boy) (5). Her excess energy, when not channelled into long walks or ice skating, expresses itself in swinging on furniture, stretching, tossing her fringe out of her eyes, and constant nervous fiddling and fidgeting. She is given to outbursts of childish enthusiasm and fits of sullenness, has a high opinion of herself and a highly stubborn streak. Her mother died when she was very young, and her sickly, impoverished father was unable to provide a suitable home, so she has latterly been brought up by her clergyman uncle and his rather narrow-minded wife. Selma has enjoyed having their student son Richard as a comrade and sparring partner whenever he is home for the holidays.

Selma's ambition is to become an art student, but her uncle and father forbid it, and would rather see her make a good match. With no power over her own fate, she is swinging between rebellious resentment and resigned submission when Squire Kristerson embarks on his courtship, in which he is aided and abetted by Selma's uncle, who swallows his misgivings about the huge discrepancy in their ages and convinces himself the marriage will be for her own good. Selma, not unnaturally, thinks Kristerson old and unattractive, but she has long been entranced by the two stylish greys that pull the carriage in which he travels round the neighbourhood, and in which she longs to ride. Her uncle knows how susceptible she is, like virtually any girl of sixteen, to material temptations, and makes sure she knows what Kristerson's wealth will be able to buy her. Of all the visions set before her, the one she finds most irresistible is that of her own horse chosen from a whole stableful, plus all the accoutrements: a smart riding habit with a train, a ladies' saddle of the latest design, and a groom to do her bidding.

With these inducements, Selma capitulates to pressure from her uncle and marries the stout, red-faced Kristerson, but in her sexual innocence is deeply shocked and repelled by the physical realities – brutalities, as she and Benedictsson perceive them – of her wedding night. She is equally shocked by the jealousy of her new husband, who likes to show her off at parties and balls but is suspicious and abusive when she dances with any younger man. In pique she gives up dancing and soon stops accompanying him to social gatherings altogether, thus depriving herself of a pleasure which was one of the few acceptable physical outlets she had left as a married woman in public. Benedictsson vividly and memorably portrays Selma's expression of her physical frustrations through her reaction when left alone in the evenings:

> Ja, hon kunde dansa omkring på mattorna, häva sig på armarna i de höga dörrposterna och finna på tusen upptåg som det vildaste barn. Och så skrattade hon högt åt sig själv. Det var så jubeltokigt... (153)

> (She would even dance around on the carpets, hang by her arms from the high doorposts, and get up to a thousand pranks like the wildest of children. And then she would laugh out loud at herself. It was such joyful madness!) (89)

Selma, now mistress of a household effectively run for her by servants, with nothing to fill her future but a little bookkeeping for her husband and charity work, is bored, disillusioned and under-exercised. Her energy is pent up as if in a coiled spring, so it is hardly surprising that at the age of nineteen she throws herself eagerly into the riding lessons the Squire arranges for her. She is delighted to be given her own young horse - whom she significantly names Black Prince - a riding master and a practice track, and also makes it her business to read all the books she can obtain on the subject. Here it should be emphasised that the money of the novel's title is a prerequisite for all Selma's riding activities and lavish equipment, which would scarcely have been available to a woman of lesser means; hers is a socially privileged position. Selma's excellent progress in riding is however interrupted by an urgent summons to her father's sickbed, where she spends some days in close confinement with him and her cousin Richard, now a final year medical student, who tends the patient until he is well out of danger from his pneumonia. The conversation between the two young people is lively and frank, not to say intimate. There is a clear attraction between them. But Selma is of course a married woman, and Richard too has recently become engaged.

The first time we encounter Selma as an accomplished horsewoman, several more years have elapsed; she is now twenty-three. We see her, glowing and self-assured after an early morning ride in crisp autumn weather. She is well aware that she and her horse will be a glorious sight for anyone watching from the house. Her playful interaction with the horse once she has dismounted, the physical intimacy of the scene, her lack of heed for the flecks of foam with which Prince is wetting her, her pet names for him, all this is not only highly suggestive but also in stark contrast to the icy aloofness with which she treats her husband, and also to the strict self-discipline she imposes on herself in Richard's company.

From Selma's subsequent conversation with Richard's wife Elvira, we learn that he is sulking because he asked if he could go riding with Selma, but she refused. As with the dancing, she will do nothing to hazard her reputation; she has even chosen her groom specifically for his ugliness, so neither the Squire nor anyone else could possibly imagine any impropriety on her part while out riding with the servant. Selma confides to Richard that she is all too aware of how beguiling a ride with him could be,[2] having often imagined it:

> Ja, du förstår, att jag tycker det måtte gå så lätt att prata under den där vaggningen, som man får på hästryggen, och vid det där klaprandet av hovar, som låter så trevligt. A vad det är skönt! Man känner värmen av hästens kropp ända ned i fötterna och runt omkring sig den friska, kalla luften... (200)

> (Well, you know, I think it must be so easy to converse as you're gently rocked, as you are on horseback, to the soothing sound of clip-clopping hooves. How lovely it is! You can feel the warmth of the horse's body right down to your feet, and the cold, fresh air around you...) (133)

The morning conversation between Selma and Elvira after Selma's ride highlights their contrasting characters, specifically in attitudes to exercise and to how a woman looks her best. Lithe, lively-minded Selma has already been out on horseback for hours and now reclines easily on the sofa, prodding the carpet with her riding crop, while the sweet but rather superficial Elvira, not even dressed, sits sleepily crimping her hair in front of the mirror. Artifice versus nature. In fact, the emphasis throughout the novel is on the naturalness of Selma's looks: her figure; her complexion; the long, close-fitting, unfussy dresses that emphasise her suppleness and vitality. Elvira tells her she should have been a man, and Selma does not entirely disagree. The problematic question - for a girl - of fearless horseriding being viewed as a badge of masculinity does surface elsewhere in Victoria Benedictsson's work.[3] It is interesting that in *Pengar* we scarcely see any male on horseback except the deformed groom. Squire Kristerson prefers the comfort of a carriage, and Richard's horsemanship remains out of our view. Being seen riding is Selma's preserve.

Would Selma like to be a man? Although she thinks a combative, comradely spirit is a better basis for a sound marriage than Elvira's sighs and tears, she still maintains she herself is meant to be a woman because she feels 'ett begär hos mig att liksom gå upp in en annan existens' (197) (such a craving to somehow submerge myself in another's existence) (130). Unlike Elvira she has no child to bring up according to her own principles; there is ambiguity as to whether this is by accident or design, but she says she has no regrets about not being a mother. She wishes she had married a man with ambition, so she could have encouraged and worked for him. We naturally conclude that the man she has in mind is Richard.

This section of the novel culminates in an intensely physical horseriding scene which shows Selma riding cross-country at breakneck speed, elated and in impressive control of her mount, but also in a sense controlling the plot: the horse is a means to an end, a tool in Selma's rapidly devised strategy for imprinting herself on Richard's memory. In this key scene, Elvira and and Richard have made their formal farewells to their hosts and set off by carriage at the end of their extended visit. Just prior to this, a private conversation between Richard and Selma has shown them both acknowledging their mutual physical attraction openly for the first time, but Selma has insisted their relationship must remain platonic. She astutely realises that this is the only way to retain his friendship in the long term. Selma knows that Richard has always admired her for her lack of conventionally demure femininity; it suddenly occurs to her that by riding swiftly across the fields she can intercept the carriage on the road and leave Richard with an unforgettable image of her, sweaty and full of vitality. Galloping across ploughed fields, recklessly leaping ditches and fences, forcing her way through brambles, she exults in being alive.

Selma here reverts briefly to the wildness and wilfulness of her youth, but now she is in addition seizing the initiative with a mature self-assurance and sense of purpose. In the saddle, by contrast with so many other aspects of her life, she is the one in control. She is later displeased with herself for having deliberately choreographed the scene, but its power and double entendre are indisputable. Perspiring, nostrils flaring, splashed with yellow mud, her horse's flanks pulsating beneath her: the description of Selma physically aroused by the thrill of the ride is an undeniably sexy one, and it is hardly surprising that it proved too much for the moral climate of the late nineteenth century. This passage was entirely removed from some subsequent editions of the novel, as was the one quoted above, in which Selma imagines the physical sensations of going out riding with Richard.

In considering horseriding as an expression of freedom in *Pengar*, it is important for the twenty-first century reader to remember the constraints of the era in which it was written. Quite apart from the censorious influences which suppressed the physicality of the descriptions of horseriding in the novel, the female rider of the day was already quite severely bodily constrained by today's standards of practical, stretchy, aerodynamic sportswear. It was expected that a lady would ride side-saddle and wear a riding habit with a long skirt. Beneath it she was very likely to be wearing rigid, restricting corsets; in *Pengar*, Selma is said always to be tight-laced for riding. A lady was also usually expected to be accompanied on her rides by a groom. The fact that even such a compromised form of liberation is so welcome to Selma is an indication of just how stultifying she finds her married life, how even her expensively furnished refuge, a study full of books, decorated with prints and statuettes of dogs and horses, ultimately proves unsatisfying.

It must be said that there is a certain ambivalence in Benedictsson's attitude to the female fashions of the time. Although her novel is an appeal for greater self-determination and freedom for women, she is clearly drawn to the severe silhouette that fashionable corsets and long skirts could achieve. The style she creates for Selma in *Pengar*, once the girl has left gangly adolescence behind, emphasises plain, dark, full-length outfits clearly meant to contrast with the fripperies and bows of conventional femininity. There are repeated references to a statuesque Selma standing firm-hipped, shapely and healthy, in outline against some paler background. Her riding habit finds favour with the narrator for enhancing her appearance, making her taller, her bust higher and her waist slimmer. Interestingly, a diary entry written by Benedictsson in 1883 sets out in detail her ideal wardrobe for the well-dressed mature woman (she was herself 33 at the time). Its proposals echo not only what Benedictsson herself is seen wearing in photographs, but also the style she chooses for Selma: simplicity and pureness of line; soft, dark fabrics; high necks and long sleeves; no bows, tassels, flowers, loose shawls or scarves; an occasional simple piece of jewellery.[4] Image - how Selma is seen, and how she sees herself - has a crucial role to play in the novel. Like her beauty, which has far more to do with an aura of freshness and health than with conventional prettiness, Selma's attire is a very personal vision on the author's part.

After her wild ride to bid Richard a memorable farewell, the fight temporarily seems to go out of Selma. There is no further mention of horseriding. She persuades her husband to take her on a trip to Stockholm, in the hope of finding distraction, but in fact this just precipitates the inevitable confrontation between them on the central issues of the book, including women's demand for more fulfilling lives, double sexual standards, and marriage as church-sanctioned prostitution. Selma vents her bitter frustration but cannot rouse her husband from his complacent self-satisfaction. He knows where the real power lies and is convinced society will condemn and ruin her if she leaves him. But her mind is made up, and once the Squire is asleep she writes a letter to Richard, asking him to enrol her at a gymnastics institute in Germany, so she can train as an instructor. Her desire for personal freedom and self-determination takes the form of further embracing the physical culture that has helped her survive her marriage.

Selma's dull-eyed husband has dismissed her advocacy of greater female independence as 'dockhemsteorier' (239) (Doll's House theories) (170). The novel *Pengar* and Ibsen's play certainly both conclude with the determined departure, actual or planned, of the main protagonist, but unlike Nora, Selma is not a mother and thus is spared the guilt of abandoning her children. She is a freer agent, with a constructive plan to earn her living, and has a firm ally in the shape of her progressively minded doctor cousin. As she writes in the letter, and as we have seen earlier in the novel, Richard knows her to be a self-disciplined scholar, a successful autodidact, although her studies have been all too theoretical. The events of the book have shown that her physical robustness and ability to master new physical education skills are not in question. Although the matter of financing Selma's studies is skated over, the reader does not seriously doubt that she could succeed at her chosen profession, as long as her husband and society's rumourmongers let her alone. It is in fact a relatively optimistic conclusion to this angry novel.

One interesting aspect of *Pengar* in terms of its celebration of female physical fitness in general and horseriding in particular is the fact that the author was probably not able to enjoy the benefits of these herself. I have not been able to find any evidence to indicate whether Benedictsson ever went riding. It is however well documented that throughout her adult life she suffered severe problems with her right leg, which hampered her mobility, even confining her to bed for a number of years. After treatment in Malmö in 1882, she made some progress and was able to walk with crutches, eventually graduating to a stick (Benedictsson 1978: 302n86). In the light of this handicap, Selma's health, agility and delight in riding can perhaps be seen as a form of vicarious wish-fulfilment or compensatory fantasy for the author. Benedictsson's longing for greater mobility is clear.

She pens a joyful poem in her diary on the occasion of the opening of the local railway line, which will allow her to travel more easily. It is a hymn to the transport of the future linking places more closely together, and in it she likens the locomotive to a horse. One verse begins: 'Jernfålen frustar och ångan sjuder' (Benedictsson 1978: 112) (The iron steed is snorting and the steam is boiling).

One could argue that in *Pengar* Benedictsson takes her vision of horse-borne liberation one stage further. When Selma is out riding full tilt on Black Prince, there is a sense of them being a single entity. As Selma is standing lost in contemplation after her morning ride and talk with Elvira, the narrator even calls her a 'hästmänniska' (200), literally a horse-person. The term is used in the context of her not being easily startled by Richard coming up silently behind her; it could be paraphrased as 'a person used to dealing with horses.' But there is an underlying ambivalence: is Selma a horsewoman or a horse-woman? The idea resurfaces in the final chapter. Before the hotel-room exchanges between Squire Kristerson and Selma reach confrontation point, the narrator describes Kristerson's look as he admires his wife, now a mature woman: 'han såg på henne med något av förtjusningen hos en sportsman, som betraktar en elegant rashäst' (231) (He looked at her with something akin to 'the delight a sportsman might feel on contemplating an elegant thoroughbred') (163). Clearly this shows him continuing to view her in a demeaning light as his chattel, a dependent creature whose intelligence and critical faculties are at animal level and thus irrelevant. But in the reader's mind it also serves once again to identify Selma, here dressed in soft black velvet and brocade, with her Black Prince. The link is further underscored by Selma herself, when she tells Kristerson how repugnant she has always found his tipsy, late-night amorous advances, adding:

> Jag måste pressa tänderna tillhopa för att inte bita omkring mig som en vildsint häst. Du visste inte, vad det ville säga att hålla sig stilla, när det inom mig jäste ett ursinnigt begär att kasta dig till marken och trampa på dig! (236)

> (I was gritting my teeth to stop myself lunging out and biting anything within reach, like a wild horse. You had no idea what it meant to keep my composure, when seething inside me there was a frenzied urge to throw you to the ground and stamp on you!) (168)

If *Pengar* were one of the fairytale-like fragments in the first volume of *Stora boken*, one could almost imagine Victoria Benedictsson letting Selma turn into a horse and gallop far away from all her tribulations. Is this the ultimate expression of a writer's vision of the horserider as a symbol of freedom?

In conclusion then, horseriding in Victoria Benedictsson's novel is so much more than just a decorous hobby or a sporting activity. It is a narrative device for mirroring the central character's development, from a naive, impressionable girl to a self-assured, frustrated woman. Riding gives Selma a legitimate excuse for escaping the constraints of the drawing room and expressing her inner self. It gives a welcome free reign to her vitality, contrasting effectively with the lack of outlet for the energies (not only physical) of a woman of her class in late nineteenth-century Sweden.[5]

References

Benedictsson, V. (1950): *Från Skåne; Pengar* (Skrifter i urval av Fredrik Böök). Stockholm: Albert Bonniers förlag.

Benedictsson, V. (1999): *Money*. Translated and with an Afterword by Sarah Death. Norwich: Norvik Press.

Benedictsson, V. (1978): *Stora boken I. Dagbok 1882-1884*. Ed. Christina Sjöblad. Cavefors. Skrifter utgivna av Lunds universitetsbibliotek. Ny följd i:1.

Benedictsson, V. (1919): 'Ur mörkret'. In *Samlade skrifter II, Berättelser och utkast; Efterskörd*. Stockholm: Albert Bonniers förlag, pp. 203-15.

Leffler, Y. (2005): 'Maskspel och mångtydighet. Berättartekniska strategier hos kvinnliga 1880-talsförfattare.' In Y. Leffler (ed.), *Det moderna genombrottets prosa*. Lund: Studentlitteratur, Lund, pp. 9-25.

Forsås-Scott, H. (2005): 'Makt och text i Victoria Benedictssons *Pengar*.' In Y. Leffler (ed.), *Det moderna genombrottets prosa*. Lund: Studentlitteratur, pp. 27-41.

Holm, B. (2002): 'Vem dog på Leopolds hotell?' *Samlaren* 123, pp. 78-110.

Sjöblad, C. and Witt Brattström, E. (1993): 'Jag vill skriva om kvinnor. Om Victoria Benedictsson.' In E. Møller Jensen (ed.), *Nordisk Kvinnolitteratur*, vol. II, Höganäs: Bra Böcker, pp. 528-39.

Witt-Brattström, E. (1993): 'Ur textens mörker: Victoria Benedictsson.' In *Ur könets mörker: litteraturanalyser.* Stockholm: Norstedts, Stockholm, pp. 67-88.

Notes

1. Page references for the Swedish quotations are to the *Skrifter i urval* edition: *Pengar*, 1950. English quotations are to the 1999 translation: *Money.* A revised edition was published by Norvik Press (2011).

2. It is not impossible that Benedictsson is here giving her own answer to Gustave Flaubert's *Madame Bovary* (1857), in which Emma succumbs to her seducer after her husband Charles Bovary sends them off for a ride together.

3. Specifically in the short story fragment 'Ur mörkret' (Out of the Darkness), written in 1888, which has been analysed by various scholars. See for example Witt-Brattström 1993.

4. *Stora boken I*, pp.176-77. This costume could in part have been devised to hide Benedictsson's own difficulties in walking and be as practical as possible, within the fashion dictates of the time, for her as a tall woman on crutches.

5. My thanks to Susan J. Bandy, who originally commissioned this essay for an anthology of literary texts about sport. The essay was translated into Danish by Lena Fluger and published in: Vicki Bjerre and Susan J. Bandy (2011): *Litterære fortællinger om idræt i Norden. Helte, erindringer og identitet.* Århus, Aarhus Universitetsforlag.

Patriarchal Consumption of the Female Body in Cecilie Løveid's *Måkespisere*

Lynn M. Houston and Ellen Rees
California State University   Universitetet i Oslo

Cecilie Løveid's intertextual use of a cookbook in her 1982 radio play, *Måkespisere* (translated as *The Seagull Eaters*, 1989), raises a provocative and complex critique of patriarchal discourse. In the dramatic text, the body of Kristine Larsen, the story's adolescent protagonist, is spoken of in terms of the meat of various fowl being prepared as dishes in the recipes recited from Henriette Schønberg Erken's classic cookbook, *Stor kogebog for større og mindre husholdninger* (*Big Cookbook for Households Large and Small*) from 1914. The recipes, recited by the disembodied voice of the cookbook author herself, serve a complex function in the narrative, giving the reader a formal structure, a recipe, by which to read and interpret the plot. Paradoxically, the cookbook both invokes a subversive tradition of embodied female knowledge and at the same time enforces patriarchal ideologies upon other women. Kristine initially reads Erken's cookbook as a dramatic text. As Løveid's play progresses, however, the cookbook's covert warnings and veiled advice ultimately fail to protect Kristine from patriarchal consumption.

The title *Måkespisere* suggests an indictment of male society whose primary desire for self-preservation is realized through the symbolic consumption of the body of a young woman in an act of cannibalism, a necessary consumption in order to maintain dominance as her claim to subjecthood threatens the status of patriarchal society.[1] In *Måkespisere*, we witness a young woman whose subjectivity is always in question; by the end of the text she is violently reduced to a non-subject through acts of consumption that are clearly marked as sexual, and which resist metaphorical readings. That is, they resist being read as purely symbolic and move toward a reading of these acts as literal destructions of a life-form through a process of breaking up, incorporation, and digestion, as

Eivind Tjønneland, who describes the text as a 'demetaforiseringsprosess' (1998: 34) (process of de-metaphorization), has also suggested. This de-metaphorization is echoed by the literally present voice of the cookbook author Erken within the text.

Scene two of the drama takes us into Kristine's family kitchen where we are introduced to her parents. Because of the patriarchal critique at the heart of Løveid's work, the young girl's relationship with her mother, the figure who directs her upbringing in – and understanding of – the social system of patriarchy, is particularly significant. Kristine's mother is afraid for her because she understands the dangers her daughter faces, but can do little to shield her. Kristine's father is equally ineffectual. He kindly but unrealistically supports Kristine's theatrical dream without giving her any concrete physical or economic support. Between the roles of the mother and the father in educating the young girl lies the cookbook. The mother, aware of the practical realities of life, feels that the cookbook is the 'eneste anledning hon (Kristine) har te utdannelse...' (1983: 22). Henning Sehmsdorf translates this as 'the only opportunity she has to learn anything...' (1989: 268), but the sense of the word 'utdannelse' implies formal education rather than simply the acquisition of skills. The cookbook tells the story that the father cannot or will not reveal as a man and that the mother is silenced from explicitly telling: that Kristine must give herself over to a submissive role or be violently dealt with by male society. On the one hand, her mother's pronouncement that the cookbook is Kristine's only chance of an education might be seen as an imposition of the traditional role of housewife on Kristine because the assumed main purpose of reading a cookbook is to learn how to cook. Yet the recipes declaimed by Erken are too elaborate and expensive for a family on the Larsens' budget. They have relevance to Kristine's situation not because they will teach her how to keep house, but because they serve a twofold role for her as an alternative dramatic narrative and as a covert warning to her about her position within the male economy.

Kristine explicitly reads the cookbook as a dramatic narrative, which thus posits the cookbook as a literary text. This opens up a reading of the cookbook as a covert sourcebook for subversion. In this interpretation we differ from the majority of Løveid scholars, such as Sigrun Borgersen (1984: 20), Wenche Larsen (2005: 124n75), Bjarne Markussen (1998: 32), Tanya Thresher (2005: 31), and Tjønneland (1998: 34), all of whom interpret Erken as a purely negative force in the text. Yet these interpretations ignore both Kristine's subversive reading of the cookbook as drama and the way in which Løveid's juxtapositioning of cookbook citations within her dramatic text casts negative light on Kristine's exploiters rather than on Kristine herself.

Cookbooks have long served as textual vehicles through which women could express themselves and write about their experiences in addition to sharing domestic knowledge and skills. Anne Bower (1997: 5-6) argues that a host of women's texts and textual artifacts from popular culture function as legitimate narratives, noting that women '[...] expressed themselves through other print and nonprint materials [in which] they not only recorded and reflected the world around them, they worked to construct their world [. . .] whether complicit with or pushing against the constraints and categories that bound them.' Bower emphasizes the revisionary power of such materials, noting that in them women could not only represent the conditions of daily life, but also comment upon and critique them. Andrea K. Newlyn examines the explicit and implicit narrative strategies present in nineteenth-century American cookbooks and private cookbook manuscripts. She argues that although the texts have an 'overtly collusive function' in supporting institutionalized patriarchal systems, the often anonymous cookbook writers nonetheless

> [...] reappropriated the cookbook form and transformed it into a locus of female artistry, empowerment, and social reform. The reappropriation of cookbooks' otherwise domestic function demonstrates not only women's efforts toward empowering themselves and the spaces they inhabited, but also reflects their development of alternative textual strategies that contest dominant conceptions of 'narrative.' (Newlyn 1999: 35)

While acknowledging that '[a]t first glance, cookbooks appear only to reproduce the period's various competing ideologies of femininity [...],' Newlyn maintains that '[...] cookbook narrative accommodates more than just recapitulations of patriarchal ideologies' (1999: 37). We find a similar tension between patriarchal complicity and feminist resistance in Løveid's use of Erken's recipes.[2] In her 2005 book on Løveid's stage dramas, Larsen points out that Løveid frequently appropriates antiquated dramatic genres such as tableaux vivants, Christian passion and morality plays, and Baroque theater (25) into her texts in order to create complex resonances that incorporate at times conflicting messages about women and their bodies in the face of patriarchal oppression. We find that the Erken cookbook functions similarly.

The cookbook becomes a legitimate narrative in the radio play. Kristine reads it as if it were a dramatic work on a par with canonical texts by

Bjørnstjerne Bjørnson and Henrik Ibsen, or even higher, given that her father has already pawned the works of these authors while keeping the cookbook. She states '[j]eg elsker å lese den kokeboken. Det var det mest spennende dramatikk. Hvordan stikke dyr, hvordan svi høns, hvordan slakte gås...' (Løveid 1983: 23) (I love reading the cookbook. Suspense and drama. How to cut animals' throats, singe hens, slaughter geese...) (Løveid 1989: 269). As a reader, however, Kristine places herself in the subject position in relation to the 'dramatikk' of the cookbook, while her social and gender status inevitably place her in the object position of the fowl.

Eating Seagulls and Sexual Consumption

The first connection between seagull eating and sexuality is made in the dialogue between Kristine and the Theater Director on the ferry in Scene Four. The Director muses on the fact that Kristine will one day eat seagulls as if he were deciding an element of the plot: he knows that she will eat them, but he must decide under what circumstances: 'De kommer dit en dag ... at De vil spise måker ... men hvorfor? For fanget frihet, overskudd, eller ... den bitre nød ... ?' (Løveid 1983: 24) (One day you will get to ... eat seagulls ... but why? Captured freedom, excess or ... necessity...?) (Løveid 1989: 270). The ellipses in his address to Kristine suggest other meanings that he may have in his mind before he decides on the words that he delivers. They also link his thoughts structurally to another question he asks Kristine during the same exchange: 'får De nok ... kjærlighet?' (1983: 24) (You get enough ... love?) (1989: 270). Although Kristine may not be conscious of it yet, her ability to get love and her ability to get food are one and the same. The Director's reflections on why Kristine will come to eat seagulls ('fanget frihet') elides Kristine and the seagulls, for a few lines earlier he had mused that sea gulls are like 'Friheten selv hentes ned fra sin sky' (1983: 24) (Freedom personified brought down from heaven) (1989: 269). When he imagines the various situations under which she might come to eat them there is an ambiguity between subject and object.

The implied sexuality of the seagull discussion segues into a scene between Kristine and the young fisherman and procurer of seagulls, Nicolay, who in a forthright manner attempts to initiate sexual intercourse with Kristine, whom he views as an appropriate partner for himself. The relationship between Nicolay and Kristine is representative of the normative production of Kristine's identity. The management of male society depends on Kristine's acceptance of her coming role as housewife and mother. Nicolay, being of Kristine's class, should be a logical choice for her mate. In the text, their amorous relationship is thwarted by Kristine's ambitions beyond becoming a housewife. When Nicolay comes to pay a clandestine visit to Kristine he enters through her window and she badgers him for being so clumsy, 'Husj, er det nødvendig å knuse rutene, Nicolay?' (1983: 26) (Hush! Do you have to break my window, Nicolay?) (1989: 272). A few lines later, as she is not being cooperative, he asks her 'Kan du og knusast, Stine?' (1983: 26) (Will you break, too, Stine?) (1989: 272). Her reply, in the midst of her rejection of his advances, 'Jeg vet ikke om jeg er helt uknuselig...' (1983: 27) (I'm not unbreakable, I imagine) (1989: 272), at once affirms her humanity and her need for participation in human society, and a repository of strength of which she is in possession, while at the same time allowing us to contemplate the odds against the success of one young woman in a struggle with such a ubiquitous and unfair system of power distribution. The exchange also clearly marks their varying levels of ambition through language usage: Nicolay calls her by a familiar nickname and speaks in a rural dialect, while Kristine appropriates the sociolect of the upper class.

This dialogue between Kristine and Nicolay offers further detail about the gendered power struggle in which they are involved as commented on in the selections from Erken's cookbook. When he comes to see Kristine, Nicolay states his purpose crudely: 'Du hev no eit hol einkvann plass, veit eg. Eg har med verkty ... Kan eg få sjå, gjøna blonden?' (1983: 27) (Got a hole someplace. And I've got my tool here ... Can I take a look, can I play with your lace?) (1989: 272-273). Her identity is reduced to a non-space, a decorated, disembodied hole. By refusing sex at this juncture, Kristine has humiliated his masculinity, making him the object of scorn and thwarting the marriage plot. Nicolay's presence demonstrates the reduction of Kristine's choices; his character expresses patriarchal desires in contrast with Kristine's desires. Religious ideology must, of course, disapprove publicly of sexual relations before marriage, but the male economy counts on it. In her economic situation, if Kristine were to get pregnant she would have to give up her dreams of something more than a life as a housewife and mother.

Just after Kristine makes Nicolay leave, the voice of Erken comments on the potential sexual consumption of Kristine from the point of view of a male economy that makes her a commodity to suit its ends:

> I alminnelighet settes der ikke stor pris på duer. Kan man skaffe seg dem til beste kvalitet, er de utmerkte, og man vil neppe skuffes. De er best fra juli til oktober. Den passende alder er når de

har fått fullstendinge fjær. Er de for unge, er de løse i kjøttet. Kjøttet er saftigst før de kan flyve. På gamle duer derimot, kan der koge en utmerket suppe... (1983: 27)

As a rule, pigeons are not considered desirable. But if of highest quality they are excellent to eat and will not disappoint. Pigeons are prime between July and October, or as soon as their feathers are grown. If too young, the flesh is soft. Pigeon flesh is moistest before the bird can fly. Mature pigeons, on the other hand, are excellent for soups... (1989: 273)

Rhetorical devices such as 'I alminnelighet,' and the impersonal pronoun 'man'(ostensibly neutral, but clearly marked as masculine) make it difficult to determine the position from which the female author Erken actually speaks. The pigeon is a direct analogy to the patriarchal perception of Kristine's body: in this economy Kristine, being from the lower classes, is not considered a desirable legitimate partner for the middle and upper class men in power. However, she is a target because of her beauty and because she has placed herself in a vulnerable and ambiguous position through her desire to become an actress in the theatre and associate with high society; in this respect she is, as is said of the pigeon above, 'of highest quality' and, later, like a hunted animal, she becomes the object of 'traps,' the most dangerous of which is sexual intercourse.

Erken further elucidates the terms of Kristine's consumption by the male economy in this passage: she describes puberty as a particular time in a woman's life when she proves most interesting for conquest, telling us that the flesh is too soft if the bird is too young but that it is at its moistest 'before the bird can fly.' Kristine seeks freedom from her situation and the restrictions placed on her by class and gender; she is critical of her parents' marriage and, as revealed to us by contributions from the chorus, she understands that marriage is a tool of the economy used to keep her subservient: 'Når du engang blir gift / bør du aldri trette med din man / men heller elske han!' (1983: 31) (Once you are married / you must never fight, / Love your man, stand by his side!) (1989: 276). It is best for the preservation of the male economy if she is dealt with before she has been given a taste of the freedom she seeks, otherwise she could prove dangerous and she might serve as a role model for other women. If she does not comply, the patriarchy must make her a cautionary example of what happens to young women that have what Erken calls 'store fordringer' (1983: 29) (exaggerated expectations) (1989: 274). The recipe from Erken functions as a warning, and it also intimates that even if Kristine should escape the fate that awaits her as an adolescent woman from the lower classes in this economy, the system will have an opportunity to deal with her later: she still risks being cooked when mature.

Feminist Resistance to the Marriage Plot

Most of the voices of the characters that speak to Kristine in this dramatic text work for or within the male economy: the chorus functions as the voice of 'everyone,' spouting clichés about women's proper behavior in marriage; the Theater Director is a gatekeeper into the world of narrative; and Nicolay, and her later lover, Olsen, represent the threat to her subjectivity posed by marriage or pregnancy. Olsen ultimately becomes the primary manager of Kristine's consumption by taking advantage of her physical deprivation. There are only three voices that offer any sort of critique of the male economy for Kristine: her mother; Erken; and the actress Magda Blanc, who, like Erken, is a real historical figure and an example of a professional woman. This is not to say that these voices provide Kristine with empowerment to help her achieve any freedom within the system, as they too imply that the only commodity she can realistically offer within the patriarchal economy is her body. Nonetheless, these three voices do seek to help Kristine understand and articulate the workings of that system.

No matter how each woman conceives of her freedom, the institution of marriage is shown as detrimental to its realization; Magda Blanc tells Kristine, 'Gift Dem aldri, Lille Larsen!' (1983: 41) (Never get married, little Larsen!) (1989: 285). In our reading of the text, this statement is critical, for it also suggests that Kristine's only chance at survival within the male economy is to deny her sexuality entirely, since female sexuality could only be sanctioned within the bounds of legal marriage, the very institution that threatens to destroy Kristine's freedom. In the context of the play, resisting the marriage plot at all is subversive. In her warning to Kristine, Magda Blanc thus suggests a systemic critique of the male economy.

This advice from Blanc is flanked in the play by a marriage proposal from Olsen and a marriage proposal from Nicolay, indicating the intense pressure on Kristine to comply. Nicolay's description of her role in their married life is telling of how little freedom she would have:

> NICOLAY: [...] Hvis du skal gifta deg me meg, Kristine, så må du gå frå teatret. Du må sitte i en stova og sjå ut glaset ... passe på om stikkelsbærbuskene få stikkelsbærkart, om de blir modne. (1983: 42)

> (NICOLAY: [...] If you want to marry me, Kristine, you've got to leave the theater. You've got to sit in your house and look out the window ... watch the gooseberries bloom and get ripe.) (1989: 286)

Their exchange reveals that her participation in the theatre has in fact provided some sort of refuge from the demands of the marriage plot, despite the sexual advances of the Director. Male objectification keeps drawing Kristine back to the body, back to her commodity value in the patriarchal economy.

Olsen's desire to possess Kristine is couched in an overtly economic discourse: his advances happen over discussion of how much food he can provide her with and how warm he can keep her. Kristine tries constantly throughout the text to get warm and to get enough food. When Olsen rents her an apartment with plenty of firewood and brings her food in exchange for sex, she falls for the 'trap' of prostitution rather than the 'trap' of marriage, against which she had been more explicitly warned. Kristine thus places herself in a far more dangerous position by engaging in sexual intercourse outside of marriage. In doing so, she faces rejection not only by explicit supporters of the male economy, but also by the three women who covertly tried to help her, her mother, Magda Blanc, and Erken.

How to Serve a Goose

Løveid's text suggests that Kristine engages in sex not out of desire, but as forced repayment for warmth and food. The sex act between Kristine and Olsen is described in terms that echo both a recipe later in the play and the call and response children's game found in the opening of the play:

> KOR: Alle mine barn kom hjem!
> KRISTINE: Jeg kan ikke!
> KOR: Hvorfor ikke det?
> KRISTINE: Ulven står bakom et tre og vifter med sin lange skarpe kniv!

KOR: Hva drikker han?
KRISTINE: Blod!
KOR: Hva spiser han?
KRISTINE: Kjøtt!
KOR: Kom allikevel! (1983: 45)

(CHORUS: All my little children come home!
KRISTINE: I can't
CHORUS: Why not?
KRISTINE: The wolf is behind a tree brandishing his long sharp knife!
CHORUS: What does he drink?
KRISTINE: Blood!
CHORUS: What does he eat?
KRISTINE: Flesh!
CHORUS: Come anyway!) (1989: 288)

Olsen here is the wolf and his sexual organ is represented as a 'long sharp knife.' The sex act is his drinking of her blood and eating of her flesh. This perverse echo of the Eucharist is the consumption of Kristine foreshadowed by Erken. Further, the reference to the children's game directs attention to reproduction, and indeed Kristine does become pregnant by Olsen.

Once the relationship is consummated, Kristine is pursued by an image of herself as a housewife, or perhaps as an embodiment of Erken as Gudrun Urd Sylte suggests (2002: 84), while the voices of her Mother and the Lady confront her:

Hun forfølger meg med en gul bunadkjole...
og et strykejern hun har puttet glødende gråstein inn i...
Hun forfølger meg innover veiene, utover myrene...
Hun glatter og stryker...
Hun glir over sengen min...over meg...
Men hun er så NYTTIG
hun samler inn strå til sengehalm
fugledun til puter
madrasser med halm og til madrasser samler hun
loppekvinner og loppemenn og lusekvinner og lusemenn
og hun glir over sengen hvor vi ligger
hvor vi ligger nakne,
stryker og glatter, glatter og stryker, og legger
blodige laken i kaldt vann, straks!
[...]

Hun kommer helt opp i sengen til oss
med bunadkjolen og strykejernet
med glødende stein inni...og kan falle!
Og inni kjolen aner jeg min egen kropp
Åh! (1983: 46-47)

(KRISTINE: She's after me in a yellow dress...
and an iron filled with glowing stones...
She follows me over roads, over swamps...
She smoothes and irons...
She glides over my bed...over me...
But she is so EFFECTIVE
she gathers straw for bedding
bird down for pillows
mattresses with straw and for mattresses she gathers
flea women and flea men and louse women and louse men
and she glides over the bed where we lie
where we're lying naked,
irons and smoothes, smoothes and irons, and soaks
bloody sheets in cold water, now!
[...]
She comes all the way into our bed
in her yellow dress and the iron
filled with glowing stone...it might fall!
And inside her dress I feel my own body.
Oh!) (1989: 288-289)

In a dramatic turn after her 'fall,' Kristine is pursued by this vision of Erken, who then becomes Kristine herself, ironing and doing chores around the house. The bloody sheets that Kristine envisions her washing represent Kristine's sexual initiation. The blood here, symbolic of feminine (re)production within the male economy, is also suggestive of other ways in which the struggle between masculine and feminine power takes place in, on, or to women's bodies: blood produced on linens by menstruation, rape, childbirth, as well as blood that can be considered the ink of a woman's body and suggestive of female 'writing' of the body.[3] After her consummation/consumption she feels, more than ever, the compulsion to accept the role of the housewife – the image literally invades her – but that avenue has been lost to her because she has had sex out of wedlock and thus broken the ambiguous rules of the male economy regarding female sexuality. Olsen takes her baby away, making it a donation to the 'Gi Føreren et barn' (1983: 48) (Give the Führer a child) (1989: 290) campaign. In a troubling ironic twist that emphasizes the social disturbance that the Nazi occupation brings to Norway, her commodified body is valued by its ability to contribute yet another body to militant patriarchy.

The voices of her mother and the respectable, upper-class lady in whose kitchen she works speak to Kristine menacingly of an act of physical torture, the laying of hot irons on her body, to cleanse her because she has 'soiled' her reputation. The threat of the torture is a particularly domestic image that echoes Erken's description of singeing geese to remove feathers, as Sylte points out (2002: 84). The women's betrayal of Kristine after her undoing by Olsen speaks to their acceptance of danger that free female sexuality poses not only to the male economy as a whole, but also to them individually as married women who hold a precarious but sanctioned role within that economy. They therefore enforce its moral code and reject Kristine. Additionally, she faces rejection by her suitor, Nicolay, and further violence at the hands of Olsen.

The recipe that follows Kristine's symbolic consumption is used by Erken, however, to convey the repulsiveness and violence of Olsen's seduction of Kristine, not to criticize Kristine. It follows an exchange between Kristine and Olsen in which she asks him if the reason he will not marry her now is because she is not pretty enough and he replies 'Mellom bena er De pen nok' (1983: 48) (You're pretty enough between your legs) (1989: 291). But this is an oxymoronic statement: it is precisely because he has been able to 'have' Kristine 'between her legs' that he is no longer interested in marrying her. Just as the beauty of the live bird, the beauty of its plumage, no longer matters when all one cares about is killing it to cook and eat it, nothing beyond Kristine's sexual body interests Olsen. Marriage, here, exists as an institution in order to control and subjugate women; however, if this control and subjugation can be realized sexually, then, as we see in the case of Olsen, marriage is no longer desirable. In her struggles against the advances from men and admonitions from women, the jealous criticism by other members of the lower class and the condescending rejection by members of the upper class, Kristine's loneliness and her lack of community of likeminded peers – in short, her isolation – precipitate her undoing. She finds no alternatives to the severely limited subject position imposed on her by the male economy.

Kristine is not a straightforwardly feminist heroine, one who might critique and triumph over the male economy, and indeed both ideological and formal ambivalence are typical of Løveid's entire dramatic production, as Larsen suggests (2005: 43). With no other community available and with the ultimate failure of the theatre group to provide her with a safe haven from patriarchal expectations, Kristine feels herself succumbing to this economy's pull. Olsen tells her that by giving up her baby she can return to the theatre. It is Olsen's decision and Kristine has little say in it. She tells of the presents that Olsen brings her while she is hiding at home with her pregnancy and then says 'Han lovet meg sko av krokodilleskinn / Sko skåret ut av hans egen rygg' (1983: 48) ('He promised me shoes made from crocodile leather. Shoes carved from his own back') (1989: 291). In the space between these two sentences Olsen is metamorphosed into a crocodile. It is an appropriate image for Olsen who is being very nice, taking care of Kristine while she is pregnant, but who will take her baby away as soon as it is born; appropriate because crocodiles are believed to shed tears before they eat their prey. The consumption of prey refers to the continued consumption of Kristine that Olsen perpetrates by taking her child away, breaking her, gutting her.

Like the carcasses of birds in the recipes, Kristine has, through the commodification of her child, had her insides removed. The last recipe given for a dish connects the violence of sexual consumption with the emotional anguish inflicted upon Kristine, suggesting that she has been dis-assembled or undone, broken, then put back together and made to look as if she were a whole person:

> ERKEN: Servering av gås.
> Ved anretningen skjæres laarene fra, brystkjøttet skjæres ut, og dette skjæres i seks stykker, legges igjen sammen, saa den ser hel ut. Fatet pyntes med fine salatblade, brunede poteter, rosenkaal, potetesreder fylde med grøntsaker, og den frukt gaasen har vært fyldt med. Gule og hvite rotfrynser legges over gaasen. Kan ogsaa serveres med rødkaal (1983: 49)

> (ERKEN: How to serve goose.
> Begin cutting at the thighs. Cut away at the breast, divide in six pieces, reassemble to look whole. Decorate the platter with lettuce, fried potatoes, Brussels sprouts, potatoes stuffed with vegetables, and the fruit with which the goose was filled. Place yellow and white vegetable ruffles over the goose. Or serve with red cabbage) (1989: 291)

The protagonist in *Måkespisere* is faced with death if she refuses to assume the role that patriarchy assigns her. Her role itself might be seen as a process of dying; she senses her own right to subjectivity and it is this sense that must die in the young woman in order for her to exist in patriarchal society. The commentary on the plot provided through the voice of Erken elucidates this view of the young woman's tenuous grounding in society. The denouement of the piece is in making this more and more apparent to the audience through her use of the cookbook narrative, which represents an alternative way of understanding Kristine's fate.

Conclusion

This reading of *Måkespisere* views the ideology expressed through Erken's recipes and disembodied voice in the text as more complicated and less unambiguously associated with patriarchal ideology than other scholars have. The plight of the meat in the recipes, to be torn apart, cut up, shredded, dressed and consumed, etc., both serves as a veiled warning to Kristine and provides an intratextual commentary on the patriarchal violence enacted on Kristine. Løveid's use of the recipes is both a formal innovation and an ambivalent critique of patriarchy and the forms it assumes in language and in literary structure. Løveid suggests that when women are limited to recipes in order to communicate among themselves, the chances of being consumed are almost insurmountable.

In *Måkespisere* we are taught to read as resistant readers through the model of Kristine's reading of Erken's recipes as drama, a drama that echoes her own tragic fate, rather than simply as instructions for the preparation of food. Although Kristine succumbs to patriarchal consumption, Løveid ultimately succeeds in reclaiming the subversive heritage of recipe writing, and suggests more complex ways of performing class and gender in dramatic texts.

References

Andreassen, V.S. (1996): 'Å plukke fjæra av unge høner: Ei lesing av *Måkespisere* av Cecilie Løveid.' In *Nordica Bergensia* 11: pp. 80-102.

Borgersen, S. (1984): 'På kant med genrene: Cecilie Løveids dramatikk.' In *Vinduet* 38 (3), pp. 19-23.

Bower, A.L. (1997): 'Bound Together: Recipes, Lives, Stories, and Readings.' *Recipes for Reading: Community Cookbooks, Stories, Histories*. In A.L. Bower (ed.). Amherst: University of Massachusetts Press, pp. 1-14.

Dinesen, I. (1937): 'The Blank Page'. In *Last Tales*. London: Penguin

Garton, J. (1993): 'Cecilie Løveid.' In *Norwegian Women's Writing 1850-1990*. London: Athlone, pp. 209-228.

Gubar, S. (1981): '"The Blank Page" and the Issues of Female Creativity.' In *Critical Inquiry*, VIII, 2 (Winter 1981), pp. 243-63.

Larsen, W. (2005): *Skuespillet om kvinnekroppen: Bildets og kroppens betydning i Cecilie Løveids dramatikk*. Oslo: Unipub.

Løveid, C. (1983): *Måkespisere. Tre spill for radio og scene*. Oslo: Gyldendal, pp. 17-51.

Løveid, C. (1989): 'The Seagull Eaters.' Trans. by Henning K. Sehmsdorf. In J. Garton and H.K. Sehmsdorf (eds.), *New Norwegian Plays*. Norwich: Norvik Press, pp. 263-293.

Markussen, B. (1998): 'Hverdagslige katastropher. Om *Måkespisere*.' In M.M. Andersen (ed.), *Livsritualer: En bok om Cecilie Løveids dramatikk*. Oslo: Gyldendal, pp. 30-55.

Newlyn, A.K. (1999): 'Challenging Contemporary Narrative Theory: The Alternative Textual Strategies of Nineteenth-Century Manuscript Cookbooks. In *Journal of American Culture* 22 (3), pp. 35-47.

Sylte, G.U. (2002): *Stykkevis og delt? Montasje og symbolikk i Cecilie Løveids Måkespisere*. Thesis. University of Bergen.

Thresher, T. (2005): *Cecilie Løveid: Engendering a Dramatic Tradition*. Laksevåg: Alvheim & Eide akademisk forlag.

Tjønneland, E. (1998): 'Fablens fragmentering – Noen strøtanker om Cecilie Løveids drama *Måkespisere*.' In *Nordica Bergensia* 17, pp. 29-37.

Notes

1. Wenche Larsen comments that the title 'gjør oss alle potensielt medansvarlige' (2005: 124, note 175) (makes us all potentially responsible).

2. The format of this analysis does not allow for a discussion of the extent to which Erken's text itself might contain traces of resistance.

3. See Isak Dinesen's 1957 tale 'The Blank Page,' and Gubar (1981).

What did Sigrid Undset inherit from Amalie Skram?
The body in *Constance Ring* and *Jenny*

Christine Hamm
Universitetet i Bergen

In 1901, the young Sigrid Undset, then unknown, wrote a letter to her Swedish pen-friend Dea. She discusses the difficulties she faces as a woman who tries to be a writer, and then exclaims:

> Alle disse fruentimmer, der laver bøger som uldstrømper og fabrikerer billeder, som skal prøve at ligne mænds. Og saa *er* der kvinder, der kan blive kunstnere – eders deilige Selma Lagerlöf, hun ser livet gjennom en kvindesjæl, saa det tindrer, for fornem til at plagiere manden, og Amalie Skram og saa gaar der her i byen en stakkars tuslete fru Anna Munch – midt i salig kvindesagens dage prøvede hun at være kvinde – og ble udpebet unisont af mænd og kvindesagskvinder. (Undset 1992: 64-66)

> (All these females who make books like woollen stockings and fabricate images that are supposed to resemble those of men. And yet there are women who can be artists. Your own wonderful Selma Lagerlöf – she sees life through the soul of a woman so it glitters, too distinguished to imitate men; and Amalie Skram; and then here in town there's poor frail Fru Anna Munch – in the midst of the glorious days of the women's movement she tried to be a woman, and was jeered at by men and feminists alike). (Page 2001: 368)

In this quotation, Undset presents at least four interesting ideas:

1) There is a difference between real artists and writers who just try to be artists. Those who just try to be artists think they can produce art in the same way as they knit socks, which means that they think they can just copy a pattern.

2) Female writers tend to copy an artistic pattern produced by men.

3) Female artists (examples are Selma Lagerlöf, Anna Munch, and Amalie Skram) differ from mere writers because they see 'life through the soul of a woman.' Sexual difference is important for the way writers produce their books: Undset even seems to claim that books written by women *should* differ from books written by men.

4) The female artist who writes from a woman's point of view tends to be harshly criticized by both men and women.

In this essay, I want to take the quotation from Undset's letter to Dea as a starting point and take a closer look at the relationship between the two Norwegian writers Amalie Skram and Sigrid Undset. Does it make sense to say that Undset followed in Amalie Skram's footsteps? The question might surprise literary scholars, since Skram and Undset are understood to write quite differently. Although they figure side by side in anthologies about Nordic women writers (Garton 1993), they differ in their literary style, in the themes they write about, and in the way they were received by the literary establishment. In addition, Skram and Undset usually end up on different sides when it comes to feminist readings. Although both writers are valued because of their strong female voices, Skram has proven to be more interesting to feminist scholars than Undset. Since the 1970s, Skram has been praised for criticising the institution of marriage, and for taking up the burning gender issues of her time (Bonnevie 1977; Engelstad 1992). Feminists had much more trouble with Undset, partly because she seemed generally to advocate in favour of marriage and motherhood (see Bliksrud 1981).

I want to argue that Skram and Undset might have more in common than has hitherto been realised. I want to focus especially on the two works which are taken to be the two artists' breakthrough novels: Amalie Skram's *Constance Ring* (1885) and Sigrid Undset's *Jenny* (1911). Both texts were recognized as important soon after they were published, but they were also ardently criticised and debated by both men and women. The reception of the two literary texts actually comes quite close to what Undset in her letter to Dea tells us about the reception of Anna Munch's writings: *Constance Ring* and *Jenny* not only provoked a disgusted reaction from the conservative critics, but they also challenged representatives of the women's movement. The magazine *Nylænde,* which had the explicit aim of promoting female writers, did not comment on *Constance Ring* (Iversen 1983: 17), and when *Jenny* was published, the women's rights club in Kristiania spend a whole evening criticizing Undset's novel. Undset was present during the debate, but she kept silent all the time. Asked later what she thought about the discussion, she smiled and said that she did not expect anything else (Slapgard 2007: 129). This seems to confirm that Undset was aware of her position as a woman writer, as someone who was supposed to be as misunderstood by other women as Anna Munch and Amalie Skram were at their time.

I now want to show that Undset probably was inspired a good deal by other Norwegian woman writers, and especially by Skram. This becomes clear if one studies the way that Undset focuses on the notion of the body. In *Jenny*, the protagonist's body is clearly shown in a different historical situation to that of Constance in Skram's novel. Nevertheless, Jenny comes to recognize that her body fundamentally is her situation, much in the same way as Constance comes to recognize that her body is her situation. Paraphrasing Toril Moi's reading of Simone de Beauvoir (Moi 1999), one could claim that both Undset and Skram are concerned with the meaning of the human body for the situation of a woman. Both writers show how a woman can despair because of her embodied life: in both texts, the female protagonist ends up taking her own life. In *Constance Ring* and *Jenny*, sexual difference becomes not so much visible by the way everything is seen through a 'woman's soul,' as Undset expressed it in her letter to Dea. Rather, sexual difference is constructed by the way the human body is shown to be the situation for the female protagonist.

Constance

Constance Ring starts with a description of the young heroine's bodily change two years after her marriage to Ring. Before she became Ring's wife, she went 'hoppende og nynnende gjennem stuene' (Skram 1993: 4) (She went skipping and humming through the house) (Skram 1988: 3). Now, her eyes 'som hadde vært så blanke og skinte så livsmodige, blev matte og rødkantede' (1993: 4) (Her eyes, once bright and full of life, were now redrimmed and dull) (1988: 4). The reader soon understands the reason for this dramatic change: the young woman is forced to give her body to her husband, whom she does not love. The first pages show that Constance tries to escape from every intimacy with Ring. As soon as she hears him coming to kiss her goodbye in the morning, she busies herself with washing her face: 'Når hun så hørte hans skritt – han kom alltid og kysset henne før han gikk på kontoret – for hun op og stod og vasket sitt ansikt med hodet nede i vannbollen' (1993: 4) (When she heard his footsteps – he always came to kiss her before leaving for the office – she would leap up and begin to wash, plunging her face into the wash-basin) (1988: 4).

From the beginning of the novel, Skram thus shows the reader that Constance's body is her situation, as well as it is in a situation. The notion of situation is important here: as Toril Moi stresses in her reading of Simone de Beauvoir's *The Second Sex*, the body is never understood as just a thing, but 'the body-in-the-world that we are, is an embodied intentional relationship to the world' (Moi 1999: 67). The body places us in different situations, but at the same time, the body is the background from which human beings perceive their situation. Human existence becomes readable as the freedom to realize certain projects which at the same time are limited by the human body. As Moi points out, the notion of a woman's body is dependent on the way she uses her freedom.

As I see it, it is not so much Constance's economic or social freedom that comes into focus in Skram's novel, but first and foremost her existential freedom, in Beauvoir's (and Sartre's and Merleau-Ponty's) understanding. Skram shows that Constance can express her subjectivity, the fact that she is a human being, only by denying her husband the right to kiss her. She takes care of her personality in taking care of her body. The text of the novel continuously stresses the fact that Constance understands her body as her situation, and that she has to act accordingly. When she finds out that Ring has an affair with her maid Alette, for instance, she first wants a divorce, but she is then persuaded by her aunt and her cousin to stay with Ring. Her condition for staying with her husband is that she can live as Ring's sister or hostess. While Ring accepts this condition to begin with, he soon starts to approach her again. Constance reacts with disgust, but cannot do anything about it. She lives a seemingly meaningless life until Ring dies in an accident.

It is only when she is re-married to Lorck, her long time admirer, that Constance starts to enjoy having sex with her husband. She no longer despises her body, and as a consequence, Constance once again turns into a lovely young woman. But this idyllic state of affairs is soon disrupted. By coincidence, Constance finds out that Lorck had had previous relationships with other women, and that he even had a child. When Constance discovers this fact, she is herself pregnant, and it particularly distresses her to think of the many brothers and sisters her child might have. She is struck by the fact of sexual difference: as a woman married to a man, she has no control over the possible number of children produced by Lorck, since the male body is not affected by childbirth in the way that the female body is. Constance understands that her situation is totally different from his: she becomes aware that her situation is determined by her female body. As a consequence of this insight, she loses her child during one of the following nights. This is, at least, how Constance herself interprets the event:

> Hun lå med lukkede øine og følte en slapp tilfredshet over det som var skjedd. Hun hadde ønsket det vilde gå således, og halvveis ventet det. Den sterke sinnslidelse hun på det siste hadde gjennemgått, var jo mer enn årsak nok. Det påkom henne en fornemmelse av frihet og lettelse; nu skulde hun da slippe for å føde til verden et pant på en kjærlighet hun ikke lenger nærte. (Skram 1993: 243)

> (She lay with her eyes closed, feeling a faint satisfaction at what had happened. This was what she had wanted – she had half expected it. The violent mental turmoil she had experienced recently was more than sufficient cause. A feeling of freedom and relief swept over her; now she didn't have to bring into the world a symbol of a love she no longer felt.) (Skram 1988: 224)

Skram points out that Constance feels free, when she no longer has to give birth to a child who was conceived with a man she no longer loves.

As soon as her love for Lorck is over, Constance becomes more and more attracted to the young musician Meier, who has pursued her ever since her life with Ring. In the final part of the novel, Skram actually describes in detail how a married woman can end up feeling sexually aroused by another man. This description alone might explain why Skram's novels were not commented on in *Nylænde*, a journal produced by women who condemned all kinds of sexual activity apart from intercourse between husband and wife. In *Constance Ring*, Skram argues against biological theories of the female body which were popular at the time, when she describes how a woman in fact could feel sexual desire all by herself:

> Constance lå for lengst i sin seng; hun jog inntrykket av optrinet mellem henne og Lorck fra sig og lukket øinene. Hun tenkte på det øieblikk Meier hadde trykket henne til sitt bryst, og hun følte hans leber dypt nede på sin hals. Hun levde det om og om igjen, og hver gang var det som hun løftedes på en bølge, mistet pusten og blev borte i svimmelhet. Til sist falt hun i søvn og drømte at hun og Meier vandret sammen i en deilig have tett omslynget, og at hun kjente hans kyss og varme ånde på sitt kinn. (Skram 1993: 284)

(Constance had long been in bed. Closing her eyes, she drove away the traces of her scene with Lorck. She thought about the moment when Meier had pulled her to his chest, felt his lips at the base of her throat. Again and again she relived it – and each time it was like being lifted by a wave that left her breathless and dizzy. At last she fell asleep and dreamed she was walking with Meier in a beautiful garden; their arms were around each other, and she could feel his kisses, his breath warm against her cheek.) (Skram 1988: 262-263)

Skram shows that women can feel bodily desire, but she simultaneously points to the responsibility which Constance feels for Lorck, to whom she is married. The body is not only desiring, but also situated socially and ethically, and this means that Constance cannot just act as she wants. First when she discovers that Lorck is unfaithful to her, she arranges a meeting with Meier, partly because she wants revenge. But after she has spend some hours with Meier, she finds out that Meier, too, has had other women in his life, and she ends up in total desperation. Now, she wants to do away with herself:

Hun følte trang til å spytte sig selv ut. Det var ikke stoff i henne til det hun hadde villet, kunde hun merke. Hun vemmedes ved sin mann, ved Meier, ved livet, men frem for alt ved sig selv. (Skram 1993: 308)

(She was sickened by herself. She didn't have the courage of her convictions, that was clear enough. She was disgusted with her husband, with Meier, with life – but above all, with herself.) (Skram 1988: 285)

The physical sensations can be read as reactions to her embodied life, and, quite logically, Constance kills herself at the end of the novel. Her death is narrated from Constance's point of view until the bitter end, and it becomes clear that she blames herself for her breakdown. She remembers that her father once had called her an egotist; in more modern terms, we would rather call her a narcissist. During the novel, Constance in fact constantly tries to be acknowledged as a human being, but the more she circles around herself the more she feels that this acknowledgment is denied to her.[1]

The novel closes with Lorck coming home and finding out that his wife is dead. The text does not gloss over the appearance of Constance's body:

Der lå hun på sin seng med åpen munn og brustne øine. Lebene var dekket av en blålig skum, som også var sivet ned over haken. Den ene hånd hang utenfor sengen og var opsvulmet på oversiden, og den tomme flaske var rullet et stykke bort over gulvet (Skram 1993: 312)

(She was lying on the bed. Her mouth hung open and her eyes were glazed. A bluish froth covered her lips and oozed down over her chin. One swollen hand dangled from the bed, and the empty bottle had rolled some distance across the floor.) (Skram 1988: 289)

Constance Ring, thus, ends with the female protagonist's physical breakdown. The body has become Constance's unbearable situation; it is invaded by men, it is supposed to produce children, it gets rid of them again. Constance's body is not treated as the picture of a human soul, but as an object seen by, and dealt with by, men. I will now show that it is a similarly estranged notion of the body that also characterizes Jenny at the end of Undset's novel.

Jenny

The first few pages of Undset's text, too, provide a picture of the protagonist's body. But, as opposed to Skram, Undset localizes the beholder of the woman's body more precisely: Helge Gram observes Jenny together with her friend Cesca in the streets of Rome. He thinks that the two women are the direct opposite of each other. While Cesca has dark eyes and hair and a rounded, petite figure, Jenny is blonde, tall and pale:

Frøken Winge var absolutt en pen pike, hun òg, men hun falt rent igjennom mot venninnen. Hun var like blond som den andre var mørk: håret, som var strøket tilbake fra den høye, hvite panne, bruste gyllent flammet under den lille grå skinnbaretten, og huden var skjært hvit og blekrød. Selv øyenbrun og vippene om de stålgrå øyne var lyse – gullbrune. (Undset 2004: 20)
(Frøken Winge was certainly an attractive girl too, but she was no match for her friend. She was as fair as the other was dark. Her hair, which was pulled back from her high, white forehead, billowed in golden flames beneath the little gray leather beret, and her complexion was a glowing pink and white. Even her eyebrows and

her lashes around her steel-gray eyes were light-colored: a golden brown.) (Page 2001: 15-16)

In the description of the two women, Undset makes excessive use of contrast (see also Eriksson 1977: 71f). While Cesca has several amorous adventures behind her, Jenny has not even kissed a man, in spite of her 28 years. It looks as if Undset wants to represent chastity through the fair, blonde woman, using the body seemingly more as a symbol than describing it as a situation. Later on, though, Jenny's chastity is undermined, something which has fatal consequences. While Cesca is shown having problems with her sexuality – she lets Jenny know that she cannot enjoy intercourse with her husband – Jenny turns out to be a very sensuous, desiring woman, longing for sexual union with a man. But at the same time she has decided that she will wait for the right man, for the man she can call her 'master'; unfortunately, as Jenny herself later interprets it, she loses patience, and becomes engaged to Helge.

Feminists have had problems with the fact that Jenny, a talented young painter who lives an unrestricted life with friends in Rome, does not appreciate her work to a larger degree. Why would Jenny have to long for a man and a family in addition to being an artist? Interestingly, though, Undset just follows in Skram's footsteps, when she describes a woman's desire in *Jenny*: Undset makes clear that desire can take over a woman's emotional life even if it is not directed towards a particular man. As Skram does in her novel about Constance, Undset stresses in her description of Jenny that desire demands an ethical effort of the woman. At a point in the novel, Jenny and Helge split up, because Helge's father has become interested in Jenny and Helge becomes jealous of his father. In this situation, Jenny is glad that she has not given herself to Helge, but has kept her chastity for the master she longs for. As she sees it, it is this longing that keeps her going, although she feels disgusted with her life after the awful break-up with Helge:

> Akk nei. Hun levde fordi hun ventet. Hun ville ikke ha en elsker, for hun ventet på sin herre. Og hun ville ikke dø, ikke nu, for hun ventet. [...] Hun kunne ikke dø slik – så fattig at hun ikke hadde en eneste elsket ting å si farvel til. Hun torde ikke – for hun måtte da tro en gang så ble det annerledes. Så fikk hun forsøke å klemme på med malingen igjen. Formodentlig ble det rent faen forresten – siden hun gikk her og var syk av forelskelse. Hun lo. Det var det hun var. Gjenstanden eksisterte foreløpig ikke – men kjærligheten, den var der. (Undset 2004: 207)

(Oh no. She kept on living because she was waiting. She didn't want a lover because she was waiting for her master. And she wouldn't die, not right now, not while she was waiting. [...] She couldn't die like this – so poor that she didn't have a single beloved thing to say good-bye to. She didn't dare, because she still believed that someday things would be different. So she had to try painting again. Presumably it would be an utter disaster, since she was walking around sick with love. She laughed. That's what was wrong with her. The object of her affection hadn't yet appeared, but the love was there.) (Page 2001: 174)

But Jenny gives up waiting anyway. Helge's father makes use of her sad situation, and for a short time, he can fill up the empty place left by his son. Although Jenny is convinced that he is not the right partner for her, and although she feels guilty for having Gert Gram leave his wife, she nevertheless does not manage to split up with Helge's father before she becomes pregnant. The discovery of being with child (Helge's half-brother) comes not as a happy insight: Undset describes it more as a recognition, as a growing understanding of what it means to be a woman. Her pregnancy lets Jenny see that men and women differ, that women do not have the same possibilities in life as men have, and that precisely for that reason they have to take care of themselves to a higher degree. Jenny's discovery of her pregnancy as a situation is stressed by Undset's description of her bodily sensations:

Hun lå en stund og forsøkte å bli herre over den motbydelige fornemmelse – vil ikke, vil ikke. Men det hjalp ikke – munnen løp full av vann. Det var så vidt hun nådde bort til toalettbøtten før oppkastingen kom. Men du store gud, var hun virkelig så full. Nu ble det likefrem flaut. Men så var det vel over også. [...] Men da hun hadde ligget litt med lukkede øyne, begynte sjøgangen igjen og svetten og kvalmen. Det var forbausende, for nu var hun virkelig ganske klar i hodet. Allikevel måtte hun opp enda en gang – . I det samme hun gikk tilbake til sengen, slo tanken ned i henne – . (Undset 2004: 229)

(She lay still for a moment, trying to win control over that abominable sensation – I won't, I won't. But it didn't help; her mouth filled with water. She barely managed to reach the chamber pot before she vomited. My God, could she really be that drunk? It was getting downright embarrassing. But surely it was over now. [...] But after she had been lying there for a while with her eyes closed, the sea swells began again, along with the sweats and the nausea. It was puzzling, because by now she was quite clearheaded. Nevertheless, she had to get up again. The moment she was back in bed, the thought occurred to her.) (Page 2001: 193-194)

This description of a pregnant woman's bodily sensations is something that Undset could hardly have copied from a male writer's text.

While the female body is thematically focused on in Skram and Undset, it is also emphasized structurally both in *Constance Ring* and in *Jenny*. Like Constance, Jenny has relations with three different men: while Constance is shown together with Ring, Lorck and Meier, Jenny is posited against Helge Gram, Gert Gram and Gunnar Heggen. Furthermore, the situation of the woman enclosed by the three men is brought out in the title of Skram's novel – Constance goes 'konstant i ring,' she walks continuously in a circle (Engelstad 1992: 56) – while it is stressed by the circular composition of the plot in *Jenny*. The story told by Undset starts and ends in Rome, and while Jenny is seen in the beginning from the perspective of Helge Gram, Jenny is described in the conclusion by Gunnar Heggen. This circle composition is even stressed by the symmetrical position of the initials of the men in Undset's text: HG-GG-GH (Eriksson 1977: 74). Thus, Undset shows structurally that she sees Jenny as much enclosed by men as Skram saw Constance, even if Jenny looks much freer to begin with. Although Jenny is an independent artist who lives alone and who earns her living for herself, her body sets limits on her life. The only time that she tries to realize a project of freedom is when she breaks up with Gert Gram and escapes to Germany, where she gives birth to her child. She even starts to paint again. But when her newborn son dies, she falls apart emotionally. Towards the end of the novel, Jenny tells Gunnar Heggen what happened to her after the death of her child. She describes her mourning mostly as a physical longing, a longing for the little body of her son:

> Og så var det bare savnet igjen – du kan ikke forstå hvordan det kjentes. Det var som hele min kropp verket av savn efter ham. – Jeg fikk betennelse i brystet, og smerten og feberen kjentes som bare savnet slo ut. – Jeg savnet ham i armene og mellom hendene og mot kinnet –. (Undset 2004: 289)

> (And then there was nothing left but loss. You can't imagine what it felt like. As if my whole body ached with the loss of him. I had an infection in my breast, and it felt as if my loss erupted into pain and fever. I missed him in my arms and in my hands and against my cheek. (Page 2001: 245)

Undset describes Jenny's experience as a mother, focusing on the body as her situation. In contrast to Constance, Jenny experiences her child as her happiness, but when he dies, the human body, again, sets limits on Jenny's freedom, since it is her child's body that is taken away from her own.

As is the case with Constance, Jenny takes her own life after a final act of sexual intercourse with a man. Jenny is raped by Helge Gram, and when he has left, Jenny's death is narrated from her own point of view:

> Hun la hodeputen over kanten av nattbordet – støtte den venstre hånd på den og skar igjennom pulsåren. Blodet kom i et sprøyt som ramte en liten akvarell hun hadde satt opp på veggen over sengen. […] Hun hadde ingen tanke og ingen angst – bare følte det som hun gav seg hen i det uavvendelige. […] Men om en stund ség der en ukjent, besynderlig fornemmelse over henne – en angst, som vokste og vokste. […] Hun tumlet ned av sengen, ravet mot døren, opp trappen til taket i blinde, til hun falt sammen på dens øverste trinn –. (Undset 2004: 313)

> (She placed her pillow on the edge of the nightstand, rested her left hand on it, and slashed the artery. Blood gushed out, striking a little watercolour she had pinned up on the wall over the bed. […] She had no thoughts and no fear – merely felt that she was surrendering to the inevitable. […] But after a moment an odd, unfamiliar sensation came over her – a fear that grew and grew. […] She tumbled out of bed, blindly staggered toward the door and up the stairs to the roof, until she collapsed on the top step.) (Page 2001: 265)

As does Constance, Jenny is finally found by the man who has been part of the reason for her destruction. Undset lets Helge see into Jenny's room:

> Han så inn – den tomme seng og de blodige laken og blodet over gulvet. Og han vendte seg og så at hun lå sammenkrøpet øverst på trappen, og at et var blod på de hvite marmortrinn. (Undset 2004: 314)

> (He looked inside – the empty bed and the bloody sheet and the blood all over the floor. And he turned around and saw that she lay curled up on the top of the stairs and that there was blood on the white marble steps.) (Page 2001: 266)

The two death-scenes are similarly horrible in both *Constance Ring* and *Jenny*. In both cases, the dead female body is not presented as beautiful and as part of an aesthetic project, as had been a tradition since the early nineteenth century.[2] Rather, in both novels the female protagonist's suicide is connected to a woman's sexual desire, and at the same time, it can be seen as an answer to the recognition of the woman that her body is her imprisoning situation. It seems to me clear that Undset must have found much more inspiration in Amalie Skram than in contemporary male writers.[3]

References

Bliksrud, L. (1981): 'Feminisme og antifeminisme i Sigrid Undsets forfatterskap.' *Norsk litterær årbok*. Oslo: Samlaget.

Bonnevie, M.B. (1977): 'Den gifte kvinnen i det borgerlige ekteskap. Belyst ved fire ekteskapsromaner av Amalie Skram.' In M.B. Bonnevie *et al.* (eds.), *Et annet språk. Analyser av norsk kvinnelitteratur*. Oslo: Pax Forlag, pp. 40-45.

Bronfen, E. (1992): *Over her Dead Body: Death, Femininity and the Aesthetic*. Manchester: Manchester University Press 1992.

Engelstad, I. (1984) 1992: *Sammenbrudd og gjennombrudd. Amalie Skrams romaner om ekteskap og sinnssykdom*. Oslo: Pax Forlag.

Eriksson, J. (1977): 'Angrepet som forvandlet seg til et forsvar. Om kvinnelighet, kjærlighet og kjernefamilie i Sigrid Undsets *Jenny*.' In M.B. Bonnevie *et al.* (eds.), *Et annet språk. Analyser av norsk kvinnelitteratur*. Oslo: Pax Forlag, pp. 65-91.

Garton, J. (1993): *Norwegian Women's Writing 1850-1990*. London: Athlone Press.

Hamm, C. (2006): *Medlidenhet og melodrama. Amalie Skrams romaner om ekteskap*. Oslo: Unipub.

Hamm, C. (2013): *Foreldre i det moderne: Sigrid Undsets forfatterskap og moderskapets grammatikk*. Trondheim: Akademika forlag.

Iversen, I. (1983): '*Kvinnelige litteraturkritikere og etableringen av en kvinneoffentlighet i 1880-åra.' Norskrift* 38.

Moi, T. (1999): 'What Is a Woman? Sex, Gender, and the Body in Feminist Theory.' In *What Is a Woman? And Other Essays*. Oxford: Oxford University Press.

Page, T. (2001) (ed.): *The Unknown Sigrid Undset. Jenny and Other Works*. Translated by T. Nunnally. Hanover NH: Steerforth Press.

Skram, A. (1988): *Constance Ring*. Translated by J. Messick with K. Hanson. New York: Seal Press.

Skram, A. (1993): *Constance Ring*. In *Samlede verker 1*. Oslo: Gyldendal.

Slapgard, S. (2007): *Sigrid Undset. Dikterdronningen*. Oslo: Gyldendal.

Undset, S. (1992): *Kjære Dea*. Oslo: Aventura Forlag.

Undset, S. (2004): *Jenny*. Oslo: Aschehoug.

Notes

1. I have argued at greater length for this reading in my book on Skram's novels of marriage (Hamm 2006).

2. Elisabeth Bronfen describes this tradition in her book *Over her Dead Body* (Bronfen 1991).

3. In my recent book on Sigrid Undset's writings (Hamm 2013), I have argued more particularly how *Jenny* could be read as a naturalist novel, as well as a critique of naturalism's deterministic picture of the body.

Janet Garton
Selected Publications

Books

Writers and Politics in Modern Scandinavia (under the name Janet Mawby). Hodder & Stoughton, London 1978. 55pp.

Jens Bjørneboe: Prophet without honor. Greenwood Press, Westport 1985. 162pp.

(Editor) *Facets of European Modernism. Essays in Honour of James McFarlane.* University of East Anglia, Norwich 1985. 372pp.

(Editor) *Proceedings of the Ninth Biennial Conference of the British Association of Scandinavian Studies.* University of East Anglia, 1992. 316pp.

Norwegian Women's Writing 1850-1990. Athlone Press, London 1993. 306pp.

Kurs i Nordens språk og litteratur. (Report on the status and quality of summer universities in Denmark, Finland, The Faroe Islands, Greenland, Iceland, Norway and Sweden.) The Nordic Council, Copenhagen 1995. 186pp.

(Editor and Translator) *Contemporary Norwegian Women's Writing.* Norvik Press, Norwich 1995. 254pp.

(Editor with Michael Robinson) *Nordic Letters 1870-1910.* Norvik Press, Norwich 1999. 422pp.

(Editor with Michael Robinson) *On the Threshold. New Studies in Nordic Literature.* Norvik Press, Norwich 2002. 489pp.

Elskede Amalie. Amalie og Erik Skrams brevveksling 1882-1899. Vol.1: 1882-September 1883, 557pp.; Vol.2: October 1883-1888, 520pp., Vol.3: 1888-1899, 597pp. Gyldendal norsk forlag, Oslo 2002.

Caught in the Enchanter's Net. Amalie and Erik Skram's letters. Norvik Press, Norwich 2003. 461pp.

Amalie Skram: Brevveksling med andre nordiske forfattere. C.A. Reitzels forlag, Copenhagen 2005. 485pp.

(Editor) *Amalie Skram: Constance Ring.* Danske klassikere. DSL. Borgen, Copenhagen 2007. 381pp.

(Editor) *Amalie Skram: Brevveksling med forlæggere.* Det danske sprog- og litteraturselskab, Copenhagen 2010. 342pp.

Amalie. Et forfatterliv. Gyldendal norsk forlag, Oslo 2011. 474 pp.

Articles, Chapters in Books

'The Collective Novel and the Rise of Fascism in the 1930s'. In *Ideas and Ideologies in Scandinavian Literature since the First World War*, ed. Sveinn Skorri Høskuldsson, University of Iceland, Reykjavik 1975. pp. 14-61.

'The Norwegian Novel Today'. In *Scandinavica* Vol.14, No.2, November 1975. pp. 101-13.

'New Directions in Norwegian Literature'. In *Review of National Literatures* Vol.12: Norway (ed. Sverre Lyngstad). Griffon House Publications, New York 1983. pp. 163-84.

'Om å snuble i sine egne lengsler. Bjørg Vik: En håndfull lengsel'. In *Norsk litterær årbok 1983*, ed. Leif Mæhle. Det norske samlaget, Oslo 1983.

'Billedbruken i Bjørg Viks novelle "Rosa og Ruth"'. In *Edda* 6, 1983. pp. 321-28.

'Women and Literature. Camilla Collett: Amtmandens døtre and the Critics.' In *Proceedings of the Conference of Teachers of Scandinavian Studies in Great Britain and Northern Ireland 1983*. University of Surrey, 1984. pp. 42-62.

(Editor) *Language and Culture Guide 6: Danish.* Centre for Information on Language Teaching and Research, London 1984. 54pp.

'A Vision of a Continual Battle: Jens Bjørneboe and the Theatre.' In *Scandinavica* Vol.14, No.2, November 1984. pp. 137-60.

'Dag Solstad and Profil: Norwegian Modernism in the 1960s'. In *Facets of European Modernism* (ed. J.Garton), Norwich 1985. pp. 349-65.

(Editor) *Language and Culture Guide 17: Norwegian*. Centre for Information on Language Teaching and Research, London 1986. 56pp.

'Angels and Demons in Norwegian Literature.' In *Proceedings of the Conference of British Scandinavists*, April 1985. Lampeter 1986. pp. 180-98.

'Women of Letters: Nineteenth century Norwegian authors in their correspondence.' In *Proceedings of the Conference of Teachers of Scandinavian Studies in the British Isles*, April 1989. Edinburgh University, 1989. pp. 94-121.

'The Economics of Journal Publishing: A Desktop View.' In Karen Brookfield (ed.), *Scholarly Communication and Serials Prices*. Bowker Saur, London 1991. pp. 46-51.

'Cecilie Løveid: Feminist Modernist Dramatist.' In Asmund Lien (ed.), *Modernismen i skandinavisk litteratur*. Nordisk institutt, Universitetet i Trondheim, Trondheim 1991. pp. 349-54.

'Kvinnelitteratur en Penelopes vev?' In *Norsk litterær årbok 1991*, ed. Hans H.Skei and Einar Vannebo. Det norske samlaget, Oslo 1991. pp. 175-81.

'On translating Cecilie Løveid.' In *Proceedings of the Ninth Biennial Conference of the British Association of Scandinavian Studies*. University of East Anglia, 1992. pp. 112-17.

'Dag Solstad and Norwegian Modernism.' In *Adam: An International Review*, ed. Miron Grindea. Nos. 498 499, London (dated 1988). pp. 70-73.

'Fra det lukkede rommet til rosebedet? Norsk kvinnelitteratur i 1970 og 80 åra.' In *Norsk litterær årbok 1993*. Det norske samlaget. Oslo 1993. pp. 178-92.

'Natursymbolikken i norske krigsdikt.' In *Literature as Resistance and Counter-culture*. Hungarian Association for Scandinavian Studies. Budapest 1993. pp. 157-61.

(1) 'Ibsen: The Middle Plays'. (2) Interview with John Barton. In *The Cambridge Companion to Ibsen* (ed. James McFarlane). Cambridge University Press 1994. pp.106-25; 217-26.

'The Flight to the South.' Norwegian Literature 1995. *The Norseman* Nos.4/5, 1995. pp. 77-82.

'Lys og skygge i Halldis Moren Vesaas' dikt.' In Ole Karlsen (ed.): *Klarøgd, med rolege drag*. LNU, Cappelen, Oslo 1996. pp. 28-40.

'Little Red Riding Hood Comes Of Age: or When the Fantastic Becomes the Feminist.' In Christopher Smith (ed.), *Norwich Papers IV: Essays in Memory of Michael Parkinson and Janine Dakyns*. University of East Anglia, Norwich 1996. pp. 289-94.

'Scandinavia.' In John Sturrock (ed.), *The Oxford Guide to Contemporary Writing*. OUP, Oxford 1996. pp. 340-360.

'Villdyrmetaforer i moderne norsk kvinnelitteratur.' In Helga Kress (ed.), *Litteratur og kjønn i Norden*, Institutt for litteraturvitenskap, Reykjavik 1996. pp. 682-87.

'"Vogt Dem for fru Collett!" Camilla Collett-portretter i egne og andres brev.' In Jorunn Hareide (ed.), *Skrift, kropp og selv. Nytt lys på Camilla Collett*. Emilia forlag, Oslo 1998. pp. 114-33.

'"Som du trænger til mig Amalie!" Amalie og Erik Skrams brevveksling 1882-1899.' In Pål Bjørby og Elisabeth Aasen (eds.), *Amalie Skram - 150 år*. Senter for humanistisk kvinneforskning, Universitetet i Bergen 1997. pp. 50-63.

'Language and Gender in the Correspondence of Amalie and Erik Skram.' In Annegret Heitmann and Karin Hoff (eds.), *Ästhetik der skandinavischen Moderne*. Peter Lang, Frankfurt am Main 1998. pp. 105-18.

'"Why do Norwegians hate Denmark so much?" National Consciousness in Amalie and Erik Skram's Correspondence.' In Michael Robinson and Janet Garton (ed.), *Nordic Letters 1870-1910*. Norvik Press, Norwich 1999. pp. 264-80.

'Vi har oplevet det meste Livet kan byde - Noen bemerkninger omkring Amalie Skrams brevveksling med Erik Skram.' In *Årbok 2001*, Amalie Skram Selskapet, Bergen 2001, pp. 32-49.

'Erik Skram'. In *Arkiv for Dansk Litteratur,* Dansk Sprog- og Litteraturselskab, Copenhagen 2002. Published electronically: www.adl.dk. Ca. 10,000 words.

'Intertekstualitet i Paal-Helge Haugen: *The Maid of Norway.*' In Anker Gemzøe *et al.* (eds.), *Fortællingen i Norden efter 1960.* Aalborg Universitetsforlag, Aalborg 2004.

'Georg Brandes og nordiske kvinneforfattere: Amalie Skram og hennes samtidige.' In Olav Harsløf (ed.), *Georg Brandes og Europa.* Det kongelige Bibliotek/ Museum Tusculanums Forlag, Copenhagen 2004, pp.203-14. Also published as "Georg Brandes e le scrittrici nordiche: Amalie Skram e le sue contemporanee", in *Studi Nordici* IX, Pisa/Roma 2002, pp. 113-121.

'Translating Ibsen: From Page to Page – to Stage?' In Sabine Coelsch-Foisner and Holger Klein (eds.), *Drama Translation and Theatre Practice.* Peter Lang, Frankfurt am Main 2004.

'Amalie Skram's Many Masks: Fragments of an Epistolary Autobiography.' In *Scandinavica* Vol.44, No.1, May 2005, pp. 5-28.

'Amalie Skram: A Norwegian Naturalist.' In Inger M. Olsen and Sven Hakon Rossel (eds.), *Female Voices of the North II*. Praesens Verlag, Vienna 2006, pp. 111-128.

'Amalie Skram og hennes samtidige. Brevveksling med norske og danske forfattere.' *Årbok 2006*, Amalie Skram selskapet, Bergen 2006, pp. 35-52.

'"Are you really going to have this person in your living-room?" Ulrik Brendel's difficult entry into Ibsen's Rosmersholm.' In Petra Broomans *et al.* (ed.), *Staging, Images and Poetics - From a Transatlantic Perspective.* Tijdschrift voor Skandinavistiek 2, 2006, pp. 77-93.

'After the Door Slams: The Depiction of Divorce in Nineteenth-Century Scandinavia.' In Karl Leydecker and Nicholas White (eds.), *After Intimacy. The Culture of Divorce in the West since 1789.* European Connections Vol.10. Peter Lang, Bern 2007.

'På fremmede scener: utvandring eller utvanning?' Plenary lecture on drama translation for International Association of Scandinavian Studies, in Maria Sibinska *et al.* (eds.), *Nordisk drama. Fornyelser og transgressioner.* Fundacja Rozwoju Uniwersytetu Gdańskiego, Gdańsk 2010, pp. 71-86.

'"Lille søde kjære Jantsekianski!" Amalie Skrams brev til sin datter

Johanne.' In Per Thomas Andersen et al. (eds.), *Brev. Til Jorunn på 70-årsdagen*. Tapir akademisk forlag, Trondheim 2010, pp. 71-82.

'Amalie Skram and Henrik Ibsen: a missing link.' In Eydun Andreassen *et al.* (eds.), *Malunarmót*. Fródskapur, Tórshavn 2012, pp. 65-76.

'Not only Ibsen. The fate of Norwegian literature in the United Kingdom.' In Helge Ø. Pharo and Patrick Salmon (eds.), *Britain and Norway: special relationships*. Akademika forlag, Oslo 2012.

'Amalie Skram og Henrik Ibsen: En forsømt anledning.' In Berit Bareksten (ed.), *Årbok 2012-13*. Amalie Skram-selskapet, Bergen 2013, pp. 45-57.

"Amalie Skram og hennes tyske oversettere." ibid, pp. 75-87.

Translations

Eleven short stories for the anthology *Slaves of Love* (ed. James McFarlane), Oxford University Press, London 1982.

Dag Solstad: "The Player", "Floating, floating" and other stories. Translated with an introduction. *Comparative Criticism* Vol.6, Cambridge University Press, 1984. pp. 229-255.

Bjørg Vik: *An Aquarium of Women*. Norvik Press, Norwich 1987.

Knut Faldbakken: *The Sleeping Prince*. Peter Owen, London 1988.

(Editor and translator) *New Norwegian Plays*. With Henning Sehmsdorf. Norvik Press, Norwich 1989.

Excerpt from Cecilie Løveid: *Double Delight*. *Dimension*, special issue on Contemporary Nordic Literature, Austin Texas 1994. pp. 404-17.

Karin Moe: "Sextext"; Sissel Lie: "Strange Things Happen When My Forest Burns"; Cecilie Løveid: "Double Delight"; Lisbet Hiide: "Adam the Dream of Lioness S". *In Contemporary Norwegian Women's Writing*, Norvik Press, Norwich 1995.

Bjørg Vik: "The Trip to Venice", in Alan P.Barr (ed.): *Modern Women Playwrights of Europe*, OUP, New York and Oxford 2001, pp. 483-510.

Kirsten Thorup: *The God of Chance*. Norvik Press, London 2013.

Kirsten Thorup

The God of Chance

(translated by Janet Garton)

The God of Chance focuses on the lives of two very different women: Ana, a career woman from Copenhagen whose work is her life, and the young Mariama, whom she meets on a beach in Gambia and who becomes a substitute for the family she has never had. The novel moves to Copenhagen and then to London as Ana brings Mariama to Europe to be educated; the girl finds the cultural shock intensely difficult, whilst Ana's obsession with her leads to her own carefully controlled life descending into chaos. The story depicts the gulf between European affluence and Third World poverty; it explores our dependence on money, our need to be in control in every situation, and the problematic relationship between sponsor or donor and recipient. The scene moves from colourful depictions of life in a luxury hotel in Africa cheek by jowl with desperate poverty to elite designer flats in Copenhagen and finally the bustling multicultural community on the streets of London.

ISBN 9781909408036
UK £11.95
(Paperback, 300 pages)

Jørgen-Franz Jacobsen

Barbara

(translated by George Johnston)

Originally written in Danish, *Barbara* was the only novel by the Faroese author Jørgen-Frantz Jacobsen (1900-38), yet it quickly achieved international best-seller status and is still one of the best-loved classics of Danish and Faroese literature. On the face of it, Barbara is a straightforward historical romance. It contains a story of passion in an exotic selling with overtones of semi-piracy; there is a powerful erotic element, an outsider who breaks up a marriage, and a built-in inevitability resulting from Barbara's own psychological make-up. She stands as one of the most complex female characters in modern Scandinavian literature: beautiful, passionate, devoted, amoral and uncomprehending of her own tragedy. Jørgen-Frantz Jacobsen portrays her with fascinated devotion.

ISBN 9781870041225
UK £9.95
(Paperback, 304 pages)

HANNE MARIE SVENDSEN

Under the Sun

(translated by Marina Allemano)

Written in 1991, *Under the Sun* is the story of Margrethe Thiede, the daughter of a lighthouse keeper in an unnamed small fishing community on the north-western coast of Denmark. We follow Margrethe through her childhood, her years as a student in the capital, her marriage to a mentally unstable man, her involvement in the peace movement, and her old age.

The novel is also about a changing community where fears of violence at sea and rampant commercialism on land are strong undercurrents. The building of a naval base and the ominous presence of foreign submarines intimidate the fishermen and their families, and an accident caused by one of these intruding vessels forms the catastrophic climax of the novel.

ISBN 9781870041621
UK £9.95
(Paperback, 256 pages)

HELENE URI

Honey Tongues

(translated by Kari Dickson)

The honey tongues of the title belong to four friends in their thirties who have known each other since school. They make up a 'sewing circle' where no sewing is done, but much exquisite food is lovingly prepared and consumed and increasingly bitchy gossip exchanged.

The novel follows their three-weekly meetings over six months, as they take turns to entertain each other; we are privy to their thoughts and memories and discover how apparently innocent actions are motivated by emotional hang-ups with their roots in childhood traumas. The tension builds towards a gourmet trip to Copenhagen to celebrate their friendship, where during an eight-course meal the masks drop and undisguised fear and loathing are revealed. Shocking secrets are unearthed as the balance of power subtly shifts from one member of the group to another. Brilliantly observed, this is female bonding at its worst, manipulative and psychotic, exposing the dependency and deceit behind the compassionate and affectionate façade.

ISBN 9781870041720
UK £9.95
(Paperback, 192 pages)